# The History and Development of the Doctrine of the Trinity

The History and

## Development

## *of*

## the Doctrine of the Trinity

Steven N. Gill

Biblical Hebrew
Academy Online

Library of Congress Control Number (LCCN) 2022901294

ISBN 9780578478784

Published by Steven Gill
In conjunction with Biblical Hebrew Academy Online
Anderson, IN

Printed in the United States of America
Artwork by Sparq Creative Solutions, LLC.

All Scripture quotations are taken from the King James Version (KJV) unless otherwise indicated.

*To all who have ever been awakened by the past, inspired by the present, or believed in the future...*

All dates in this volume are written using the B.C.E. – C.E. designations, as opposed to the more traditional B.C. – A.D. This was a formatting decision and does not reflect a personal bias against the traditional format by the author. Because this book covers many important dates crossing back and forth between millennia, the designations B.C.E. and C.E. allowed the author to record important dates with ease and accuracy throughout the writing process with less room for error. While he understands that this format has been used in modern academia to avoid religious affiliation, such biases did not motivate the author's decision in this instance. Throughout this book, the modern usage may be understood accurately by the reader to mean: Before Christian Era (B.C.E.) and Christian Era (C.E.).

# TABLE OF CONTENTS

# INTRODUCTION

On the eastern border of the Italian peninsula lies a city that is home to many of the oldest traditions of Western thought and religion. Sitting atop the northern coast of the Adriatic Sea just east of Verona is *La Serenissima* herself—the most serene jewel of the renaissance. Venice, whose borders have been called home by Marco Polo, Vivaldi, and Pope Gregory XII, holds a unique place in the history of the world as an inspiration to the adventurous, creative, and religious spirit of mankind. The city of canals has served as a muse to painters and sculptors for centuries, and in much the same way, has arrested the attention of historians who seek to better understand the seemingly less tangible but altogether more real aspects of human existence.

On the east end of the Piazza San Marco sits one such example of human achievement and beauty that epitomizes the splendor of the city. It is perhaps the most famous religious structure of Venice—Saint Mark's Basilica. Framed by the grandeur of Doge's Palace and the stoicism of Campanile, the nine-hundred-year-old basilica is visited by millions of tourists each year.[1] Although centuries of wars, fires, and renovations have brought the expanded church to its present form, much of the basic structure of the building remains intact.[2] Originally constructed in the ninth century by the Doge, the present design exists largely as eleventh-century successor to the original.[3] Today the basilica stands as one of the great triumphs of Middle Age architecture and serves as one of the most significant examples of Byzantine art and culture still in existence.

---

[1] Paris, Natalie. "Venice mulls ticketing system for St. Mark's Square to combat overcrowding." The Telegraph. Last modified May 3, 2017. https://www.telegraph.co.uk/travel/news/venice-to-charge-tourists-ticket-enter-st-marks-square/#:~:text=The%20city%20attracts%20more%20than,how%20better%20to%20protect%20it.

[2] "Basilica di San Marco." Last modified , 2021. http://www.basilicasanmarco.it/storia-e-societa/la-basilica-funzione-politica-e-religiosa/?lang=en.

[3] Ibid. (2) *(The Doges and the Basilica).*

One cannot walk through Saint Mark's Basilica without coming away with an appreciation for the Byzantine influence which pervades it. The intricately colored marble, which covers so much of the surface of the structure's surface, as well as the great columns brought to the city sometime after the fourth crusade, recalls an era that placed a premium on architectural beauty and was possessed by a longing for Greek revivalism.[4]

Yet situated on the south-west corner façade to the right of the primary entrance of the basilica is an image that has puzzled historians for centuries. Although it is attached to one of the most famous Byzantine structures in history, this curious piece reflects something that is not Byzantine at all. Covering this particular corner of Saint Mark's is a porphyry two-piece stone addition, depicting the Roman tetrarchy. These four rulers shared the burden of imperial rule of the Roman Empire in the waning years of the third century.[5] It is significant to note the addition of the image of the tetrarchy to the great Christian basilica of Venice, because none of the four tetrarchs depicted on the statue were ever Christians themselves.

Throughout the third century, the Roman Empire suffered a great deal of civil strife that resulted in dozens of men vying for control over the territories and many claiming to be the legitimate successor of the Roman emperors. When it became clear that no one man was going to possess sovereign authority over the empire and survive, the power of the throne was split among four men. Dominant of these four rulers was Diocletian—the last of pagan Rome's great Augusti. Depicted at his side in the image on Saint Mark's façade are Galerius, the companion ruler of Diocletian in the East, along with Maximian and Constantius, who ruled the Western portion of the empire.

Diocletian—or *Diocles* ("to the glory of Zeus") as he was called at birth—is largely considered the last of the great Roman emperors.[6] Although a strong ruler and a shrewd politician, Diocletian was a cruel persecutor of Christians in the third

[4] Ibid. (2) *(The Fourth Crusade)*.
[5] Smarthistory: YouTube. Last modified May 1, 2013.
https://www.youtube.com/watch?v=Dui5V8TZYbE.
[6] Strauss, Barry. *Ten Caesars*. New York: Simon & Schuster, Inc., 2019. (p.265).

century. Among the many stories of Christian martyrs throughout history, few are to be compared with those who were slain during the rule of Diocletian.[7]

Galerius—the offspring of the god Mars, child to the consort of a serpent[8]—was perhaps the most responsible party in the great religious persecutions which occurred during the reign of Diocletian. Although a lesser Caesar, Galerius seemed to rule with a heavier hand than his master. Under the influence of his mother Romula, Galerius ordered the destruction of Christian houses of worship, made the practice of Christianity illegal in the empire (a policy which he would later reverse at his death), and ordered the execution of Christians throughout the land.[9]

In the West, the situation for Christians was not greatly improved. Under the leadership of Maximian, Christian churches were torn down, and their leadership was largely imprisoned or executed. Constantius, Caesar and right hand to Maximian in the West, ruled with perhaps the mildest approach toward the persecuted religion. Nevertheless, the political climate for Christians remained bleak.[10]

And so, the question remains, just how did these four rulers come to be depicted on the side of so great a bastion of Christian history?

If one were to examine the stonework of the four tetrarchs closely, they would find that each of the Augusti depicted on the porphyry (Diocletian and Maximian) are bearded, while the two Caesars (Galerius and Constantius) are not. The beards on the Augusti recall a Hadrian-like emphasis on the reinstitution of Greek culture in the empire, as beards were donned most commonly by Greek men, while the men of ancient Rome kept a clean shave.[11] Recall as well the most senior of the four tetrarchs was Diocles—a Greek name given to him at his birth that synonymized the ruler with Zeus, greatest in the Greek pantheon,

---

[7] Foxe, John. *The New Foxe's Book of Martyrs*. North Brunswick, NJ: Bridge-Logos Publishers, 1997. (p.28).
[8] Ibid. (6) (p.272).
[9] Grant, Michael. *The Roman Emperors*. New York City: Simon & Schuster, Inc., 1997. (p.221).
[10] Ibid. (6) (p.278-280).
[11] Ibid. (6) (p.176) *(Hadrian the Greek)*.

as opposed to Jupiter, who was his Roman counterpart.[12] It is significant to note the Greek-ism of the Augusti at this time in history because it was Greek revivalism that inspired the successor of the tetrarchs to re-found the Roman Empire permanently in the East, and recast the dominant culture of the era in the mold of the ancient Greek city of Byzantium.

It is also important to emphasize the dominance of Greek thought during the time of the tetrarchs because it recalls the question asked in this introduction: Why are four pagan emperors—four persecutors of Christians—enshrined on the corner of Saint Mark's Basilica?

The answer to that question is deeply intertwined with the subject matter of the book you are reading. Although they did not know it at the time, each of the four tetrarchs would each play an important role in codifying the most universal doctrine of the religion that they despised. *The History & Development of the Doctrine of the Trinity* is a long and storied journey throughout the ancient world which will lead the reader into the most epic times of Ancient Greece and Rome, as well as Egypt, Syria, and Israel. It is not a story that can be told with a handful of names and dates, although many may attempt to reduce the subject to such triviality. It requires a patient examination of what an older world believed about the gods, what one civilization believed about One God, and how the two worlds collided at the turn of one of the most important millennia in human history.

There is a challenge to documenting the history of things that have been venerated by mankind. The loftier the subject matter, the greater the challenge. When dissecting the foundations of religious thought in the world, it is not difficult to appear irreverent, even accidentally, to those who have embraced the subject matter to which the historian has devoted himself. In fact,

---

[12] Hamilton, Edith. *Mythology*. New York: Grand Central Publishing, 1942. (p.46).

it may appear impious to some even to suggest that certain religious thought has a history at all. Our devotion as spiritual thinkers to faith in the inerrancy and infallibility of holy texts sometimes leads us to place similar faith in the inerrancy and infallibility of the traditions of the men and women who embraced those texts. That is, of course, not a long tenable idea. While it may be admirable—even honorable—to live life with the belief that the Scriptures through which we orient our lives have been perfectly and divinely pieced together, it is not as reasonable to assume that the human beings who read those Scriptures are equally perfect or divine. Christians, specifically, have long embraced this notion, not as a fringe element of religious thought, but as an essential core of church doctrine: The Scriptures may be perfect. But the human beings who read them and interpret them every day are not perfect.

In acknowledging the principle of human fallibility comes the inevitable necessity of maintaining a spirit of humility. When examining human history, it is not possible to work from the principle of inerrancy. Human beings miss the mark at times, and that does not diminish the sincerity or even the reality of their faith. Human beings hit the mark too, and that is worth acknowledging.

Nevertheless, coupled with the responsibility to acknowledge human fallibility is the willingness to realize its implications. There are deep and abiding principles about religious thought to be discovered throughout this book that do not always square with dogma. Yet, when considered closely, they may lead the reader to a still greater and more meaningful relationship with the faith they so closely hold to their heart. For the non-religious, I hope the historical accounts discussed provide a great source of enjoyment for the reader. The epochs of history covered in this book tell some of the most incredible stories of human achievement, transcendence, and adventure that have inspired generations of thinkers. For believers, I hope it enhances your understanding of how we got here.

The doctrine of the trinity has unified Christian believers all over the world who would otherwise have almost nothing else in common. Although the term "trinity" appears nowhere within the

Jewish or Christian canon of Scriptures, it nonetheless stands as the centerpiece of modern Christian theology. Catholics and Protestants have long debated the role of grace in eternal salvation, the importance of works and sacraments, as well as other standards of piety in the Christian life. Yet, the doctrine of the trinity has stood the test of time. While almost every dogma of Christianity finds variance in meaningful ways throughout the world, trinitarianism is a characteristic of Christian thought on which many denominations find common ground. Catholic or Protestant, the trinity is something many have been able to unify around. Yet, it has not always been so.

In the first five centuries following the establishment of the church, the doctrine of the trinity was one of the most hotly contested beliefs in Christian thought. Even in the many centuries that followed, the trinity was by no means an uncontested doctrine. Although considered by many Christians to be an area of common ground between believers today, it was not so at the beginning of the church.

Throughout the last one hundred years or so, the history of the doctrine of the trinity has become a source of great interest to Christians all over the world in numbers not seen in centuries past. Although many books have been written on the theological and hermeneutical elements of trinitarian thought, a codified history of its development is an endeavor that I hope will serve as a meaningful contribution to the discussion of the subject in generations to come.

One of the most challenging aspects of historical writing is creating relevant boundaries for the subject matter at hand while not leaving too much beyond the border that will force the reader to rely heavily on private interpretation. In this work, I have attempted to map an essential and relevant guide to the development of the doctrine of the trinity throughout history without extending needlessly into the less certain and more interpretative aspects of its ideological framework. A great deal of writing may be done on spiritual interpretations of the Christian trinity and their theological implications. However, that is not the primary function of this book. The doctrine of the trinity as it stands today has clear and precise definitions which may be reasonably traced to specific people and places that gave place to its rise.

The opening chapters of this work focus centrally on the birth of Hellenism in the Near East, as I have found it to be the most helpful starting point when trying to understand the prevailing political and religious thought during the waning years of the Western Roman Empire in the third century and the beginning of Byzantium in the fourth. This is important, because it was during this period that the doctrine of the trinity was officially codified under Emperor Theodosius in 381 C.E. Ancient Greece and Rome are focus points of this work because they were the two great epicenters of civilization from 400 B.C.E. to 400 C.E. It is not the intention of the author to be reductionist—only to create reasonable boundaries for the subject matter at hand that may be discussed thoroughly in one volume.

The birth of Hellenism in the East is a helpful starting point when trying to frame the history of the doctrine of the trinity for other reasons as well. When studying the prevailing religious beliefs of the first four centuries, it is impossible to separate the pagan beliefs of the Romans from those of the Greeks that preceded them. In studying the origins of Hellenism in the Near East and Asia Minor, the reader comes away with a stronger understanding of the world that the Romans (and, by extension, the Christians) inherited.

Following the movement of Hellenism around the world, the book will take the reader through one of the most transitory periods of Israel's political history, as well as the great epochs of the Roman Empire, and the subsequent impact that they had on the Christian church. Last, the book settles on the subject matter discussed at the opening of this introduction—the peculiar era of the Roman tetrarchy, and the birth of the Byzantine Empire which followed it.

The content of this book serves as a literal account of the events that influenced the creation of the trinitarian statement articulated by the Nicene Creed in the fourth century and the ideological history of the beliefs that contributed to its present form. From ancient Greece to Byzantium, the seven centuries of religious thought examined in this work serve to illuminate the origins and spread of one of the most significant and ubiquitous theologies in the world.

# CHAPTER I

## Alexander the Great

## &

## The Persian Campaign

It is not always simple to determine the starting point of a particular epoch. Nevertheless, there are occasions where history gives us a moment, the significance of which is difficult to mistake. One such example is the birth of Alexander the Great in 357 B.C.E. It is nearly miraculous what Alexander accomplished in such a short amount of time on earth. Although he began his life as merely a prince in Macedonia, he had effectively conquered the known world by its end. In just twelve years, Alexander solidified his role as the hegemon of Greece, took back Greek city-states and territories that enemies of his kingdom had occupied throughout Asia Minor, and supplanted the King of Persia as ruler of the Near East.

Alexander was the child of Philip of Macedon and Olympias of Epirus. The sentiment that Philip conquered Greece while Alexander conquered all the rest may be an over-used one, but it is not necessarily overstated. Philip of Macedon was responsible for unifying the loose confederation of Greek city-states in a manner not seen before in the history of Greece. His quest to become the hegemon of Greece re-galvanized the territories as a regional power, and it set the stage for Alexander's conquest of Persia.

The Persians and the Greeks had a long and storied history of fighting, dating back most memorably to the battles between Xerxes and Sparta in the fifth century B.C.E. After the Spartans were driven out of Thermopylae in 480 B.C.E., Alexander I of Macedon (from whom Alexander the Great likely received his namesake) made allegiance with the Hellenes, giving Macedonia the legitimacy that it needed to build a meaningful legacy in

Greece.[1] By the time Philip came to power in 359 B.C.E., it was apparent that there would be no triumph over the Persian invaders without a unified Greece. Philip of Macedon saw within himself a man up to such a task. While both an absolute-ist in his approach to power and ruthless in his tactics,[2] Philip was also quite an effective leader. During his twenty-three-year reign, Philip consolidated total power over the largest portions of Greece, including Athens. Although his totalitarian control created much resentment in the city-states (eventually leading to his assassination in 336 B.C.E.), Philip of Macedon was as much responsible for the Greek conquest of Persia as his more famous son, Alexander the Great.

When Alexander came to power in 336 B.C.E., Macedonia was already situated atop the hierarchy of the Greek territories. Alexander believed it was his duty to fulfill the mission that his father had left behind, returning the territory in Asia Minor occupied by Persian invaders to their rightful Greek leadership. Further still, Alexander wanted to bring the Persian Empire itself to its knees, even if he had to travel into unknown parts of the world to do it. When examining the childhood of Alexander, it is not surprising that the young man had such visions of grandeur from a young age. His mother, Olympias, claimed that her son was the offspring of Heracles himself, and by extension, Zeus.[3] This claim to demi-god status by Olympias for her son was augmented by her participation in the cult of Zeus and her belief that her destiny had been sealed in a dream which foretold that she would produce such a child. Tradition taught that Olympias was herself the offspring of *echis* (snake), manifestly Achilles, and that she was the consort of a serpent, producing offspring the likes of which would conquer the world. Such religious beliefs caused great rifts between Olympias and Philip, potentially even contributing to the assassination of the latter in 336 B.C.E.[4]

Alexander's grandiose ambitions were quickly realized after the death of his father when he assumed his role as ruler of

---

[1] Cummings, Lewis V. *Alexander the Great.* New York: Grove Press, 1940. (p.7).
[2] Demosthenes, *Olynthiacs* II, (Sect. XV).
[3] Ibid. (1) (p.53-54).
[4] Athenaeus, XIII, (p. DLVII).

Macedon, leader of the League at Corinth, and commander of one of the most powerful military forces in the world at that time. With little standing between himself and his visions, Alexander set his sights on the long-awaited vengeance against Persia.

In order to understand the process of Alexander's systematic conquest of Asia Minor, Persia, and the Ancient East, one must have an appreciation for the feuding history of the two dominant empires at that time. In the mind of Alexander, his travels to the east were not a taking, but a taking *back*. Persia had long occupied territories once controlled by the Greeks, and Alexander had it in his heart to restore those areas to the Greek domain. In many ways, Alexander saw himself not as a conqueror at all, but as a liberator. At least, at first.

In his journeys through Asia Minor, Alexander made it his custom to show great benevolence to those areas which he captured (or re-captured) in the name of Greece. A common practice during his entry into a Persian-occupied Greek territory was to lavish great gifts on the Greeks who had maintained faithful allegiance to the traditions of Hellas. He would rebuild their infrastructure, levy taxes on the Persians, and re-institute Greek leadership in the area. But his most consistently repeated act of kindness to the occupied Greek territories during the campaign through Asia Minor was to rebuild Greek temples and houses of worship.[5] Alexander understood that politics was downstream of culture and that culture was downstream of religion. Where the Greek religion was allowed the thrive, the Greek culture would quickly follow suit. Ousting Persian influence from the territories meant disassociating the religion of the Persians from the area.

It is important to recognize the premium that Alexander placed on the restoration and spread of Greek religion. Alexander the Great had been raised to believe that he was himself a god. Or, at least, the son of one. Specifically, Alexander claimed to be the offspring of Heracles, situating himself squarely in the house of Zeus. It is of Zeus which the *Iliad* says,

---

[5] Ibid. (1) (pp. 136-137).

I am mightiest of all. Make the trial that you may know. Fasten a rope of gold to heaven and lay hold, every god and goddess. You could not drag down Zeus. But if I wished to drag you down, then I would. The rope I would bind to a pinnacle of Olympus and all would hang in air, yes, the very earth and the sea too.[6]

Not for nothing was Alexander intentional about synonymizing himself with the most premier god of the Greek pantheon. In himself, Alexander saw the next hero of Greece, the true successor of Heracles. The first of his own Twelve Labors would be the liberation of those cities that had been contaminated by Persian influence for generations.

During the days of Alexander the Great, Darius III reigned over the Persian Empire. The Persian Empire from 560 B.C.E. until 330 B.C.E. was ruled by kings known as the Achaemenid Dynasty, which was founded by Cyrus the Great in the sixth century B.C.E. As the Babylonian Empire declined during the reign of King Belshazzar, the Persian Empire took center stage in the Near East as the most dominant power of the region.[7] Darius III was the last of the Achaemenid kings, although it was unlikely that he (or anyone else) knew that at the time.

Upon reaching the outskirts of the Persian Empire with his army, Alexander showed such fearlessness that one wonders if youthful ignorance did not contribute to his success in some ways. The Macedonian forces were outnumbered, far from home, and

---

[6] Homer, the *Iliad*, (scroll VIII, line I).

[7] Daniel (Ch.5).

- It is not known with certainty that the King Darius mentioned in Daniel chapter six was Darius I of the Achaemenid Dynasty, however it seems plausible that he was indeed the same Darius. In Daniel chapter five it is said that Daniel traveled out of Israel during the Babylonian exile in 586 B.C.E. with many other Jews. Given the fact that Darius I reigned from 522-486 B.C.E., it is entirely possible that Daniel was a man of his mid to late seventies by the time the Babylonian Empire fell to the Persians, and that Darius knew Daniel personally as the Bible seems to suggest.

without sufficient resources to sustain a long campaign in foreign territory when they arrived at their first great battle—the Granicus River. There they faced off against the Great King's army. At Granicus was one of Darius III's most reliable leaders, and one of Alexander's most formidable opponents, Memnon of Rhodes.[8] While historical accounts of the battle are colorful and are likely written to paint the victors in the best light, it is difficult to come away with any understanding of the battle that does not depict Alexander as brash, if not reckless, in the mind of the reader. Of particular interest is his encounter with Spithradates, an enemy soldier who would have killed Alexander at Granicus had it not been for a dramatic intervention of one of Alexander's trusted men.[9] It is difficult to imagine a world without Alexander the Great in the history books, but had it not been for Cleitus at Granicus, the hegemon of Greece may only have been remembered as Alexander of Macedon. Nevertheless, Alexander the Great he was, and he continued to press forward in his campaign against Persia.

After his second crucial victory over Memnon at Halicarnassus (the last great general to serve under King Darius III), Alexander was determined to take the fight to Darius himself and march in Susa. Located near the Zargos Mountains in modern-day Iran, Susa served as the capital city of the Persian Empire for generations.

Although Alexander knew that he would ultimately have to march on Susa before his conquest of the Persians would be complete, it was apparent early in the campaign that Darius would not relinquish his control of the region without a fight. So begins the story of the famous battle at Issus between the two great kings in 333 B.C.E.

Issus would be the first of two great clashes between Alexander the Great of Macedon and Darius III of Persia, and it is certainly the most memorable. Fought along Gulf of Issus (Alexandretta) in what is today modern Turkey, the battle of Issus is remembered as Alexander's signature triumph over the

---

[8] Ibid. (1) (p.128).
[9] Arrian, *Anabasis,* Book I, (Ch. XV).

Persians, and the victory which would solidify Greece's revenge upon the Achaemenid kings.

Although the battle between Alexander and Darius was long expected, the timing and location of the battle came as a surprise to both parties. Darius had hoped to fight Alexander in Syria, but when it became apparent that Alexander's army could not be goaded into battle there, Darius settled on Cilicia, whose broad coastal plains would make an acceptable substitute that could adequately accommodate the size of his great army. Although ancient sources are somewhat unreliable for accurate figures concerning the size of each king's army, it can be safely assumed from all accounts that the Persian Army outnumbered the Macedonian's at least two to one. The situation was made all the more strenuous for Alexander when Darius surprised the Macedonian king by cutting off his supply lines from the north, thus limiting Alexander's ability to regroup and fight the battle on his terms.[10] Nevertheless, Alexander kept a level head in the crisis. Although the timing and location was not what Alexander expected, he was able to control the situation enough to force the army of Darius to fight in a narrow along the Pinarus River. This gave Alexander a distinct advantage, as the Persian Army was vast and not entirely mobile. Without wasting time, Alexander turned his army quickly toward the Persian forces, and chose to face the enemy head-on.

Ironically, it was the Greek mercenaries fighting on behalf of Darius who gave the Macedonians the most grief during the battle at Issus. While the Persian army was not incompetent, it lacked the experience of the Greek fighters. Furthermore, Darius made a tactical error early in the battle by moving the cavalry on his left wing near the foothills over toward his right to break through the Macedonian forces just off the coast of the gulf. When he did this, it created a gap on his left wing that Alexander (already well-positioned for such a move, as seen in figure 1.1) felt confident he could capitalize on.[11] Breaking through the enemy lines, Alexander

[10] Strauss, Barry. "Issus." Antiquitas. Last modified November 7, 2019. https://podcasts.apple.com/us/podcast/antiquitas/id1442027700?i=100045619 3534.
[11] Ibid. (1) (p.162-165).

charged head-on toward Darius himself on horseback, cutting down Persian enemies that stood in his way.

While ancient accounts of the battle at Issus vary in degree concerning the devastation of the battle, one detail of the clash of kings remains constant: Alexander charged Darius personally and did not hesitate to put himself in harm's way to capture or kill the head of the Persian Empire. The bravery of Alexander at Issus is reminiscent of his apparent recklessness at the Granicus River, but once again, Alexander came out on top. The story of Alexander's charge against Darius reads like something out of an old myth or legend, but there is no reason to assume that the events described did not transpire in precisely the way that they have been handed down to us by the ancient writers. In fact, from what can be gathered about Alexander's personality, the charge at Issus seems entirely within the realm of expected behavior by the Macedonian king. Modern historians have pieced together the moment that vividly paints the picture of Alexander's first run at Darius:

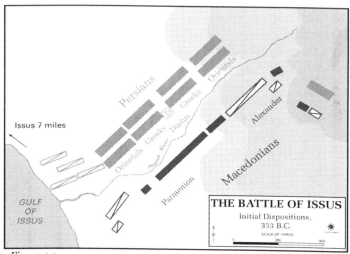

*Figure 1.1*

The Persians on the left having broken in route, Alexander found himself on the flank of the Greek phalanx. Turning to the left he fell upon them like a thunderbolt and cut his way through, then, seeing Darius far ahead of him in his great four-horse chariot, he turned toward his imperial enemy. The Persian nobles and bodyguard threw themselves in the path of the attacker, only to be swept aside or cut down and trampled underfoot. Our chroniclers say that the bodies of the Persian dead piled high before their king. The raging Macedonian king, now that his enemy was at least within range of his eyes, would not be halted. Oxathres, brother of Darius, threw himself upon Alexander, who slew him as casually as if he were merely a minor obstacle in the way of an accomplishment...As his gleaming Nemesis swept forward, Darius could stand it no longer; he turned his chariot and drove away at top speed, accompanied by only a few of his bodyguard. He fled away across the plain in his chariot, but as soon as he reached the rough foothills, he abandoned the vehicle, and, leaving in it his mantle, shield, and bow, continued the flight on horseback...In disgust, the [Persian] cavalry broke off the engagement and joined the rest of the Persian army in headlong flight. As soon as the rout was complete Alexander started in pursuit of the Great King, and Ptolemy Lagus, who accompanied him, later wrote that so great was the number of slain that in the pursuit they crossed a ravine on a dam of corpses.[12]

So it was that Alexander had defeated his great Persian adversary. The battle at Issus would not be the last time that these two foes met on the battlefield; however, Issus was the last serious opposition that Alexander faced in his march to Susa. Shortly after the second battle between the two opposing forces in 330 B.C.E., Darius III died. The death of the Great King meant that a power vacuum would soon be filled. And to the victor go the spoils. Soon after the death of his enemy, Alexander would forever cement his legacy as the man who had avenged Grecian honor, destroyed the Persians, and conquered the known world in just a few short years.

---

[12] Ibid. (1) (p.164).

But understanding how Alexander was able to unify such vast swaths of territory and bring together peoples of Greek, Egyptian, and Persian blood under one umbrella requires more than a mild grasp of the military history which precipitated it. It also demands an appreciation for the religious fervor that motivated Alexander and many other leaders in the fourth century B.C.E.

Remember that Alexander was not himself without a belief in the gods. In fact, he saw within his own person their earthly successor. In the mind of Alexander, he was the liberator of the Grecian way. As the son of Philip, he had an obligation to lead the people of Macedonia and Greece at large. But as the offspring of Heracles, he was duty-bound to bring Macedonia and greater Greece to the rest of the world as well. Alexander did not take kindly to territories that resisted his moves to spread Hellenism around the world. Of particular interest is Alexander's encounter with the Jewish people living in Israel during the post-Babylonian Exilic Period. After the battle of Issus, Alexander marched his army toward Tyre. While there, Alexander sent a message to the high priest of Jerusalem named Jaddua requesting Jewish assistance in the siege on Tyre. When the high priest refused, having sworn allegiance to Darius III and his forces, Alexander made a vow to sack Jerusalem as punishment for the refusal. Yet astonishingly, Alexander's anger was assuaged by none other than the writings of the Jewish religion itself. Upon reaching the gates of the city, Alexander marveled at the fidelity of the people and was shown a prophecy that foretold of the days when a man of Javan (Ionia) would free the people from Persian rule.[13] Alexander

---

[13] It is difficult to know with certainty which prophecy Alexander was shown that softened his heart to the Jewish religion. However, it very likely that the prophetic reading came from Daniel chapter eight. In Daniel 8:5, the prophet is shown a he goat that conquers a ram in battle. Later, in Daniel 8:19-21, the prophet is told by the angel Gabriel that the goat represented the Grecian Empire, while the ram represented the Persians and the Medes. Another prophecy of interest during Alexander's encounter with the Jews is Zechariah chapter nine, which tells of a day in which the city of Tyre will be sacked and destroyed. Furthermore, the prophecy specifically mentions a Jewish conflict with the people of Greece.

was so greatly moved by this prophecy that his anger against the Jews was stayed, and he allowed the people to continue their religion and way of life unmolested by the Greeks.[14]

While it is understood that Alexander remained true to the Greek cults all of his life, it is remarkable how much deference he seemed to show the Jews. The story of Alexander's encounter with the high priest of Jerusalem and the people of Israel illustrates a peculiar regard that Alexander had for certain religious traditions of the peoples around him. In the mind of the Grecian king, it was not acceptable for the hegemon of Greece to defile the gods as the Persian Zoroastrians had done. For Alexander, unity required a measure of respect for the religious beliefs of the peoples of the world, at least in as far as his personal interests were concerned. Persian Zoroastrianism did not receive such generous treatment by Alexander, but his regard for the Jewish religion had utility. According to the temple leadership of Israel, their God had ordained Alexander's victory over Persia. Whether this claim was sincere or motivated by self-preservation, it had its desired effect on Alexander. In fact, there is no reason to assume that Alexander's decision to leave Israel alone during his conquest was not motivated by a legitimate fear of the Jewish God. Afterall, in the mind of Alexander, the God of Israel had chosen the king for the very destiny that Alexander had already believed was the will of the gods of Greece as well. His willingness to forgo conquest in Israel is senseless outside of this understanding; Alexander probably believed that the prophecies of the Israelites were true. Israel was a relatively small nation with no military force that could challenge the Greeks of that era. Alexander could have made quick work of destroying Judaea, but he didn't. Where hay could be made, Alexander allowed the sun to shine. Israel would not be the last nation to experience such magnanimity from Alexander. There were other occasions where the king showed deference to the gods of the lands the Greeks conquered, even if such deference meant recasting the cults of the Greeks in the mold of the surrounding nations at times.

---

[14] Josephus, *Antiquities of the Jews*, Book XI, (Ch. XII), and Niese's Geschichte der griech, und makedon. Staaten, (p.83).

Herein lies the challenge of being both the sovereign of a nation as well as an expansionist—how does one bring together the newly conquered territory with the old homeland? The most naturally understood response to such conflict between the conqueror and the conquered is tyranny. Do what the king says or face the consequences. But such an aggressive tactic is not always so simple, and it can create more problems for a leader than it solves. The primary motivation behind conquest is the expansion of influence and resources. Tyranny and civil strife can cost a leader both in a very short amount of time. For a peaceful transition of power to take place in such a situation, the culture, lifestyle, and religion of the conquered must be respected to some degree. If not, rebellion is sure to ensue. However, in showing such respect, one may alienate their own constituency in the process. The Greeks had their religion to consider too, and it was certainly the one that was to be more highly prioritized. In order to understand how Alexander accomplished such a recasting of Greek culture in the image of the world around him, it is helpful to briefly examine a few fundamental principles concerning what much of the ancient world believed about the gods.

The practice of subjugated territories amalgamating the most ideal portions of a particular cult or god into a more unified religious principality was not uncommon in the old world, even before the days of Alexander the Great. The ancient Babylonians worshiped a god named Marduk, but Marduk was not "a" god at all. Marduk was a projection of more than fifty gods, known by more than fifty names, and was regarded as the master of as many forces in the world. Because religious compromise is generally preferable to war or other forms of social conflict, territories that expanded or were expanded into had to find a way to bridge the gap between the various pantheons that existed in the nations around them.[15] Perhaps one region venerated Baal as the chief of

---

[15] Peterson, Jordan B. Kings, Ideals, and Marduk. Last modified August 18, 2020. https://youtu.be/BfqYGhncoeE.

its deities, and another honored the Egyptian Horus. Rather than forcing a showdown between the peoples of the two gods, the cults would find a place of compromise. One might think of it this way: If I worship god "A" and you worship god "B" then by extracting the most essential portions of the two, we can create god "C" to personify both god "A" and god "B" at the same time. The characteristics that last the longest ultimately find their place in god "C" singularly, until eventually god "D" will need to be formed as well, and so on.

The practice may seem foolish to some, but if you can conceive of a world where the gods are not all-powerful and often in conflict with one another, then the behavior of the ancient world becomes more rational, at least in principle. The gods were more or less images of archetypes in the world as understood by their worshipers. Just as we do today, the peoples of ancient Greece, Egypt, and Babylonia were watching one another act in the world and trying to understand what patterns of behavior were the most ideal to imitate. They were paying attention to what vices were most common, as well as what virtues. The most repeatedly recognized patterns of being were often personified into a single principality (a god). That principality represented a force that competed with other forces for dominance in the world, each remaining critical to the structure of the whole.[16] This act of religious amalgamation also made it possible for societies to remain cohesive that would otherwise have very little in common. As long as each portion of the new community felt that its gods were being appropriately honored, the particular images, practices, and names became less relevant. At least, that is how it appears when read from a more modern perspective. This also informs our understanding of the deification of human beings in the ancient world, which was certainly not an uncommon practice. Particularly among the ruling elite, it was almost essential that the ruler possess some form of god-like status.

---

[16] Peterson, Jordan B. The Jordan B. Peterson Podcast-Introduction to the Idea of God. Last modified April 20, 2020. https://podcasts.apple.com/us/podcast/the-jordan-b-peterson-podcast/id1184022695?i=1000471222601.

Perhaps it is difficult for the modern reader to understand, particularly in the western world, but it was not so far-fetched an idea for Alexander to claim to be a god among his peers. At least, not in his time. One must remember that the Greek pantheon of gods consisted of a plethora of competing forces, none of which were necessarily omnipresent and certainly not omnipotent. The idea of a "God above gods" is a conception of the divine, which is to be found first and foremost in the Jewish and later Christian religions. But it was not a Greek sentiment, nor was it very common in the peoples of the ancient Near East (with, perhaps, the exception of the Zoroastrians, which will be discussed later in this chapter). In the ancient world, gods could be challenged and even defeated.

Alexander may have considered himself to be in the family of Zeus, but Zeus had enemies. Zeus could be opposed, as could his son Heracles. Alexander was no different. In order to be a god Alexander did not need omnipotence, because the gods of Greece were not omnipotent. He did not need omnipresence, because the Greek pantheon was not omnipresent, at least not in an existential sense. However, he did have to embody a particular purpose of the gods. Alexander had to be the personification of a very particular kind of telos, and it was a personification that he would be possessed by until his death.

Nevertheless, the religious zeal of the Macedonian king would not get the better of the political side of Alexander. And politician he was. After the death of Darius III in 330 B.C.E., Alexander could claim a vast new empire as his own. That empire included the coveted land of Egypt, and Egypt had many gods. When he traveled through Asia Minor liberating Greek cities from Persian influence, it was the modus operandi of Alexander to rebuild Greek temples and re-institute the cult of Zeus where the Persian Zoroastrians had attempted to uproot the Greek way of life. But the further east he traveled, the more that this practice became challenging for the Macedonian king. In Asia Minor, Alexander was a liberator. When the cult of Zeus was re-established in that region, it was to the great joy and relief of the people whose land the Persians had occupied. But in Egypt, Alexander was not a liberator. He was a conqueror, and that meant that Greek sympathizers were likely harder to come by. While the Egyptians welcomed Alexander as the king, they were not prepared to relinquish their gods. Thus, the challenge was presented to Alexander the Great: how is one to honor his god and the god of another at the same time? Alexander's behavior in Egypt revealed wisdom beyond his years in many ways. He did not enter Egypt with the attitude of a Greek imperialist bent on imposing his will on the Egyptian people. As in Israel, Alexander showed deference to the Egyptian pantheon and found subtle yet meaningful ways of paying homage to their gods. One modern historian offered this explanation of Alexander's behavior upon his entry into the land of Egypt:

> It is certain that Alexander in Egypt either showed perfect understanding of the psychology of conquered peoples or acted upon excellent advice in adopting the course of action that he did. He officially and publicly offered sacrifice to the [Egyptian] gods and to the bull Apis, who was not a god but a sacred animal of the cult of Ptah. It may be that Alexander, though officially offering sacrifice to the gods of Egypt, was really sacrificing to the gods of Greece. The Egyptian gods had long been equated in the Greek mind with their own, Ammon with Zeus, Osiris with Dionysus, Horus with Apollo, and so on...By these and subsequent acts, such as ordering the rebuilding of the sanctuary of the temple of Karnak and the temple at Luxor, Alexander identified himself with the preservation of the gods and religions, thereby removing immediately a very possible seed of rebellion and discontent.[17]

Like all successful politicians, Alexander understood that people are generally averse to change, particularly change that happens too quickly. Of all the ancient peoples of Alexander's time, it appears that the Greeks understood this principle better than most. For the Greeks, it was not sacrilege to synonymize the gods of the surrounding nations with the gods of Greece, so long as in

---

[17] Ibid. (1) (p.191).

the mind of the adherent, the true identity of the god remained sound. In her classic work on mythology, Edith Hamilton writes,

> The Zeus of song and story has been made by combining many gods. When his worship spread to a town where there was already a divine ruler the two were slowly fused into one.[18]

In other words, it is possible (indeed likely) that Alexander saw his actions in Egypt as divinely ordered of Zeus and paid tribute to him accordingly in the name of Ammon. In fact, it is known from the accounts of Plutarch and Strabo that Alexander visited the oracle of Ammon in the temple erected at the oasis of Siwah. Upon entering the shrine,

> The king alone was suffered to enter the temple in ordinary dress; his retinue was compelled to change their clothes. All others stood outside to listen to the delivery of the oracle, Alexander alone inside. Oracles are not given here, as in Delphi and Branchidae, in words, but for the most part in gesture and symbols, the prophet assuming the character of Zeus (Ammon). This, however, was said distinctly in words by the prophet to the king, that he, Alexander, was the son of Zeus.[19]

At the oracle of Ammon, the gods were not necessarily combined to create a new god, but they were harmonized to express a unity of divine power. It was not improper in the eyes of either the Greek king or the Egyptian oracle to capitulate on the name of the deity responsible for Alexander's conquest. This recalls the practice of the ancient Mesopotamian peoples that worshiped Marduk. Compromise is preferable to war, particularly if such compromise does not appear to offend. Because much of the pre-Christian world's understanding of the gods was primarily articulated in terms of power, identity of the gods in the nominal sense was always secondary. This was particularly true of the Egyptian god

---

[18] Hamilton, Edith. *Mythology*. New York: Grand Central Publishing, 1942. (p.21).
[19] Strabo, *Geography*, Book XVII (Ch. I, Sect. XLIII).

named Ammon, to which Alexander paid homage in the name of Zeus. Thus, Zeus was honored in Ammon and Ammon in Zeus.

In Egyptian mythology, Ammon was both self-created and sat apart from the rest of the hierarchy of the gods. In some ways, Ammon was considered to exist distinctly from all other powers. Because mystery surrounded the cult of Ammon, he was easily synchronized and associated with other Egyptian deities. By the dawn of the New Kingdom, Ammon was most closely associated with the Egyptian Ra, god of the sun.[20] The unique beliefs about Ammon and Ra influenced the Egyptian understanding of the power of the Pharaohs as well. Because Ammon was considered the unknown god, and he existed beyond the boundaries of the visible and expressive, Ra became the "unknown revealed" to the Egyptian people. In other words, Ra was a knowable representation of an otherwise unknowable God. He was both god of the sun, as well as "Ammon revealed." This impacted the Egyptian beliefs about the Pharaohs because it was accepted by many that the Pharaohs were themselves offspring of the gods. Specifically, the Pharaohs were the children of Ra.[21] Through this claim, the Pharaohs could, in a sense, be considered a visible expression of Ammon as well. Their power was associated with that of Egypt's greatest god, thus strengthening their claim to divine right.

This understanding was not unlike the Greeks in their belief that the great kings were the offspring of the Olympian pantheon. Remember that Alexander's mother claimed to be the consort of a serpent possessed by the gods, therefore Alexander had familial relation to the demi-god Heracles. It is also worth noting that

---

[20] "Deities in Ancient Egypt - Amun." Rosicrucian Egyptian Museum. Last modified , 2021. https://egyptianmuseum.org/deities-amun.
[21] Sacks, Jonathan. *Covenant & Conversation - Exodus: The Book of Redemption.* Jerusalem: Maggid Books, 2010.

- The Egyptian Pharaohs known as Rameses were an expression of this belief. The suffix "meses" being interpreted "son of." Quite literally, the Rameses were the "sons of Ra."

Ammon, in his many forms, was also known as the god of the air.[22] In Greek tradition, Zeus was the god of the sky and the clouds,[23] which likely bolstered the relationship between the two gods in the mind of the Egyptians and the Greeks. When Alexander visited the oracle of Ammon, the tacit relationship between the two gods became more real. Ultimately, this culminated in the unification of the two in what has become known as Zeus-Ammon.[24] Figures 1.2 and 1.3 depict a sculpted image of one representation of this unified god. The two dominant features of this particular bust are the beard and the horns. Beards were donned most commonly by Greek men in Asia Minor and the Near East,[25] while the horns added to the sides of the head of Zeus Ammon reflect the dominant expression of Ammon-Ra during this time period, which often included the body of a man with a ram's head. The image accurately illustrates characteristics that would have been recognizable to both Greek and Egyptian viewers.

When reflecting on the practice of unifying deities, it may be tempting to assume that the ancient world had a dim or even childish view of religion. But it is difficult to discern with certainty that this was the case. The people of Alexander's time understood that there are great forces at work in the world and that human beings did not create them. That takes humility to acknowledge, and so in some sense it may be proper to think of the Greeks, Egyptians, and other cultic worshipers as a people having a longing for something that was true but not knowing precisely what it was.

It is true that many of the Greek gods were characterized as forces in nature, but not just in the elemental sense. The Greeks recognized archetypes of human behavior and they paid a great deal of attention to patterns in the world. Their understanding of the gods was greatly informed by such inquiries. While the idea of one supreme God which ruled over the rest was not common in ancient Greek thought, the practice of combining certain of their

---

[22] Ibid. (20).
[23] Ibid. (18).
[24] Liebieghaus Skulpturen Sammlung. Last modified , 2010. https://www.liebieghaus.de/en/antike/head-zeus-ammon.
[25] Strauss, Barry. *Ten Caesars*. New York: Simon & Schuster, Inc., 2019. (p.176).

gods suggests that, at least in principle, the Greeks knew that there were forces at work which seem to transcend the gods themselves.

*Figure 1.2*                    *Figure 1.3*

Although polytheistic in practice, the fact that Alexander chose to show deference to the religion of the Jews without being familiar with its finer theology, as well as his willingness to truncate Greek traditions concerning the cult of Zeus for the sake of the Egyptian people, shows that the modern understanding of ancient religion is, at best, obscured.

While much of what the ancient world believed about the gods remains unclear, there is one thing that can be known from Alexander's trip to the oracle of Ammon—it had its desired outcome. Alexander became the new king of Egypt without causing a civil war. For this accomplishment alone, Alexander deserves tremendous credit for his skills as a politician. The priests of the Egyptian pantheon were very powerful figures among the ruling class of Egypt, yet they did not protest Alexander's claim to kingship. Whether out of political expedience or a genuine trust of the man, the religious leaders of Egypt accepted Alexander's rule as the divine will. While Greeks would continue to understand the supreme power as it was expressed through Zeus, the Egyptians would continue to honor Ammon. And both would honor Alexander the Great's reign as the unified will of their gods.

The fact that Alexander was willing to pay homage to Zeus in the name of Ammon was augmented by his subsequent willingness to embrace the ancient titles traditionally placed upon the Egyptian king as well. The following passage taken from Ulrich Wilcken's work on the subject includes translation from hieroglyphic writings dating to the era:

> Of the five titles customary from the middle of the third millennium B.C. the first, fourth, and fifth were given to Alexander. As 'Horus' (I) he was called 'the strong prince' (2); also with the addition 'he who hath laid hands upon the lands of the foreigners,' or 'the protection of Egypt' (3). As 'King of Upper Egypt and King of Lower Egypt' (4), he was called 'beloved of Ammon and selected of Ra'; and finally as 'son of Ra' (5), he was called 'Alexanderos.' Here the Horus title, 'he who hath laid hands upon the lands of the foreigners,' seems to have been invented for Alexander, whereas the other two titles are frequent before his time. These titles prove two things of Alexander, his special sovereignty over Egypt, and his consequent deification.[26]

These examples and others guide the modern reader to a higher understanding of Alexander's savvy as a politician. Still, they also tell us a great deal about his prioritization of the Greek religion. For Alexander, Hellenism transcended time and place. It could be absorbed into any nation, so long as the fundamental structure of it remained intact. This is, perhaps, why Alexander's great religious benevolence was not shared with the Persian Zoroastrians. Unlike the Egyptians, who, like the Greeks, worshiped a pantheon and regarded the dominion of each

---

[26] Wilcken, Ulrich. *Alexander der Grosse*. Germany: Quelle & Meyer, 1931.

individual god in the context of certain shared traditions, the Persian religion was unique to its time and location.

Although the name "Zoroastrian" ultimately came to refer to those who followed the teachings of Spitama Zarathustra (Zoroaster) some fifteen hundred years before Christ, the religion itself can be traced back to the Mazdayasnianism of the Aryas who lived in the Media Atropatene region and predated Zoroaster. While their exact origin is not known, the Mazdayasnianism referred to in the teachings of the Zoroaster is regarded as belonging to a quasi-monotheistic people who spoke out against the worship of the sun and the moon, which had become popularized among the people of that region.[27] According to the Aryas, those who practiced sun and moon worship had become idolatrous, acknowledging the power of creation more than the creator. Zoroastrianism taught that there was a Good Spirit and an Evil Spirit at work in the world and that these two spirits, while in conflict, were not equals. While this description of Zoroastrianism has led some historians to surmise that the religion was the basis for what became known as Persian dualism, such an assumption appears reductionist at best.[28] According to the Avesta and the Pahlavi texts (Zoroastrian religious works), the beliefs of the Mazdayasnian peoples did not perceive good and evil as equal spiritual forces in the world. In fact, contrary to the principles of dualism, Zoroastrian texts seem to suggest a belief in the Good Spirit as the supreme power at work in the world and unrivaled.[29]

> Ahura-Mazda, (All Knowing Lord) through omniscience, knew that Ahriman (destructive spirit) exists...The Evil Spirit, on account of backward knowledge, was not aware of the existence of Ahura-Mazda...He [Ahura-Mazda] sets the vault into which the Evil Spirit fled, in that metal; he brings the land of hell back for the enlargement of the world...So it is declared that Ahura-Mazda is supreme in omniscience and goodness,

---

[27] Kapadia, Shapurji A. *The Teachings of Zoroaster*. London: Aziloth Books, 2013. (p.16).
[28] Qualben, Lars P. *A History of the Christian Church*. New York: Nelson and Sons Pub., 1958. (p.105-106).
[29] Ibid. (27) (p.24).

and unrivaled in splendor...Revelation is the explanation of both spirits together: one is he who is independent of unlimited time, because Ahura-Mazda were and are and ever will be; While Ahriman in darkness, with backward understanding and desire for destruction, was in the abyss, and it is he who will not be.

While the Zoroastrian religion did experience fracture and fragmentation throughout the centuries culminating in the formation of many break-away religious doctrines, (such as dualism), the fundamental beliefs of the Mazdayasnian were not principally dualistic. Good and evil were not on equal footing in the minds of these ancient people. In fact, the Zoroastrian religion seems to have acknowledged a subordination of evil to good as a force in the world, an idea that was not particularly common for its time.

The Zoroastrian emphasis on good works as a signal commitment of righteous people to their relationship with God raises questions about their ethnic origins as well. Zoroastrianism predates Christianity and Islam significantly, but its early relationship to the dominant monotheistic religion of the world during the days of Alexander the Great (Judaism) is less certain. In the Jewish tradition, there were monotheistic gentiles even before the days of Abraham who did not participate in the idol cults of their generation.[30] Even after the calling of Abraham in Genesis chapter twelve there are numerous references to gentiles who feared the God of the Israelites,[31] or at least were not like the rest of the gentile idol worshipers around them. While there does not appear to be any direct connection between Zoroastrianism

---

[30] The book of Genesis leads the reader to understand that Noah, a gentile, was a righteous man who feared the God of heaven.

[31] In Genesis, Noah is depicted as a god-fearing man in an otherwise godless world. In Exodus, the reader is made to understand that two Egyptian women named Shiphrah and Puah who worked as midwives to the Hebrews refused to carry out an immoral order against the Jews. Again, in Exodus there is made mention of Jethro, the father-in-law of Moses, who was a priest in Midian that feared the God of Moses yet was not a Hebrew himself. In the book of Joshua, the reader finds Rahab the Canaanite harlot who acknowledges the power of the Israelite God. Furthermore, the patriarch of the dominant monotheistic peoples of today (Abraham) was a man from Ur of Chaldees, who according to Hebrew tradition, was the son of an idol merchant.

and Judaism in any meaningful historical sense, the monotheistic qualities of the early Mazdayasnian peoples are peculiar. It is the opinion of the author that it is at least conceivable that these Persians had a distant relationship with the proto-Hebrew cultures of the ancient world that had received some traditional understanding of God as described in the book of Genesis. Nevertheless, the Zoroastrians largely evolved into a form of Persian dualism and seemed to abandon whatever monotheistic tendencies they may have once had.

The Zoroastrians also seemed to place a premium on a personal commitment to good character and holiness, something that would have seemed superstitious to the Greeks of Alexanders time. In Khordah-Avesta,[32] the following is said concerning their god's behavior toward those who are good and evil:

> He is in possession of all good things, spiritual and worldly, such as good mind, immortality, health, the best truth, devotion and piety, and abundance of every earthly good. All these gifts He grants to the righteous man who is upright in thoughts, words, and deeds. As the ruler of the whole universe, He not only rewards the good, but He is a punisher of the wicked at the same time.

While the belief that the gods had the power to punish and reward was not a novel one in fourth century B.C.E. Greece, the belief that the gods only did so according to a man's good and evil works was certainly not a Greek notion. Furthermore, the role of the ancient Persian god in the creation of the world[33] would have seemed foreign to the Greek cults around the western world at that time. These examples and others perhaps shed light on understanding Alexander's ambivalence toward the Persian religion.

Perhaps the most objectionable belief of the Zoroastrians in the mind of Alexander was their commitment to abstaining from the worship of the sun and the moon. As the ancient religion of the Aryas began to become corrupted in the mind of Spitama

---

[32] Khordah-Avesta is the prayer book of the Parsi people, who are modern observers of Zoroastrianism from the Indian subcontinent.
[33] (Yaîçna I).

Zarathustra, he began to warn his followers against the influence of the Evil Spirit in the world. According to Zoroaster, the peoples' tendency to worship and adore the created elements or manifestations of the Ahura-Mazda, instead of the god himself, was not pleasing to this god. In contrast to the Aryas, Zoroaster used the word daêva (Sanskrit for "light" or "to shine") to describe the wicked idolatry that the people were practicing. In Greek, the word daêva is translated as "Zeus."[34]

In light of this, it is not difficult to understand what objections Alexander the Great may have had to the Zoroastrian religion. This is to say nothing of his personal vendetta against the Persians as a nation and his desire to exact vengeance on them for their storied wars against Greece. The Zoroastrians placed a premium on good thoughts and good works, and they believed that there was a divine connection between the soul of a man and his good standing with God. By contrast, the Greeks tended toward a sort of paganism that was probably more synonymous with the sun and moon worship so despised by Zoroaster than with the more spiritual religion of the Mazdayasnians. The cult of Zeus in particular had a reason to feel that Zoroastrianism was dangerous to their way of life. Specific references to the worship of the sun, moon, and stars were made by Zoroaster, and they were not reverent. In fact, Zoroaster considered the worship of such things to be a work of the Evil Spirit in the world. Apollo was the god of light in Greece. Zeus was the god of the wind and the skies, and associated with the light. Alexander had temples constructed in the honor of both gods before his death, to say nothing of the fact that Alexander believed himself to be a peer of these gods. Dishonor to these cults was a dishonor to Alexander himself. This, perhaps, explains why Alexander treated the Zoroastrians with a greater degree of harshness than he had treated the Jews when he arrived outside the gates of Jerusalem. His familiarity with Zoroastrianism was much keener than his understanding of Judaism. Furthermore, there was no historical score between the Greeks and the Jews which needed to be settled. The same cannot be said for the Greeks and the Persians.

---

[34] Ibid. (27) (p.22-23).

Although his behavior toward the Jews and the Persians were exceptions to the rule, Alexander the Great was a master of assimilating nearly every culture that he dominated to the traditions of Hellenism. Because of his willingness to adapt the Greek religion to the principal deities of the world around him, he ensured that the over-arching structure of Greek religion remained intact. And remain intact it did. When he encountered a religious structure that could not (or would not) conform to the principles of Hellenistic religious dogma, that religious structure was generally dismissed as superstitious or dangerous and ultimately ostracized from society. Even Judaism would not stand unmolested for long. In the centuries following Alexander's death, Judaism came under the pressure of Greek persecution due to its incompatibility with Hellenism, a subject which will be discussed in greater detail throughout chapters three and four of this book. Hellenism demanded a principled acceptance of the idea of assimilation itself. The mystery and mythology surrounding the Greek and Egyptian cults made such assimilation much more palatable to the citizens of those regions during the days of Alexander the Great. But the unique religious beliefs of the peoples living in the region of modern Syria, Iran, and Israel made assimilation to the Greek way of life much more difficult. The tension between Hellenism and these regions would come to a boiling point throughout the rise and fall of the Seleucid Empire.

Alexander's talent as a military commander took him a long way in his march through the Persian Empire. But his understanding of the need for religious cohesion is no less responsible for his success as a conqueror. By the end of 330 B.C.E., Alexander had convinced much of the known world that his self-proclaimed deification was not without merit.

Nevertheless, Alexander's claim to god-like status did not go unchallenged in his homeland. After his campaign through India, Alexander returned to Babylon to reaffirm political alliances between himself and the Persians, as well as quell unrest that had been stirred up by his long absence. Upon his return, he demanded that the Greek states inside the League of Corinth recognize him as a son of the now officially unified deity, Zeus-Ammon. The response of the Greek states to the demand by the new ruler of the known world was ambivalent at best.

> Megalopolis hastened immediate recognition of his godhead and even erected an altar to it. Sparta acceded unwillingly and with bad grace. Athens was furious at the order. Demosthenes still blindly hated Alexander's equally blind militarism, and blindly failed to recognize that the order emanated, not from Alexander the hegemon of Greece, but from Alexander the king of Macedonia, pharaoh of Egypt, King of Persia and Babylonia, and lord of all Asia, who was also prospective lord of the world. Demosthenes inveighed sarcastically upon the order, but accepted it: 'Let him be the son of Zeus if he wishes, or the son of Poseidon for all I care.' Lycurgus the orator exclaimed bitterly: 'What kind of god is this Alexander, at whose temple one must purify himself on going out instead of before entering?' Demades seems to have been the only realist. Instead of kicking against the pricks, he proposed that Alexander be worshipped as the thirteenth of the Olympian gods, as an aspect of Dionysus, whose legendary exploits he had surpassed. When the matter was hotly debated in the assembly, he, mindful of the unwisdom of opposition to the conqueror's expressed demands, warned them 'to take care lest in guarding heaven they lose earth.'[35]

The less-than-enthusiastic response by so many of the Greek states and the leaders within them may reveal something important about religious beliefs of the Greeks. While many acquiesced to Alexander's demand of deification, many did so only begrudgingly.

The relationship between politics and religion in the ancient world is perhaps difficult to understand for modern readers, particularly in the West. To the Greeks, Alexander had become

---

[35] Ibid. (1) (p.424).

arrogant, even filled with delusions of grandeur. And yet, his claim that he was a god was not met with heavy resistance either. It is evident from the written accounts of the Grecian reaction to Alexander's demand for deification that the role which power played in understanding the Greek and Egyptian religions was at least a complicated one. While many may have dismissed Alexander's claims privately, they honored him publicly. Whether it was out of a sincere fear of the gods or political expedience, it matters very little—the outcome was still the same. In the ancient world, to have power was tantamount to the favor of the gods. The two were not easily separated. Alexander may have seemed delusional to his critics, but they still likely regarded his conquest of Persia as divinely ordained. In this regard, they saw Alexander as an instrument in the hands of the gods, and he was not to be challenged. The very act of conquest had earned Alexander the right to make the claims that he did, delusional or not.

The more religiously fervent followers of Alexander may have even acknowledged Alexander as the vessel of Olympus. Just as Heracles had brought order to so much of the known world by founding cities and establishing Greek dynastic rule, so too had Alexander. Sincere believers or not, the Greeks understood that Alexander was in charge, and no one could dismiss how much he had managed to accomplish in ten short years.

No less mysterious than his life is the death of Alexander the Great. Upon his return to Babylon, tradition says that Alexander had been warned by Chaldean priests that his trip to Babylon would be his last.[36] Not willing to succumb to the priests and their pleas that he not come by the way he was determined to go, Alexander entered the city and engaged in weeks of drunken feasts, parties, and other excessive behaviors. On June 3, 323 B.C.E. we are told that Alexander began a fever and severe

---

[36] Ibid. (1) (p.440).

headache which did not abate for more than a week.[37] By June 13, 323 B.C.E. the great king was dead.

In ways still being discovered today, Alexander the Great changed the world. His journeys through Asia Minor, Persia, and the rest of the Near East created a ripple effect that would have far-reaching consequences. It is said that upon being asked who he would leave his empire to, Alexander's last words were "*Kratisto*" (to the strongest). If this is true, it may be said that Alexander received his last dying wish. Generations of civil war among Alexander's military leaders who were anxious to take their share of the vast empire ensued due to Alexander's untimely death. Had it not been for Alexander's conquest, it is unlikely that the later Roman Empire would have ever become as vast or as influential as it ultimately did, as the Romans practiced the adoption of Hellenic culture, augmenting its influence. After the death of Alexander, his empire was fractured into three major pieces because he had left no clear heir to his throne. In what became known as the Macedonian (Antigonid), Seleucid, and Ptolemaic Empires, civil war broke out between the three smaller kingdoms. These broken and weakened versions of Alexander's vast empire created the catalyst that Rome needed to win the first of the Punic Wars less than a century after Alexander's passing. Whether or not this feat could have been accomplished against a unified Alexandrian Empire is a question that will never be answered. Nevertheless, in one of history's great ironies, Alexander was responsible for both the great conquest that made him famous and the downfall that destroyed his empire. Alexander as a conqueror, had unified much of Greece, expanded the kingdom, and enlarged its influence. But his decision to name no heir led to the deterioration of the Grecian Empire, allowing Rome—the Hellenized outgrowth of Greece—to rise.

In the generation immediately following the death of Alexander, the Seleucid Empire was one of the three major kingdoms created as a consequence of the civil war between Alexander's generals. The Seleucid Empire galvanized Hellenism in the territories of Syria, Western Asia, and Israel. As will be

---

[37] Arrian, *Anabasis,* Book VII, (Ch. XXVIII).

discussed in the following two chapters, the rise and fall of the Seleucid Empire set the stage for the most influential religious movement in the history of the world. But in order to understand just how the Seleucid Empire's formation influenced the birth of certain religious revolutions in the first century, we must first examine the religious conflict that precipitated it. In the first two centuries B.C.E., great conflict arose between Hellenism and Judaism. Israel, which had been largely left alone by Alexander the Great, would not experience such benevolence under the tutelage of the Seleucid Greeks. The conflict between Judaism and Hellenism created the catalyst for the various religious sects and geo-politics of first-century Israel that would eventually culminate with the rise of Judaism's most influential Rabbi and His followers known in later years as the Christians.

# CHAPTER II

## The

## Seleucid

## Greeks

Although each part of Alexander the Great's fragmented empire played an important role in shaping religious and cultural thought in the waning years of the millennia, the Seleucid and Ptolemaic Empires had the most direct influence in Syria and much of the Near East following Alexander's death. Examination of the Seleucid Empire's existence, brief though it was, is an essential step in understanding the religious climate of Israel and the surrounding nations before and throughout the time of Jesus Christ. The religious zeal of Alexander, his prioritization of the cult of Zeus, and the overarching devotion of his followers to the spread of Hellenism had a sustained influence on the world for centuries following the decline of Grecian rule. While Hellenism was not entirely novel to western Asia before Alexander's conquests, it was by no means the primary culture of the region. Even after the battles of Granicus and Issus, it was not certain that Hellenism would succeed in supplanting the religious cultures already long established in the areas which Alexander had conquered. As discussed in chapter one, the further east that the Greeks traveled, the more diverse the world's religions were revealed to be. Nevertheless, Hellenism did take root in the Near East, and that is primarily because of influence of the Seleucid Empire.

The abrupt passing of Alexander the Great created a power vacuum in the vast empire that had to be filled. Unifying territories that stretched from modern-day Athens to India, Egypt to Turkmenistan, and the Caspian Sea to the Red Sea was not a task that was likely to succeed without the ability of a leader to claim divine right by birth. Because divine right could not be found among Alexander's children (he had left no legitimate heir), that allowed just one other option for claiming dominion over the territories—military might.

Alexander had many trusted generals who had served alongside him since his departure from Macedonia in 334-333 B.C.E., but among the most influential of these generals was Seleucus I Nicator. Like Antigonus (and later Lysimachus) in Macedonia, or the forces of Ptolemy in Egypt, Seleucus considered himself to be the rightful heir of Alexander's legacy, not by birthright, but through military strength. Upon Alexander's death, these generals fought for the territories of Asia Minor, Egypt, and Syria in an effort to solidify and legitimize their claims to kingship. Seleucus represented the kingdom covering Syria, Babylon, and parts of the Near East; Ptolemy was the most influential in Egypt, the Near East, and northern Africa; Lysimachus made his claims in Asia Minor and Macedonia.[1]

Although Seleucus I Nicator was successful in bounding the territory that became known as the Seleucid Empire, it was by no means certain that such an empire would ever exist at all. After an unsuccessful attempt at claiming Macedonia for himself, Seleucus returned to the familiar region of Babylon to establish himself as its rightful king.[2] In unstable territory, a warrior has a decision to make in his conquest: Does one continue to seek expansion through force of might, or is it more effective to use benevolence as a means of obtaining favor with the surrounding peoples? Much like Alexander, Seleucus showed political savvy in his decision not

---

[1] Kosmin, Paul J. *The Land of the Elephant Kings: Space, Territory, and Ideology of the Seleucid Empire*. Cambridge, MA: Harvard University Press, 2018. (p.31).

[2] The Hellenistic Age Podcast: The Seleucid Empire - Syrian Nights, Macedonian Dreams. Last modified November , 2020.
https://podcasts.apple.com/us/podcast/the-hellenistic-age-podcast/id1377920930?i=1000500359954.

to continue pursuing conquest of India in the East as a means of obtaining kingship in that region. Instead, Seleucus chose diplomacy. In 305-304 B.C.E., through what eventually became known as the Treaty of Indus with the king of India, Chandragupta Maurya, Seleucus established the eastern border of his empire without going to war with another world power.[3] But the treaty with Chandragupta did more than ensure stability in Seleucid territory—it defined the terms of the kingdom itself. Before the settlement with India, Seleucus as a recognized regional power was not necessarily self-evident. His kingship was not secure and certainly not well established yet. By making peace with India and defining his eastern frontier, Seleucus had cleverly situated himself as the recognized king of the territories between India to his east, and Macedonia to his west.

Although founded in Babylon, the eastern capital of the empire known as Seleucia-on-the-Tigris would eventually be recognized as the epicenter of Seleucid territory. The reluctance to establish Babylon as the capital of the empire was in partly due to the fact that Babylon was too recognizable of a city and had too much history to be easily renamed or to re-cast in the Seleucid mold. The deeper the roots of the tree, the more difficult it is to move. So it was, Babylon could not easily be altered in the minds of the people living in that region. It had its own identity.[4] Furthermore, Syria was much closer to the Greek mainland, and Seleucus I Nicator may have founded his kingdom in Babylon, but his heart remained in Macedonia.

Given that the Seleucid Empire's tenure in the Near East was so brief, it is remarkable to consider just how large of a footprint the empire left on the world. In fact, of the three break-away kingdoms founded after Alexander's death, it is the Seleucid's which modern historians regard as the most prolific of city builders.[5] Their constructions outlived them for generations, creating much of the map that would later be inherited by the

[3] Ibid. (1). (p. 33).
[4] Ibid. (2).
[5] "The Hellenistic Age Podcast." Hellenistic Cities-Colonization, Urbanization, & Hellenization. Last modified December 9, 2019. https://podcasts.apple.com/us/podcast/the-hellenistic-age-podcast/id1377920930?i=1000459147232.

Roman Empire. Although their stewardship of the region was short lived, the Seleucids left their mark on the world.

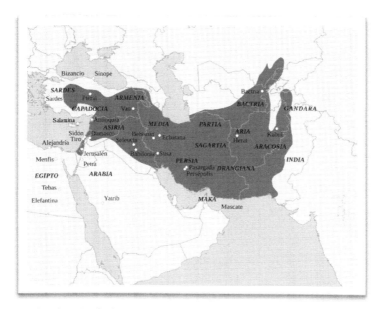

*Seleucid Empire, third-century B.C.E.*                    *Figure 2.1*

Significant cities mentioned as late as the first century C.E. within the framework of the New Testament writers were founded by the Seleucids, including the Laodicean cities, Tarsus, Antioch, and others.

> The Seleucid kings pinned their empire into place with colonial settlements. It is a historical commonplace, and rightly so, that the dynasty's most transformative and historically significant undertaking was its establishment of new urban foundations across the Hellenistic Near East...Colonization was a continuous theme of Seleucid kingship, in both the practical actions of individual monarchs and the legitimizing discourses that enunciated them. The scale of these urbanizing activities is breathtaking, far outpacing those of the Ptolemaic and Antigonid neighbors in number and importance and prompting in ancient and

modern historians the bureaucratic recoil into lists. So, Appian estimates that Seleucus I Nicator founded sixteen Antiochs, five Laodiceas, nine Seleucias, three Apameas, and one Stratonicea in addition to more than twenty cities named after Greek *poleis* (if anything, an understatement). Many more were established by Antiochus I, Antiochus II, Seleucus IV, and Antiochus IV and a few others by Seleucus II, Antiochus III, Demetrius II, and Demetrius III.[6]

Founding cities is one thing, but the sustainability of the Seleucid model is impressive, particularly for its time. Still today, the evidence for the Seleucid's prioritization of the Hellenization of the area they ruled can be found in the ancient ruins of many Middle Eastern countries, including Iran and Syria. For an empire that so briefly ruled, it left a lasting impact.

Recasting the Near East in the mold of the Greeks was not a simple task. As examined in chapter one, much of the area occupied by the Persians, Medes, and the Jews had deep and abiding religious traditions that conflicted with Hellenism. But the fragmented empire created the opportunity for ambitious men to take the task upon themselves, particularly in the context of conquest. The work of Hellenizing the land of Israel began with the Ptolemaic Empire's influence on the region, but it was the Seleucid kingdom that transitioned the spread of Hellenism from an act of willful cultural assimilation to one of imposition and conquest. The Seleucid rulers who played their part in the active spread of Hellenism were numerous, but none were quite as effective in the early stages of the empire as Demodamas.

Demodamas served as a general in the Seleucid military during the reigns of both Seleucus I Nicator and his son Antiochus I.[7] His most significant contributions to the establishment of the Seleucid Empire manifested in the form of establishing new cities

---

6 Ibid. (1) (p.183).
7 Ibid. (1) (p.62).

around the occupied territory, but not necessarily in the way that the modern reader might expect. Traditionally considered, conquest is generally understood in terms of military might, coercion, benevolence, or a combination of the three. It is difficult to imagine any great empire being established without these elements at work on some level. But ideology is no less powerful of a tool in the arsenal of conquerors, and Demodamas seemed to understand that principle quite well. Religious ideology in particular fueled the founding of cities by Demodamas, and it was a religious ideology that would have a deep and abiding impact on the world in the centuries that followed.

Drawing from writings of Pliny the Elder,[8] in which Pliny states that Demodamas set up altars to the god Apollo as an act of demarcating territory, modern historians have pieced together a basic understanding of the actions of Demodamas in city-founding, as well as the motives behind them.

> Pliny identifies the source he follows here as Demodamas himself: the Milesian general wrote an autobiographical account of his military activities in Central Asia. The erection of altars at a watery edge (fluvial or oceanic) was a thank-offering to the gods, a memorial to achievements, and, above all, a bounding of territory...Accordingly, Demodamas' altars should be understood as a spatializing gesture: they indicate the edge of Seleucid sovereignty in this region and identify the Iaxartes (mod. Syr Darya) river as the kingdom's north-eastern boundary.[9]

The emphasis here is on the setting up of religious altars as a method of demarcating territory, instead of a military garrison or outpost. While this practice was not new to Demodamas' time, it was utilized by the Seleucids early and frequently in drawing the boundaries of the Seleucid Empire. For Demodamas, where the worship of Apollo began, the old kingdoms ended. Establishing dominion through the building of altars was effective because where the kings could not be, the gods and their followers could

---

[8] Pliny the Elder, *The Natural History*, Book VI (Ch. XVIII).
[9] Ibid. (1) (p.62).

be. Religious zeal is a powerful thing in the hands of faithful followers. If altars could be erected to the gods that the Seleucids feared, then they would be more apt to occupy the territory, perhaps even defend it from invaders. In this way, territory could be secured by trust in the religious fervor of the citizens to protect sacred territory, as well as the nationalism associated with the Greek pantheon. Remember that Greek religion and government could not be easily separated from one another. In the minds of the people, the kings were divinely ordained leaders.

Harvard University's Philip J. King Professor of Ancient History and author Paul Kosmin says,

> Demodamas' spatializing operation not only distinguished Seleucid from non-Seleucid territory. By honoring Apollo of Didyma (also known as Branchidae), the main god of Miletus, Demodamas bracketed this far-flung corner of the Seleucid kingdom with Miletus, the Aegean, Old World Greece, and everything they stood for.[10]

For Demodamas, the principal discipline that must be exercised over a given territory was no different than Alexander the Great's belief about annexing new territory: association. What Alexander accomplished on a macro-scale, Demodamas accomplished on a micro-scale: Hellenization through association. By erecting altars to Apollo, Demodamas took the most meaningful first step in assimilating new territory—changing what the general populous believed about power in the region. Specifically, he did so by attempting to influence what the people believed about which gods were really in charge. And, by extension, which kings. So it was, Demodamas was able to bound the sovereignty of Antiochus throughout Central Asia using his expedition to the Iaxartes.

Demodamas decision to use the construction of altars to establish dominion and, more importantly, boundaries in a given territory

---

[10] Ibid. (1) (p.63).

was an effective one. Altering the religious climate of the Near East had generational influence, and it is essential to understanding the religious structure of the first century during the advent of Christianity. However, the question may be asked, why was the god Apollo honored as opposed to the other gods of Greece? Demodamas wouldn't have taken any action of his own accord— he was a man under orders. Seleucus I Nicator and his son Antiochus I ruled the empire in the days of Demodamas. Given Alexander the Great's relationship to Zeus, it isn't obvious that Seleucus or Antiochus would have benefited from diverting from Alexander's course. Afterall, Seleucus wanted the eastern world to respond to the Seleucid Empire as the proper ancestor of the Alexandrian. Each empire created in the power vacuum left behind by Alexander the Great was challenged to set themselves up in the eyes of the people as the rightful descendant kingdom. It would seem obvious to prioritize the veneration of Zeus-Ammon in this context, particularly where establishing territorial borders was concerned. But using religion in politics had limits, even in the ancient world. Although Zeus-Ammon was the premier deity of the Alexandrian Empire, Seleucus had his own legacy to consider. And although Zeus-Ammon was worshiped more broadly, the citizenry was not ignorant to the stories of the gods. Imitation of the Alexandrian legacy would not fulfill the objectives of the Seleucid Empire. Like all empires, the Seleucids needed an origin story that would be received well throughout the world. In order to build a meaningful relationship with the territories they had conquered, the Seleucids needed to be able to transcend might—there must be right as well. And convincing the territories that the Seleucids had come to power by divine right required a belief in the relationship between Seleucus and Olympus that went beyond his connection to Alexander. Seleucus may have been the king, but what did that mean? Like all stories, Seleucus' empire needed a context, a history, even a purpose. And Seleucus had a history with the cult of Apollo, just as Alexander did with Zeus and Heracles.

The story of Apollo, like many of the gods of Olympus, is broad and cannot be reduced to a single interpretation of power or will. At times, Zeus was the god of the sky and the air, as well as the god of the rain. Zeus was also equated with the sun god in many traditions and was a unifying figure of power in the Greek pantheon who could not be reduced to a single form. Apollo was much like Zeus in this way. His full name, "Phoebus Apollo," meant "The brilliant" or "The shining one." In many religious traditions around the world, "the sun" and "the light" were not necessarily one and the same. This belief was true in ancient Greece as well. Although Apollo was the god of the light and was often associated with the sun, he was not truly the sun god, at least in as far as the two could be separated. "Light" in Greece did not just mean illumination. It was the primary symbol of truth, so Apollo was known as the god of truth as well.

> The son of Zeus and Leto (Latona), born in the little island of Delos. He has been called "the most Greek of all the gods." He is a beautiful figure in Greek poetry, the master musician who delights Olympus as he plays on his golden lyre; the lord too of the silver bow, the Archer-god, far shooting; the Healer, as well, who first taught men the healing art. Even more than of these good and lovely endowments, he is the God of Light, in whom is no darkness at all, and so he is the God of Truth. No false word ever falls from his lips.[11]

The relationship between light and truth is a reoccurring theme in many ancient religious works, and its use in Greece perhaps informs our understanding of why the Seleucids chose Apollo to mark territorial boundaries. Light and darkness are the most fundamental ways of demarcating boundaries, and insofar as the light went, so too went the kingdom. As far as the light touches— that is the border of the kingdom.[12] Where darkness begins, the

---

[11] Hamilton, Edith. *Mythology*. New York: Grand Central Publishing, 1942. (p.25).
[12] Dr. Jordan Peterson's discussions on the relationship between light and darkness and the example used in the story of *The Lion King* greatly informed my understanding of this principle as an archetype in history. For more on the

empire ends. And so, the empire itself becomes the representation of light in the land, and the god of light is the beacon of the boundary.

Apollo was not just the god of light; he was also the god of truth. And the connection between these two things is not easily separated in the Ancient Greek mind. Edith Hamilton writes,

> Apollo at Delphi was a purely beneficent power, a direct link between gods and men, guiding men to know the divine will, showing them how to make peace with the gods; the purifier, too, able to cleanse even those stained with the blood of their kindred. Nevertheless, there are a few tales told of him which show him pitiless and cruel. Two ideas were fighting in him as in all the gods; a primitive, crude idea and one that was beautiful and poetic. In him only a little of the primitive is left.[13]

The portrayal of Apollo as one who was mostly good but also given to cruelty and pitilessness is a very human image of the god of light and truth. Like all of the gods of Olympus, Apollo was neither omnipotent nor omniscient. He was, at times, both good and bad. Anthropomorphism is the attribution of human characteristics and behaviors to things that are otherwise not human. Olympus was depicted as a place of the gods, but the gods also bore a resemblance to men. Zeus was at times deceived and given to bouts of lust. The Nine Muses played the Lyre of the god of truth, but they knew how to say things that were lies yet appeared to be true as well. Apollo was benevolent but could also be cruel. And so, the war inside all men was reflected in their perception of the gods.

Like Alexander and Zeus, Seleucus I Nicator had a peculiar relationship to Apollo that almost certainly would have influenced his decision to venerate the god of light in his newfound empire.

Just as Alexander's mother had claimed to have been impregnated by Zeus through the form of a serpent, so too had

---

subject, I highly recommend his latest book *Beyond Order* as well as its companion volume, *12 Rules for Life.*
[13] Ibid. (11) (p.26-27).

Seleucus mother Laodice claimed to have consorted with Apollo, and that Seleucus was the offspring of that union.

> The merit of Seleucus was well known, and his birth had been attended with extraordinary circumstances. His mother Laodice, being married to Antiochus, a man of eminence among Philip's generals, seemed to herself, in a dream, to have conceived from a union with Apollo, and after becoming pregnant, to have received from him, as a reward for her compliance, a ring, on the stone of which was engraved an anchor, which was visible on the thigh of Seleucus when he was born, made this dream extremely remarkable.[14]

Here, Seleucus' claim to divine right as king may be understood. Leaders were not leaders without the consent of the gods in the ancient world, and like Alexander, Seleucus knew that he needed a divine sponsor. When Demodamas set up altars to Apollo, it was as much a statement about Seleucus and his son Antiochus as it was about the boundaries of the kingdom.

The erection of altars to the gods and the spread of Hellenism through the construction of theaters, civic buildings, and restoration of pagan temples was not a novel feature of the Seleucid Empire but one of its primary functions. For the Seleucids, religion was the signal form of completed conquest. The more Hellenized an area became, the more assured the Seleucids could be of their place in the world. Incorporating the worship of Apollo and the rest of the Olympian pantheon was essential to growth in the minds of the Seleucid Greeks. Religious dominion was tantamount to military or political might.

Seleucid strategy was different from the tactics of the previous generation. During the reign of Alexander, it was not uncommon to see the king himself adopt the culture or religious practices of conquered territories. (Recall in chapter one our examination of Alexander's behavior in Egypt.) But that was not so for the Seleucids. While Alexander practiced confidence in his Macedonian identity, insomuch as he was not swayed from the

---

[14] Marcus Junianus Justinus, *Epitome of the Philippic History of Pompeius Trogus.* Book XV, (Ch.IV).

Greek-ism of his empire, the Seleucids were less certain in their role as conquerors. Some historians have surmised that the frantic Hellenism of the Seleucids was, perhaps, motivated by the fragility of the still freshly formed empire and ethnic insecurity possibly created by their detachment from the Greek mainland.[15]

Whatever its motivations, Hellenism spread like wildfire in the Near East primarily due to its evangelism by the Seleucid Empire. The enthusiastic Hellenism of the Seleucids would lead to a cultural and religious boiling point in one of the smallest, yet most significant territories ever ruled by the Seleucid kings.

Remember that Jerusalem and the greater area of Judaea were left essentially to themselves during the expansion of Alexander the Great's empire. Although a small and seemingly insignificant region comparatively speaking, Judaea repeatedly appears in the history of the Greeks and later the Romans as an area of political, cultural, and religious tension. That tension largely began during its vassalage to the Seleucid Empire.

The land of Judaea came under the tutelage of the Seleucids officially sometime between 202-200 B.C.E. during the Fifth Syrian War. By 175 B.C.E., Antiochus IV Epiphanes had ascended to the throne of the Seleucid Empire, and he possessed a great deal of animosity toward the Jews and their religion. More than any of his predecessors or successors, Antiochus IV sought to dispel Judaism from the area and Hellenize the land of Judaea once and for all.

In order to understand the motivations of Antiochus IV Epiphanes, it is helpful to examine his background and the cultural influences that informed much of his behavior.

Antiochus IV Epiphanes was born in 215 B.C.E. and was the third son of Antiochus III the Great.[16] Antiochus IV is remembered more than any other Seleucid king for his Hellenizing policies and

---

[15] Ibid. (1) (p.118).
[16] "Antiochus IV Epiphanes." Britannica. Accessed October 15, 2021. https://www.britannica.com/biography/Antiochus-IV-Epiphanes

his vehement attitude toward the Jewish people and their religion. But the source of his love for Hellenism, as well as his hatred of the Jews, did not necessarily begin in the Seleucid Empire. Antiochus' father, Antiochus III the Great, made war with Rome between 192-188 B.C.E. in what became known as the Roman-Seleucid War. After being defeated by the Romans, Antiochus IV served as a hostage to the Romans in his father's debt and as a bargaining chip over the Seleucid kingdom.[17]

While a prisoner of Rome, a fondness for Roman culture grew within Antiochus IV. The toga became his traditional garb, and he adopted the gladiatorial games which he eventually brought to Daphne.[18] Antiochus is also said to have outfitted his army in Roman armor.[19] Although the Seleucid Empire worshiped Zeus as its premier deity even during the days of Antiochus IV, the ancient historians also record that he constructed a temple to the Roman Capitoline Jupiter as well (Rome's equivalent to Zeus).[20]

By the time Antiochus IV usurped his brother Seleucus IV as the king of the Seleucid Empire, constant wars between the Seleucids and the Ptolemaic Empire, as well as the Macedonians and the Romans, had weakened Antiochus' ability to create a lasting Seleucid presence in Alexandria and lower Egypt which he had long coveted.[21] Against his will, Antiochus retreated from his battles with the Roman and Ptolemaic forces in 168 B.C.E. to preserve his kingdom in Syria.

The territory of Judaea and the surrounding area had once been conquered by Antiochus III but guardians of Ptolemy VI's empire in Egypt had taken the region back some time before 173 B.C.E. Antiochus IV prioritized conquest of Judaea because of its strategic location in his battles with the Egyptians, as well as its place in his family's legacy. However, continued disturbances in Judaea against the Seleucids forced Antiochus IV to withdraw from his battles with the Ptolemaic Empire and quell the Judaean rebellion against his empire. Eventually, Antiochus was forced to retreat from his battles with the Ptolemies completely. This

---

[17] Ibid. (16).
[18] Ibid. (1) (p.228).
[19] Polybius, *Histories*, Book XXX, (Ch. XV).
[20] Livy, *Periochae*, (XLI).
[21] Ibid. (16).

perhaps informs our understanding of why Antiochus hated the Jews and why he persecuted their religion as much as history seems to suggest. To Antiochus, the Jews were responsible for dissolving his last chance at dominance over Egypt.

Under Antiochus III, the land of Judaea enjoyed much of the same autonomy which the region had experienced under Alexander the Great. There were no mandates against their laws, culture, or worship. But Antiochus IV battles with the Ptolemaic forces seemed to be the final push that changed the status quo between the Seleucids and the Jews. Antiochus IV Epiphanes was a fervent proponent of Hellenism, perhaps the most passionate that the Seleucid Empire had known. As discussed in chapter one, the tension between Judaism and Hellenism began almost immediately upon first contact between the two worlds. When Alexander wrote to the Jews requesting assistance in his fight against the Persians, the Jewish leadership resisted. According to tradition, Alexander showed up to the gates of Jerusalem, likely with the intentions of razing the city and offering sacrifices to Zeus in their temple as punishment for their slight against him. He was then met with religious resistance, not a military force as one might expect.

For the Jews, laws and customs could not be so easily separated from religion. As Seleucid influence in the region of Judaea grew, it created a bifurcation in the culture of the Jews, which ultimately culminated with the creation of two of the more famous sects of Judaism mentioned by the New Testament writers called the Pharisees and the Sadducees. The tension within Jewish culture in the second century B.C.E. existed largely between those willing to adopt the traditions and customs of Hellenism and those who wanted to conserve traditional Judaism as the dominant culture of the region.

To understand the willingness of some Jews to adapt to the culture of surrounding nations during the time of the Seleucids, one must remember that after the exile into Babylon in 586 B.C.E., many Jews were scattered throughout Syria, Egypt, and Asia Minor. Generations of Jews were born, lived, and died in areas with little to no influence of traditional Judaism in their daily life. Even Jews who remained in and around the land of Judaea had no temple to worship in for a generation. After the construction of the Second Temple, the restored structure bore little resemblance to that of the former.[22] The new temple was much smaller, and it lacked a great deal of the furniture that had made Solomon's Temple so special to begin with. After the Jews began to return to their homeland from areas occupied by the Persians sometime around 516 B.C.E., many of them had few personal attachments to the religion of their fathers.

*Figure 2.2*    *Photo by Steven Gill, 2016*

*Bnei Hezir tomb (left) and the tomb of Zechariah (right) located in the Qidron Valley of Jerusalem. These memorials likely dating to the late first century B.C.E. or first century C.E. illustrate the great influence of Greek architectural forms embraced by the Jews.[23]*

---

[22] Ezra 3:11-13 says that the foundation of the newer temple was much smaller than that of Solomon's Temple. Furthermore, it can be assumed from the second book of Maccabees that the Ark of the Covenant was never restored to the Second Temple. In fact, it is still missing to this day. Historical accounts such as Josephus also record that the Second Temple was largely empty by the first century, and was missing the seven golden candlesticks as well.

[23] I took this photo in October, 2016. Although constructed long after the deaths of the men that they honor, these memorials constitute some of the clearest examples that archeology has to offer concerning the influence of Hellenism in Seleucid and Roman occupied Jerusalem. Large colonnade structures typified Greek style and was later adopted by the Romans.

While some remained faithful to the study of Torah, keeping of holy days, and following dietary restrictions, others did not. The influence of Hellenism in the land of Judaea brought about the introduction of gymnasiums, theaters, and Greek literature to the land. While Hellenism in the Near East pre-dated the Seleucids by centuries, its pervasiveness during the reign of Antiochus IV was only augmented by his hatred of Judaism. While much of the interactions between Judaism and Hellenism were incidental in the generations prior to the Seleucid kings, under Antiochus, the culture of the Greeks was forced upon the Jews in ways not known in the past. Still, many Jews willingly accepted the ways of the Greeks.

Many Jews living in Judaea when Antiochus ruled had already adapted to Hellenism and were opposed to the conservative religious resistance in the Jewish leadership.

> Jews became exposed to and thoroughly engaged with the Greek culture that prevailed in the various communities in which they settled. And not only in the diaspora.[24] Greek towns sprang up in Palestine itself, from Akko to Gaza on the Mediterranean coast, in the Lower Galilee, and in various sites on both sides of the Jordan. Hence, even the Jews of Judaea could not and did not isolate themselves altogether from the pervasive aura of Hellenism. For many Jews, especially in the diaspora, the close contact with the institutions, language, literature, art, and traditions of Hellas reached the point where they lost touch with Hebrew itself. The translation of the Hebrew Bible into Greek, probably in Alexandria sometime in the third or second century B.C.E., reflects the need of Jews settled abroad for several generations for whom Greek was the primary, perhaps sole, language and for some of whom education gave greater familiarity with Plato than with Moses. The Jewish involvement with Hellenism in the period from Alexander the Great to the destruction of the

---

[24] Diaspora refers to the dispersion of Jews outside of their ancestral homeland of Israel. Still today, Jews who choose not to live in Israel are referred to as diasporic communities.

Second Temple in 70 C.E. was a central, even defining, characteristic.[25]

The internal struggle within the leadership of Jerusalem eventually came to a head with the persecution by Antiochus IV Epiphanes against the religion of the Jews. When he returned to the area of Judaea after his failed subjection of Alexandria and southern Egypt, Antiochus IV's frustrations with Judaea began to manifest. The books of the Maccabees, the ancient record of the Jewish Revolt against the Seleucids, highlight the gradual capitulation of the Jews to Hellenism, and the aggression of Antiochus against their way of life.

> So Alexander reigned twelve years, and then died. And his servants bare rule every one in his place. And after his death they all put crowns upon themselves; so did their sons after them many years: and evils were multiplied in the earth. And there came out of them a wicked root Antiochus surnamed Epiphanes, son of Antiochus the king, who had been a hostage at Rome, and he reigned in the hundred and thirty and seventh year of the kingdom of the Greeks. In those days went there out of Israel wicked men, who persuaded many, saying, let us go and make a covenant with the heathen that are round about us: for since we departed from them we have had much sorrow. So this device pleased them well.[26]

It is probably noteworthy that the writer of Maccabees would emphasize the deterioration of the Jewish people's faithfulness to their homeland before mentioning the actions of Antiochus. As will be seen, Antiochus IV committed grave atrocities against the Jews. Yet, the wound of Hellenism upon the Jews was, at least in part, self-inflicted. According to the author of the first book of the Maccabees, there were men of Israel who made the conscious decision to seek out an accord with the Greeks, and their decision was primarily motivated by self-interest. "For since we departed

---

[25] Gruen, Erich S. "Hellenistic Judaism." In *Cultures of the Jews*, edited by David Biale, 78-79. New York: Schocken Books, 2002.
[26] 1st Maccabees 1:7-12 (KJV).

from them we have had much sorrow." This statement is likely a reference to those who had once lived in the diaspora or, at least, under the rule of the Greek-occupied territories. Whether a simple justification for wicked behavior or an intense frustration with the quality of life in the land of Judaea (the truth is usually somewhere in the middle), there were Jews that were not only pleased to live under the rule of the Greeks but actively sought it out.

> Then certain of the people were so forward herein, that they went to the king, who gave them license to do after the ordinances of the heathen: Whereupon they built a place of exercise at Jerusalem according to the customs of the heathen: And made themselves uncircumcised,[27] and forsook the holy covenant, and joined themselves to the heathen, and were sold to do mischief.[28]

The specific practices of the Greeks which the Jews adopted, such as gymnasium building and becoming "uncircumcised," were not necessarily motivated by a fear of Antiochus. At least, not at first. According to the author of First Maccabees, these practices were an attempt to participate in a culture they seemed to admire. But the capitulation of certain Jews to the lifestyle of the Greeks was not without its consequences. The Hellenized Jews received opposition from their more conservative peers, and the push back only further weakened the already fragile state against the Seleucid king.

> And after that Antiochus had smitten Egypt, he returned again in the hundred forty and third year, and went up against Israel and Jerusalem with a great multitude, and entered proudly into the sanctuary, and took away the golden altar, and the

---

[27] This act of "becoming uncircumcised" is likely a reference to the wearing of false foreskins by Jewish men so that they might participate in the gymnasiums of the Greeks. Activities such as athletic competition, theatrical productions, etc. were often performed in the nude. Because circumcision was not practiced by the greater culture, it was revolting to the Greeks to look upon. In an effort to conceal their Jewish identity and become more accepted members of the Hellenized culture, Jewish men would practice the buying and selling of artificial foreskins. For more on this, see Eric Meyers in *Cultures of the Jews* (p.170).
[28] 1st Maccabees 1:13-15 (KJV).

candlestick of light, and all the vessels thereof, And the table of shewbread and the pouring vessels, and the vials. And the censors of gold, and the veil, and the crown, and the golden ornaments that were before the temple, all which he pulled off...Her sanctuary was laid waste like a wilderness, her feasts were turned into mourning, her sabbaths into reproach her honour into contempt. As had been her glory, so was her dishonour increased, and her excellency was turned into mourning. Moreover king Antiochus wrote to his whole kingdom, that all should be one people, And every one should leave his laws: so all the heathen agreed according to the commandment of the king. Yea, many also of the Israelites consented to his religion, and sacrificed unto idols, and profaned the sabbath. For the king had sent letters by messengers unto Jerusalem and the cities of Juda that they should follow the strange laws of the land, And forbid burnt offerings, and sacrifice, and drink offerings, in the temple: and that they should profane the sabbath and festival days: And pollute the sanctuary and holy people: Set up altars, and groves, and chapels of idols, and sacrifice swine's flesh, and unclean beasts: That they should also leave their children uncircumcised, and make their souls abominable with all manner of uncleanness and profanation: To the end they might forget the law, and change all the ordinances.[29]

Antiochus' extensive actions against the Jewish religion inform the modern reader about power of religion in the ancient world to sway a culture, even a nation. For Antiochus, the dissolution of the Jewish religion was essential to the subjection of the region. But persecution was not an end unto itself for the Seleucid king. Assimilation was the primary goal of the actions which Antiochus took against Israel. "To the end that they might forget the law, and change all the ordinances." By making circumcision illegal, Antiochus ensured that the next generation of Jews did not look any different from the next generation of Greeks. By forbidding the celebration of their holy days, he disrupted the Jewish

---

[29] 1st Maccabees 1:20-22;39-49 (KJV).

calendar. By demanding that the sacrifices to their God cease, he attempted to disconnect the Jewish people as an ethnicity from their religious identity, which had heretofore been indistinguishable from one another.

It is ironic that Antiochus's methods of assimilation caused the fracture in Judaea that he was trying to avoid. According to the writer of Maccabees, Antiochus sent out an order that the people of Judaea (and, presumably, the surrounding territories he annexed) must abandon their own laws and customs in favor of the laws of Hellenism.

> Moreover king Antiochus wrote to his whole kingdom, that all should be one people, and every one should leave his laws: so all the heathen agreed according to the commandment of the king. Yea, many also of the Israelites consented to his religion, and sacrificed unto idols, and profaned the sabbath.[30]

The ordinance that everyone "leave their laws" was not confined to bureaucratic behavior or taxation and property procedures. The author situates the command of the king primarily in the context of religious practices and holy days. In other words, this was an instance of forced consent to a specific set of values. It was mandatory conversion to the religion of the Seleucids.

In circumstances where a particular set of actions is mandated or forbidden, the result is often precisely the opposite of what the prevailing authority intended. Remember that the motivation of the king was that all the people should be "one." Unity was the intent, but chaos was the result. Why was this so?

Unity through coercion cannot be achieved without resistance, even in the most favorable of circumstances. At least, not any unity that can endure for a meaningful amount of time. But it was nearly impossible in the situation of the Jews. Although there is no doubt that the tyranny of Antiochus created problems in other areas of his kingdom, the specific pressure he placed upon the Jews to conform to Hellenic culture was certain to create instability in the region from the start. Judaism, at its core, is a

---

[30] 1st Maccabees 1:41-43 (KJV).

religion of distinction. In the Law of Moses, God gives many commandments concerning how men ought to behave in the world and what men ought to do. But there are also many commandments concerning what men ought *not* to do. There are commands to participate in certain religious practices, as is the case in many religions. But there are also many commands to abstain from certain practices. The stringency of Jewish law put the religious Jews diametrically at odds with the laws of Antiochus. When the king demanded that all men be one, the laws of the Jews demanded that they be different.

Judaism is not just a religion concerned with what men should do, but what they should not do. There are certain behaviors common to the rest of the world that, according to the Law of Moses, were not to be considered common among the Jewish people. Some of these commandments concerned abstaining from the worship of other gods,[31] avoiding certain foods,[32] and honoring certain days of the week as sacrosanct,[33] all of which the Seleucid king had demanded that the Jews abandon. These laws were not just given to make the Jews more righteous in the eyes of God— they were also given to make the Jews separate and distinct from the rest of the world. Separate-ness and distinct-ness were not just bi-products of Judaism. In some cases, they were the very express intention of the law itself.[34] For the Jews, the command from Antiochus was no different than asking the Jews to cease from existing. And, to a large degree, that is exactly what Antiochus seemed to desire. In the mind of the king, the people would accept Hellenism as the singular culture of the nation, or they would no longer be a people at all.

---

[31] Exodus 20:1-5.
[32] Leviticus 7:19.
[33] Exodus 20:8-9.
[34] Exodus 11:7. According to the Exodus account, the plague of the death of the firstborn was specifically to separate the Jews from the Egyptians. "That you may know how the LORD does put a difference between the Egyptians and Israel."

Of course, persecution is effective only to the degree to which it dismays the most faithful to the cause that it seeks to destroy. In some cases, the faithful are not dismayed but emboldened. So it was in Judaea. What followed the aggressive actions of Antiochus came to be known as one of the most important rebellions in Jewish history—The Maccabean Revolt.

According to the first book of Maccabees, a man named Matthias, along with his five sons, was responsible for routing the Seleucid rulers out of the land of Israel for a time and re-establishing the traditional practices of Judaism in the land. It is worthy of note that the rebellion of Matthias did not begin with military action by Antiochus against the Jews, nor was it sparked by a particularly cruel incident of behavior by the followers of Antiochus against the Jewish people. According to the writer of Maccabees, Matthias was a ruler of the people who dwelled in Modin. When one of the king's officers approached him about paying homage to the gods of Greece in the sight of the people as a symbol of his loyalty, Matthias refused. During his act of defiance against Antiochus' officer, a fellow Jew approached the altar erected to one of the idols of Greece in Modin and sacrificed on it according to the king's command. When Matthias saw this, he zealously attacked the Jew, slaying him on the very altar which he had intended to sacrifice.[35]

This act of defiance against the religion of the Greeks sparked the revolution that would culminate in the creation of one of Judaism's most famous holy day celebrations, Hanukkah. After Matthias' actions against the Seleucids, he, his sons, and freedom fighters from the land of Israel waged war against the Antiochian intruders. Though their reprieve was short-lived, they eventually won independence from the occupation of the Seleucid forces.

The Maccabean Revolt, named after Judas Maccabeaus, son of Matthias, was the military and political action taken against the Syrian Greeks by those Jews who wanted to throw off the culture of Hellenism from the land of Judaea. After the death of Matthias, his son Judas became the leader of the revolt against the forces of Antiochus IV Epiphanes. The celebration of Judas Maccabeaus'

---

[35] 1st Maccabees 2:1-24.

forces taking back the temple mount from the Seleucid invaders became known as the Feast of Dedication, or, as it is more familiarly called today, Hanukkah. According to tradition, when Judas Maccabeaus and his forces took back the temple, they were determined to restore the holy site to its ritual purity. When they arrived at the temple, there was only one cruse of uncontaminated oil that could be used for the ritual purification. As the purification would take eight days, one cruse of oil was not sufficient to complete the task at hand.[36] Yet, when they burned the oil that they had, the cruse did not run dry for eight days.[37] Hanukkah celebrates that miracle, along with the Jewish resilience in the face of persecution.

The Maccabean Revolt is significant to the discussion of the development of religious thought in the land of Israel before the first century. Although Antiochus' actions against the Jews were numerous and some unbelievably cruel,[38] the primary emphasis of the Maccabean record is not the need for political or economic restitution but religious restoration. The revolt is framed squarely around the fight against Hellenism and its impact on the land of Judaea. As will be discussed in the following chapter, although the Maccabean Revolt was a success for its time, the fruit of its labor was short-lived. Hellenism became deeply embedded in the culture of the land of Judaea, and it would not be easily dismissed.

In 164 B.C.E., Antiochus IV Epiphanes died. His legacy of tyranny and cruelty left an indelible mark on his generation. Contemporary writers refashioned his name, Epiphanes (meaning

---

[36] It is interesting to note that the miracle of the oil does not appear in the books of the Maccabees from which the story of Hanukkah is most popularly known. The traditional story of the oil that burned for eight days has been preserved in other texts such as the Talmud, but it was not included in the historical account of the Maccabean Revolt.

[37] Telushkin, Joseph. *Jewish Literacy*. New York: William Morrow and Co., 1991. (p.575-576).

[38] 1st Maccabees 1:60-61 says Antiochus had women and children put to death who participated in the act of circumcision. Mothers were executed, while the infants were hung from their necks.

"God manifest"), to *Epimanes* ("insane") as a means of protest during his lifetime. After his death, the Seleucid Empire never found long-term stability again. Between the reign of Seleucus I Nicator and Antiochus IV Epiphanes, some vied for power in the kingdom and were willing to kill to get their way. But the epicenter of the kingdom remained stable, and the relationship between king and country was, on the whole, agreeable. After the death of Antiochus IV, the relationship between the Seleucid kings and their subjects deteriorated at a rapid pace. Special interest rulers took on independent conquests against the heirs of the house of Seleucus. Territories occupied by the Seleucid kings began to rebel, minting their own coins that did not include the faces of the Seleucid kings or their appointed rulers.[39] Continued rejection by the colonies and instability surrounding the throne ultimately led to the collapse of the Seleucid Empire less than a century after the death of Antiochus IV. In 64 B.C.E., Pompey of Rome annexed the territories occupied formerly by the Syrian kings. Alas, the Seleucid Empire was no more.

There are lessons to be learned from the harsh treatment Antiochus IV exhibited against the Jews contrasted with that of Alexander the Great. It could be argued convincingly that had Antiochus left the Judaean province to its own devices, it likely would have adopted the practices of Hellenism of its own accord. Hellenism was not new to the region during the reign of Antiochus, and its acceptance in the land of Judaea had already created civil strife and instability in Israel. The Jews were in Hellenism, and Hellenism was in the Jews. As was the typical strategy of Alexander the Great, benevolence and deference proved to be the force multipliers needed to supplant a culture successfully. Alexander was able to unify vast swaths of territory because rather than forcing the areas he occupied to conform to Hellenism in a literal sense, he simply conformed Hellenism to the locality (remember the merging of "Zeus-Ammon"). Thus, instead of making the Persian territories wholly Greek, they merely became "Greek-ish." So it was in Israel.

---

[39] Ibid. (1) (p.248).

Antiochus IV's tyranny and severity may have forced the Jews into the worship of the Greek cults and caused them to abandon the religion of their fathers in the short term, but it also gave them a common enemy. Backing your enemies into a corner is only an effective strategy if you are willing to see their demise through to the end. If control and not destruction is the goal, appeasement is a better strategy. Because if your opposition is not willing to conform, and they have nowhere to turn, they will fight back. The actions of Alexander the Great and those of Antiochus IV Epiphanes seem to have proved that. Nevertheless, tactics aside, Hellenism made its home in Israel. Centuries after the death of Antiochus, a Greek revivalist from Naissus (modern Turkey) would learn the lessons necessary from the great Macedonian and Seleucid kings to unify his empire behind another religion that would have a vast impact on Judaea as well.

Understanding the Seleucid Empire's impact on the world in the fourth to first centuries B.C.E. can be a challenging task for a number of reasons, not the least of which is that the empire did not exist for very long. Second, there is much to be desired in the way of primary source material that can be drawn from its time. However, what can be known of the Seleucids is that they were largely responsible for drawing the map of the Near East in which Jesus and His followers lived. The Seleucid Empire's enthusiastic construction informs New Testament geography of new cities, including Antioch, Laodicea, and Tarsus. Furthermore, the rapid expansion of Hellenism in the Near East by its Seleucid evangelists led to some of the most significant theological controversies discussed by the New Testament writers. The events that ultimately contributed to the creation of the doctrine of the trinity are indebted to the expansion of the Seleucid Empire. The ideology and the geography surrounding the formation of what would come to be known as the Catholic (universal) church owe much of its history to the world that was shaped by the Seleucids and later the Romans.

The next chapter will examine the influence of Hellenism in Jewish thought and the lasting impact of Hellenic culture in the land of Israel just before the birth of Christ. Centuries after the death of Antiochus IV Epiphanes, Christian theological debates would rage between men such as Tertullian and Origen, Eusebius and Eustathius, Servetus and Calvin. Many of the most controversial aspects of Christian thought discussed by these men were informed by the spread of Hellenism in the Near East and Asia Minor to one degree or another. To that end, it may be argued that the Seleucid Empire was at least partially responsible for what would eventually become the vast splintering of Christian theology from its otherwise Judaean roots.

Christianity, as a movement, was founded by the Jews, but the Jews of the first century cannot be reduced to a single religious sect or cultural box. Theological heterodoxy abounded in first-century Judaea after the vast spread and influence of Hellenism during the Seleucid and Roman Empires. Thus, before one can rightly sort out Christianity, one must first sort out the Judaism which precipitated it. Not all religious thinkers at the turn of the millennia embraced Hellenism, but many did. Understanding how the birth and spread of Hellenism in the Near East influenced the land of Israel and, by extension, the Christians, may provide the necessary contrast to see the outlines of what would eventually become the formation of a comprehensively trinitarian religion.

# CHAPTER III

Hellenism
&
Jewish Thought


There is a story in the Mishnah[1] that illustrates the problem that Hellenism presented for the Jews of the late first century B.C.E. and the early first century C.E. In the rabbinic tale, Rabbi Gamaliel is washing in the Bath of Aphrodite at Acco. When he is confronted by a Greek man about his behavior, citing the biblical mandate to forgo association with the idols of the land,[2] Rabbi Gamaliel responded by saying, "I did not come into her borders, she came into mine!" The rabbi explains that the Aphrodite which adorned the bath house was surely not an idol, since it sat in such an irreverent place. Rather, the image of Aphrodite was simply ornamentation put upon the bath.

For Rabbi Gamaliel, his washing in the Bath of Aphrodite was an inevitable consequence of the world in which he lived—a necessary evil. The bath itself did not constitute an idol; it simply included the image of one as a form décor. But as Eric Meyers points out in his entry on the subject matter at hand, it is not what adorns the bath but the bath itself which proved the pervasive nature of Hellenism in Jewish life.

> Bathing is not worship and statues are not idols! Yet, by going to the public bath in the first place, Gamaliel, the titular leader of the rabbinical caste, engaged in behavior that clearly reflects the influence of Greco-Roman culture. For Gamaliel, though, the bath is not a foreign institution: "I did not come into her borders, she came into mine!" The very exchange

---

[1] *Mishnah* is a compilation of rabbinic literature including legal opinions and debates that was assembled likely in 200 C.E. by Rabbi Judah the Prince.
[2] Deuteronomy 13:17.

between the rabbi and the Greek philosopher, fictional thought it may have been, also attests to the sense the Jews had of participation in the discourses of wider culture.[3]

Public bath houses were not a Jewish invention. The public bath served as a central communal institution of ancient Greece, and it was adopted later by the Romans as a standard feature of everyday life. For Gamaliel, the primary emphasis of the conversation with the Greek man was not fixated upon whether or not the public bath ought to exist—that much was assumed—but whether or not the Aphrodite which adorned the bath constituted a form of idolatry. Even the conversation between Gamaliel and the philosopher only serves to bolster the Greek imagery of the story. Public discourse in the *poleis* played one part in the long tradition of the Greek debate and forum.

This story from the Mishnah reveals to the modern reader that the relationship between Hellenism and Judaism was complex, and the religious attitude toward Hellenism in Israel, just before and during the turn of the millennia was not homogenous. As discussed in the previous chapter, there were those in Judaea that found a home in Hellenism and had no interest in preserving the religion of their fathers. However, the more traditional Jewish sects also had their influence. Since neither group was going away, the hybridization of Hellenism and Judaism in the dominant culture began to take shape.

After the Maccabean Revolt, more traditional observers of Judaism enjoyed a period of reprieve from the oppressive version of Hellenism put upon them by the Seleucids. Still, while the oppression faded, the Hellenism stayed. Although the Seleucid Empire faded into the background less than a century after the death of Antiochus, the influence of Hellenism was much more

---

[3] Meyers, Eric M. "Jewish Culture in Greco-Roman Palestine." In *Cultures of the Jews*, edited by David Biale, 135. New York: Schocken Books, 2002.

permanent in the region. Rome adopted many of the traditions of Hellas, although as in every culture that adopted the ways of the Greeks, it had its unique features. The Greek pantheon was adopted by Rome generations before the annexing of Judaea, and its role as the epicenter of Roman religion and culture, albeit under other names, would last for centuries. Jewish participation in the gymnasium, theatrical productions, bath houses, and other forms of Greek culture were only the surface evidence of Hellenistic influence in the region. Much deeper and intricate forms of cultural assimilation took place in the Jewish psyche, to the extent that it began to transform their interpretation of Jewish identity.

> The Jews, it might better be said, redefined their heritage in the terms of Hellenistic culture itself. They engaged actively with the traditions of Hellas, adapting genres and transforming legends to articulate their own legacy in modes congenial to a Hellenistic setting. At the same time, they recreated their past, retold stories in different shapes, and amplified the scriptural corpus itself through the medium of the Greek language and Greek literary forms. The challenge for the Jews was not how to surmount barriers or cross boundaries. In a world where Hellenic culture held an ascendant position, they strove to present Judaic traditions and express their own self-definition through the media of the Greeks—and to make those media their own.[4]

As with so many battles, time has a way of redefining the objectives of the conflict. Hellenism had a deep and abiding impact on Judaea, and as assimilation expanded, Jewish self-identity began to suffer. Because eliminating Hellenism from the region altogether was not a realistic goal even for the most religiously devout, redefining acceptable levels of assimilation became more common practice (hence the story of Gamaliel at the bath house of Aphrodite). Participation in the everyday activities of Greek culture was probably not avoidable, but certain steps

---

[4] Gruen, Erich S. "Hellenistic Judaism." In *Cultures of the Jews*, edited by David Biale, 80. New York: Schocken Books, 2002.

could be taken to mitigate how much influence Hellenism had on the religion of the Jews. This conflict between traditional beliefs and assimilation to new ones created a major split in Judaism, culminating in the formation of a new dominant Jewish sect during the waning years of the old millennia.

The two leading groups of religious Judaism became known as the Pharisees and the Sadducees. The Pharisees represented the old guard that had remained true to traditional Jewish beliefs while the Sadducees represented a progression out of Jewish norms, and into a new hybrid religion. While these terms are likely familiar to the Christian reader, their origins are somewhat less understood in modernity, at least in the West. Christianity situates the identity of the Pharisees and the Sadducees squarely in the context of their relationship to Jesus Christ and His followers in the first century, but they have a long and storied history that predates the New Testament by nearly two centuries.

After Judas Maccabeus and his forces took back the temple from the Seleucid forces, it seemed as though Jewish identity apart from the Greeks would have some staying power in Judaea. But, as stated previously, the Jews were in Hellenism, and Hellenism in the Jews. Although the Maccabean Revolt began as a political and cultural protest against the forced conversion to the religion of the Greeks brought on by Antiochus IV Epiphanes, it took less than a generation for the priorities of the new Jewish leadership to shift.

A ruling class arose in Israel known as the Hasmonaean kings.[5] The brother of Judas Maccabeus named Simon declared himself *hegemenos* and high priest[6] after the taking back of the temple, thus setting the stage for future leaders to violate the Jewish prohibition against kings becoming priests and priests becoming kings.[7] Future generations of Hasmonean kings did precisely that, coming to its apex likely during the reign of Alexander Jannaeus (103-76 B.C.E.). As time progressed, it became easier for the Hasmonean rulers to assume greater

---

[5] "Hasmonaean" refers to the family clan of Hashman, from whom the Maccabees descended. For more on this, see Meyers in *Cultures of the Jews* p.143.
[6] *Hegemenos* was a Greek term used to refer to the supreme leader. Alexander the Great bore this title, as well as his father Philip of Macedon.
[7] 1st Maccabees 14:41-42 (KJV).

amounts of power, and they were ultimately responsible for corrupting the very revolution they had begun. The Hasmonean's decision to adopt a Greek vocabulary of rulership had its consequences as well. Terms such as *hegemenos, strategos,* and even *sanhedrin*[8] were Greek terms adopted by the Jews to define the structure and boundaries of Jewish authority, and they were not cohesive with traditional Jewish practices concerning how to govern. But Hellenism influenced the Hasmonaeans in more ways than terminology.

> [The Hasmonaeans] took Greek names and adopted foreign symbols such as the sun, anchor, caduceus, and cornucopia in imitation of other regimes, seeking to combine old with the new, the religious with the political. Despite their ideology of ethnic and religious nationalism, the Hasmonaeans had no qualms about conforming to the conventions of the Hellenistic world.[9]

As the reign of the Hasmonaeans became more Hellenistic in practice and corrupted by the kings who had attempted to hijack the priesthood for themselves, Jewish dissent against their leadership became more common. According to the Hebrew Bible, the priesthood of Israel descended (and *must* descend) from the lineage of Aaron. The Hasmonaeans, though Levites, were not legitimate heirs of the priesthood.[10] Nor were the Hasmonaeans decedents of King David, and their decision to assume the office of the High Priest for themselves created animosity with the religiously devout of Israel. At its peak, the corruption of the office of the High Priest by the Hasmonaeans led to the selling of the office to the highest bidder.[11] The corrupted priesthood was in

---

[8] While often thought of as a Jewish office because of its role in the New Testament, the sanhedrin was not a Jewish creation. It was a term for jurisprudential and private political council created by Alexander the Great in the fourth century B.C.E.

[9] Ibid. (3) (p.145-146).

[10] Aaron was from the tribe of Levi, hence all priests were Levites. However, not all Levites were priests.

[11] Wolbe, Yaakov. "Heresy, Hedonism and Hatred: The Rise of The Sadducees." The Jewish History Podcast. Last modified January 11, 2017.

charge of the temple order, which only augmented the tension between those who had thrown in their lot with the Greeks and the Romans, and those who wanted a biblical Jewish identity and political sovereignty. The temple was the holiest site in Jerusalem, and the more traditional Jewish sect despised its contamination by the idolatrous practices of Greece. Those who maintained stewardship over the temple order and had sympathy for the role of Hellenism in Israel were primarily the Sadducees. The more religiously conservative that wanted no part with the assimilation of the Sadducees were known as the Pharisees, or "separated ones," although this term was placed on them only after the assimilation of the Sadducees. The Sadducees were greatly influenced by the Greek political leadership of their time and cultivated many views on Judaism that were not in step with traditional Jewish norms. These views included their beliefs about the Scriptures, which according to the Sadducees, were limited to the books of Moses and were also open to a great deal of private interpretation by the reader.[12] The Sadducees also possessed variant views on the afterlife and the resurrection of the saints of God. According to the Sadducees, there would be no resurrection of the soul after death, giving license to the body to behave as it saw fit while it was alive. Their liberalized view on the consequences (or lack thereof) of behavior in the physical realm and the condition of their eternity in the spiritual realm would have a ripple effect leading into the first century C.E.

The novel beliefs of the Sadducees contrasted with traditional Judaism lends credibility to the claim that the Pharisees did not represent a novel Jewish sect themselves, but that they were the core from which those who assimilated to the greater culture chose to depart. While other religious sects would spring up throughout Judaea's vassalage to the Roman Empire including the Essenes (Qumranites) and the Zealots, the division between the Pharisees and the Sadducees provides somewhat a summary

---

https://podcasts.apple.com/us/podcast/the-jewish-history-podcast-with-rabbi-yaakov-wolbe/id1151634104?i=1000379837347.
- It is estimated that the office of the High Priest was sold more than three hundred times during this era.
12 Ibid. (11).

representation of the ideological and religious battles which raged in the land of Israel at the turn of the millennia.

Understanding how Hellenism infiltrated Judaism to the degree that it did has been a subject of much debate among historians. Part of the reason for this is that Hellenism can be difficult to define, just as the precise definition of Jewish identity has historically been grappled with as well.

> At one level, Hellenism has to do with the ethnic and cultural construct of "Greek-ness." Thus, the fifth-century B.C. historian Herodotus records a speech from an Athenian delegation that identifies as one of the reasons for their failure to come to terms with the Persian Xerxes the Athenians' own "Greekness"...defined in terms of "common blood, common language, altars of gods and sacrifices shared in common, and common ways of life" (Herodotus, *Hist.* 8.144.2 [cf. Isocrates, *Paneg.* 50]).[13]

Although Hellenism greatly informed the religion of the Greeks, it could not be reduced simply to Greek religion. Nor could it be defined only as Greek ethnicity or culture. Hellenism was the encapsulation of Greek-ism as expressed throughout the world in all of its various shades and degrees. Greek in root, but not limited to the Greeks. Because of this, many cultures found ways to incorporate Hellenism into their pre-existent culture and thus bend their world into a new image that also seemed to reflect the old. Judaea was no exception to this practice. Throughout the waning centuries of the old millennium, there arose Jewish writers who retold Jewish stories through Greek mediums. Some of these stories were biblical tales refashioned in the mold of the Greek mind. Others were novel creations of their own that used

---

[13] Downs, David J. "Hellenism." In *Dictionary of Jesus and the Gospels*, edited by Joel B. Green, Jeannine K. Brown, and Nicholas Perrin, 376. Nottingham, England: InterVarsity Press, 2013.

traditional Jewish tales to color in an otherwise Greek outline. Examination of these Greek-influenced versions of Jewish traditions can offer helpful insights into the Jewish psyche during the Hellenistic Age, and under the tutelage of the Romans.

There is a great deal of evidence to suggest that the Jews were heavily influenced by their Syrian Greek and Roman peers in their written works, as the retellings of biblical stories frequently appear during and after the Hellenistic Age in Judaea. One such example is a work called the *Testament of Job*.

Set at the end of Job's life, the story depicts Job as a man gathering together his seven children to tell them the story of the suffering he had experienced early in his life. Departing from the biblical text early, the *Testament of Job* attempts to paint Job in a heroic light, telling the reader that Job knew from the beginning of his walk with God what price he would have to pay for his righteousness. This deviates from the biblical story, which unlike the *Testament of Job*, emphasizes Job's lack of knowledge concerning why he had been made to suffer. In the *Testament of Job*, much like Abraham, Job is said to have despised the idolatry of the nation that he lived in.[14] In attempting to destroy the idols of his age and lead his people closer to the true God, Job is visited by an angel of the Lord, who warns him that the more he stands for righteousness, the more that Satan will work against him. When Job asks the Lord to help him destroy the idols of Satan, the archangel responds to Job by saying,

> Thus speaketh the Lord: if thou undertakest to destroy and takest away the image of Satan, he will set himself with wrath to wage war against thee, and will display against thee all his malice. He will bring upon thee many severe plagues, and take from thee all that thou hast. He will take away thine children, and will inflict many evils upon thee. Then thou must wrestle

---

[14] Although not included in the biblical account of Abraham's life, the *Midrash* says that Abraham's father named Terah was a seller of idols. To prove the powerlessness of such idols, Abraham destroys the statues and icons in his father's shop and blames it on one of the idols. When Terah objects to Abraham's story, saying that there is of course no way that an idol came to life and destroyed the other idols, Abraham responds with agreement, and questions his father's willingness to worship idols that are indeed so powerless.

like an athlete and resist pain, sure of thy reward, overcome trials and afflictions.[15]

Despite the great suffering that it will bring upon his life, Job stands up against the idolatry of the land. The *Testament of Job* paints Job as an advocate for truth among an idolatrous people.

Although this particular story about Job was written long after Job would have lived, it is illuminating when trying to understand how the ancient world received and re-told the story of Job throughout history. In the *Testament of Job*, Job's sorrowful plight was brought on by his heroism—a willingness to be made a martyr by defying the power of Satan. The role of Job-as-hero throughout this retelling of Job's story signals the Greek influence on the ancient biblical account. The hero who suffers tragedy in the name of virtue, faithful to a higher cause—even when they are made to fight against supernatural powers—is a Greek motif, reflected in stories such as Prometheus, Odysseus, and Heracles. That Job remains the protagonist in this tale—likely more than one thousand years after his death—may reveal how the man named Job was admired by the Hellenistic cultures which inherited his story, or perhaps a version of it.

From the biblical account of Job, the reader understands that Job knew nothing about the reasons for his suffering, and even after petitioning God for such answers, Job received none. That is a notable difference between the biblical account and the retelling. While many of the broad strokes of the story of Job remain similar between the two stories, the mindset and the motives of Job evolve in the *Testament of Job* in a way that is not necessarily consonant with the biblical version. In the Bible, Job is a righteous man who Satan despises for his righteousness. Job does not provoke the evil in his life in the Bible, and although he remains faithful to God

---

[15] James, M. R. (2000). Testament of Job. In *Wesley center online*. Retrieved from http://wesley.nnu.edu/sermons-essays-books/noncanonical-literature/noncanonical-literature-ot-pseudepigrapha/testament-of-job/

- The phrase, "thou must wrestle like an athlete" almost certainly places the *Testament of Job* in the category of books written to reshape the stories of Judaism into Greek forms. Athletic competitions were foreign to Judaea until the influence of the Seleucids.

despite his circumstances, he questions why he has been made to suffer in the first place.[16] In the *Testament of Job*, Job knowingly provokes the evil to come in his life, and he does so unapologetically. While in the biblical account, Job is targeted for his righteousness, in the later story, Job is the one who takes the initiative against evil itself. In the former account, he is in a defensive position. In the latter, he is on the offense. This difference may tell the reader something about the Jewish mindset during the time of the Hasmonean kings.

Likely written between the first century B.C.E. and the first century C.E., the *Testament of Job* is written with Greek motifs but to a Jewish audience. The alterations made to the original story by the author may inform the modern reader as to the psyche of the Jewish people while under Greek and Hasmonean rule. Suppose the person of Job may be synonymized with Jewish identity more broadly in the *Testament of Job*. In that case, it may be inferred that his willingness to shoulder the burden of defending righteousness and conquering evil resonated with the Jewish *ethos* of the first century. In a time of rebellion against wicked authorities, Job-as-tragedy would not suit the situation. Instead, the *Testament of Job* offers a different perspective for the reader entirely. Job-as-hero. Why is this so? It is unlikely that the writer of the *Testament of Job* desired to be blatantly contradictory to the Scriptures in his story. However, the recasting of Job into a Greek medium does point to a Hellenized Jewish culture. The significance of the retelling also served the purpose of revealing to the reader what the Hellenistic Jewish world believed to be the character and virtue exhibited by Job throughout his life. By situating Job in a place of resiliency and virtue, his became an inspirational theme that an oppressed Jewish identity could rally behind. Job-as-hero is a remarkable image painted by the first-century retelling.

Not unlike the story of Rabbi Gamaliel at the Bath House of Aphrodite, the *Testament of Job* complicates the Jewish relationship to Hellenism in the first centuries B.C.E. and C.E. Job

---

[16] The closing chapters of Job not only emphasize the unknowable nature of Job's trials, but also offer criticisms of Job for his insistence on trying to know such answers at all (see Job ch.37-ch.40).

remained the protagonist of the story and is regarded as one having heroic virtue and courage. (A bolstered Jewish identity amid an idolatrous and corrupted society.) Yet the fact that the story was refashioned at all from its traditional biblical structure to that of a more Greek (nearly comedic) form reveals the influence of Hellenism on Jewish thought, regardless of how much they may have sought to avoid such a perception.

Other Jewish traditions were fashioned in the Hellenistic mold in less subtle ways. Among the more well-known Jewish creations in the Greek genre is a work called *Exagoge*. This literary work comes to us from an author known only as Ezekiel. The story follows the Exodus account and retells the events following the basic structure of the Bible. But *Exagoge* departs from the traditional narrative in not-insignificant ways. The story exemplifies Hellenic influence as it pertained to the Jewish religion in particular, and it may serve as an example of the sorts of things which motivated the great hostility that formed between the Pharisees and the Sadducees.

> Moses, in dialogue with his father-in-law, reports a puzzling dream in which he had a vision of a great throne high upon a summit extending to the cleft of heaven. There a noble man sat with diadem and a great scepter, summoned Moses to him, handed him the scepter and diadem, and departed from the throne. From that spot Moses had a view of the whole earth, both below it and above the sky, and a multitude of stars fell on their knees. Moses' father-in-law provides a most heartening interpretation of the dream: it is a sign from God that Moses will lift up a great throne, will issue judgements, and will serve as guide to mortals; the vision of the whole world, things both below and beyond God's firmament, signifies that Moses will perceive what is, what has been, and what will be. This striking passage corresponds to nothing in the book of Exodus...And some approximations can be found

in the Bible: a few fortunate figures received visions from God in their dreams, and still fewer actually glimpsed a throne. But nothing quite like the sight seen by Moses in *Exagoge*. Nowhere does God relinquish his seat to anyone else.[17]

According to the interpretation of Moses' father-in-law, the vision which Moses is said to have had meant that he would achieve a quasi-divine state, and that he will be lifted above the rest of humanity to guide them. The reader can infer this from the simple contrast created by Jethro[18] between Moses and the rest of mankind: that he will serve as a guide to mortals. Jethro's interpretation implies that in the context of his vision, Moses was not mortal himself. The picture which *Exagoge* paints is one of Moses as a divine intermediary between God and men, but with divine characteristics (mortal men do not know the past, present, and future together). In this way, *Exagoge* departs from the biblical depiction of Moses and situates Moses in a messianic role, not only for the Jews, but for the entire world. The image of the stars bowing before Moses recalls the imagery of Joseph in the book of Genesis,[19] but as Gruen states, in no other story is God said to have relinquished His throne. The similarities between *Exagoge* and the biblical narrative are only nominal. In principle, *Exagoge* departs widely from the biblical presentation of Moses and creates the office for Moses as that of a surrogate god, apparently dethroning the true God. While the Jews had no affection for Antiochus IV Epiphanes, this presentation of Moses is not unlike Antiochus' views concerning himself and a host of other Greek kings, including Alexander the Great. Recall that Alexander claimed to be the successor of Heracles, thereby making himself the joint offspring of Zeus. Seleucus I Nicator believed similar things of himself related to his relationship with Apollo.

Greek notions of royal divinity perhaps inform the modern reader as to the effect which their beliefs had on the Jewish psyche

---

[17] Ibid. (4) (p.81-82).
[18] Jethro, also known as Reuel, was the father-in-law of Moses according to Exodus 3:1.
[19] Genesis 37:9.

concerning their own leaders too. The divine ordination of kings was practiced in ancient Israel, dating back to their first king named Saul.[20] But the divine identity or the divine characteristics of kings was not something that biblical Judaism embraced. The Hebrew Bible is filled with stories of men being led by God, ordered by God, and even appointed by God. But nowhere in the biblical tradition are men said to have legitimately become gods themselves. In fact, the biblical presentation of the kings of Israel is exceptionally human, detailing their moral and spiritual failures to a degree not often seen in other cultures.[21] In this way, Hellenic influence is evident in Ezekiel's *Exagoge*. The difference in the narrative of Ezekiel's tale is that Moses is the god-king who unseats the true God. Moses is given the power to see things which were and things which are to come, and he does so as God's oracle or intermediary.

There is some irony to the presentation of Moses as a quasi-divine figure in Jewish literature, particularly at the time in which *Exagoge* was written. According to the book of Deuteronomy, it was Moses who warned the Israelites that there would come a day when they would ask God to give them a king so that they could be like the rest of the nations which were around them, although it was not God's express will that they have one at all. According to Moses, any king who would sit on the throne in Israel must be an Israelite, write a copy of the Law for himself, and he must not allow his heart to be lifted above his fellow Israelite.[22] Yet, it is the presentation of Moses in *Exagoge* which detracts the most from these requirements. Moses is intentionally portrayed as one lifted above his fellow man that he might lead mortals. He unseats God, illustrating a fundamental violation of the Law. And the use of Greek medium only emphasizes the non-Jewish nature of the characteristically Greek story that Ezekiel tells.

---

[20] 1st Samuel 9:15.

[21] 2nd Samuel tells the story of David's moral failings concerning his affair with Bathsheba and his murder of Uriah. In 1st Kings 16, Ahab is regarded as a king that was more evil than any other in Israel. Even the most well-regarded kings in the history of Israel such as Hezekiah have their faults recorded in the books of the kings as well. Indeed, no other nation seems to have recorded their failures so thoroughly as the ancient Israelites.

[22] Deuteronomy 17:14-20.

Although fictional, in the eyes of Pharisees, this story was likely an abominable presentation of Moses. *Exagoge* positions Moses in a lofty place within the Jewish psyche, confirming the zeal for Jewish identity among the people in a land controlled by the heathens in the first centuries B.C.E. and C.E. Yet just as the *Testament of Job, Exagoge* seems to betray its traditions through its expression in another. A longing for Jewish identity augmented the complexities of Hellenic influence in Jewish life yet also diluted the identity that many Jews were trying to preserve.

In some cases, compatibility between Hellenism and Jewish thought found their most meaningful expression through the writings of thought leaders, as opposed to playwrights or entertainers. One such example may be found in the work of Philo of Alexandria. Philo was born sometime around 20 B.C.E. in the Hellenized Egyptian city of Alexandria. Philo belonged to the class of Jews born outside the historic land of Israel yet maintained their Jewish identity in gentile lands. His contributions to the process of blending the Greco-Roman and Jewish worlds were among the most significant of his time. The teachings of Philo may have even been largely responsible for the Greek response to Christianity in the first century, to say nothing of the Jewish response as well.

To understand the method of Philo in bridging the Hellenistic and Judaic worlds, it is helpful to note that the Jews and the Greeks had very different beliefs about the metaphysical world and what constituted reality. For many of the Greeks at this time, the spiritual world and material worlds were distinct from one another, and true reality was primarily understood in terms of what may lie beyond the physical, seeable, tangible world. This included their understanding of human existence; the soul and the flesh were distinct, each possessing its own nature.

For the Jews, however, the physical and spiritual worlds were connected. In this way, the soul was not something that could be separated completely from the actions of the body, because the outer reflected the inner. For the Greeks, this was not necessarily the case. The soul was something apart from and distanced from the body, existing as a separate entity entirely.

The bifurcation of the metaphysical and the physical world in the Greek mind is essential when examining Philo. He was among the most prominent Greek writers of his time to embrace a more allegorical approach to the Hebrew Scriptures which disconnected it from literal interpretations which the Jews had historically accepted.

> In his symbolical interpretations Philo only partially took the same road as the Rabbis. The symbolism of numbers and, so far as the Sanctuary was concerned, that of colours, and even materials, may, indeed, be said to have its foundation in the Old Testament itself. The same remark applies partially to that of names. The Rabbis certainly so interpreted them. But the application Philo made of this symbolism was very different. Everything became symbolical in his hands, if it suited his purpose: numbers (in a very arbitrary manner), beasts, birds, fowls, creeping things, plants, stones, elements, substances, conditions, even sex—and so a term or an expression might even have several and contradictory meanings, from which the interpreter was at liberty to choose.[23]

Edersheim's emphasis in the above passage is on the form which biblical interpretation took in the hand of Philo, not the act of interpretation itself. The principle that portions of Scripture were intended to represent spiritual axioms and that those axioms could be rightly understood by looking at the physical world they impacted was a very traditional belief for the Jews of Philo's time. But Philo diverted from the traditional course in his decision to make the entire processes of studying the Scriptures *principally* interpretative. For Philo, the spiritual and physical worlds could be disconnected in such a way that the boundaries for interpretation existed only in the mind of the interpreter. Thus,

---

[23] Edersheim, Alfred. *The Life and Times of Jesus the Messiah.* 3rd ed. Vol. 1. Grand Rapids, MI: Wm. B. Eerdmans Publishing Co.,, 1973. (p.43).

even portions of the text that were intended to be read in a literal sense, or at least not in a highly symbolic sense, were taken to be symbolic anyway.

If you can conceive of a world in which there is a spiritual realm that lies beyond the physical that is perceived to be the more real, more true, or most important, then the methods of Philo do not seem so beyond the bounds of reason. However, the more liberal interpretative practices of Philo were not necessarily consonant with the greater Jewish culture. For the Jews, the physical world was not something to be ignored or dismissed as only a shadowy reflection of what was real.[24] Instead, what happened in the physical world directly related to the spiritual and could even alter the conditions of what may lie beyond the physical realm. Thus, there were limits to interpretative practices. Symbolism and allegory had to reflect consonance with the physical world. A correlation between the two was necessary for interpretation to be considered sound.

For Philo, the physical world as it was described in a particular passage of Scripture possessed only a distant relationship to the deeper meaning. In some cases, the deeper meaning of a specific passage of Scripture may be contradictory to the words of the text itself. If this were the case, it only served to bolster the belief that what lies beyond the physical was more true than the physical.

Thus, the connection between words and reality was loosened. There was less emphasis on what the words in a particular passage meant, or what they should have meant, and more focus was placed on the idea of what they *could* mean. The two are not the same. As Edersheim points out, "a term or an expression might even have several and contradictory meanings, from which the interpreter was at liberty to choose." For Philo, this practice was not an academic fallacy but a key to deeper spiritual understanding.

---

[24] This is akin to Plato's "shadowy cave" analogy. For more on this, see:
- Schenck, Kenneth. *A Christian Philosophical Journey*. Marion, IN: Triangle Publishing, 2014. (p.8).

Philo was an intellectual deeply influenced by Grecian Stoic thought. This was important to his understanding of the origin of all things, the biblical creation narrative, and other religious archetypes. Much like other Greek thinkers of Alexander's time, the Stoics believed that there was matter in the universe that pre-existed the gods, and that matter, although ruled by the gods, could resist them too.[25] Although Philo was essentially monotheistic in his approach to religion, the idea of pre-existent matter which was formed by the power of Potencies that were not necessarily created by God but shared consubstantiality with Him was not beyond the bounds of reason for Philo.[26] This likely informed Philo's understanding the *logos*, which he wrote of often, and was even addressed by later Christian writers.

The Potencies as understood by Philo may be regarded as something distinct from yet emanating from the unknowable or distant God. Remember that for the Greeks, the most extraordinary powers of the universe were not searchable in human understanding. Although the gods of the Greek pantheon were knowable (in some cases, though not all), the Titans were much more elusive.[27] According to the Egyptians, this is similar to the relationship between Ammon and Ra, as discussed in chapter one. Ammon, the one distant from all things—Ra, Ammon revealed. Eventually, the emanations were personified in human flesh; thus, Alexander claimed demi-god status for himself, and the Egyptians claimed that the Pharaohs were children of Ra.

Making the unknowable knowable was not just a byproduct of Greek myth and later philosophy. It may be understood as one of its primary functions. For Philo, the challenge was applying these principles to the God of the Israelites to create cohesion and consonance between two competing ideologies in the Near East. To do this, Philo chose the cult of light as understood by the

---

[25] See (Ch. 1).

[26] Ibid. (22) (p.50-51).

[27] Hamilton, Edith. *Mythology*. New York: Grand Central Publishing, 1942. (p.17-18).

- According to the Greeks, some of the Titans were only known by the pre-existent forces that they embodied, such as Ocean.

Greeks to describe the Potencies of Stoic thought in relationship to Judaism.

The Potencies, as explained by Philo, bore a relationship to God in the same way that light beams share a relationship with true light or the sun. Thus, the light emanating from the sun may not be said to be the sun precisely but also cannot be separated from it. Similarly, he described the Potencies as waters that flow from a spring, or breath coming from the human lungs. It is interesting to note Philo's decision to express the relationship between Potencies and God in terms of sun and sunlight, as well as other natural forces. The conception of Potencies being characterized by light reappears in the writings of Philo, possibly guiding the reader to an understanding of other dominant religious influences of the era. The cult of Apollo maintained a strong presence in the Ptolemaic and Seleucid kingdoms and continued under the auspices of Rome. Philo likely used the familiar imagery of the cult of light as a means of imitating concepts his audience would have been familiar with.

These Potencies were the creative forces that brought about matter's existence, but they were not necessarily God Himself. Again, in Greek thought, there was a belief that even those things that the Gods created could challenge or oppose them, and in this way, it would not be proper to think of the Potencies as manifestations of God. Rather, they were principalities empowered by God.

> They were immanent in God, and yet also without Him— motions on the part of God, and yet independent beings. They were the ideal world, which in its impulse outwards, meeting matter, produced this material world of ours. They were also the angels of God—His messengers to man, the *media* through whom He revealed Himself.[28]

It should not be assumed that Philo's primary motivation was to reconcile Judaism and Hellenic thought. Perhaps it was, but his work merely reflects the dominant culture of the world in which

---

[28] Ibid. (22) (p.46).

he lived. As a philosopher, Philo did the work of philosophy. It is unnecessary to seek out an ulterior motive on the part of the writer. As will be discussed in later portions of this book, the battle between traditional Jewish thought and Hellenism would continue well beyond the death of Philo and even beyond the Roman Empire.

The relationship between Greek culture and Jewish identity expanded beyond the boundaries of pen and parchment. The political relationship between the two worlds became much more unified during the close of the Seleucid Empire and throughout the beginning of Roman occupation of the Judaean province. This melting together of two worlds is perhaps typified by the actions of Aristobulus, son of Hyrcanus, in the late second century B.C.E.

Aristobulus came to power soon after the death of his father, John Hyrcannus, in 104 B.C.E., and although his reign was short, Josephus includes the story in his *Antiquities*. Aristobulus exemplifies the conflict presented by this chapter, as his love of Jewish identity and his desire for Hellenism were at odds with one another in many ways.

> But Aristobulus repented immediately of this slaughter of his brother; on which account his disease increased upon him, and he was disturbed in his mind, upon the guilt of such wickedness, insomuch that his entrails were corrupted by his intolerable pain, and he vomited blood...whereupon he shed many tears, in that disorder of mind which arose from his consciousness of what he had done, and gave a deep groan, and said, "I am therefore, I perceive, to be concealed from God, in the impious and horrid crimes I am guilty of...In saying which last words he died, having reigned a year. He was called a lover of the Grecians: and had conferred many benefits on his own country, and made war against Iturea, and added a great part of it to Judaea, and compelled the

inhabitants, if they would continue in that country, to be circumcised, and to live according to the Jewish laws.[29]

The passage from Josephus in chapter twelve begins by presenting Aristobulus' profound grief at the error he made in executing his brother, having done so only by the trickery of his queen.[30] But the author's emphasis when summing up the significance of the life of king Aristobulus is primarily in the context of his love of the Grecians and his expansion of the territory of Judaea into gentile lands. What is so striking about the account of Josephus is that it emphasizes Aristobulus' affection for Hellenism, as well as his pride in national identity. "He was called a lover of the Grecians." Aristobulus possessed a measure of affection for the invaders of the land of his people. Yet this did not diminish Jewish identity in the eyes of the king.

When Aristobulus conquered the Itureans, he made their citizenship conditional upon every male being circumcised and abiding by the laws of the Jews. Thus, the practice Antiochus IV Epiphanes once outlawed was restored during the reign of the Hasmoneans—but not by driving out the Greeks. The demand placed upon the Itureans was not enforced on all the Greeks living in greater Israel. It likely was done in the case of the Itureans only because the region which they occupied belong to historic Israel in the mind of the Judaean kings.[31] Nevertheless, the fact that it was done at all—circumcision restored and enforced—illustrates the struggle to retain Jewish identity amid an increasingly non-Jewish land. Perhaps more than any other territory, Judaea defined Hellenism as it was practiced in the rest of the world: Greek-ish, but not completely without its own identity.

---

[29] Josephus, *Antiquities of the Jews*, Book XIII, (Ch. XII.).

[30] Ibid (29). (Ch.XI).

[31] Iturea was situated just north of Galilee, southwest of Damascus. At its peak, the Davidic kingdom of Israel stretched as far north as Sidon, and slightly further east than Ramoth Galaad.

The Hellenization of Judaea and its impact on the religion of the Jews just before the turn of the millennia culminates with the rise of Herod the Great in the first century B.C.E. It is this same Herod of which it is said he sent out an order into the province that all the children under the age of two among the Israelites should be murdered, as he was paranoid that a prophecy predicting an end to his kingship would come to pass.[32]

Herod the Great was not Jewish according to traditional Jewish heredity laws.[33] Ethnically speaking, Herod was an Edomite whose father Antipater had served as a high-ranking official in the Roman government. Herod's grandfather was forced to convert to Judaism during the reign of the Hasmoneans, likely in similar circumstances to that of the Itureans mentioned earlier.[34] It is not surprising, then, that a great fondness for Greek culture characterized Herod's rule. Nor is it surprising that he possessed less passion for Jewish ethnicity and nationality than many of his predecessors. After Rome annexed Judaea in 63 B.C.E., they set Herod up as their proxy ruler in the region. Knowing that his allegiance to Rome would remain sound given his father's ties to the empire, the Romans gave Herod much latitude in the province. Herod used his hegemonic freedom over the area to build new edifices in the Greek style and institute greater Greco-Roman culture in Jerusalem.

During his reign, Herod instituted games every fifth year in Judaea to honor Caesar. Caesarea was established as an homage to the man Herod perceived to be the ruler of the world. Although many Jews despised the games and the theater for their culturally pagan ties, Herod insisted that theaters be constructed in Judaea as well.[35] Still today, the ruins of the theater constructed at Caesarea Maritima can be visited in the land of Israel (see Figure 3.1). Classical Greek structures typified Herodian-Era

---

[32] Matthew 2:1-17.
[33] Telushkin, Joseph. *Jewish Literacy*. New York: William Morrow and Co., 1991. (p.429).
  - According to Jewish law, one is only a Jew by birth if their mother is a Jew. Thus, even if one is born to a Jewish father, intermarriage with a non-Jewish woman would prevent the child from being a Jew halakhically.
[34] Ibid. (3) (p.147).
[35] Josephus, *Antiquities of the Jews*, Book XV (Ch. VIII).

constructions, and Herod's fondness for *Thymelici* (Greek musical theater) caused productions to be put on around the province. This included performances in the nude, which some Jewish men desired to participate in, so much so that they concealed their circumcision in order to do so.[36] Herod imported wrestlers, actors, musicians, and other artists from all over the world, bringing more classical Greek elements into the Judaean frame.[37] While it was protested by the greater Jewish community in Judaea that such behavior was abominable for a Jewish king, Herod saw Grecian restoration and construction throughout the land as a way of legitimizing the region as a recognizable power in Rome. Furthermore, Herod the Great had no nostalgic ties to an older portrait of Israel that many of his subjects longed for. His disconnection with the greater Jewish psyche eventually culminated with an assassination attempt (and probably more than one) against the king. After hearing of threats against his life, Herod sent spies throughout the land to root out any plots that may have been in the works to kill the king.

*Figure 3.1*

*The theater at Caesarea Maritima, constructed during the reign of Herod the Great, (37-4 B.C.E.) (Photo credit Eyal Bartov.)*

When one spy infiltrated a group of ten men who were about to carry out an attempt on Herod's life, the king had them executed.

---

[36] See (Ch. 2) (Note 26).
[37] Ibid. (29).

Public outrage at the spying actions of Herod caused an uproar, and the spy who infiltrated the assassin's group was killed. The killing of the king's spy motivated an especially cruel act against the people, of which it is said that Herod had certain women tortured and killed to determine who the culprits were.[38] If Josephus is to be believed, most of the Judaean province despised Herod by his death.

In addition to his Greco-Roman architectural and cultural revolution, Herod the Great imported priests from Egypt (or Babylonia, the source is not certain) to serve in the temple.[39] As the Pharisees already hated the impurity of the Sadducee order, this action likely only have served to amplify the tension between the two worlds. In step with his Hellenizing of the Judaean province came the most historically notable act of Herod the Great—the renovation of Zerubbabel's Temple.

When the Israelites rebuilt the temple of Jerusalem in the late sixth century B.C.E., it was significantly smaller than its tenth-century predecessor. According to Ezra's account, the Second Temple had smaller foundations than Solomon's Temple,[40] and many other accounts inform the modern reader that the Ark of the Covenant, the most critical piece of the structure, was not present in the Second Temple either.[41] Nevertheless, the temple remained the holiest site in Jerusalem, and it was the epicenter of Jewish social life as well.

The Herodian structure was nearly double that of the Solomonic temple (Josephus, J.W. 1.401-2), though exact measurements, at least of the court of the Gentiles, differ in the sources (cf. m. Mid. 2:1; Josephus, Ant. 15.391-403). It was an irregular structure, broader on the north than south, surrounded by a stone wall with several gates (Josephus, Ant. 15.410-20; cf. m. Mid. 1:3), a porch on the east side (Jn 10:23;

---

[38] Ibid. (29).
[39] Mishnah Parah (3.5a).
[40] Ezra 3:9-13.
[41] According to 2nd Maccabees, the prophet Jeremiah buried the Ark of the Covenant and the Altar of Incense in a cave before the Babylonian invasion of 586 B.C.E. Josephus' Antiquities of the Jews also says that the Second Temple was largely empty compared to Solomon's Temple.

Acts 3:11) and open spaces where some commerce occurred (Mt 21:12 par.; Jn 2:14-16). Here was the location where Jesus ministered to the blind and lame (Mt 21:14) and overturned the money tables (Mt 21:12 par). Increasing the size required extensive topographic reconfigurations, including filling in the valleys to the west and north, and part of the Kidron Valley to the south. Modern archeological analysis suggests that the retaining wall for the Temple Mount was 1,590 feet (west) by 1,035 feet (north), by 1,535 feet (east) by 912 feet (south).[42]

Whether Herod's motivation behind renovating the temple was purely religious or not is unclear. What is known is that at a time when the most religiously devout in Israel saw Herod's reign as a threat to their existence, Herod wanted to assuage their concerns by building an edifice unlike any other in Israel's history. Ironically, the reconstructed temple reflected the very Greek culture that the Pharisees had come to despise so much. As shown in Figure 3.2, Herod's renovated temple was designed differently than Solomon's, including large colonnade structures throughout the site reflecting the generations of Greek influence on its reconstruction.

Josephus states that around the entirety of Herod's Temple were spoils taken from heathen nations and that those things had been dedicated to the temple by Herod.[43] When examining many of the dominant design features of the Herodian structure, it is evident that the king desired to make an edifice not so much suited for the work of the Levitical priesthood as for the admiration of the surrounding nations.

[42] Gurtner, Daniel M. "Temple." In *Dictionary of Jesus and the Gospels*, edited by Joel B. Green, Jeannine K. Brown, and Nicholas Perrin, 940. Nottingham, England: InterVarsity Press, 2013.
[43] Josephus, *Antiquities of the Jews*, Book XV (Ch. XI).

*Figure 3.2*

*An artistic rendering of what Herod's Temple may have looked like in first-century Israel. A model of the temple may be seen at the Israel Museum.*

And indeed, it is recorded that many leaders from Near East came to Judaea to witness the gaudy structure constructed by Herod.

> Now in the western quarters of the enclosure of the temple there were four gates; the first led to the king's palace, and went to a passage over the intermediate valley; two more led to the suburbs of the city; and the last led to the other city, where the road descended down into a valley by a great number of steps, and thence up again by the ascent; for the city lay over against the temple in the manner of a theatre, and was encompassed with a deep valley along the entire south quarter; but the fourth front of the temple, which was southward, had indeed itself gates in its middle, as also it had the royal cloisters...This cloister had pillars that stood in four rows one over against the other all along, for the fourth row was interwoven into the wall, which [also was built of stone]; and the thickness of each pillar was such that three men might, with their arms extended, fathom it round, and join

their hands again, while its length was twenty-seven feet, with a double spiral at its basis; and the number of all the pillars [in that court] was a hundred and sixty-two. Their chapiters were made with sculptures after the Corinthian order, and caused an amazement [to the spectators], by reason of the grandeur of the whole.[44]

Herod's renovation of the Second Temple into a more Greek-like structure was not met without resistance. Combined with his decision to import priests that did not belong to the inheritance of Aaron, it was believed by many religious sectarians of the first century that the temple order had become exceedingly corrupted and was operating in direct contradiction to the Law of Moses.

One such group included the Essenes who resided in the area surrounding the Dead Sea, on the outskirts of greater Judaea in the first century. The Essenes were primarily responsible for writing the documents which came to be known as the Dead Sea Scrolls, discovered in the 1940s by a Bedouin who stumbled upon the caves where the scrolls had been preserved for two millennia. The scrolls included manuscripts of many biblical works and codes for sectarian life in the Qumranite community. Some of the Dead Sea Scrolls date as far back as the early Seleucid Empire. Their contribution to the modern understanding of the culture and political climate of the first centuries B.C.E. and C.E. are extremely valuable. Included in these scrolls were writings that spoke out against the temple order of first-century Judaea. Viewed as a corrupted class by the Essenes, *The Damascus Document* states,

> They also defile the sanctuary, for they do not separate clean from unclean according to the Law...Furthermore they marry each man the daughter of his brothers and the daughter of his sister, although Moses said, "Unto the sister of your mother you shall not draw near; she is the flesh of your mother" (Lev. 18:13)...Also they have corrupted their holy spirit, and with blasphemous language they have reviled the statutes of God's

---

44 Ibid. (42).

covenant, saying, "They are not well founded." They continually speak abhorrent things against them...[45]

According to the Essenes, those in charge of the temple order during the days of Herod were known as "boundary shifters" who had deemed ancient Jewish traditions as antiquated and had liberalized much of what the Pharisees and the Essenes considered to be sacrosanct.[46] In terms of their treatment of the temple and their behavior as priests, both were reviled by the Qumranite community repeatedly in the writings of the Dead Sea Scrolls.

The stage is set for the New Testament by the waning years of the first-century B.C.E. The immersion of the Near East in Hellenism during the conquests of Alexander the Great, the birth of Hellenic cities in greater Syria, Judaea, and Asia Minor by the Seleucids, and the response of Judaism to the religious influence of surrounding nations all contributed to the political and cultural climate in which Jesus and His followers lived. Throughout the first three chapters of this book, the journey from Macedonia to Judaea has been only a brief example of how cultures separated by centuries remained deeply connected through religious thought. It is remarkable to consider the principally similar methods of Alexander the Great, Seleucus I Nicator, Antiochus IV Epiphanes, and even Herod the Great in assimilating the people they ruled to the culture that they lived in. Recall that in chapter one, we examined how change that happens too quickly is quickly opposed. But the ability of each generation to recast themselves in the mold of the Greeks while maintaining a shade of an older

---

45 Geniza A+B, 4Q268, *The Damascus Document* (Wise, Abegg Jr., & Cook translation).

    • (4) refers to the cave number in Qumran the scroll was discovered in. (268) refer to the manuscript number taken from that cave.

46 Ibid. (45) 4Q266, *The Damascus Document*. (Wise, Abegg Jr., & Cook translation).

identity is remarkable. That is, perhaps, the very definition of Hellenism. It was effective because rather than destroying each culture that in infiltrated, Hellenism changed with the culture. Thus, the tent got larger, and therefore the outgroup got smaller. The smaller the outgroup, the less resistance can be expected. In this way, many nations, including the Jews, could participate in communities that they had heretofore not known. Where familial or religious ties were once necessary to maintaining a cohesive society, communal identity through participation in the greater culture could supplement those more traditional relationships.

Yet Hellenism in and of itself is not to be blamed entirely for the sectarianism of Judaea at the turn of the millennia. Assimilation of any kind tends to alienate as much as it unites. Many Jews were ready to adapt to the political climate of their time in each generation, regardless of the consequences it may have had on the religious traditions of their fathers. That was not a behavior unique to its time—according to the biblical narratives, in nearly every generation of its existence, the Jews struggled to preserve their covenantal identity. Hellenism presented many opportunities for assimilation to the greater culture, but assimilation is also a choice.

The religious adaptations of Alexander to the cult of Ammon and Seleucus I Nicator's emphasis on the cult of Apollo in bounding Seleucid territory reveal the adaptability of the Greek religion to its expanding influence. Through philosophy, Greek culture formed easily to the various pantheons, traditions, and liturgical practices of the territories it occupied.

The vast city and temple construction projects of the Macedonian, Ptolemaic, and Seleucid kings laid the foundation for what would eventually become the primary geography and epicenters for the religious cults of the Greeks (and later the Romans) in the Near East as well. Jupiter, the Roman representation of Zeus, remained dominant in the Roman pantheon long after the first century. Phoebus Apollo as well. These Greco-Roman gods would be recast as archetypes of the metaphysical realm through philosophical disputations on spirit and light in the century of Christ, as well as many after. As discussed in this chapter, the writings of men such as Philo of

Alexandria evidence a Semitic culture that was already becoming taken with the notions of the Stoics and had a mind to apply Greek philosophy to the traditions of Moses through the principles of the cult of light.

The influence of Greek architecture changed the physical landscape of the world that the Jews lived in as well. It would not be proper to imagine Israel as portrayed by the prophets in the Old Testament when trying to conceive of the world in which Jesus Christ lived. During the time of Christ, Israel was architecturally a reflection of the Ptolemaic and Seleucid world which had occupied it for centuries (recall Figures 2.2 and 3.1). At the very least, it was a messy amalgamation of the old world and the new. This was reflected in the dominant languages of the region as well. Greek, Aramaic, and Latin were all common in the Judaean province of the first century.[47] Thus, to say there was a single dominant culture in Israel during the time of Christ is reductionist at best.

Both within Judaism itself and in the greater region of Judaea and Samaria, sectarianism existed. Battles raged between the Seleucid holdouts and the Romans. There were Zealots in Judaea fighting against the Hasmoneans. The conflict between the Pharisees, Sadducees, and Essenes abounded during the time of Christ, and this was primarily due to the influence of the Greeks in the centuries leading up to His birth. If the Sadducees were perceived as assimilators, boundary movers, and capitulators of Judaea by the Pharisees, the Pharisees were dismissed as the faux-pious, the out of touch, or the cynical by the Sadducees. And neither was suited to lead the religious world of Judaea out of conflict, according to the Essenes.

All of this would allow a new sect to arise that would become the most famous and enduring of the first century. Their leader did not attach himself to any particular religious or political order of His time. His followers contended actively with both Jewish and Roman opposition in the early stages of their movement. By the

---

[47] John 19:20. The writer states that the inscription written above the cross of Jesus was done in Hebrew, Greek, and Latin. However, the word "Hebrew" here likely refers to Aramaic, which was a Syrian dialect of the Hebrew language that contemporary speakers used. Paleo-Hebrew was not in common use during the first century, however religious communities probably continued to use it in liturgy and other isolated instances.

end of the first century, they were known as the ones who had "turned the world upside down."

# CHAPTER IV

## Early Christian Opposition

## to

## Hellenism

In those days came John the Baptist, preaching in the wilderness of Judaea, And saying, Repent ye: for the kingdom of heaven is at hand.[1]

The preaching of John the Baptist was not, as it may be easily assumed, primarily directed toward the conversion of Jews to the Christian church. In the days of John the Baptist, As a sect, Christianity did not exist yet. Although John did not believe himself to be the equal of Jesus, he was the forerunner of Jesus. John baptized Jesus, foreshadowing the practice of Christian baptism in the name of Jesus Christ, which would follow the ministry of John. John was also martyred before the birth of the church as well, and thus did not see Christianity as it was understood in the book of Acts come to pass in his lifetime.

Yet, John the Baptist is remembered as a primarily Christian figure in history nonetheless, and that is largely because of his personal relationship to Jesus Christ,[2] as well as his emphasis on the importance of Jesus as the true Messiah who would usher in Israel's redemption. Since John died before the church was born into the world in the book of Acts, and he was also a devout believer in Jesus as the Messiah, it may not be improper to think of John the Baptist as an intermediary figure between Old and New Testament Israel. John was a prophet, fulfilling the message

---

[1] Matthew 3:1-2 (KJV).
[2] According to Luke's Gospel, John the Baptist was the cousin of Jesus (see Luke 1:36).

of Isaiah which foretold of the days when a voice would cry out from the wilderness to prepare the way of the Lord.[3] But he also represented a movement into something new. John was radical for his time, and his words were not always well received. His religious piety ultimately contributed to his execution by Herod Antipas in the early part of the first century.[4]

Thus, situating John in the New Testament is a complex process that does not fit neatly into any single ideological framework. John represented both the old and the new, making him exceptionally valuable to the New Testament church.

Knowing the background of John is beneficial to understanding the message that John the Baptist preached. In the New Testament, it is said that John came out of a wilderness community of the Judaean desert.[5] Although it cannot be known with precise certainty where John lived, the Judaean desert is likely a reference to the land of the Qumranites, situated around the Dead Sea.

*Figure 4.1*                                    *Photo by Steven Gill, 2016*

*Qumran, 2016. The Dead Sea, visible in the background, is believed by some to be the final resting place of the ancient cities of Sodom and Gomorrah.*

---

[3] Isaiah 40:1-3. This prophecy is explicitly said to have referred to John the Baptist according to John's Gospel (John1:15-23).
[4] Mark 6:24-38.
[5] Luke 1:80; Matthew 3:1.

Whether or not John lived in Qumran specifically is not critical to our understanding of the culture John would have been familiar with. What is known about the wilderness communities of the Judaean desert is that they were the preferred dwelling places of the sectarian group known as the Essenes. Recall from chapter three that the Essenes were one of the numerous splinter groups which separated from the dominant religious community of Israel during the reign of the Hasmoneans. The Essenes were critical of the religious establishment in Israel.[6] They believed in an era of messianic fulfillment in which the Children of Light would conquer the Children of Darkness, ushering in an age of righteousness and peace for God's people.[7] It is also known that these wilderness dwellers were regular practitioners of *mikvah*,[8] and their baptism pools have been discovered in and around the area of the Dead Sea in recent decades. When studying the behavior and travels of John the Baptist according to the New Testament, it is not out of the question to assume that he belonged to the sect of the Essenes. According to the gospel accounts, John practiced ritual immersion, but this was not precisely the same as Christian baptism.[9] John's baptism was an act of spiritual confession and cleansing, but it was not considered sufficient in the Christian model, as followers of John were said to have been rebaptized after his death.[10] The theory of a Qumranite background for John also fits comfortably with his preaching. The

---

[6] See notes (45-46) in chapter three.

[7] 1QM, 4Q491-496, *The War Scroll*, 4Q285, 11Q14, *The War of the Messiah*. (Wise, Abegg Jr., & Cook translation).

[8] *Mikvah*, was the act of ritual cleansing by water immersion in Judaism. Given its consistent use by John the Baptist in the gospels, it is fair to assume that John belonged to one of the Essene communities that practiced ritual cleansing. As a matter of religious rite, *mikvah* was likely the forerunner for Christian water baptism. The Christian baptism practiced by the followers of Jesus Christ was associated with the actions of John the Baptist (see Acts 19), thus lending credibility to the theory that *mikvah* was the earlier form of spiritual cleansing through water immersion.

- Figures 4.2 and 4.3 were taken in 2016 on an excursion to the ancient Dead Sea communities. Ritual baths were discovered just a short walk from the Qumran caves in which the Dead Sea Scrolls were discovered. Figure 4.2 includes an entry by Josephus in his work on the war of the Jews in which he details the ritual bathing practices of the separatists.

[9] Matthew 3:6.

[10] Acts 19:3-5.

writings of the Dead Sea Scrolls are highly critical of the corrupted religious order of first-century Jerusalem. The ministry of John the Baptist was in consonance with this criticism.

*Figure 4.2*                    *Figure 4.3*

*Photos by Steven Gill, 2016*

John is said to have referred to the Pharisees and the Sadducees alike as a generation of vipers[11] and called them to repentance.

The criticisms of John against the religious order of his time cannot easily be separated from the Hellenization of the land of Israel that precipitated it. Recall from previous chapters how the most religiously devout of Judaea believed that traditional Judaism had become contaminated by heathen influence, culminating with the Greek-ification of their temple and their city. Jerusalem had once been the epicenter of Jewish piety in the land of Judaea, but generations of political and cultural upheaval had turned it into a powder keg of ideological tension that would eventually explode before the close of the first century.

---

[11] Matthew 3:7-8.

Early Christian opposition to Hellenism begins with John the Baptist because John was the first man recorded in the New Testament to point to Jesus and His teachings as the answer that the land of Judaea needed to right the religious corruption of Israel. The teachings of John also encapsulate the beliefs of the Essenes and other religiously conservative groups like them who saw the religious leadership of Jerusalem as out of step with true Jewish values.

> Now in the fifteenth year of the reign of Tiberius Caesar, Pontius Pilate being governor of Judaea, and Herod being tetrarch of Galilee, and his brother Philip tetrarch of Ituraea and of the region of Trachonitis, and Lysanias the tetrarch of Abilene, Annas and Caiaphas being the high priests, the word of the God came unto John the son of Zacharias in the wilderness. And he came into all the country about Jordan, preaching baptism of repentance for the remission of sins;...Then said he to the multitude that came forth to be baptized of him,[12] O generation of vipers, who hath warned you to flee from the wrath to come? Bring forth therefore fruits worthy of repentance, and begin not to say within yourselves, we have Abraham to our father: for I say unto you, that God is able of these stones to raise up children unto Abraham...And the people asked him, saying, what shall we do then? He answereth and saith unto them, He that hath two coats, let him impart to him that hath none; and he that hath meat, let him do likewise. Then came also publicans to be baptized, and said unto him, Master, what shall we do? And he said unto them, Exact no more than that which is appointed you. And the soldiers likewise demanded of him, saying, And what shall we do? And he said unto them, Do violence to no man, neither accuse any falsely; and be content with your wages.[13]

---

[12] In Matthew's account of the same story, the writer specifically states that there were Pharisees and Sadducees among the crowd that came to listen to John (Matthew 3:1-10).
[13] Luke 3:1-3; 7-8; 10-14 (KJV).

The interaction in the passage above between John the Baptist and a crowd which had gathered to hear him speak tells us a great deal about the former's religious priorities. John is primarily concerned with acts of repentance (turning away from sins) in his message to the crowd, and John situates repentance squarely in the context of ethical behavior. Furthermore, the command to repent is given to the Pharisees and the Sadducees, not just the people generally (see note 12). There is also an emphasis on the Jewish identity of the people who gathered to hear John preach. "Do not say within yourselves, we have Abraham to our father." John's statement implies that this objection would have been a likely response by the people to his preaching had he not chastised them to do otherwise. In other words, it was expected that the people would seek justification primarily through ethnic or cultural affiliation, as opposed to spiritual purity.[14]

Such prioritization of ethnic identity among the Jews was seen in prior generations during the reign of the Hasmoneans. Recall from chapter three, Aristobulus conquered the Itureans and made their citizenship conditional upon every male being circumcised. Despite this command, it has also been shown that the Hasmoneans were not deeply concerned with maintaining all the other traditions of their fathers. Circumcision was undoubtedly part of the Law of Moses; however, there were other conditions placed upon maintaining the covenantal bond between the Jews and their God. These additional conditions were less emphasized during the Hasmonean era, and that is the problem John seems to address in the aforementioned passage. When Herod the Great came to power in the first century B.C.E., he had no apparent affection for the Jewish religion. Although he was certainly circumcised, as his grandfather was first forcibly converted to Judaism in generations prior, Herod's Judaism was primarily expressed in ethnic and cultural terms. For Herod, Judaism stopped at nationhood in the nominal sense. Ethical and spiritual Judaism were less important. His attachment to Greek life and his willingness to ignore various commandments concerning holiness

---

[14] According to the book of Genesis, Abraham had at least eight children (Genesis 25:1-12), although only one was in the covenant of God (Isaac). Thus, being a child of Abraham alone did not constitute a covenantal relationship with God.

and personal piety was evidence of his detachment from religious Judaism. Herod had gentile priests imported from other nations to serve in the temple. He refashioned the temple itself into the mold of Hellenic culture. Herod had all children in the kingdom under two years old murdered to prevent a perceived threat to his reign. These actions were expressly forbidden according to the Law of Moses, but, for Herod, they did not necessarily inform or diminish his Jewish identity. When John says, "God is able to raise up children to Abraham from these stones," he is attempting to correct a misunderstood approach to Jewish identity: It is not enough to be biologically or culturally Jewish—to be pleasing to the God of our fathers, you have to live differently than the world around you.

When John is speaking with the crowd, he not only implies that obeying ethical commandments is essential to religious identity, but he seems to suggest that they are critical to Jewish identity itself, or, at least, that the two cannot be easily separated. Three different groups of people (the general crowd, which included the Pharisees and the Sadducees, followed by the publicans and the soldiers) question how they can act on repentance, but John does not respond with a command to go and offer sacrifices at the Temple Mount or to perform various customary ritual acts. He offers them a guide to ethical behavior. Both would have aligned with the Law of Moses, but from John's perspective, only one was missing in Jewish life.

The separation of Jewish identity from Judaism itself cannot be blamed entirely on the influence of Hellenism in the region, as the problem predated John the Baptist by nearly a millennium.[15] Nevertheless, the blending of the Greco-Roman and Jewish cultures augmented the issue in the first century in ways not known before in centuries prior and presented new challenges to

---

[15] In the book of Joshua, two tribes of Israel named Gad and Reuben and one half-tribe named Manasseh decided not to establish residence in the land of Canaan that had been promised to them by God as their ancestral homeland. Because of this, they were disconnected from the altar of sacrifice used by the Jews to fulfill their ritual obligations according to the book of Leviticus. Because they still wanted to be considered Jews but did not want to live in the Jewish homeland, they set up a faux altar called Ed, nearly causing a civil war among the Israelites. Ed served to remind their children that they were still Jews, even though they did not live within the borders of Canaan.

religious Jews like John. Neither the House of Herod nor the Caesars were legitimate heirs of king David. The priests that offered service in the temple were not the offspring of Aaron. And the *Sanhedrin*, which governed local Jewish affairs, was not a biblical court. All of these problems could be traced back to the influence of the Greeks and later the Romans on the land of Judaea. Many of these issues were the subject of John's preaching.

John's criticism of the moral deterioration of the Judaean province was not limited to the religious leaders of the territory. The book of Mark tells the story of John's subsequent arrest and execution by Herod Antipas, and both were a direct consequence of his preaching against the king's moral corruption.

Philip of Ituraea was the brother of Herod Antipas. From Mark's gospel, it can be gathered that Herod likely engaged in an affair with his brother's wife, leading to an eventual marriage between Herod and his former sister-in-law. Herodias, as she is known in the gospel account, did not like the fact that Herod listened to the preaching of John. When John spoke out against the wrongful marriage of Herod to Herodias, she arranged to have him thrown into prison and eventually executed.[16]

Herod's violation of the Law of Moses concerning his marriage to Herodias was not beyond the bounds of reasonable criticism in the eyes of John the Baptist. Although the Herods were ethnically Edomites, they were still converts to Judaism. From the perspective of John, that conversion came with a responsibility to uphold the laws and customs of the Jewish people. Monogamy was instituted in the Roman Empire as early as 18 B.C.E. and backed by such documents as the *lex Julia* and the *lex Papia Poppaea*. However, divorce was still permissible

---

[16] Leviticus 20:10-21 details the various commandments concerning an unholy marriage according to Jewish law. Herod violated Leviticus 20:21 which says, "and if a man shall take his brother's wife, it is an unclean thing..."

under Roman law in some circumstances.[17] Given the fact that Herod Antipas embraced the Roman approach to the marriage laws allowing his sister-in-law's divorce (and his subsequent marriage to her) as opposed to the Jewish approach, it is fair to assume that he did not prioritize Jewish law. Here again, lies evidence of the Hellenic influence on Jewish thought in the first century. Herod Antipas was likely just as disconnected from his Jewish identity as Herod the Great was before him. However, Herod Antipas did possess some appreciation for the preaching of John the Baptist. Herod Antipas was considered ethnically Jewish but behaved like the Greco-Roman culture he ruled. Thus, a conflict between two worlds is again seen: A nostalgia for the old world, combined with a love of the new.

John the Baptist was the forerunner of Jesus, and in the eyes of many, John's criticisms of Judaea's religious order defined his ministry as anti-establishment. So too, Jesus was perceived to be an outsider due to his criticisms of the Pharisees and the Sadducees. In many ways, Jesus was much more critical of the religious establishment of Judaea than John ever was. Yet, some distinction must be made between the criticisms of Jesus against the religious leadership more broadly and traditional Judaism as a doctrine.

Although no date is given for His birth in the gospel accounts, some ancillary information concerning the world of the first century can inform the modern reader as to when Jesus of Nazareth may have been born. Given the fact that the death of Herod the Great can be drawn from numerous historical sources[18] and that he was still alive when Christ was born, it can be safely assumed that Jesus was likely born sometime between 6-4

---

[17] Scheidel, Walter. "Monogamy and Polygyny." Princeton Ed.. Last modified January , 2009. https://www.princeton.edu/~pswpc/pdfs/scheidel/010903.pdf.
[18] Josephus records the death of Herod the Great in 4 B.C.E. (the thirty-seventh year of his reign) in *Antiquities of the Jews*, Book XVII (Ch.VIII).

B.C.E.[19] An early date for the birth of Christ is also supported by the fact that the New Testament states that Caesar Augustus (Octavian) was the ruler of the Roman Empire at the time when Mary and Joseph are said to have traveled back to Joseph's hometown of Bethlehem.[20]

Modern perspectives of Christianity are sometimes quick to characterize Jesus as a revolutionary against traditional Judaism who was in favor of casting off the restraints of the old Law of Moses in favor of a newer and more liberalized covenant. But this perspective is primarily based on a common misunderstanding that Jesus was, Himself, an aggressor against the Law of Moses. On the contrary, the portrait of Jesus in the New Testament is one of a man in harmony with the Law of Moses but out of step with the contemporary Jewish psyche as well.

> Then spake Jesus to the multitude, and to his disciples, saying, the scribes and the Pharisees sit in Moses' seat: All therefore whatsoever they bid you observe, that observe and do; but do not ye after their works: for they say, and do not. For they bind heavy burdens and grievous to be borne, and lay them on men's shoulders; but they themselves will not move them with one of their fingers.[21]

Matthew's gospel situates the primary concerns of Jesus in the context of hypocrisy, not religious practices. In fact, Jesus told His listeners that they should follow what the scribes and Pharisees said that the people ought to observe and do. However, it is the *behavior* of those same scribes and Pharisees which Jesus was not pleased with. Not their preaching. Thus, to Jesus, the message can be right, and the messenger wrong.

---

[19] A date this early for the birth of Christ would conflict with the traditional belief that Jesus was crucified in 33 C.E. Nevertheless, it can be known with a reasonable amount of certainty that Herod the Great died in 4 B.C.E. Given the fact that Herod issued an edict to have all children in the region of Bethlehem under two years old killed, and that Mary and Joseph fled to Egypt after this order was given and returned with their child after Herod's death, an early date for the birth of Christ fits the timeline of the New Testament.

[20] Luke 2:1.

[21] Matthew 23:1-4 (KJV).

Jesus placed a premium on the observance of the Law and the Prophets, but much like John, He emphasized fulfillment of the ethical and spiritual commands of the Scriptures, not just ritual observance of particular rites. Thus, when asked by one of the Pharisees what the greatest commandment was, Jesus gave a two-fold response of "love of God" and "love of neighbor" as the chief commandments on which all the Law and the Prophets depended.[22] This approach to the Law of Moses was not out of step with the Old Testament Scriptures. In the book of Jeremiah, the prophet wrote that God did not command the Exodus generation of Israelites concerning the observance of burnt offerings and sacrifices. Instead, he says that God gave commandments concerning obedience to His voice.[23] Of course, the Exodus generation received the Law of Moses that detailed the various commandments concerning ritual observance, so the words of the prophet can be confusing without a holistic understanding of the Abrahamic covenant. Just like the Israelites who made the Exodus from Egypt, it can be easy for modern readers of the Hebrew Bible to come away with the understanding that God's covenant with Abraham and Moses was established with the highest emphasis being placed upon the proper observance of certain rituals, holidays, etc. But that is not precisely true. Of the original Ten Commandments, only one concerned the observance of a particular ritual or holiday as sacrosanct.[24] The remaining nine all deal exclusively with ethical behaviors and moral boundaries. Fidelity to God and fellow man are the two most highly emphasized themes of the Ten Commandments, the same

---

[22] The specific wording and pattern of the response of Jesus is interesting in Matthew 22:37-40. The first century B.C.E. Rabbi named Hillel was once approached by a would-be convert to Judaism and asked a similar question. Hillel gave the response, "Whatever is hateful unto you, do not do unto your neighbor. The rest is commentary, now go and study." The act of summing up the whole Torah in a single axiom was common to the schools of Hillel and Akiva in the generations following their deaths, of which Jesus may have been a part.
[23] Jeremiah 7:22-23.
[24] "Remember the sabbath day, to keep it holy" (Exodus 20:8 KJV) is the only commandment given in the original ten that concerns a form of ritual observance. It is interesting to note that many modern Christian denominations have adopted all the original Ten Commandments as essential to their own spiritual purity as well, except the one regarding the Sabbath day. Some regard the weekly attendance of their local church assembly as a symbolic fulfillment of this commandment.

message that Jesus was attempting to convey in the New Testament. While it is honorable to fulfill ritual commands and to adhere to strict observance of certain holidays ordained by God, the ritual aspects of the Law of Moses were intended to inform the more significant theme of the Law—spiritual purity.

After the Maccabean Revolt, the struggle for Jewish identity that took place in Judaea created an attitude of strict adherence to portions of the Law of Moses that informed Jewish ethnicity and nationhood (i.e., holidays, circumcision, maintaining the lunar calendar, and the borders of the kingdom, etc.) but other aspects of the Law were neglected. From the perspective of Jesus, those parts of the Law that had been neglected were the most important, and they were the cause of a great deal of the internal struggles among the Jewish people.

The corrupted religion and culture of Judaea was of great concern to Jesus, particularly in Matthew's gospel account. Where the Jews were concerned, the dismissal or diminishing of the value of the Law of Moses was the problem, not the solution to these concerns. Thus, the following exchange between Jesus and the Sadducees illuminates the fight between the greater culture which had evolved out of Seleucid and Hasmonean influence and those who attempted to remain religiously devout:

The same day came to him the Sadducees, which say there is not resurrection, and asked him, saying, Master, Moses said, If a man die, having no children, his brother shall marry his wife, and raise up seed unto his brother. Now there were with us seven brethren: and the first, when he had married a wife, deceased, and having no issue, left his wife unto his brother: Likewise the second also, and the third, unto the seventh. And last of all the woman died also. Therefore in the resurrection whose wife shall she be of the seven? For they all had her. Jesus answered and said unto them, Ye do err, not knowing the scriptures, nor the power of God. For in the resurrection they neither marry, nor are given in marriage, but are as the angels of God in heaven. But as touching the resurrection of the dead, have ye not read that which was spoken unto you by God, saying, I am the God of Abraham, and the God of Isaac, and the God of Jacob? God is not the God of the dead, but of the living.[25]

Matthew prefaced his account of the interaction between Jesus and the Sadducees, reminding that the Sadducees did not believe in a resurrection, and he did so for a purpose. The inquiry of the Sadducees is cast in an insincere light by the writer, as they are said to have asked Jesus to enlighten them as to the technicalities of marriage in the coming resurrection that they did not believe in anyway. In other words, the Sadducees were trying to "trip up" Jesus by pointing out that the resurrection could not be a real thing insofar as they understood the laws of marriage. It would create conflict with earthly principles regarding the relationship between a man and his wife. From the perspective of the Sadducees, because it would be impossible to say with certainty who the woman in their hypothetical question would belong to in the afterlife, it must follow that the afterlife did not exist. According to Jesus, the fallacy of the Sadducees is that they believed that the woman must belong to any husband at all. Furthermore, Jesus pointed to the Sadducees lack of understanding of the Scriptures more broadly as the reason for their hermeneutical fallacy.

"Ye do err, knowing not the scriptures, nor the power of God." The condemnation of Jesus against the Sadducees concerns their ignorance of the same religion they claimed to be stewards of. This error by the Sadducees supports the Maccabean claim that the Sadducees had become an illegitimate religious authority that was not deeply concerned with maintaining liturgical purity or biblical wisdom. Jesus perceived that the Sadducees did not understand the resurrection because they were not familiar with the Scriptures, which supported the traditional belief in the eternal nature of the soul.[26] Not for nothing that it is only after the rhetorical bruising that Jesus gave the Sadducees that the

---

[25] Matthew 22:23-32 (KJV).
[26] The statement by Jesus in Matthew 22:32 is probably a reference to Exodus 3:6, in which God said that He was still the God of Abraham, Isaac, and Jacob, long after the three patriarchs had passed away. The continued reference to the patriarchs in the Old Testament in the present tense suggests that their existence continues in a spiritual form, although physically they are gone.

Pharisees became interested in what Jesus had to say.[27] Although only a passing comment in Matthew's account, it further supports the claim that the Pharisees and the Sadducees were two religious groups at odds with one another in the first century.

The criticisms of Jesus against the Sadducees specifically are detailed in other accounts of Matthew's gospel, culminating with His entry into the temple at Jerusalem, of which the Sadducees were the keepers.

> And Jesus went into the temple of God, and cast out all them that sold and bought in the temple, and overthrew the tables of the moneychangers, and the seats of them that sold doves, and said unto them, It is written, My house shall be called the house of prayer; but ye have made it a den of thieves.[28]

Recall from chapter three that during the construction of Herod's Temple, the outer portions of the structure had become epicenters of commerce and trade since they were open to more of the general public. The irreverent treatment of the most holy site in Jerusalem angered Jesus. His uncharacteristic outburst against the temple order may shed light on the severity of the corruption among the Pharisees and the Sadducees. Remember that Herod the Great had imported priests from gentile nations to serve in the temple, and for this act alone, Jesus may have taken great issue. Furthermore, the office of the high priest, in particular, had become a political pawn in Judaea, bought and sold to the highest bidder.[29] Jesus directed ire against moneychangers and those who bought and sold doves specifically[30] and referred to them as thieves. While it has been supposed that this may have been a reference to their corrupt business practices generally, it is also worthy of note that, again, the practice of buying and selling

---

[27] In Matthew 22:34, the writer says that only after Jesus had left the Sadducees speechless did the Pharisees call him "master" and ask Him more sincere questions.
[28] Matthew 21:12-13 (KJV).
[29] See (Ch. 2).
[30] Doves were a traditional fowl offering according to Levitical Law (Leviticus 1:14).

sacrifices was a novel departure from the Law of Moses and was not consistent with traditional Judaism.

The book of Leviticus opens with commandments concerning the correct behaviors concerning animal sacrifices brought to the temple. In Leviticus 1:2, there is no allowance made for the practice of buying and selling of sacrifices. Instead, it is assumed that when a sacrifice is made on behalf of someone, the sacrifice will be brought personally by the individual to the priesthood, who would then oversee its proper use. The fact that Matthew's gospel depicts a scene at the temple in which certain sacrifices were either bought or sold offers one of two possibilities: Either the priesthood was selling sacrifices that people brought to them rather than offering them upon the altar, thus robbing the public; or the people were not bringing sacrifices at all, but purchasing them at the temple, limiting their personal obligations in the process of sacrifice and ultimately robbing God. In either case, the practice was foreign to traditional Levitical practice as described in the Hebrew Bible, and Jesus was not pleased with what He saw.

Jesus was not completely disassociated from the various sects of first-century Judaea. Just as John could be easily identified with the Essenes, Jesus, too, could be associated with an unlikely peer group: the Pharisees.

This association can be surprising considering that throughout the New Testament, Jesus was very critical of the Pharisees. Nevertheless, the Bible does offer some evidence to suggest that, even if He did not consider Himself a Pharisee in the most-strict sense, the world around Him associated Jesus with the traditions of the Pharisees.

When the Sadducees came to power in the second century B.C.E., their liberalized theology was perceived as a threat to traditional Judaism by many religious Jews. The bifurcation of the two groups culminated with a break between the keepers of the temple order and the teachers of the Hebrew Bible. In the Old Testament, the priesthood generally operated in harmony with the

Scriptures; the work of the two could not be easily separated. In the New Testament, that was not necessarily the case. While there were, no doubt, some priests who remained pious in so far as they understood in keeping the Law of Moses, many did not. Thus, a sect of Jews arose which desired more strict observance to the Law and the Prophets than the corrupted Hasmonean leadership embraced. This group came to be known as the Pharisees.

Among the Pharisees were the teachers of the Scriptures. These teachers, known as rabbis, were considered by many to be the true keepers of traditional Judaism. Because the temple was an integral part of Jewish life and essential to observance, it never completely disappeared from the life of the Pharisees. But a greater emphasis was placed upon the preaching and teaching of the Law of Moses in synagogues,[31] as well as communal prayer and fellowship. Synagogues are not mentioned in the Old Testament, as they came into use primarily with the rise of rabbinic Judaism. After the first century, the temple order dissolved, and rabbinic Judaism became the permanent spiritual authority in Jewish life.[32] Although other sects arose in the centuries that followed the time of the Pharisees, such as Hasidism and Chabad, the authority of the rabbis remained a constant in Jewish life. In this way, it may be helpful to think of observant Judaism today as an outgrowth of

---

[31] "Who Invented the Synagogue?." Chabad.org. https://www.chabad.org/library/article_cdo/aid/74339/jewish/Who-Invented-the-Synagogue.htm.

[32] Wolbe, Yaakov. "Rabbis, Renaissance and Reclamation: Jewish History of the Mishnaic and Talmudic Eras." The Jewish History Podcast. Last modified April 13, 2021. https://podcasts.apple.com/us/podcast/the-jewish-history-podcast-with-rabbi-yaakov-wolbe/id1151634104?i=1000375348977.

- It has been argued convincingly by some historians that the survival of rabbinic Judaism explains why the books of Maccabees were left out of the Hebrew Bible during the later canonization process. The books of the Maccabees tell the story of the reclaiming of the temple, culminating with the rise of the Hasmonean kings. Because the Sadducees were an outgrowth of Hasmonean influence, it makes sense that the rabbis chose not to include the stories of their heroic deeds in the Hebrew Bible. After the temple was destroyed by the Romans in the first century, the Sadducees no longer had political power and eventually dissolved as a sect completely. Rabbinic Judaism supplanted the temple order as the religious ruling class of the Jews. The rabbis were responsible for the final canonization process of the Hebrew Bible. Leaving out the tales of the Maccabees may be understood as a final slight against the Sadducee order, which the rabbis believed to be a grotesque movement of assimilation and compromise. Thus, history was written by the victors.

the Pharisee sect. Pharisee simply means "separated one."[33] In this way, first century rabbinic Judaism reflected a protest against the more liberal drift of the greater culture, particularly the Sadducees.

The reason it is not improper to think of Jesus as one who belonged to the sect of the Pharisees (or, at least, one who was often associated with them) is the overwhelming evidence for His relationship to traditional Judaism. The teachings of Jesus reflect a deep knowledge and conviction for adherence to the Law of Moses. His use of parables as a primary teaching method was consonant with rabbinic Judaism and His ability to sum up the spirit of a particular commandment in a few words.[34] It does not seem apparent from the New Testament that Jesus embraced the isolationist perspectives of the Essenes, and the liberalism of the Sadducees was antithetical to the character displayed by Jesus in the gospels, as well as His reverence for the Law of Moses. Furthermore, the amount of time that Jesus spent teaching in the synagogues (there are more than twenty references to such instances in the New Testament) suggests a strong relationship with the Pharisees, as well as their admiration for His knowledge of the Scriptures.

Throughout the gospel accounts, Jesus is referred to as a rabbi many times. These references seem to confirm His role as a teacher of the Scriptures insofar as it was understood in the first century. From what can be gathered about the standard practices of that period, the readiness of the public to identify Jesus in the role of a rabbi places Him firmly in the camp of the Pharisees.

However, if Jesus was a Pharisee, that raises questions about some of the stories in the New Testament as well. Jesus is very critical of the Pharisees in the New Testament, and in some cases, His rebukes against them are even more potent than those against the Sadducees. To a degree, this legitimizes the notion that Jesus did not ride for the brand of any particular sect of Judaism nominally. Still, it may also shed light on what the primary goals of His teachings were insofar as the Jews were concerned.

---

[33] Strong's number: g5330, *Pharisaios*: a separatist, i.e. exclusively religious.
[34] See note 19.

Then came to Jesus scribes and Pharisees, which were of Jerusalem, saying, Why do thy disciples transgress the tradition of the elders? For they wash not their hands when they eat bread. But he answered and said unto them, Why do ye also transgress the commandment of God by your tradition? For God commanded, saying, Honour thy father and mother; and, He that curseth father or mother, let him die the death. But ye say, Whosoever shall say to his father or his mother, It is a gift, by whatsoever thou mightiest be profited by me; And honour not his father or his mother, he shall be free, Thus have ye made the commandment of God of none effect by your tradition.[35]

If the most significant problems with the Sadducee sect stemmed from ignorance or assimilation, the greatest issues with the Pharisee sect were rooted in guile and sanctimony. The emphasis the Pharisees placed on knowledge and piety created a religious elite that seemed to have become too clever by half in the eyes of Jesus. In some regards, the Pharisees were utterly rightful in their teachings. Recall what Jesus said later in Matthew 23:1-4: "Whatever the Pharisees teach you to observe and do, do it." Thus, in one respect, the Pharisees were the rightful heirs of Moses. And yet, in the eyes of Jesus, their strict adherence to the letter of the law did not measure up.

In the above passage, the disciples of Jesus are accused of breaking certain traditions of the Jews by not washing their hands before they eat. But before Jesus addressed that objection, (He does so later) He responded pointedly to the Pharisees with a question of His own. His comments concern the fifth commandment: honor thy father and thy mother. In the context of the narrative, it seems that honoring father and mother could be avoided according to the Pharisees by paying tribute to the parents or to the temple in the form of money.[36] It is possible that

---

35 Matthew 15:1-6 (KJV).
36 In Mark's gospel, this tribute is called "Corban." This was probably a temple offering and likely refers to a monetary pledge made to the priesthood in exchange for the responsibility of caring for one's parents in old age. According to Jewish law, children must care for their parents when they become too old to care for themselves. However, it seems that in this context, the Pharisees endorsed an

the offering was regarded as a sort of charity that could be contributed to the priesthood, who would then offer certain services to elderly parents that could not take care of themselves. Or, it could be a simple reference to giving money to one's parents as a way of absolving one's self of the responsibility of more direct honor, such as quality time, affectionate words, and assisting with needs. Giving money to someone is an easy way soothe the conscious after treating them poorly, or to justify not offering more meaningful attention or care.

Jesus criticized the Pharisees acceptance of this practice as a form of offering lip service to the commandments of God without actually obeying them. "This people draweth nigh unto me with their mouth, and honoureth me with their lips; but their heart is far from me."[37] The irony of this passage is that it is evident the Pharisees were familiar enough with the fifth commandment to know that it ought to be obeyed. Still, they found a way to reduce obedience to a fairly meaningless task. In this way, the Pharisees could say that the commandment had been fulfilled and demand very little of themselves in the process. Hence, too clever by half.

Perhaps that is why the Pharisees received such severe responses from Jesus in the New Testament as opposed to other groups of people. The Pharisees were familiar enough with the Scriptures to know the commandments and teach them to others, but not convicted by them enough in their hearts to obey them personally. To whom much is given, much is required,[38] and from the perspective of Jesus, the Pharisees had been given a great deal. Jesus could rightly say that the Pharisees paid lip service to the commandments in that they did believe that father and mother must be honored. But how they claimed to honor father and mother violated the spirit of the law altogether. In this way, it may be understood that the Pharisees maintained ritual observance to the commandments of the Law of Moses yet were not abiding by them in the sense that they were originally intended. This is the most common objection that Jesus presents to the ways of the

---

effective legal "loophole" allowing children to offer their parents money rather than care through the form of temple offerings.

[37] Matthew 15:8 (KJV).

[38] Luke 12:48.

Pharisees in the New Testament. While the Sadducees never cared enough for the Scriptures to learn about the yoke of heaven, many of the Pharisees knew the yoke of heaven but cast it off.

There is another Christian in the New Testament who was also known as a Pharisee. His journeys throughout Asia Minor as well as his letters to the Christian churches constitute some of the most meaningful examples of early Christian battles with the influence of Hellenism in the first century.

Saul of Tarsus, as he was known before his conversion to Christianity, was likely born sometime in the first ten years of the Christian millennium. At the peak of the Persian Empire, Tarsus served as the capital city of the Cilician satrapy. After Alexander the Great defeated the Persian forces in the late fourth century B.C.E., Tarsus came under Seleucid control, being renamed for a time "Antioch-on-the-Cyndus."[39] When the Romans came to power in the middle of the first century, Tarsus resumed its role as the capital city of the Cilician province. Tarsus enjoyed a great deal of autonomy while under the tutelage of the Roman Empire, which was likely due to its enormous influence in the region as an epicenter of trade, commerce, and culture. Evidence of Tarsus' great affluence in the first century can also be demonstrated by the fact that when Saul, later Paul, was arrested by the Roman authorities, he appealed his case by invoking *civis romanus sum*— I am a citizen of Rome—which offered the right to appeal one's case to Caesar where severe penalties were concerned.[40] Paul could not have been a Roman citizen unless his father was either a freeborn native of Rome or an extremely influential provincial citizen.[41] Because the first is unlikely given that the family was Jewish, it is apparent that Paul's family belonged to the societal

---

[39] Xenophon, *Anabasis,* Book I (Ch. II Sect. XXIII).
[40] Acts 22:25. Paul's invocation of this right lends credibility to the notion that Tarsus enjoyed greater privileges than Judaea in the Roman Empire, and that Paul was from the upper-crust of Tarsus. No such invocation is seen in the case of any of the other Christian apostles who were known to have lived in Judaea.
[41] See A.N. Sherwin-White, *The Roman Citizenship* (Oxford,[2] 1973).

elite of Tarsus. To be a Roman citizen in Paul's case was exceptionally rare. While it cannot be known with certainty just how he obtained it, there is no doubt that such status assisted him in his missionary journeys later in life.

More prominent than his Roman citizenship, it is Paul's identity as a Jew which stands out in the New Testament. Unlike Jesus, the reader does not have to assume Paul's relationship to the Pharisees—he says so himself.

> ...If any other man thinketh that he hath whereof he might trust in the flesh, I more: Circumcised the eighth day, of the stock of Israel, of the tribe of Benjamin,[42] an Hebrew of the Hebrews; as touching the law, a Pharisee;[43]

More than a Roman, Paul was a Jew. There are repeated references to Paul's use of the Law and the Prophets to convert his fellow Jews to Christianity. His familiarity with the Scriptures comes out often in his letters to the churches, most notably in First Corinthians, in which Paul used the story of the Exodus to illustrate certain principles of New Testament conversion.[44] Paul's role as a Pharisee and his understanding of Greco-Roman culture proved to be valuable assets to his ministry in the New Testament. As a Pharisee, Paul had credibility with religious Jews living in

---

[42] While it is often believed that only the tribe of Judah was spared after the Exilic Period of Israel's history, the Bible actually names three tribes of Israel that remained vibrant in the post-Exilic Period. According to 2nd Kings, the entire Northern Kingdom of Israel was wiped out in the eighth century by the Assyrian armies. There were eleven tribes of the Israelites represented in The Northern Kingdom of Israel (Reuben, Simeon, Levi, Issachar, Zebulun, Ephraim/Manasseh, Gad, Asher, Dan, Naphtali, and Benjamin). On the surface, this would mean that only the descendants of Judah could have survived into the first century. However, it is known from the books of Chronicles that a portion of the tribe of Benjamin seceded from the Northern Kingdom and chose instead to dwell in Judah after the civil war between the loyalists to Saul and the followers of David (1st Chronicles 12:29). Furthermore, the tribe of Levi was not allotted any land of its own in the book of Joshua. Instead, it was spread out across the lands occupied by the Northern Kingdom and Judah alike (Joshua 13:14), thus there would have been Levites living in Judah during the Assyrian exile as well. Although confusing at first glance, the Bible is very clear in the end: The tribes of Judah, Levi, and Benjamin all had representation in first century Judaea.
[43] Philippians 3:4-5 (KJV).
[44] 1st Corinthians 10:1-11.

Judaea and Asia Minor. As a citizen of Rome, Paul had the attention of the Greeks as well.

The Jews who lived in Tarsus could trace their heritage back to the early diasporic communities which sprung up around the Near East after the Babylonian Exile in 586 B.C.E. The fact that Saul of Tarsus was born in such a city perhaps informs the modern reader how he was such an effective evangelist for Christianity in Asia Minor and other Hellenized territories. Paul understood the greater culture of the Roman Empire in ways that the Christians who had been primarily isolated to the Judaean province did not.

There are many examples of Paul's familiarity with Hellenic culture early in the New Testament accounts of his life and in his letters to the churches. Among the earliest of these examples is in one of Paul's missionary journeys with Barnabas, during which the two encountered citizens of the Lycaonian city of Lystra.

> And there sat a certain man at Lystra, impotent in his feet, being a cripple from his mother's womb, who never had walked: The same heard Paul speak: who steadfastly beholding him, and perceiving that he had faith to be healed, said with a loud voice, Stand upright on thy feet. And he leaped and walked. And when the people saw what Paul had done, they lifted up their voices, saying in the speech of Lycaonia, The gods are come down to us in the likeness of men. And they called Barnabas, Jupiter; and Paul, Mercurius, because he was the chief speaker. Then the priest of Jupiter, which was before their city, brought oxen and garlands unto the gates, and would have done sacrifice with the people. Which when the apostles, Barnabas and Paul, heard of, they rent their clothes, and ran in among the people, crying out, and saying, Sirs, why do ye these things? We also are men of like passions with you, and preach unto you that ye should turn from these vanities unto the living God, which made

heaven, and earth, and the sea, and all things that are therein:[45]

Perhaps more than any other, this story included in the book of Acts lends a great deal of understanding to the direct tension between Christianity and Hellenism in the first century. When Paul and Barnabas came to Lystra, it is apparent from the reading that the cult of Jupiter resided in that city. While ministering in that area, Paul encountered a lame man who had enough faith to be healed. After Paul lifted up his voice and commanded the lame man to get up, he did. This incident caused a stir among the people of Lystra, and they perceived that Paul and Barnabas were themselves visitations from the gods. "And they called Barnabas, Jupiter; and Paul, Mercurius, because he was the chief speaker." The pagan designations for Paul and Barnabas are interesting. In the New Testament, Paul is easily assumed to be the leader of whatever Christian circle he associates himself. Other than Jesus, Paul may be considered the primary focus of the New Testament. Yet it is Barnabas, not Paul, who is called Jupiter. Jupiter—the greatest among the Roman gods. On the surface, it seems that Paul should have rightly been associated with Jupiter, but he wasn't. But this was not a mistake in identity by the people of Lystra. In fact, it demonstrates that the people possessed a very thoughtful understanding of the Greco-Roman pantheon.

First, it must not be assumed that Paul was the chief among the apostles when our selected narrative took place. By the fourteenth chapter of the book of Acts, Paul had only been a Christian convert for a short amount of time. Acts chapter eight details the conversion of Paul to Christianity, but like all converts, Paul spent a fair amount of time under the leadership of others who were more experienced than himself. During his missionary journeys, Barnabas was Paul's first major traveling partner and was probably a convert himself as early as the fourth chapter of Acts. While it is only speculative, it is possible that Barnabas traveled with Paul as the more experienced apostle of the two. Of course, if this were the case, Paul outgrew the relationship rather

---

[45] Acts 14:8-15 (KJV).

quickly, as he would eventually become the premier apostle of the New Testament. In this way, it may not be wrong to consider Barnabas the Jupiter of the relationship.

Regardless of whatever role Barnabas may have played in the ministry of the two apostles, it is evident from the reading why Mercurius was chosen as the associative god of Paul. Mercury was the Roman representation of the Greek god called Hermes. Mercury/Hermes was the messenger of Zeus (Jupiter)—the god of divine words and interpretation.[46] This characterization of Mercury probably explains the phrase, "because he was the chief speaker." In the eyes of the Lycaonians, Paul was the mouthpiece of the gods. He represented mediation between the heavens and the earth through divine oration. The context of his words also concerned the heavens and the earth as well, likely only serving to bolster their superstitions.

Interesting as it may be to know that Paul was regarded as a god in Lycaonia, his response to the Greek beliefs becomes vital in the context of this chapter.

> ...Sirs, why do ye these things? We also are men of like passions with you, and preach unto you that ye should turn from these vanities unto the living God, which made heaven, and earth, and the sea, and all things that are therein: Who in times past suffered all nations to walk in their own ways. Nevertheless he left not himself without witness, in that he did good, and gave us rain from heaven, and fruitful seasons, filling our hearts with food and gladness.[47]

What is the difference between what the Greeks believed about the gods in the first century and what the Christians believed about Jesus Christ? Although brief, Paul's response to the people of Lystra offers some insight on the subject.

First, it must not be assumed that the Greeks or the Romans ever embraced a single "all-powerful" god at all. Neither Zeus nor Jupiter possessed that quality. Even the titans were numerous,

---

[46] Hamilton, Edith. *Mythology*. New York: Grand Central Publishing, 1942. (p.30-31).
[47] Acts 14:15-17 (KJV).

and their powers considerably distributed. In this way, Paul's response served as a sort of contrast between traditional Greco-Roman notions about the spiritual world and the Judeo-Christian one. "We also...preach unto you that you should turn from these vanities unto the living God, which made heaven, and earth, and the sea, and all things that are therein." Wittingly or not (though probably the former) Paul addressed the primary powers of the Greek pantheon in his summation of the qualities of the true God. Contrasted with Zeus, the god of the wind and the skies, the Christian God ruled the heavens. Contrasted with Poseidon or Neptune, Paul's God was the master of the seas and was the ruler over them.[48] Hephaestus, Artemis, or Apollo, it did not matter—none could be compared with the God of Israel. One step further—Paul's God did not just rule the forces which had been attributed to the Greco-Roman pantheon—He *created* them. That is important too.

It is not said of the gods of Olympus that they were creative forces. Obscure beliefs surrounding the role of the titans during the formation of matter may be drawn from various texts (something like Philo's Potencies), but the gods were not creators themselves. In his message to the people of Lystra, Paul describes his God with unqualified power. He is both the maker of the rules and the ruler Himself. That diverged from the Greek notions drastically.

Another example of Paul's contention with greater Hellenic culture is illustrated in the seventeenth chapter of Acts, fresh upon Paul's arrival to the city of Athens.

> Now while Paul waited for them at Athens, his spirit was stirred in him, when he saw the city wholly given to idolatry. Therefore disputed he in the synagogue with the Jews, and with the devout persons, and in the market daily with them that met with him. Then certain philosophers of the Epicureans, and of the Stoicks, encountered him. And some said, What will this babbler say? Other some, He seemeth to be a setter forth of strange gods: because he preached unto

---

[48] Ibid. (45).

them Jesus, and the resurrection. And they took him, and brought him unto Areopagus, saying, May we know what this new doctrine, whereof thou speakest is? For thou bringest certain strange things to our ears: we would know therefore what these things mean.[49]

Not for nothing is Paul widely considered the apostle to the gentiles. Athens was far from Tarsus and still further from Jerusalem. It is remarkable to discover diaspora communities in Greece as well. From the account in Acts, it seems apparent that there was a synagogue in Athens where Paul spent time teaching and disputing. In Athens, Paul also encountered two very popular schools of philosophy in the first century known as the Epicureans and the Stoics. Both Epicureanism and Stoicism were highly influential in their time, and Stoicism has even made a comeback in popularity in recent years.[50] Stoicism embraced the belief that the world possesses a good nature and that human beings ought to live in accordance with that nature, submitting to those things which are natural for man to do. For the Stoics, living in the bounds of virtue could be cultivated from the self. Control is the primary emphasis of the philosophy. Or, at least, embracing the principle that there are some things that can be controlled, and some that cannot.[51] In this way, the Stoics adopted a neutral attitude to both pleasure and pain in the world. Events that caused pain were not painful because they were evil but painful because they were perceived that way.

Disassociated with traditional Athenian beliefs about the gods, the Stoicism of Paul's time was not a religion in and of itself but a way of viewing the world in the context of a particular set of beliefs. Stoics and Epicureans were both materialists, denying the existence of things without form, sometimes characterized as

[49] Acts 17:16-20 (KJV).
[50] Rutledge, David. "The Rise of Modern Stoicism." ABC's The Philosopher's Zone. Last modified November 17, 2014.
https://www.abc.net.au/radionational/programs/philosopherszone/modern-day-stoicism/5896364.
[51] Ibid. (50).

spiritual or other-worldly.[52] Interestingly, some have suggested that there were no degrees of virtue in the ancient Stoic mind, in the sense that one might understand them today. One was either irredeemably good or irredeemably bad in so far as they lived in or out of accordance with nature.[53] This sort of dualistic approach to existence without a belief in the gods (or a God) seems difficult to reconcile in the modern mind.

Epicureanism was different. Epicureanism emphasized an attitude of maximizing happiness through pleasure. While academics have not generally understood this to mean that the Epicureans were pure hedonists, one can see where such a philosophy may create problems, especially in the context of a world without moral limits.[54] Assuming that the natural state of man will draw him to live in harmony with his fellow man through the pursuit of happiness sounds simple until what makes one man happy puts him out of harmony with another man's happiness.

Modern examinations not-withstanding, Paul addressed both schools of philosophy in his sermon on Mars' hill.

Then Paul stood in the midst of Mars' hill, and said, Ye men of Athens, I perceive that in all things ye are too superstitious. For as I passed by, and beheld your devotions, I found an altar with this inscription, TO THE UNKNOWN GOD. Whom therefore ye ignorantly worship, him declare I unto you. God that made the world and all things therein, seeing that he is Lord of heaven and earth, dwelleth not in temples made with hands; Neither is worshipped with men's hands, as though he needed any thing, seeing he giveth to all life, and breath, and all things; And hath made of one blood all nations of men for to dwell on all the face of the earth, and hath determined the times before appointed, and the bounds of their habitation; That they should seek the Lord, if haply they might feel after him, and find him, though he be not far from every one of us: For in him we live, and move, and have our being; as certain

---

[52] Hanselman, Stephen. "Stoicism vs. Epicureanism." Daily Stoic. https://dailystoic.com/stoicism-vs-epicureanism/.
[53] Becker, Lawrence. *A New Stoicism*. Princeton, NJ: Princeton University Press, 1997.
[54] Ibid. (52).

also of your own poets have said, for we are also his offspring. Forasmuch then as we are the offspring of God, we ought not to think that the Godhead is like unto gold, or silver, or stone, graven by art and man's device.[55]

In step with his address to the Lycaonians, Paul built his argument to the Athenians on the premise of an all-powerful God, something that was not a common belief in ancient times. Just as Paul was critical of the idolatry in Lystra, so too was he displeased with the idol worship he witnessed in Athens. His criticisms of their attributions to "THE UNKOWN GOD" are interesting. It seems that the ancient Greeks understood that there was an underlying force behind even the gods at Olympus, at least in the context of the things that they did not understand. Potentially directed at the philosophers, Paul emphasized the creative work of his God in Athens too. "God that made the world and all things therein...and hath determined the bounds of their habitation." Such a thought was antithetical to the materialist beliefs of the Stoics and the Epicureans (something without form created that which has form).

Perhaps Paul's most remarkable rhetorical device in the story of Mars' hill is his use of Greek materials to support his arguments against the Greek notions themselves. "For in him we live, and move, and have our being; as certain also of your own poets have said," is a quote from the fifth century Greek poet Epimenides.[56] Paul did not dismiss the words of Epimenides either. From his perspective, the poet's words served to confirm the very thing he was trying to tell the Athenians—that by the God of Israel, all things that have been, are, and will be, consist.

Paul's missionary journeys took him to cities such as Antioch, Philippi, and Macedonia; he traveled throughout the regions of

---

[55] Acts 17:22-29 (KJV).
[56] Epimenides, *Cretica*.

Galatia, Phrygia, Neapolis.[57] He abode two years in Ephesus, teaching in the school of one called Tyrannus.[58] Paul even went to Athens itself and likely spent his final days in the city of Rome.[59] The geography of Paul's missionary journeys was attributable primarily to the vast construction projects of the Seleucids and later the Romans. Many of the places where Paul traveled owed their existence to a world cast in the Hellenistic Age. His opposition to their religious and cultural values is evident in nearly every account of his travel through Asia Minor. In his letter to the Colossian church, Paul warned Christian believers against being enticed by philosophy and the traditions of men,[60] something which will be discussed in greater detail throughout the next chapter.

In accordance with John the Baptist and Jesus Christ, Paul was critical of the religious sects of the Jews in the first century. In one particularly humorous account, Paul pits the Pharisees and the Sadducees against one another in an argument over belief in the resurrection of the saints. The result of the argument illustrates the fact that sectarian divisions in first-century Judaea were much more substantial than even disagreements over the identity of Jesus of Nazareth.

> And the high priest Ananias commanded them that stood by him [Paul] to smite him on the mouth...And they that stood by said, Revilest thou God's high priest?...But when Paul perceived that the one part were Sadducees, and the other Pharisees, he cried out in the council, Men and brethren, I am a Pharisee, the son of a Pharisee: of the hope and resurrection of the dead I am called in question. And when he had so said,

[57] Acts 16:11.
[58] Acts 19:9.
[59] Although tradition says he ran to his own execution, it is not actually known precisely when or how the Apostle Paul died. The book of Acts closes with Paul on house arrest, awaiting his opportunity to give an appeal of his arrest to Nero. Historians have surmised that perhaps Paul made his appeal, whereupon he was released and continued to travel into the area of Britain or Spain, preaching the gospel until his death. Others have embraced the idea that Paul's request was never heard in Nero's final years as Caesar, and he was executed during the Jewish Revolt (see chapter 6). For more on these discussions, see F.F. Bruce's *Paul: Apostle of the Heart Set Free*.
[60] Colossians 2:8.

there arose a dissension between the Pharisees and the Sadducees: and the multitude was divided. For the Sadducees say that there is no resurrection, neither angel, nor spirit: but the Pharisees confess both. And there arose a great cry: and the scribes that were of the Pharisees' part arose, and strove, saying, We find no evil in this man: but if a spirit or an angel hath spoken to him, let us not fight against God. And when there arose a great dissension, the chief captain, fearing lest Paul should have been pulled in pieces of them, commanded the soldiers to go down, and to take him by force from among them, and to bring him into the castle.[61]

Paul was arrested and brought before councils and kings in the book of Acts for his part in the growth of a new sect known as "the way,"[62] which believed that Jesus of Nazareth was truly the Christ. When Paul was brought before Ananias the high priest in the aforementioned passage, he cleverly situated himself in the camp of the Pharisees, knowing that identification with one of the sects which were before him was likely to infuriate the other. Specifically, Paul cried out amid the crowd that the only reason he was being persecuted in this instance was for his belief in the resurrection of the dead and the world to come. That was a clever play, as Paul had also perceived that he was surrounded by Sadducees who disagreed with the Pharisees about the resurrection, angels, and the afterlife. His outburst caused such a stir that he was escorted away from the mobbing crowd promptly taken to the castle.

The behavior of the Pharisees during Paul's trial before Ananias is astounding. There is no hint in the account of Acts that Paul had friends in the crowd or that the Pharisees were sympathetic to his position. Before Paul mentioned the resurrection, everyone in the crowd gathered around him was content to allow him to be beaten and publicly humiliated. But

---

[61] Acts 23:2-10 (KJV).

[62] Acts 16:17; 18:26; 22:4 all refer to the followers of Jesus as belonging to something known as "the way." In Acts 24:14 and Acts 24:22 Paul uses the phrase to refer to the sect to which he belonged. While general, this was probably a common method of referring to followers of Jesus before the word "Christian" came into common usage.

after Paul mentioned the resurrection, the Pharisees immediately cast doubt on the accusations thrown at him. "We find no evil in this man: but if a spirit or an angel hath spoken to him, let us not fight against God." Paul went from being a heretic to a hero in the span of just a few moments, which can be attributed only to his casting in his lot with the Pharisees. In my estimation, this serves to confirm the idea that the divide between Pharisee and Sadducee, religious and secular, was stronger than the tension between Christians and Jews in the Judaean province. Harsh persecution of the Christian way did not find its fullest expression at the hands of the Jews but the Romans. In Paul's time, the war with Hellenism was still raging among the various religious sects in Judaea.

Hellenism was an influential force in the Judaean province of the first century. Some of the most pointed criticisms of the religious classes by John, Jesus, and Paul were directly informed by how much Greco-Roman culture had manipulated the priorities of the religious world. Because they tended towards secularization, the Sadducees represented a significant departure from traditional Judaism itself. The Pharisees, for their part, may have kept more traditional ties to Judaism, but in their frustration with the Sadducees, they became more enamored with the letter of the Law of Moses than with the spirit of it. The Essenes became isolationists, awaiting the impending apocalypse. And the Zealots became radicalized into violence.

The emergence of Christianity presented Judaea, and eventually the world, with a new religious class that did not fit neatly into the mold of any of its predecessors. Paul summed up the role of Christianity in the first century in his first letter to the Corinthians.

Where is the wise? Where is the scribe? Where is the disputer of this world? Hath not God made foolish the wisdom of this world? For after that in the wisdom of God the world by wisdom knew not God, it pleased God by the foolishness of preaching to save them that believe. For the Jews require a sign, and the Greeks seek after wisdom: But we preach Christ crucified, unto the Jews a stumblingblock, and unto the Greeks foolishness; But unto them which are called, both Jews and Greeks, Christ the power of God, and the wisdom of God.[63]

---

[63] 1st Corinthians 1:20-24 (KJV).

# CHAPTER V

## First Century Perspectives

## on

## Jesus of Nazareth

Hermeneutical aspects of this chapter will not be exhaustive, but examination of the various beliefs concerning the person of Jesus of Nazareth in the first century inform later theological developments that contributed to the articulation of the doctrine of the trinity in the centuries that followed. The identification of Jesus of Nazareth as the Christ happened first and primarily among the Jewish population of Judaea and the surrounding territories; however, there was a bifurcated opinion among the Jews concerning Jesus' identity. Both perspectives are important to our discussion. The Semitic-messianic understanding greatly informed the gentile believer's point of view, and it eventually became the most dominant in the Christian domain. Still more complex are the perspectives of non-believing gentiles. Just as the non-believing Jews, gentiles who dismissed the messianic identity of Jesus had their own unique beliefs about who Jesus was.

When Jesus came into the coasts of Caesarea Philippi, he asked his disciples, saying, Whom do men say that I the Son of man am? And they said, Some say that thou art John the Baptist: some, Elias; and others, Jeremias, or one of the prophets. He saith unto them, But whom se ye that I am? And

> Simon Peter answered and said, Thou art the Christ, the Son of the living God.[1]

Fortunately, first-century Christian perspectives on the identity of Jesus of Nazareth are easier to come by than others. The New Testament possesses a great deal of interpretation of the Hebrew Bible and correspondence between believers concerning the person of Jesus. The passage from Matthew includes one of the earliest direct statements by the disciples of Jesus connecting His person and "the Christ." *Christos*[2] is the Greek word included in the New Testament associated with the Hebrew Messiah, referred to variously in the Old Testament as the arm of God,[3] the son of God,[4] and the salvation of God.[5] Messianic beliefs were diverse during the first century, and it was not obvious to any sect just who the Messiah would be.

> For unto us a child is born, unto us a son is given: and the government shall be upon his shoulder: and his name shall be called Wonderful, Counsellor, the mighty God, the everlasting Father, The Prince of Peace. Of the increase of his government and peace there shall be no end, upon the throne of David, and upon his kingdom, to order it, and to establish it with judgement and with justice from henceforth even for ever. The zeal of the LORD of hosts will perform this.[6]

---

[1] Matthew 16:13-16 (KJV).
[2] Strong's number: g5547.
[3] Isaiah 40:9.
[4] Proverbs 30:1-3.
[5] Isaiah 12:2-3.
[6] Isaiah 9:6-7 (KJV).

- Interestingly, in recent years it has become more common among scholars to be skeptical of Isaiah 9:6 with regards to its messianic references. Some have suggested that the passage was only a reference to the son of the prophet himself. However, the more traditional interpretation of the passage does seem to be more in sync with messianic beliefs. There are two direct references to an everlasting kingdom in Isaiah 9:6-7, something that does not seem to fit neatly if referring to an earthly ruler during the time of Isaiah. Furthermore, the description of the king to come as "the mighty God" and "the everlasting Father" are exceptionally lofty terms that do not appear often in the Hebrew Bible and almost never reference a king. In any case, if Isaiah 9:6 was intended to refer to an earthly ruler of Israel, it is apparent that the words of the prophet were not fulfilled in his lifetime, as no king of Israel was ever said to have established an everlasting

Isaiah described the Messianic Era as a time when the throne of David would be raised, and an everlasting kingdom of peace would be established. This prophecy arrested the Jewish psyche in the first century, as it was a time of great political turmoil and cultural upheaval. If ever the time was ripe for messianic fulfillment, the first century seemed to fit the bill.

As discussed in prior sections of this book, there were disagreements between the Pharisees and the Sadducees concerning nature and the soul. The Pharisees believed in the existence of a spirit world beyond the material realm and embraced the idea of a resurrection. By contrast, the Sadducees were much less open to such ideas and rejected the idea of a spiritual or eternal nature.[7] The differences between the two sects informed their beliefs about the identity of the Messiah as well.

Because of their openness to the idea of a spiritual existence, the Pharisees tended toward a belief that the Messiah would be a spirit sent to relieve Israel of its oppressors and usher in an era of peace and spiritual purity. Given the Hebrew Bible's consistent association of the Messiah with God Himself, it was not outside the bounds of reason for the Pharisees to believe such things.

> Behold, God is my salvation; I will trust, and not be afraid: for the LORD JEHOVAH is my strength and my song; he also is become my salvation. Therefore with joy shall ye draw water out of the wells of salvation. And in that day shall ye say, Praise the LORD, call upon his name, declare his doings among the people, make mention that his name is exalted. Sing unto the LORD; for he hath done excellent things: this is known in all the earth. Cry out and shout, thou inhabitants of Zion, for great is the Holy One of Israel in the midst of thee.[8]

---

government of peace. The major historical events immediately following the death of Isaiah were largely characterized by the Babylonian Exile in 586 B.C.E.

[7] Lang, Jeremy L. "From the Foundation of the World: The Establishment of the Oneness in Genesis." In *ALJC Oneness & Baptism Symposium 2021*, edited by Nathan S. Whitley, 30-31. Memphis, TN: Assemblies of the Lord Jesus Christ, 2021.

[8] Isaiah 12:2-6 (KJV).

More than nearly any other book of the Hebrew Bible, Isaiah tells of an era of messianic fulfillment and the restoration of Zion. Isaiah was also the prophet that spoke of the days when a forerunner would go before the Messiah preaching repentance and restoration of holiness. The Christians understood that person to be none other than John the Baptist.[9] "Behold, God is my salvation...He also is become my salvation." Not without reason did the Pharisees associate the coming Messiah with a spiritual being. God is frequently associated with salvation in the Old Testament, and in many instances, the two are completely intertwined; however, what sort of salvation God would bring was not necessarily as obvious.

I, even I, am the LORD; and beside me there is no saviour.[10]

Drawing from Isaiah, messianic fulfillment is situated in the context of salvation. God is both referred to as the one who "becomes" salvation, as well as salvation itself. Thus, the two are not so easily separated in the mind of the reader. If the Messiah were going to be a king, he would be a king sent by God, led by God, possessed by God—perhaps even identifiable with God.

There were miraculous deeds associated with the coming of the Messiah as well.

Strengthen ye the weak hands, and confirm the feeble knees. Say to them that are of a fearful heart, Be strong, fear not: behold your God will come with vengeance, even God with a recompence; he will come and save you. Then the eyes of the blind shall be opened, and the ears of the deaf shall be unstopped. Then shall the lame man leap as an hart, and the tongue of the dumb sing:...[11]

The early Christians were convinced that the miracles performed by Jesus of Nazareth served as evidence of His Messiahship. Although from John's gospel, the reader may gather that there

---

[9] Isaiah 40:3.
[10] Isaiah 43:11 (KJV).
[11] Isaiah 35:3-6 (KJV).

were many things that Jesus did throughout His life that were not recorded in any of the biographical materials associated with the gospels,[12] specific stories were recorded to confirm His role as the Messiah to future readers. In the fifth chapter of Luke, Jesus causes a lame man to walk.[13] In John chapter nine, He opens blind eyes.[14] In Mark's seventh chapter, Jesus unstops deaf ears and causes a dumb man to speak.[15] And in one of the most famous passages of the New Testament, Jesus raises His good friend named Lazarus from the dead in John chapter eleven.[16]

Other ancillary stories associated with Old Testament prophecies are included in the gospel accounts of Jesus' life as well. For example, when Matthew tells the story of Herod the Great's plot to kill all the children under the age of two in his kingdom, he emphasizes that Joseph and Mary fled to Egypt, thus fulfilling the prophecy that the son of God would be called out of Egypt.[17] When Luke told the story of Peter's sermon in the book of Acts, he included this statement by Peter later:

> Repent ye therefore, and be converted, that your sins may be blotted out, when the times of refreshing shall come from the presence of the Lord; And he shall send Jesus Christ, which before was preached unto you: Whom the heaven must receive until the times of restitution of all things, which God hath spoken by the mouth of all his holy prophets since the world began. For Moses truly said unto the fathers, A prophet shall the Lord your God raise up unto you of your brethren, like unto me; him shall ye hear in all things whatsoever he shall say unto you. And it shall come to pass, that every soul, which will not hear that prophet, shall be destroyed from among the people.[18]

---

[12] John 21:25.
[13] Luke 5:17-39.
[14] John 9:6.
[15] Mark 7:33-36.
[16] John 11:38-44.
[17] Hosea 11:1.
[18] Acts 3:19-23 (KJV).

The story included in the sermon refers to the words of Moses in Deuteronomy.[19] Its inclusion by Luke in the book of Acts suggests that the audience of Peter embraced messianic theology, at least insomuch as they could understand the reference. Furthermore, the connection made between the words of Moses and the identity of Jesus of Nazareth seemed to resonate with the crowd—more than five thousand were added to the Christian sect that day.[20]

The rapid expansion of Christianity at its inception was due primarily to common Judaism's association of the deeds of Jesus of Nazareth with the Messiah that the Hebrew Bible prophesied about. The association is important, because when the gospel was extended to the gentiles, they had little or no familiarity with the Hebrew Bible to give context to the actions of Jesus. Had the gospel first spread among the gentiles, the behavior of Jesus would have seemed strange—even bizarre. The preservation of the Law of Moses and the Prophets into the first century galvanized Jewish support for what eventually became Christianity. In other words, it was Jesus' adherence to Judaism that caused Christianity to burst onto the scene so rapidly, not His departure from it. Gentile Christianity likely could not have thrived without the broad foundation constructed for it by the Jewish disciples of Jesus. Indeed, all of the first Christians were Jews.[21] Jesus-as-Messiah is the principle from which all other first-century perspectives on Jesus of Nazareth extend, positive or negative. Either He was or He wasn't.

For the early Christians, their belief in Jesus-as-Messiah was intertwined with their belief in Jesus-as-God, which created animosity between many Jews and Christians. In the Christian mind, Jesus-as-God was not so far-fetched from the perspective of

---

[19] Deuteronomy 18:15.
[20] Acts 4:4.
[21] The first gentile convert to Christianity is described in the tenth chapter of Acts. It is estimated that the conversion of Cornelius occurred somewhere between seven and fourteen years after the birth of Christianity.

the Hebrew Bible. Remember that even the Pharisees associated the coming Messiah with a spiritual being who would act as a deliverer. From the Christian perspective, if there was no savior besides the God of Israel, then it stood to reason that the Messiah would be an express manifestation of that God. Indeed, this exact claim is made about Jesus in Paul's first letter to his disciple named Timothy.

> And without controversy great is the mystery of godliness: God was manifest in the flesh, justified in the Spirit, seen of angels, preached unto the Gentiles, believed on in the world, received up into glory.[22]

Related to their belief in Jesus-as-God were the various views associated with salvation and the person of Jesus Christ. The soteriology[23] of the early Christians was highly Jesus-centric. When water baptism became an integral part of Christian conversion, it was done exclusively in the name of Jesus Christ.[24] Evidence for the Christian emphasis on the deity of Jesus Christ regarding water baptism may be seen in the behavior of the disciples (later apostles) after their commissioning at the end of the gospel of Matthew. In Matthew 28:19, Jesus commanded His disciples that they ought to go into all the world and baptize people in the name of the Father, and of the Son, and of the Holy Ghost. When the disciples obeyed this command, they did so by baptizing new converts in the name of Jesus Christ. Thus, the high Christology of the first-century church is made evident by this fact: either the apostles of Jesus Christ misunderstood the command, or they believed that the name of Jesus was, in fact, the name of the Father, the name of the Son, and the name of the Holy Ghost.

Still greater emphasis is placed on the identity of Jesus-as-God in the epistle to the Colossians.

---

[22] 1st Timothy 3:16 (KJV).
[23] Concerning the doctrine of salvation.
[24] Acts 2:38; Acts 10:48; Acts 19:5.

> Beware lest any man spoil you through philosophy and vain deceit, after the tradition of men, after the rudiments of the world, and not after Christ. For in him dwelleth all the fulness of the Godhead bodily. And ye are complete in him, which is the head of all principality and power.[25]

Paul's letter to the Colossian church seems to support the notion that the early Christians identified the person of Jesus Christ with the totality of the Godhead. "For in him dwelleth all the fulness of the Godhead bodily. And ye are complete in him..." Throughout the epistles, some associative descriptions are made of Jesus as "the Son of God" but never as "God the Son." That is important because the fullness of the Godhead referred to in the second chapter of Colossians suggests a wholeness—a singularity—in the identity of God that later Christian theological developments did not necessarily emphasize. For the early Christians, the name of Jesus encapsulated that wholeness, at least with regards to His divine identity. Distinctions made in the New Testament between Father and Son should probably not be regarded as an early Christian belief in dualism or a separation of the Godhead into distinct persons. For the first century church, the Father and Son were not different persons but associative descriptions of God's action in the world.[26] If Father and Son were intended to refer to separate persons of God in the literal sense, other distinctions in the Godhead would have to have been made as well that were not.

> For I would that ye knew what great conflict I have for you...That their hearts might be comforted, being knit together in love, and unto all riches of the full assurance of understanding, to the acknowledgement of the mystery of God, and of the Father, and of Christ;[27]

---

[25] Colossians 2:8-10 (KJV).
[26] John 14:9 sums up the "Father and Son" discussion well in the New Testament. Certain disciples of Jesus were also uncertain of the relationship between the two. Jesus clarified the confusion by stating that He and His Father were one, and if you had seen Jesus, then you had seen the Father as well.
[27] Colossians 2:1-2 (KJV).

In the same Colossian letter, Paul distinguished between "God" and "the Father," something foreign to even more liberal developments in Christian doctrine, if taken to mean a literal separation of personhood.[28] The novel distinction of "God and Father" happens again in the book of James.

> If any man among you seem to be religious, and bridleth not his tongue, but deceiveth his own heart, this man's religion is in vain. Pure religion and undefiled before God and the Father is this, To visit the fatherless and widows in their affliction, and to keep himself unspotted from the world.[29]

Again, the writer used the phrase, "God and the Father." Given the consistent Christian emphasis on the oneness of God throughout the New Testament,[30] as well as Jesus' commitment to the traditional Deuteronomic view of the personhood of God,[31] it would seem intellectually dishonest to assume that the Father and Son language of the New Testament was written in order to bifurcate the Godhead. More than likely, it was used to disclose the humanity of Jesus Christ while continuing to associate His Messiahship with the God of Israel. Father and Son language may be an anthropomorphic description of how God acts in the world, but not a literal representation of His otherwise omnipresent identity.

In the letter to the Colossians, the harmony of Jesus of Nazareth with the God of the Israelites reaches its apex. Whether Paul presented a high Christology to the predominantly gentile church of Colossae because of their ignorance concerning the Hebrew Scriptures or because of their own battles with Greco-Roman paganism, the result was the same—a presentation of Christ as both the creator and the redeemer of the world.

> For this cause we also, since the day we heard it, do not cease to pray for you, and to desire that ye might be filled with the

---

[28] Later Christian developments emphasized a distinct identity between Father, Son, and Spirit, but never between God and Father.
[29] James 1:26-27(KJV).
[30] Ephesians 4:4-5.
[31] Matthew 22:36-40.

knowledge of his will in all wisdom and spiritual understanding; That ye might walk worthy of the Lord...Giving thanks unto the Father, which hath made us meet to be partakers of the inheritance of the saints in light: Who hath delivered us from the power of darkness, and hath translated us into the kingdom of his dear Son: In whom we have redemption through his blood, even the forgiveness of sins: Who is the image of the invisible God, the firstborn of every creature: For by him were all things created, that are in heaven, and that are in earth, visible and invisible, whether they be thrones, or dominions, or principalities, or powers: all things were created by him, and for him: And he is before all things, and by him all things consist. And he is the head of the body, the church: who is the beginning, the firstborn from the dead; that in all things he might have the preeminence. For it pleased the Father that in him should all fulness dwell;[32]

Paul presented Jesus as the one whose blood redeems the world and who created all things. Jesus is called the "image of the invisible God," and by the close of the passage, Paul again emphasizes the fullness of God in Christ.

Coming from a Pharisee, the words of the Colossian letter are astounding. Early Jewish converts to Christianity did not disassociate the Messiah from the God of Israel, possibly due to the Pharisee's presentation of the Messiah as a spiritual savior. Although only conjecture, it seems at least possible that the Biblical disclosure of the identity of Jesus of Nazareth is why Pharisees were more apt to convert to Christianity than the Sadducees in the New Testament accounts.[33]

---

[32] Colossians 1:9-19 (KJV).

[33] Acts 15:5 informs the reader that there were believers in Christ from the Pharisee sect. Of course, it is also known that Paul was himself a Pharisee. In fact, the book of Acts closes with Paul doing a home-Bible study with the chief of the Jews while on house arrest. By contrast, some of the greatest conflicts between Christianity and Judaism happened during the apostles encounters with the Sadducee sect (see Acts chapters three and four).

Perspectives of non-believers on the person of Jesus of Nazareth are perhaps even more intricate than that of the Christians. Jews and Greeks alike had their doubts about the Messiahship of Jesus of Nazareth, but for different reasons.

The camp of unbelieving Greeks and Romans appeared primarily in the form of the cult of Dionysus. Dionysus was, and remains, the most popular god of the Greek pantheon. More pages telling the stories of Dionysus have been discovered than any other tale told of Olympus.[34] Christian conflict with the pagan cult abounded for centuries after the resurrection. The theological battles with the Dionysian cult specifically left a permanent mark on Christian thought (more on that later). For now, a brief discussion of the origins of the Dionysian cult will illuminate the cause of the tension between the Greco-Roman and Christian religious worlds.

There is no doubt that similarities can be found between the stories of Jesus of Nazareth and Dionysus. Mythology was the common religious vernacular of the first century Near East. In this way, some of the language used by the New Testament writers may be understood as an attempt to frame the gospel in terms that the Greeks could understand. As discussed in prior portions of this book, even the Jews were not immune to the influence of Hellenism on their religion. Even before the birth of Christ, the cult of Dionysus was pervasive in Judaea. During the reign of Antiochus IV Epiphanes, the Jews were commonly subjected to forced-idolatry as a means of assimilation. Second Maccabees details one instance in which the Jews were forced to honor Dionysus at the behest of the king.[35]

> Against this backdrop of mythology as cultural currency, there is good reason to suspect that the Gospels portrayed Jesus in ways that would have appealed to their audiences' propensity to see mythological allusions, even though the primary

---

[34] Scott, James M. "Gods, Greek and Roman." In *Dictionary of Jesus and the Gospels*, edited by Joel B. Green, Jeannine K. Brown, and Nicholas Perrin, 329-334. Nottingham, England: InterVarsity Press, 2013.
[35] 2nd Maccabees 6:7.

conduit of meaning in the text undoubtedly was OT and Jewish tradition.[36]

The similarities do not mean that the pagan cults were the source of early Christian terminology by any means, but they were, perhaps, the background against which distinctively Christian usage was forged and first heard. Myth was the popular vernacular for its time. It may even relate to John's use of the term *logos* in the opening of his gospel account.[37] Quite simply put—the first century Christians lived in a Greek world. The dominant languages of the empire were Greek and Latin, with Aramaic only remaining popular primarily in the Syrian and Judaean provinces. First-century Judaea was saturated in Hellenism, and so the use of particular terminology was bound to be interpreted in the Greek form, even if that was not the express intention of the New Testament writers.

Having that in mind, there are important differences between the story of Dionysus and Jesus of Nazareth—one very important difference in particular—that accurately illustrates why the tension between the Greco-Roman cults and the Christians was so severe, and why it ultimately led to deadly persecutions against Christianity by the Romans in the centuries to follow.

Dionysus was the last of the gods to enter the Greek pantheon, likely sometime between the ninth and eighth centuries, B.C.E. Dionysus was unique among the gods of Olympus in that he was the only one said to have had one divine parent, and one that was human.[38] For the Greeks, this was the first of many parallels that could be made between Jesus and Dionysus. The most frequently appearing argument by non-believing Greeks concerning the identity of Jesus of Nazareth was that He was, in fact, not the Jewish Messiah at all, but Dionysus. Such comparisons between the two continued long into the second century, culminating with the writings of the Apologists, which will be discussed in later

---

[36] Ibid. (34) (p.330).
[37] See discussion on Philo, (Ch. 3).
[38] Hamilton, Edith. *Mythology*. New York: Grand Central Publishing, 1942. (p.62).
- Other heroes of Greek myth were said to have both human and divine parents, but none of them were identified with the elite gods of Olympus.

chapters. For the Greeks, the virgin birth of Jesus by Mary was correlative to what they already believed about Zeus and his human bride named Semele.[39]

Dionysus was the god of wine, worshipped alongside Demeter, the goddess of harvest. It is possible that the agrarian nature of many of the parables that Jesus told augmented the Greek comparison of Jesus to Dionysus. Specifically, the miracle of water being turned into wine by Jesus probably contributed to this belief.[40] Interestingly, of Dionysus, it is said,

> Everywhere he taught men the culture of the vine and the mysteries of his worship and everywhere they accepted him as a god until he drew near to his own country.[41]

This description of Dionysus is not unlike Jesus, of whom the gospels say that although He did many great miracles around Judaea and Samaria, when He entered into His home country His ministry was largely rejected.

> But Jesus said unto them, A prophet is not without honour, but in his own country, and among his own kin, and in his own house. And he could there do no mighty work, save that he laid his hands upon a few sick folk, and healed them.[42]

From reading Euripides' *Bakkhai*, one comes away with the understanding that the worshipers of Dionysus were apt to do so while traveling through the wildernesses and far-away places such as forests and mountains. This distinguished Dionysus from the other gods of Olympus, who preferred to be worshiped in temples.[43] Just as Dionysian worship was unique for its time, the disciples of Jesus are also said to have acted in similar ways. Their worship and admiration of Jesus is described variously throughout the New Testament as happening while on journeys, in wildernesses, gardens, and seas.

---

39 Ibid. (38).
40 John 2:1-11.
41 Ibid. (38) (p.63).
42 Mark 6:3-5 (KJV).
43 Ibid. (38) (66).

Perhaps the most jarring comparison between Dionysus and Jesus of Nazareth concerns the arrest narratives; however, significant differences situate Jesus and Dionysus on opposite sides of each other in their stories. First, the arrest of Dionysus.

Greek myth says that Dionysus was arrested and brought before one named Pentheus, who was the king of Thebes, the birthplace of Dionysus. Pentheus had no knowledge of Dionysus' status as one of the gods, and ordered his arrest for being a cheating sorcerer. Although onlookers warn the king that he has arrested a god, Pentheus is not impressed and resumes his treatment of Dionysus.

> Dionysus was led in before him by a band of his soldiers. They said he had not tried to flee or to resist, but had done all possible to make it easy for them to seize and bring him until they felt ashamed and told him they were acting under orders, not of their own free will...The fetters would not keep fastened; the doors unbarred themselves. "This man," they said, "has come to Thebes with many wonders—" Pentheus was now blind to everything except his anger and his scorn. He spoke roughly to Dionysus, who answered him with entire gentleness...He warned him that he could not keep him in prison, "for God will set me free."[44]

The story of the arrest of Dionysus bears some similarity to the story of Jesus in the gospels, but with some important differences too. The correlations and disparities were likely visible to Greeks living in the first century. From the Christian perspective, it was the *difference* between Jesus and Dionysus that probably served to convert the Greek mind to the Jewish Messiah, as opposed the similarities.

> And they that had laid hold on Jesus led him away to Caiaphas the high priest, where the scribes and the elders were assembled. But Peter followed him afar off unto the high priest's palace, and went in, and sat with the servants, to see

---

[44] Ibid. (38) (p.68-69).

the end. Now the chief priests, and elders, and all the council, sought false witness against Jesus, to put him to death; But found none...And the high priest arose, and said unto him, Answerest thou nothing? What is it which these witness against thee? But Jesus held his peace. And the high priest answered and said unto him, I adjure thee by the living God, that thou tell us whether thou be the Christ, the Son of God. Jesus saith unto him, Thou hast said:[45]

Like Dionysus, Jesus was arrested and is said to have kept His peace and not resisted the accusations that were levied against Him. But the similarities between the two stories essentially end there. In the story of Dionysus' arrest, the guards who participated regret their actions and explain to Dionysus that they were only following orders. By contrast, those who brought Jesus before the high priest actively sought false accusations against Him because they despised Him so much. When the guards attempted to shackle Dionysus, the fetters "would not keep fastened." No such miraculous intervention happens after Jesus is bound and brought before the high priest and later to the governor. Furthermore, after Pentheus addresses Dionysus, Dionysus warns the king that God will save him from his situation. This could not be more different from the account of Jesus in the New Testament, of whom it is said that although "He was led like a sheep to the slaughter, He opened not His mouth."[46] In fact, when Jesus is hung on the cross, onlookers mocked Him because He would not take Himself down off the cross, nor did it seem that His God would intervene to assist him.[47]

The most significant divergence in the tales of Dionysus and Jesus of Nazareth comes from their sentencing narratives. After the arrest of Dionysus, legend says that he escaped from prison, and was responsible for bringing great doom upon Pentheus.

Pentheus went to pursue the god's followers among the hills where the maidens had fled when they escaped from prison.

---

[45] Matthew 26:57-64 (KJV).
[46] Acts 8:32.
[47] Matthew 27:43.

Many of the Theban women had joined them; Pentheus' mother and her sisters were there. And there Dionysus showed himself in his most terrible aspect. He made them all mad. The women thought Pentheus a wild beast, a mountain lion, and they rushed to destroy him, his mother first. As they fell upon him he knew at last that he had fought against a god and must pay with his life. They tore him limb from limb, and then, only then, the god restored their senses, and his mother saw what she had done. Looking at her in agony the maidens, all sobered now, the dancing over and the singing and the wild wand-waving, said to one another, In strange ways hard to know gods come to men. Many a thing past hope they had fulfilled, and what was looked for went another way. A path we never thought to tread God found for us. So has this come to pass.[48]

Here, Dionysus is depicted as both beneficent and brutal in the ancient Greek myth. After confronting Pentheus, Dionysus arranges to have the king torn apart as punishment for his treatment of the god. The gruesome nature of Pentheus' death notwithstanding, the actions and consequences of Euripides' tale are a direct contrast to the actions of Jesus of Nazareth.

And when they had platted a crown of thorns, they put it upon his [Jesus'] head, and a reed in his right hand: and they bowed the knee before him, and mocked him, saying, Hail, King of the Jews! And they spit upon him, and took the reed, and smote him on the head. And after that they had mocked him, they took the robe off from him, and put his own raiment on him, and led him away to crucify him...They gave him vinegar to drink mingled with gall: and when he had tasted thereof, he would not drink. And they crucified him, and parted his garments, casting lots...And set up over his head his accusation written, THIS IS JESUS THE KING OF THE JEWS.[49]

---

[48] Ibid. (38) (p.69-70).
[49] Matthew 27:29-37 (KJV).

Upon the arrest of Dionysus, others are condemned to death by the god for their treatment of him. It is said that he made the women mad, and they tore his accuser limb from limb. Because they fought against Dionysus and put him in prison, they were forced to pay with their lives.

By contrast, when Jesus is arrested, He is condemned to death instead. According to the governor of Judaea there was no criminal fault in Jesus for which He should have been sentenced to death,[50] yet Jesus died anyway. For non-believing Greeks, this was probably the tipping point that set them permanently at variance with the Christians. After all, if Jesus was really who the Christians claimed that He was, why on earth did He not exact justice the day He was arrested, and destroy His accusers like Dionysus? What sort of God would choose to die in the place of peasants?

From the Christian perspective, this was not a mystery of Christian theology—it was one of its primary features.

> Where is the wise? Where is the scribe? Where is the disputer of this world? Hath not God made foolish the wisdom of this world? For after that in the wisdom of God the world by wisdom knew not God, it pleased God by the foolishness of preaching to save them that believe. For the Jews require a sign, and the Greeks seek after wisdom: But we preach Christ crucified, unto the Jews a stumblingblock, and unto the Greeks foolishness; But unto them which are called, both Jews and Greeks, Christ the power of God, and the wisdom of God.[51]

Christian evidence that Jesus of Nazareth is God manifested in the flesh did not come from the belief that He could take Himself down off the cross. Instead, it was found in the fact that He chose to remain *on* the cross when He did not have to. In this way, it may rightly be said that the gospel of Jesus Christ was a stumbling block to the Jews, but it was foolishness to the Greeks. Dionysus killed his enemies; Jesus forgave His.

---

[50] Matthew 27:23.
[51] 1st Corinthians 1:20-24 (KJV).

To the Greeks, gods did not die for men; men died for the gods. Almost certainly, the Greeks who converted to Christianity realized the contrast between the behavior of Jesus and the traditional stories of Dionysus. From a theological perspective, where Greek literary forms were used, this could have been the intention of the gospel writers, and by extension, Jesus. Just as the Judaism of Jesus served to persuade the Jews, the Greeks had their own traditions through which they interpreted the gospels. That the Greeks could find essential differences in a recognizable story was spiritually significant.

Theories aside, one near certainty is that the variety contained within the gospel accounts was intended to reach a broader and more diverse audience than only the immediate crowds of the Judaean province. And, indeed, it did.

Jewish perspectives on Jesus of Nazareth in the first century were perhaps not as simple as they are often portrayed by modern scholars. As stated earlier, the Jews may have been the first group to reject Jesus as the Christ, but they were also the first group to receive Him. That complicates the discussion surrounding common Judaism's dismissal of a messianic identity for Jesus. Just as the Greeks, some Jews believed, and some did not. For the unbelieving Greeks, the gospel was foolishness. For the unbelieving Jews, it was a stumbling block. For Christians, Jesus of Nazareth fulfilled every prophecy that foretold the coming of the Messiah. From the circumstances surrounding His birth, His many miracles, His preaching and travels, to His triumphant entry into Jerusalem, His death on the cross, and His resurrection, Jesus proved His Messiahship in manifold ways to His followers.

Jews who remained unconvinced that Jesus was the Christ did so primarily for two reasons. The first was that because Jesus did not throw off the tyranny of Rome and re-establish the earthly kingdom of David, He could not therefore be the foretold saving king. The second was a dismissal of the claim that Jesus is the God of Israel manifested in the flesh. Ironically, both major objections to Jesus' Messiahship by unbelieving Jews were also the primary arguments in favor of His Messiahship by the Jews that believed. Christians would point to biblical accounts such as the book of Psalms for prophetic assurances that the Messiah would be crucified, and therefore He had to be a man.[52] They would use Isaiah to emphasize His deity, and prove that only God Himself could be the Messiah of Israel;[53] The writings of the minor prophets would serve as confirmation that it was sin that Israel needed to be saved from, not Rome.[54]

However, unbelieving Jews were not entirely out of touch with Jesus' followers. The question, "what constitutes the kingdom?" was asked by the disciples as well.

> And being assembled together with them, commanded them [Jesus] that they should not depart from Jerusalem, but wait for the promise of the Father, which, saith he, ye have heard of me. For John truly baptized with water; but ye shall be baptized with the Holy Ghost not many days hence. When they therefore were come together, they asked of him, saying, Lord, wilt thou at this time restore again the kingdom to Israel? And he said unto them, It is not for you to know the times or the seasons, which the Father hath put in his own power..."[55]

It is worth noting that in His final address to His disciples, Jesus did not dismiss the belief that the kingdom of Israel would be restored. The disciples followed Jesus for over three years. It is apparent that they did not feel His ministry invalidated the possibility of Israel's restoration as a kingdom. Instead, Jesus responded by telling them that it was not yet time for them to

---

[52] Psalm 22.
[53] Isaiah 9:6; Isaiah 43;11.
- In the book of Acts, the disciple named Philip taught the Ethiopian eunuch that Jesus was the Christ using the book of Isaiah.
[54] Although Christian theology emphasizes that the salvation of God is spiritual, and that sin was the foe that Christ defeated on the cross, it is also commonly believed among Christians that Christ will return to the world He created and rule the earth as a king as well. In this way, the Jewish perspective on the coming of the Messiah is, perhaps, not completely incompatible with Christian theology.
[55] Acts 1:4-7 (KJV).

know what was going to happen. While it was not the only objection made to His Messiahship by the unbelieving Jews, it is interesting to note that Christian eschatology is not necessarily out of step with the belief in the restoration of Jewish sovereignty over their homeland. It is the Christian presentation of Jesus-as-God that continues to fuel the disagreement today.

Ironically, one of the last major objections to the claim that Jesus of Nazareth is the Messiah was made on the grounds that if He is the Messiah, His name would have been included in the Hebrew Bible. That claim is, perhaps, the most puzzling one of them all. On the one hand, no explicit reference is made to Jesus of Nazareth, son of Mary and Joseph, cousin to John the Baptist in the Old Testament. On the other hand, the Hebrew word for salvation is יְשׁוּעָה, pronounced, "yešûʻâ." In English, we would say "Jesus." Thus, Isaiah 12:2 included at the beginning of this chapter could be read:

> Behold, God is my salvation; I will trust, and not be afraid: for the LORD JEHOVAH is my strength and my song; he also is become my Jesus.

And there is no doctrine more fundamental to the first-century Christian perspective, nor to the contemporary Christian faith, than this belief: that the salvation of God is come in the person of Jesus of Nazareth.

# CHAPTER VI

## The Jewish Revolt

In the middle of the first century C.E., the outcry against the tyranny of the Roman occupation reached a boiling point in the Judaean province. Armed garrisons were attacked; palaces were destroyed. The rebels set up provisional leaders to guide the revolt to its desired result—ending the Roman occupation of Judaea.

One of those leaders was a man named Joseph ben Matthias. Matthias had been instrumental in the fight against Nero's forces and had recently been appointed as the rebel governor of the province. But the rebellion could not long withstand Nero's legions, and the emperor decided that enough was enough. Instead of relying on his regional governors to put down the Jewish rebellion, Nero sent in one of his most skilled military strategists—General Titus Flavius Vespasianus, popularly known today as Vespasian.[1]

Vespasian was a commoner in the Roman Empire who rose through the ranks of the military and eventually began rubbing shoulders with the nobility through his cunning and determination. He did not come from royal blood. In fact, Vespasian had never even been to Rome. But where military matters were concerned, the plebian from Sabine could be relied upon to execute his objectives with excellence.

When General Vespasian invaded the territory of Judaea, the Jews did not give up their homeland without a fight. Vespasian was injured during the assault on Gamla,[2] just above the Sea of Galilee. Nevertheless, the Romans prevailed, and, for a time, the Judaean revolt was no more.

---

[1] Strauss, Barry. *Ten Caesars*. New York: Simon & Schuster, 2019. (p. 109).
[2] Josephus, *Wars of the Jews*, Book III (Ch.VII)

Governor Matthias was taken captive along with tens of thousands of other prisoners. Given Matthias' high status among the rebels, there was little doubt that he would be sent back to Rome and summarily executed for his crimes. Not only had Matthias broken Roman laws, but he had served as an inspiration to others in the province to do so as well. His execution was not just punishment—it was a message to the Jewish Revolt. So, the arrangements were made to have Joseph ben Matthias sent back to Rome where he would spend his final days.[3]

But before Matthias was executed, he had a message for the Roman general that he felt could not wait. If historians are to be believed, the urgent message was a prophecy. One that changed the course of the Roman Empire forever. Before he could be executed, Joseph ben Matthias told Flavius Vespasian that even though he was not of noble birth, he would one day be the emperor of Rome. Whether or not this prophecy was intended to deceive Vespasian into showing lenience to Matthias, or was a sincere gesture meant to inform the king that Matthias had heard from God about the future of Rome, it matters very little now. Because just two short years later, the prophecy of Joseph ben Matthias concerning the future of Flavius Vespasian came true.[4]

In 68 C.E., the Roman Senate decided it had endured enough of Nero's reign. While beloved for a time, Nero's eccentric behavior caused him to fall quickly out of favor with the Roman people. He had become a narcissist who was more concerned with entertainment than governance. He fancied himself a singer, participated in chariot races, and put on plays for the general public. This behavior was considered undignified by the Roman Praetorian Guard, and the Roman establishment despised him for what they perceived to be an emasculation of the throne. Rumors abounded throughout the empire that Nero had set the city of Rome on fire so that it could be rebuilt as Neropolis (the city of Nero).[5] Although he attempted to blame the fire on the Christians, many suspected that Nero had ordered the firing of the city himself.

---

[3] Ibid. (1) (p. 117).
[4] Ibid. (1) (p. 117).
[5] Tacitus, *Annals*, Book XV.

Fantasy and decadence marked Nero's last years...Nero's building projects, lavish games, and generous gifts to the people and the soldiers were expensive, as were the costs of rebuilding after the Great Fire, and the wars in Armenia, Britain, and Judea. In response, Nero inflated the currency. The silver content in Roman coins decreased by about 10 percent, but it was not enough. Someone had to pay...Meanwhile the emperor made time to do something to disgust his opponents. Still mourning Poppaea [Nero's deceased wife], he found a young male freedman who resembled her. He made the young man dress like her. Then he had him castrated and, finally, during his tour of Greece, Nero married him.[6]

These erratic behaviors and many others caused public trust in Nero to deteriorate, ultimately resulting in his being declared a public enemy in 68 C.E. Nero fled his would-be assassins for a time but quickly realized he could not survive. He committed suicide outside the city of Rome, ending the first imperial dynasty of the Roman Empire—the noble house of Augustus.

The void that Nero's death created on the throne of Rome could not be filled by one of his successors, as he had none. So, just as in the days of Alexander the Great, what could not be claimed by right was decided by might. And the words of the Historian Tacitus were fulfilled: "The secret of the empire was now divulged, that an emperor could be made elsewhere than in Rome."[7]

In 69 C.E., the crown changed hands four times, ultimately landing on Flavius Vespasian, the commoner for Sabine. The prophecy of Joseph ben Matthias was fulfilled, and no one could tell whether the rebel governor from Judaea was responsible for it or not.

Some Romans thought Matthias to be a spy. Many Jews considered him a traitor to their cause. Regardless of the truth, Matthias found favor in the court of Vespasian and received

---

[6] Ibid. (1) (p.103).
[7] Tacitus, *The Histories*, Book I (Ch. IV).

Roman citizenship rather than execution as a reward for his allegiance to the new emperor. He even lived in the Roman palace under government protection. Matthias was commissioned to write a complete history of the Jewish people and document the various wars of the Judaean province dating back to the time of the Seleucids. As a final act of honor for his service, the new emperor ordered that Matthias be given a new name. No longer would the rebel governor from Judaea be known as Joseph ben Matthias. Instead, he would become part of the elite class of Roman citizenry, and his new name would become cemented in the annals of history.

That new name was Flavius Josephus.

Many present-day Christians remember Flavius Josephus as a valued historian whose writings have contributed significantly to the field of Christian apologetics concerning history and archeology. But some may be surprised to find that Flavius Josephus was once the governor of the very rebellion that he wrote about in his *Wars of the Jews*. The works of Josephus are cited often in this book, as they constitute some of the most thorough primary source material known to date concerning the first-century Roman Empire.

Some scholars have been skeptical of Josephus' account of the events of the rebellion in the first century, given the turn-coat nature of his own life. However, there is little evidence that his later status as a Roman historian greatly influenced his interpretation of the events he was party to in Judaea. In fact, Josephus appears sympathetic to the Jewish cause in his writings, perhaps lending credibility to the notion that the prophecy told in the opening of this chapter was only fiction, and Josephus was himself a prisoner of the Roman Empire commissioned only to document the story of a conquered people.

While opinions concerning his character vary, they do not diminish the value of Josephus' written works for modern historians. Minimal primary source materials still exist from the first century. The works of Josephus have contributed a significant amount to the contemporary understanding of the turn of the millennia and the standard practices and governance of the Roman Empire in the first century. Throughout the rest of this chapter, I will draw on Josephus' account of the Jewish Revolt as well as several contemporary historians to illuminate its importance to our subject matter.

The Jewish Revolt changed the governance of the Roman Empire forever and its attitude toward the Jews in the centuries that followed. Furthermore, the revolt in which Josephus participated was not the last rebellion of the Judaean province against Roman occupation. There would be another challenge to Roman authority in the region, and the second rebellion had a lasting impact on the relationship between Jews and Christians as well.

The revolt of the Jews against the Romans was not caused by a singular event. During the days of Greek occupation under the reign of Antiochus IV Epiphanes, there were many conflicts over sovereignty among the Jewish people. Israel was historically a kingdom of its own, and to suffer vassalage to a greater power was perceived by the religious as an affront to the anointed line of kings. Secularists who took no issue with assimilation abounded, which also complicated the relationship between Jews. Some were uninterested in restoring the Davidic kingdom of Israel. Others felt that without sovereignty, the Jews were no better off than they were in the days of the Babylonian exile. Such internal struggles manifested most apparently in the divisions between Pharisee and Sadducee, but there were additional sectarian movements in Israel as well. When Herod the Great came to power, his tyranny precipitated some of the most notable actions against Roman authority in the first century, including a failed assassination attempt.[8]

---

[8] See (Ch. 3).

Tension between the Romans and the Jews may have reached its apex during the invasion of Vespasian but it existed long before Vespasian or even Nero came to power. To understand precisely how the conflict reached its boiling point, it is helpful to examine some of the infighting of the special interest groups of Judaea and how they impacted the Roman attitude toward the region.

Although many Jews wanted the Romans out of the province, that did not mean that all the Jews agreed about who should be in charge instead. Some remained loyal to the Hasmonean dynasty. Others believed that leadership belonged in the hands of the courts. And, of course, some wanted to be kings themselves. Instability in the land created the opportunity for competing forces to claim power for themselves in the Judaean province. When rebellions began to spring up more frequently in the early part of the first century B.C.E., they were sometimes spurious in their motives, and it was not always clear what the intended result was. In Idumea, two thousand of Herod's veteran soldiers came together and armed themselves against those of the king's party. In Sepphoris of Galilee, one man named Judas gathered a small force together and broke into the royal armory, stealing Roman equipment and weapons.[9]

In Perea also, Simon, one of the servants to the king, relying upon the handsome appearance and tallness of his body, put a diadem upon his own head also; he also went about with a company of robbers that he had gotten together, and burnt down the royal palace that was at Jericho, and many other costly edifices besides, and procured himself very easily spoils by rapine, as snatching them out of the fire. And he had soon burnt down all the fine edifices...At this time it was that a certain shepherd ventured to set himself up for a king; he was called Athrongeus. It was his strength of body that made him expect such a dignity, as well as his soul, which despised death; and besides these qualifications, he had four brethren like himself. He put a troop of armed men under each of these his brethren, and made use of them as his generals and

---

[9] Josephus, *Wars of the Jews*, Book II (Ch.IV).

commanders, when he had made his incursions, while he did himself act like a king, and meddled only with the more important affairs.[10]

When Herod's tyranny became most insufferable, special interest groups such as the ones described by Josephus, vied for control over their localities. After this particular series of rebellions, the Roman general Publius Varus became indignant toward the province, resulting in one of the most brutal executions recorded by the Roman Empire.

Upon Varus's reception of the letters that were written by Sabinus and the captains, he could not avoid being afraid for the whole legion [he had left there]. So he made haste to their relief...Varus sent a part of his army presently to Galilee, which lay near to Ptolemais, and Caius, one of his friends, for their captain. This Caius put those that met him to flight, and took the city of Sepphoris, and burnt it, and made slaves of its inhabitants...Emmaus was also burnt, upon the flight of its inhabitants, and this at the command of Varus, out of his rage at the slaughter of those that were about Arius. Thence he marched on to Jerusalem, and as soon as he was but seen by the Jews, he made their camps disperse themselves; they also went away, and fled up and down the country. But the citizens received him, and cleared themselves of having any hand in this revolt, and said that they had raised no commotions, but had only been forced to admit the multitude, because of the festival, and that they were rather besieged together with the Romans, than assisted those that had revolted...But Varus sent a part of his army into the country, against those that had been the authors of this commotion, and as they caught great numbers of them, those that appeared to have been the least concerned in these tumults he put into custody, but such as were the most guilty he crucified; these were in number about two thousand.[11]

---

[10] Ibid. (9) (Ch. IV).
[11] Ibid. (9) (Ch. V).

Against this backdrop, the reader may now better understand the Jewish hatred of the Roman occupation. Josephus records that two thousand Jews of the resistance were crucified as a result of the various uprisings in the region of Galilee and Jerusalem. Even by modern standards, that is an alarmingly high number of executions. Although crushed by Varus, the unrest in the province did not go unnoticed by Caesar. Such a violent rebellion led to a hearing taking place in Caesar's court between 7-4 B.C.E. in which certain representatives of the revolt were permitted to plead their case.

When the rebels came before Caesar, they framed most of their grievances in the context of Herod's behavior, complaining about his violations of their laws, and the barbarity of his governance.[12] When Herod died, the hope was that his son Archelaus would be a more reasonable leader of Judaea. Precisely the opposite was the case. Archelaus began his reign with the murder of three thousand citizens and showed signs of being even more cruel than his predecessor.[13]

After hearing out the rebel pleas for relief, Caesar Augustus ordered Herod the Great's kingdom to be divided among three rulers. Archelaus would receive half the kingdom, and he could resume his reign if he proved himself to be a better king than the Judaeans claimed. In the meantime, the other half of the kingdom would be divided among two rulers familiar to readers of the New Testament. Herod Antipas, and his brother Philip.

Reasons for the unrest of the Jewish people during the reign of Herod the Great have been discussed in previous chapters, but Herod was not the only ruler who mismanaged Judaea during the first century.

When Nero came to power in the middle of the first century, he appointed a very incompetent governor over the region who

---

[12] Recall that it was Herod the Great who ordered the execution of all children under the age of two due to his paranoia of losing control of the kingdom.
[13] Ibid. (9) (Ch. VI).

abused the taxation system of the province severely. At one point, he decided to confiscate a large amount of silver from the temple in Jerusalem, in all likelihood to pay back debts that he owed to Caesar. His defilement of the temple motivated an insurgency among the religiously devout. As a protest to their mistreatment, the Jews ceased from offering sacrifices to God for the welfare of the Roman people and the emperor. Zealot fighters also destroyed a garrison stationed in Jerusalem.[14]

All of this was happening against the backdrop of a religiously fractured province. Many of the incidents recorded by Josephus in his *Wars of the Jews* happened after the birth of Christ. The religious conflict between the Jews, the Greeks, and the Christians was only augmented by the political conflict that had been raging in Judaea for more than a century. One may easily wonder why the Romans did not raze Jerusalem sooner than they did, as it also caused a great deal of political turmoil in Rome. But Judaea was not an insignificant territory for the Roman Empire. The coastal region of the Mediterranean was valuable to the empire for trade and commerce, and it offered strategic significance for the military.

For more than sixty years, Rome proved unable to control Judaea. The cruel treatment of Christians throughout the first century C.E. contributed to Nero's inability to control the Judaean province. As discussed earlier, many believed that Nero intended to dismantle the city of Rome and reconstruct it as a city built in his own image called Neropolis.

Historians may never know with certainty if destroying Rome was Nero's intention. If it was an accident, then the Great Fire of Rome could not have been more poorly timed, given his ambitions to construct a new city in his own name. One thing is certain: the timing of the Great Fire of Rome was suspiciously in line with Nero's political aspirations.

---

[14]Ibid. (1) (p.96).

The blaze broke out in 64 C.E., at the Circus, which joined the Palatine Hill to the Caelian Hill in the city of Rome. Historians claim the fire spread so quickly it engulfed the entire length of the Circus, consumed the level portions of the city, and moved into the hills faster than the flames could even be addressed by those attempting to put the fire out.

> Added to this were the wailings of terror-stricken women, the feebleness of age, the helpless inexperience of childhood, the crowds who sought to save themselves or others, dragging out the infirm or waiting for them, and by their hurry in the one case, by their delay in the other, aggravating the confusion.[15]

To make matters worse, while the blaze raged in Rome Nero had traveled to Antium and was on stage acting out the destruction of Troy.[16] The timing of the Antium performance in correlation to the fire in Rome aggravated rumors that Nero played a part in setting the city on fire. Suspicions turned into accusations when citizens were forbidden to extinguish the flames in certain parts of the city by a number of individuals who claimed they were acting on orders.[17] Some have suggested that these individuals were primarily interested in looting and made up the story about being ordered to prevent the flames from being extinguished. Still, one can imagine the punishment that would have awaited such individuals if they were caught lying about orders from the emperor. The benefits do not seem to outweigh the costs in such a scenario. If Occam's Razor is to be trusted, there is little doubt that Nero set fire to the city out of delusional grandeur.

When Nero returned to Rome, he made the construction of his new palace top priority, aggravating the public distrust of his role in the crisis. When it became apparent to Nero that he was unlikely to avoid the accusation that he had intentionally set fire to Rome, he devised a new strategy. Nero shifted the blame to a

---

[15] Ibid. (5).

[16] Given his propensity for narcissistic behavior and his flair for the dramatic, the acting out of the destruction of Troy was viewed by many to be Nero's unique way of romanticizing what he had done to Rome. If Nero did not set fire to the city, the production of the destruction of Troy was, at the very least, poorly timed.

[17] Ibid. (15).

class of people who were already hated by much of the public for their radical new religion: the Christians.

> ...All human efforts, all lavish gifts of the Emperor, and the propitiations of the gods, did not banish the sinister belief that the conflagration was the result of an order. Consequently, to get rid of the report, Nero fastened the guilt and inflicted the most exquisite tortures on a class hated for their abominations, called Christians by the populace. Christus, from whom the name had its origin, suffered the extreme penalty during the reign of Tiberius at the hands of one of our procurators, Pontius Pilatus, and a most mischievous superstition, thus checked for a moment, again broke out not only in Judaea, the first source of the evil, but even in Rome, where all things hideous and shameful from every part of the world find their centre and become popular. Accordingly, an arrest was first made of all who pleaded guilty; then, upon their information, an immense multitude was convicted, not so much of the crime of firing the city, as of hatred against mankind. Mockery of every sort was added to their deaths. Covered with the skins of beasts, they were torn by dogs and perished, or were nailed to crosses, or were doomed to the flames and burnt, to serve as nightly illumination, when daylight had expired.[18]

The historian named Tacitus, from whom the account of the accusation of the Christians comes, was not a Christian himself. His claim that some Christians confessed to the firing of Rome should probably be taken with caution, as it is not unusual to find exaggerated accusations of criminal conduct among ancient writers who detested the Christians. As Tacitus says in his account of the incident, the greater portion of Christians were not even arrested for the firing of the city, let alone executed for it. In large measure, the Christians were already an out-group in Roman culture, and Tacitus states they were executed for their "hatred of mankind." Thus, their arrest was not intended to bring justice for

---

[18] Ibid. (15).

the city's destruction, but to distract the population into rallying against a common enemy. From the emperor's point of view, preferably an enemy that did not include himself.

It is entirely possible that upon arrest and torture, certain Christians willfully confessed to setting Rome on fire. It is generally understood that people are apt to say anything while under torture simply to stop the suffering. But even if this were the case, it did not change the fact that before the Christians were killed, the greater populous already had a suspect in mind. The people were not easily swayed into believing Nero's false accusations. Although the Christians served as a distraction for a time, a plot against Nero's life soon ensued. A leader in the Praetorian Guard by the name of Subrius Flavus, along with Sulpicius Asper, Lucanus Annaeus, and Plautius Lateranus, all connected to the Roman nobility, worked together in a plot to depose Nero. Unfortunately, their scheme failed, and it would be four more years before Nero was forced into exile where he eventually committed suicide.

The firing of Rome and the plot against the Christians is important to our subject matter because the time period correlates with the martyrdom of many notable New Testament apostles, including Peter and Paul. Of Peter, it is said that he was sentenced to crucifixion,[19] whereupon he requested that it be done upside down, because he was not worthy to be executed as his Lord had been. Of Paul, it is said that he was martyred around Rome after Nero's accusation against the Christians.[20] The allegations of Nero sparked what eventually became known as the ten epochs of

---

[19] Although there is no record of the death of either Peter or Paul in the New Testament, the historical account of Peter's execution handed down by Hegesippus does seem to correlate with the prophecy of Jesus regarding the manner in which Peter would be martyred (John 21:18-19).
[20] Foxe, John. *The New Foxe's Book of Martyrs*. North Brunswick, NJ: Bridge-Logos Publishers, 1997. (p.7-8).

persecution against the Christians.[21] It is important to remember that the Christians were not the only religious group that the Romans persecuted during this time. The Jews also endured Roman oppression during the first century. Separating the two is not simple. Recall that when Tacitus detailed the accusations against the Christians, he reminded the reader that it was a movement that began in Judaea, a province already hated for its rebellious behavior against the empire.

The relationship between the Jews and the Christians throughout the first century was a complicated one. The New Testament records that the early Christians worshipped alongside their fellow Jews in synagogues.[22] Even as late as the second century it is recorded that this behavior was fairly common between the two groups.[23] In what was known as the Tannaitic Period in particular, Jewish Christians regularly attended synagogue services and were active in rabbinic disputations of the Scripture.

> ...There are echoes in tannaitic literature of actual discussions or debates that were carried on between these Christians and the rabbis. These early Palestinian Christians may have been much closer to the rabbis than the later tradition wishes us to remember. They had their own halakhic interpretations that were of interest to certain rabbis. Indeed, the same Rabbi Eliezer is said to have listened favorably to a piece of law from the mouth of a min [Christian]—which was perhaps one reason that he himself was suspected of heresy. In fact, the story of Eliezer, as well as other rabbinic stories of dealings with Jewish Christians, demonstrate that the split between Judaism and Christianity did not occur as early and as definitively as is often believed. Christians continued to frequent synagogues throughout the second century (and undoubtedly much later as well).[24]

---

[21] Bernard, David K. *A History of Christian Doctrine*. Vol. 1. Hazelwood, MO: Word Aflame Press, 1995. (p.44).
[22] Acts 14:1; Acts 17:10-12.
[23]Meyers, Eric M. "Jewish Culture in Greco-Roman Palestine." In *Cultures of the Jews*, edited by David Biale, 169. New York: Schocken Book, 2002.
[24] Ibid. (23) (p.168-169).

While it may seem strange to consider for contemporary readers, early Christianity was not dismissed as antithetical to monotheism by the Jews of this time-period. The Christians and the Jews may have disagreed about whether or not Jesus of Nazareth was the Messiah, but they agreed about the sovereignty and singularity of the God of Israel. Furthermore, later tensions between the two groups over concepts such as the sacraments or the doctrine of the trinity had not formed yet, because those doctrines did not exist yet. In doctrine and liturgy, early Christianity resembled the religion of the Jews in meaningful ways, and this probably contributed to the Roman hatred of the Christian religion.

Nevertheless, there were also great disputations between Jews and Christians as well. As evidenced in the previous entry, the writer admits that Rabbi Eliezer conversed openly with Jewish Christians and considered their opinions on the Scriptures. On the other hand, Rabbi Eliezer was also called a heretic by some of his fellow rabbis. Thus, the relationship between the two groups remained tense, even as it had been in the first century.

It is possible, even likely, that at least for a time, the persecution of the Roman Empire against the inhabitants of Judaea was a unifying force in the relationship between Jews and Christians. Both were hated by the empire and forced into exile from their Jewish homeland in 70 C.E. after the destruction of the Second Temple. Although many Jews and Christians disagreed about the Messiahship of Jesus of Nazareth, there is a great deal of evidence to suggest that early Christians living in the first century were benevolent to their Jewish brothers and sisters. Even in the New Testament, Paul included an admonishment to the Christians residing in Rome that they ought not think themselves better than the Jews, but pray for them, and remember that they were still beloved by God.[25]

---

• For primary source evidence concerning these sorts of encounters between Jewish Christians and the early rabbinate, see *Tosefta Hullin* 2:24.

[25] Romans (Ch. 11).

The siege by Vespasian resulting in the end of the first revolt of Judaea occurred between the years of 66-68 C.E.

> Judaea had simmered for decades under oppressive Roman rule, with its high taxes and customs duties, an army garrisoned in Jerusalem, and favoritism toward the non-Jewish communities in the land. Various Roman insults to the Temple in Jerusalem created the impression of Rome as a "kingdom of arrogance." Poor Jews resented the pro-Roman Jewish upper classes.[26]

The events surrounding the attack on Jotapata led to the incident of Vespasian being hit by dart in a battle with the Jews that was described at the opening of our chapter. As governor and military general, Joseph ben Matthias (Josephus) decided to hole up in a fortified location of the city after the Roman forces had surrounded their position. Assuming their demise but not willing to surrender without a fight, the Jews fended off the Romans for a time, but it could not last. Vespasian's forces overpowered the Jewish position, and the conquest of the remainder of Judaea ensued.[27] Josephus was eventually captured, and Vespasian continued his march toward Judaea.

While Vespasian was preparing for his siege of the city of Jerusalem, he received word that Nero had committed suicide. This event temporarily shifted the priorities of the Roman general, as Nero had left no heir to take his place, and it was not necessarily apparent who would become the new emperor. Galba, the imperial governor of Spain, had been declared emperor by his men, and many had sworn allegiance to him. But there were others who understood that no man had a legitimate claim to the throne, and so the decision would ultimately be made by strength of arms. Whichever of Nero's generals could secure the loyalty of the military, that man was certain to become the new emperor of Rome.

---

[26] Ibid. (1) (p. 116).
[27] Ibid. (9) Book III (Ch. VII).

Wherefore Vespasian put off at first his expedition against Jerusalem, and stood waiting whither the empire would be transferred after the death of Nero. Moreover, when he heard that Galba was made emperor, he attempted nothing till he also should send him some direction about the war: however, he sent his son Titus to him, to salute him, and to receive his commands about the Jews. Upon the very same errand did king Agrippa sail along with Titus to Galba; but as they were sailing in their long ships by the coasts of Achaia, for it was winter time, they heard that Galba was slain, before they could get to him, after he had reigned seven months and as many days.[28]

Although Vespasian remained loyal to Nero as Caesar, it is unlikely that he was grieved to hear the news of Nero's death. There is a fair amount of evidence to suggest that, if the two were not adversarial in public, Vespasian was at best ambivalent toward Nero. Once, when Nero had decided to put on a public performance himself, Vespasian is said to have fallen asleep while Nero was singing, causing some consternation between the two leaders. Probably not coincidentally, Vespasian was sent to Judaea less than a year after the incident.[29]

Perhaps telling is the fact that Vespasian sent his son Titus to Galba. Vespasian may not have known that he was going to be emperor, but the possibility of it had almost certainly crossed his mind, particularly on news of the death of Nero. Vespasian showed foresight in his decision to stay out of the fray in Rome until the politicians had their fill of those clamoring for the throne. There would be three men before Vespasian who would vie for control of the empire.[30]

More than any other man, Vespasian's greatest asset in his ascension to the throne was the loyalty of the army. But Vespasian had something else that the people were restless for—a son. Vespasian was not a young man when the siege of Jerusalem

---

[28] Ibid. (9) Book IV (Ch. IX).
[29] Grant, Michael. *The Roman Emperors.* New York: Simon & Schuster, 1985. (p. 51).
[30] Galba, Otho, and Vitellius.

began, and it was known even by his most ardent supporters that if he became emperor, his rule would be short-lived. Titus was another military man that the army respected and had served under his father in Judaea. Furthermore, his youth ensured that if Vespasian were to die soon after becoming emperor, the power dynamic in Rome would remain stable. Four leadership changes in less than one year offered more than enough chaos to motivate the populous to choose a leader who could offer some stability. They found that stability in Vespasian and Titus.

While the changing of the guard at Rome slowed the destruction of the Judaean province for a time, it would not last. After his father became emperor, Titus resumed the siege of Jerusalem. In 70 C.E., the temple was desecrated with sacrifices made to the ensigns and then set on fire. According to Josephus, this event took place during the feast of Pentecost, which traditionally celebrated the giving of the Law at Mount Sinai.[31]

Although the Romans completely razed the Second Temple and the rest of Jerusalem in 70 C.E., that was not the final struggle between the competing forces. Jewish survivors of the final siege on Jerusalem fled to the fortress of Masada, located around the region of the Dead Sea. They were in number about 960. Astoundingly, these survivors managed to remain fortified in their position at Masada for nearly three years. The fact that the Romans did not give up on destroying the relatively inconsequential group of fighters that had holed up in Masada perhaps reveals the great animosity the Romans felt toward the Jews at this point in history. The Jews were among the first legitimate provinces of the Roman Empire to rebel against the Caesars. Although skirmishes and battles had long been the norm along the borders of the Roman Empire, particularly in the north, Judaea was considered a benign region that was probably not expected to cause as much trouble as it eventually did.

---

[31] Ibid. (9) Book VI (Ch. V).

When it became clear to the fighters at Masada that the Romans were going to breach the fortress, they decided to destroy themselves rather than be enslaved by the Roman forces. The leader of the Masada fighters named Elazar be Yair is said to have given a final word to the Zealots, which was passed on to the diaspora by a woman who survived the mass suicide.

> "Since we long ago resolved," Elazar began, "never to be servants to the Romans, nor to any other than to God Himself, Who alone is the true and just Lord of mankind, the time is now come that obliges us to make that resolution true in practice...We were the very first that revolted [against Rome], and we are the last that fight against them; and I cannot but esteem it as a favor that God has granted us, that it is still in our power to die bravely, and in a state of freedom." ... "Let our wives die before they are abused, and our children before they have tasted slavery, and after we have slain them, let us bestow that glorious benefit upon one another mutually."...After this oration, the men killed their wives and children, and then each other.[32]

Although Judaism condemns suicide, the last stand at Masada has been considered an act of bravery, as the Zealot fighters chose to die free rather than be made slaves by a pagan empire.

After Masada, it seemed that the Jews would retreat from the history books as so many nations that the Romans conquered had done. But Masada was not the end of the story for the Jewish rebellion.

In 117 C.E., the emperor named Hadrian ascended to the throne of the Roman Empire. Historians regard him as "Hadrian the Greek" because of his deep and abiding affection for the Greek culture in which he was raised and his longing for Greek

---

[32] Telushkin, Joseph. *Jewish Literacy*. New York: William Morrow and Company, Inc., 1991. (p. 141-142).

revivalism in the Roman Empire. As in so many places in the empire, Hadrian attempted to reinstitute Greek norms where they had been abandoned throughout the provinces. One such place, was Judaea.

Recall that Judaea was once a bastion of Greek culture, owing to the influence of the Seleucids and later the Hasmoneans in the centuries before Hadrian's reign. In Judaea, Hadrian saw an opportunity to revive Hellenism and restore the province to its Alexandrian legacy.

Whether or not the actions of Hadrian in Judaea specifically sparked what became known as the Bar-Kokhba Revolt in the second century C.E. cannot be known with certainty. What is known is that, at a time when the Roman Empire was putting pressure on Jerusalem to become more Hellenized, a new revolt rose against them led by a man named Simeon Bar-Kokhba.[33]

A precise timeline of when Bar-Kokhba came to power is difficult to come by, but it is generally accepted that his forces organized against the Romans between 132-135 C.E. Of the revolt it is said that more than five hundred thousand Jews lost their lives in the struggle against Hadrian's army, the death toll rivaling even that of the war against Vespasian just sixty-two years earlier. Simeon Bar-Kokhba was a charismatic leader of the Jews, and it is recorded that even prominent rabbis of the era, such as Akiva, enlisted in Bar-Kokhba's forces. Because Jerusalem had been so severely destroyed after the siege in 70 C.E., Galilee became the new center of Jewish life in the region. From Galilee began the codification of the Hebrew Scriptures, and rabbinic Judaism flourished where the sects of the Sadducees and Essenes began to fade.[34] Remarkably, the Bar-Kokhba revolt achieved enough success against Hadrian's military that, for a time, they were able to sustain quasi-independence in Judaea, even going as far as to mint their own coins at the height of their power, as shown in figure 6.1.[35] Nevertheless, the Bar-Kokhba Revolt, much like its

---

[33] Ibid. (32) (p.145).
[34] Ibid. (23) (p. 163).
[35] "Ancient Coins: Bar Kokhba." Coin Archives. Accessed November 15, 2021. https://www.coinarchives.com/a/results.php?search=bar+kochba.

predecessor, did not last. Just as Masada before it, the Bar-Kokhba revolt is remembered for both its bravery and its foolhardiness. Jewish scholars today have supposed if the rebellion had not happened, it is possible that Jewish life in Judaea may have had more staying power than it ultimately did. One thing is certain—the Bar-Kokhba Revolt greatly reduced the number of Jews living in Judaea after the second century.

*Figure 6.1*                                    *Coin from the Bar-Kokhba era*

The Roman historian Dio Cassius provided a detailed description of the Roman general's [Julius Severus] strategy: "He was reluctant to fight the enemy face to face after seeing their great numbers and desperate anger. Instead, his practice was to have his numerous soldiers and officers capture them singly or enclose and besiege them in their fortified palaces, thus depriving them of food supplies. In this way he was able, by degrees and with little risk, to frustrate, immobilize, and destroy them. Very few [Jews] were saved. Fifty of the Jews' strongest fortresses were destroyed by the Romans, and nine hundred and eighty-five of their most important settlements razed. Five hundred and eighty thousand Jews were slaughtered in battles and skirmishes, and countless numbers died of starvation, fire, and the sword. Nearly the entire land of Judea lay waste."[36]

---

[36] Ibid. (32) (p.146).

The Bar-Kokhba revolt is, perhaps, more critical to our subject matter than even the Judaean Revolt of the first century. The reason being that, although the Bar-Kokhba Revolt ultimately failed, the impression of its leader left a permanent mark on the Jewish psyche. Religious leaders such as Rabbi Akiva regarded Simeon Bar-Kokhba as the true Messiah. It is likely that this only served to inflame tensions between Jews and Christians in the second century.

Recall from earlier reading that, up until the second century C.E., it was not uncommon to find Jews and Christians worshiping together in synagogues, particularly in the region of Galilee.[37] Although Jews and Christians disagreed on many things, they shared a common bond through their veneration of the Hebrew Bible as the inspired Word of God, as well as their mutual conflict with the Roman authorities. In the historical examination, evidence of Christians in Jewish houses of worship become less frequent after the Bar-Kokhba Revolt. Although it did not cease entirely, it is probably not a coincidence that the relationship between Jews and Christians deteriorated more rapidly after the second rebellion against Rome. This likely happened for a number of reasons.

First, the forces of Julius Severus absolutely decimated what was left of the dominant settlements in Judaea during 135 C.E. So extensive was the damage, so complete was the destruction, that the Romans renamed Judaea *Syria Palestina*, to completely disassociate the Jewish people from the region.[38] By renaming the province after the historical enemies of Israel, Hadrian was likely sending a message that the Jews would not soon forget—the Jews had been defeated for the last time. Because Judaea (now Palestine) had become a wasteland of wars and poverty, many Jewish Christians likely migrated from the area into regions with larger Christian communities such as in Asia Minor or Northern Africa.

---

37 See (Ch. 5).
38 *Palestina*, or, in Hebrew, *Pelesheth*, which means, "Land of the Philistines." Likely as a last slight against the Jews for the trouble they had caused for the Romans, Hadrian renamed the Judaean province after the historical enemies of the Davidic Kingdom of Israel, the Philistines.

Figure 6.2

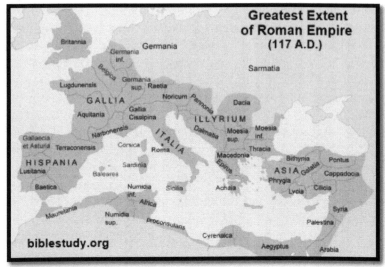

Second, the elevation of Simeon Bar-Kokhba to the status of Messiah likely dissolved whatever consonance remained between the Jewish Christians and the rebel communities of Galilee and the surrounding areas. From the Christian perspective, it was one thing to question whether or not Jesus of Nazareth was the Messiah. The disciples and later the apostles dealt with the same questions in their time, and it was a primary point of debate between Jews and Christians that would last for centuries. However, it was another thing altogether to claim that someone else was, in fact, the Messiah. The veneration of Simeon Bar-Kokhba to the position of Christ would not have been received well by Jewish or gentile Christians living in and around Judaea during the revolt. Although it is not explicitly named as the reason for the final split between Jews and Christians living in the area, it is the opinion of this author that it likely contributed to their parting of ways. From the perspective of the New Testament writers, it would not have been acceptable for Christians to have spiritual fellowship with groups that believed in a false Christ.[39]

---

[39] In Matthew 24:24, Jesus warned that there would come a time when false Christs would arise in the earth, and that they would deceive many people after His death. In 2nd Corinthians 11:4, Paul warned the church not to receive another

Still, it is known that some synagogues continued to welcome Christians beyond the second century, as the events which precipitated the bifurcation of the two into permanently separate and distinct religions as opposed to only differing sects had not happened yet. Institutionally speaking, it would be another two-hundred years before the church was permanently disassociated from its Jewish roots by Roman leadership.

The Jewish Revolt precipitated a great deal of bitterness against the Jews among the Roman authorities. The Jewish fight for sovereignty, combined with the advent of Christianity, contributed to unprecedented religious conflict in the Roman Empire that created hostility against the province and the people that introduced Judaism and Christianity to the world. Jews were an easy target for the Roman elite because of their uprisings against Herod the Great, Nero, and Vespasian. Christians were hated because they too came from the Jews, and they brought a religion that the Romans thought foolish to their homeland. Both were blamed for destabilizing the empire.

Before the various rebellions in the Judaean province, the top of the Roman Empire remained relatively stable. In the one hundred and twelve years that passed between the death of Julius Caesar in 44 B.C.E. and the death of Nero in 68 C.E., the throne changed hands just four times. Over the next fifty years, the throne would change hands nine times (from Galba to Hadrian). In the first eighty years of the third century, the throne changed hands no less than twenty-six times, with other estimates as high as sixty times.[40]

---

Jesus, another spirit, or another gospel than the one which was preached in the New Testament—the gospel of Jesus Christ.

[40] "List of Roman Emperors." Britannica. Accessed November 8, 2021. https://www.britannica.com/topic/list-of-Roman-emperors-2043294.

- It is not necessarily clear what constituted an emperor at this point in history. Factoring in whether or not the emperor in question had received endorsement from the Senate, if other men claimed to be the legitimate ruler, and the response of the military to the emperor's leadership, the

Of course, the instability of leadership in the Roman Empire cannot be blamed entirely on the Jewish Revolt or on the advent of Christianity. But each played a part in turning the status quo upside down. Nero's inability to control the Judaean province contributed to his decision to inflate the currency, as his two and three front war campaigns became expensive for the empire. He was forced to send Vespasian and his son Titus to crush the rebellion in Judaea, which only further inflamed tensions between the two worlds. It is probably not a coincidence that Vespasian became famous among military men for his campaigns in the Near East. It was those same military exploits for which he was exalted to the imperial throne.

Furthermore, Tacitus makes it known that although the citizens of Rome did not believe it, Nero blamed the firing of Rome on the Christians. When they were executed, the Great Fire was not invoked to justify their martyrdom. Rather, historians remark that their "hatred against mankind" motivated such harsh penalties as were incurred upon them. Jew and Christian were synonymous terms in the first-century Roman psyche. To kill one was not greatly different from killing the other. Both were hung on crosses around the empire. Both were sent to the Colosseum. And both perished under the sword of Roman tyranny.

After more than half a million Jews were slaughtered in the Bar-Kokhba Revolt, the Christians became the new primary target of Roman hatred culminating in the various epochs of persecution mentioned earlier in the reading. Those persecutions contributed greatly to the subject matter of our next chapter—Hellenism in Christian life. The cult of Dionysus presented real opposition to the Christian gospel, to say nothing of the fact that Christianity was illegal to practice in most of the empire until the fourth century. It was also during this period that relations between Jews and Christians dissolved more quickly. That becomes important to our discussion as well. Hellenism, persecution, and a lack of institutional legitimacy in the Roman Empire fueled the flames of

---

number does fluctuate in a way that leaves some aspects open to interpretation.

what would become some of the first recorded Christian infighting. By its end, Christianity would suffer from an identity crisis very similar to the one that the Jews endured under the Seleucid Greeks. The struggle to remain faithful to the traditions of Judaean Christianity in a pagan empire was a battle that raged for centuries after the fall of the province. That struggle was significantly impacted by the destruction of Jewish sovereignty in the Near East.

# CHAPTER VII

## Hellenism

### in

## Christian Life

Just as the Jews before them, the Christians struggled to retain their identity in an increasingly Hellenized world. Greek influence in Christian thought was only augmented by the fact that, unlike Judaism,[1] Christianity was a religion that prioritized conversion. Because of this, the influence of cultures outside of Judaea was not just an anomaly of Christianity, but one if its primary features. Bringing together every corner of the world into one faith also meant facing competing conceptions of God and righteousness from every corner of the world. The New Testament writers were not oblivious to this problem. They emphasized to the churches of Asia Minor that they were responsible for keeping the gospel of Jesus Christ pure, not allowing outside influences to contaminate the doctrine they had first received from Judaea. Paul, the chief evangelist to the gentiles in the New Testament, even went as far as to write,

> But though we, or an angel from heaven, preach any other gospel unto you than that which we have preached unto you, let him be accursed. As we said before, so say I now again, If any man preach any other gospel unto you than that ye have received, let him be accursed.[2]

After the Bar-Kokhba Revolt, Christians became further disconnected from their Judaean roots. Christianity spread

---

[1] Telushkin, Joseph. *Jewish Literacy*. New York: William Morrow and Company, Inc., 1991. (p. 509-510).
[2] Galatians 1:8-9 (KJV).

broadly into the surrounding nations until it eventually became a predominantly gentile religion. During this period, between 130 C.E. and 250 C.E. Christianity also began to produce writers known as the Apologists.[3] The Apologists were best known for composing written defenses of the Christian faith that could be submitted to the Roman authorities where Christians were being persecuted. As the Judaean Christians were much fewer in number throughout the empire by this point in history, many of these Apologists were Greek writers who had either converted to Christianity or were sympathetic to the Christian's situation.

The most common accusation brought against Christians was that they were atheists trying to introduce a novel religion to the empire.[4] The accusation of atheism was likely levied on the grounds that the Christians did not offer animal sacrifices to the gods of the Roman pantheon (or any pantheon), and that was a novel departure from traditional religious practices historically speaking. Even the Jews had a temple where sacrifices could be made until 70 C.E. The Christian emphasis on faith, combined with their belief in spiritual redemption through the death, burial, and resurrection of Christ on the cross, was considered superstitious by many in the Roman elite classes.

The Apologists were generally critical of pagan cults in Rome, and for this, they were respected by the Christians and, at times, even the Jews. This, of course, did not earn them any credibility with the Romans. Like many Christians living in the Roman Empire throughout the first and second centuries C.E., the Apologists who could be arrested were often executed.

The Apologists' writings may have been well intended, but they also reveal fractured priorities between different factions of Christians in the second century that were complex. Some of the Apologists show very little understanding of the New Testament writings, and they do not appear to be familiar with traditional beliefs surrounding Christian conversion. Being more than one

---

3 Bernard, David K. *A History of Christian Doctrine*. Vol. 1. Hazelwood, MO: Word Aflame Press, 1995. (p. 43).

4 Kelly, John D. "Apologist." Britannica. Last modified October 20, 2021. https://www.britannica.com/topic/Apologist.

hundred years removed from the ascension of Christ, the Apologists that did not grow up in or around the Judaean province had only a vailed comprehension of the Hebrew Bible as well. This fact complicates contemporary examination of their work. Defenses of the faith written by Jewish Christians would have looked very different from those written by the Greeks and the Romans. One had a background informed by the Hebrew Bible; the other was largely influenced by Greek philosophy. Since philosophy became the primary method of interpreting the Scriptures from the perspective of the Apologists, this becomes important to our discussion in this chapter.

Many Christian denominations hold the Apologists in high regard, and there is no doubt that their actions were brave in the second century. Nevertheless, their writings are not necessarily the best source for understanding dominant Christian doctrine or theology at the turn of the millennia. The Apologists were inconsistent in their approach to doctrine, and often relied upon their own background and education to interpret the Scriptures. For gentiles living in the Roman Empire of the second century, that background and education were almost always Hellenistic.

Among the most popular writers of the Apologist's era was Justin Philosopher, known in later years as Justin Martyr. Justin is unique among the Apologists because although he was born in Flavia Neapolis, Judaea, around 100 C.E., he was not a Jew.[5] Justin was raised in a pagan environment, but his Judaean residence also afforded him the opportunity to become familiar with the Hebrew Scriptures as well. Such familiarity comes out in his writings, which we will examine at length in this chapter.

Nevertheless, Justin's work raises questions for Christians as well. While it is evident that Justin was a very educated man in his time, it is not necessarily evident that he ever considered himself

---

[5] "Saint Justin Martyr Christian Apologist." Britannica. Accessed November 9, 2021. https://www.britannica.com/biography/Saint-Justin-Martyr.

a Christian in the traditional sense. As his name suggests, Justin was a philosopher and continued to be one until his death. His work greatly influenced generations of Christian writers who wanted to reconcile Roman religion and literary themes with Christianity. Justin represents a joining of two worlds in the second century that heretofore had been at odds with one another. Greek philosophy, and Christianity.

Recall from chapter four that the early Christians of the New Testament resisted the influence of the Stoics and the Epicureans.[6] In later writings, Paul warned Christians about being lured into philosophy, which he equated with deceitfulness.[7] Yet for Justin, in Christian thought, philosophy was not something to be avoided but embraced. Justin's *First Apology* and his *Dialogue with Trypho* are the two greatest primary sources for evidence of Greek influence in second-century Christian thought. They also reveal internal debates happening within Christianity itself during the second century.

Justin's *Dialogue with Trypho* is, perhaps, the most valuable of Justin's writings when trying to determine what, precisely, Justin believed about Christianity. The dialogue between Justin and an un-converted Jew named Trypho consists of debates over the value of the Law of Moses, the identity of Jesus Christ, and the relationship between the Jews and the Christians. The dialogue is crucial, because it represents some of the earliest primary source material regarding relations between Jews and Christians after the Bar-Kokhba Revolt. From Justin, we learn that Christians were worshipping in synagogues as late as the second century. In the work we also find that many Jewish Christians continued to observe the Law of Moses, something which comes up multiple times in the debate with Trypho.[8] But the most critical material in Justin's *Dialogue with Trypho* is his discussion on the person of Jesus Christ and his disagreements with Trypho on the Creator's identity. *Dialogue with Trypho* is also the most thorough written account of Justin's conversion to Christianity, and his conversion is probably the best place to begin an examination of his theology.

---

[6] See notes (Ch. 4).

[7] Colossians 2:8.

[8] Justin Martyr, *Dialogue with Trypho,* (Ch. XLVII).

First, it must be said that Justin considered himself, first and foremost, a philosopher. Even after his conversion, Justin emphasized the importance of philosophy in guiding a man to happiness. Although influenced by many schools of thought throughout his life, Justin cites Platonic philosophy as that which arrested his attention the most.

> "I will tell you," said I, "What seems to me; for philosophy is, in fact, the greatest possession, and most honourable before God, to whom it leads us and alone commends us; and these are truly holy men who have bestowed attention on philosophy...I surrendered myself to a certain Stoic; and having spent a considerable time with him, when I had not acquired any further knowledge of God...I left him and betook myself to another who was called a Peripatetic...But when my soul was eagerly desirous to hear the peculiar and choice philosophy, I came to a Pythagorean, very celebrated...but reflecting again on the space of time during which I would have to linger over those branches of learning, I was not able to endure longer procrastination. In my helpless condition it occurred to me to have a meeting with the Platonists, for their fame was great. I thereupon spent as much of my time as possible with one who had lately settled our city,—a sagacious man, holding a high position among Platonists,—and I progressed, and made the greatest improvements daily. And the perception of immaterial things quite overpowered me, and the contemplation of ideas furnished my mind with wings..."[9]

Thus, the philosophical background of Justin Martyr was extensive, and it seems apparent from his opening remarks to Trypho that he was a man in search of the highest philosophy he

---

[9] Justin Martyr, *Dialogue with Trypho* (Ch. II).

could attain.[10] This is important, because after his apparent conversion to Christianity, Justin did not dismiss his prior training in philosophy but claimed that it informed his understanding of Christianity. Of his conversion, Justin says that he wandered to a field not far from the sea to meditate when an unnamed man approached him in the same spot and began to converse with him about the merits of philosophy as a discipline in life.[11] During that conversation, the unnamed man asked Justin to describe God, upon which Justin responded that God is that which always maintains the same nature, and in the same manner, and is the cause of all other things.[12] Justin's decision to describe God as a force and not necessarily characterize Him through religious association was probably informed by his philosophical training up to that point. God as the "unmoved mover" is a rational explanation, not one associated with any specific religion or doctrine. Furthermore, when the man asked Justin if philosophy makes happiness, Justin responded by saying, "Assuredly, and it alone."[13]

Justin's philosophical discussion with the unnamed individual continues for eight more chapters, after which Justin confesses that he does not possess as keen an understanding of the things which the unidentified man speaks as he thought.

> "When he had spoken these and many other things...he went away, bidding me attend to them; and I have not seen him since. But straightway a flame was kindled in my soul; and a love of the prophets, and of those men who are friends of Christ, possessed me; and whilst revolving his words in my mind, I found this philosophy alone to be safe and profitable. Thus, and for this reason, I am a philosopher."[14]

---

[10] The explanation has been abbreviated from the cited text in this work for brevity's sake, but it is interesting to note that Justin seemed to consider the Pythagorean school to be the worthiest of his attention. He only dismissed it because he felt he did not have the proper skills necessary to utilize it, such as training in music, astronomy, and geometry.
[11] Ibid. (8) (Ch. III).
[12] Ibid. (8).
[13] Ibid. (8).
[14] Justin Martyr, *Dialogue with Trypho* (Ch. VIII).

*Dialogue with Trypho* is the most thorough account of Justin's conversion to Christianity. Although his *First Apology* offers a comprehensive examination of Christian doctrine as Justin generally understood it, only *Dialogue with Trypho* is so intensely personal. It informs the reader about the man Justin Martyr as he was. In his *First Apology*, Justin attempts to speak for Christianity more broadly. In his *Dialogue with Trypho*, he is speaking for himself.

The description of Justin's conversion is a novel departure from other Christian conversions as described in the New Testament. The book of Acts offers some of the most detailed descriptions of both Jewish and gentile conversions to Christianity in the first century. For example, the tenth chapter of the book of Acts tells the story of the conversion of an Italian man named Cornelius. After God sends the Apostle Peter to preach the gospel to Cornelius and his house, the Bible says,

> While Peter yet spake these words, the Holy Ghost fell on all them which heard the word. And they of the circumcision which believed were astonished, as many as came with Peter, because that on the Gentiles also was poured out the gift of the Holy Ghost. For they heard them speak with tongues, and magnify God. Then answered Peter, Can any man forbid water, that these should not be baptized, which have received the Holy Ghost as well as we? And he commanded them to be baptized in the name of the Lord. Then prayed they him to tarry certain days.[15]

The description of the conversion of the house of Cornelius is consonant with prior conversions in the book of Acts. When the Jews who were with Peter witnessed the event concerning the gentiles, they were astonished because the gentile's conversion appeared identical to their own, described in the book of Acts chapter two.

---

[15] Acts 10:44-48 (KJV).

And when the day of Pentecost was fully come, they were all with one accord in one place. And suddenly there came a sound from heaven as of a rushing mighty wind, and it filled all the house where they were sitting. And there appeared unto them cloven tongues like as of fire, and it sat upon each of them. And they were all filled with the Holy Ghost, and began to speak with other tongues as the Spirit gave them utterance...And they were all amazed, and were in doubt, saying one to another, What meaneth this?...Then Peter said unto them, Repent, and be baptized every one of you in the name of Jesus Christ for the remission of sins, and ye shall receive the gift of the Holy Ghost...they that gladly received his [Peter's] word were baptized.[16]

In the case of both gentiles and Jews, conversion to Christianity was characterized by faith in the gospel, repentance from old deeds, water baptism in the name of Jesus Christ, and being filled with the gift of the Holy Ghost, evidenced by speaking in other tongues. The book of Acts also includes examples of individuals who were already disciples of Jesus Christ during His earthly ministry but had not yet participated in the full initiation of Christianity as described in earlier Acts accounts.

And it came to pass, that, while Apollos was at Corinth, Paul having passed through the upper coasts came to Ephesus: and finding certain disciples, He said unto them, Have ye received the Holy Ghost since ye believed? And they said unto him, We have not so much as heard whether there be any Holy Ghost. And he said unto them, Unto what then were ye baptized? And they said, Unto John's baptism. Then said Paul, John verily baptized with the baptism of repentance, saying unto the people, that they should believe on him which should come after him, that is, on Christ Jesus. When they heard this, they were baptized in the name of the Lord Jesus. And when Paul had laid his hands upon them, the Holy Ghost came on them; and they spake with tongues, and prophesied.[17]

---

[16] Acts 2:1-12; 38-41 (KJV).
[17] Acts 19:1-6 (KJV).

The Acts 19:1-6 account is interesting because it suggests that there was, in fact, a correct way that Christians ought to be initiated into the faith. Although the Ephesians who Paul encountered were said to have been disciples already, they were still not truly converts in the mind of Paul. Although he did not dismiss their prior devotion to the teachings of John the Baptist or even Jesus, Paul emphasized the need for the disciples at Ephesus to be baptized again, this time in the name of Jesus Christ. The disciples complied immediately, and, afterward, received the Holy Ghost in the same fashion as the Jews of Acts chapter two and the gentiles of Acts chapter ten.

In all three examples of New Testament conversion, crossing both Jewish and gentile traditions, none are said to have happened in the way that Justin Martyr described his own. When the New Testament Christians received the gift of the Holy Ghost, they spoke with new tongues, prophesied, and magnified God. After interacting with the unknown man, Justin recognized Christianity as a new philosophy and magnified his office as a philosopher. Justin admits that his appreciation for the prophets and the friends of Christ was intensified after his conversation with the unknown man,[18] but nowhere does Justin claim to have spoken in other tongues. In no place is he said to have repented of any past sins. Perhaps the most astounding difference between the conversion of Justin Martyr and that of earlier Christians is although every example of conversion to Christianity is characterized by water baptism in the name of Jesus Christ in the New Testament, there is no record of Justin Martyr's baptism in his description of his conversion.

The fact that Justin did not include any account of his baptism in his *Dialogue with Trypho* does raise questions about what Justin Martyr believed about Christian conversion. In the narrative of Justin and the unknown man, Justin offered exceptional detail regarding the philosophical debate he participated in with his visitor, spanning more than five chapters

---

[18] The reason for this being that the unknown man instructed Justin in the wisdom of the prophets, juxtaposed with Greek philosophy in their conversation. For more on this, see *Dial.* (Ch. III-V).

of writing. Yet on the question of Christian initiation, he effectively reduces the process to an elevation of the mind to a higher philosophy. In the mind of Justin, that higher philosophy was Christianity.

Given Justin's background, it is not surprising to find such a heavy influence of the Greek thinkers in his writing. Judaea was a Hellenized province long before Justin was born. The works of thinkers such as Philo of Alexandria were popular in the region, to say nothing of the Stoics, Platonists, and the Epicureans. But the early Christians did not share Justin's intense love for philosophy. None of the New Testament churches are said to have characterized their faith in terms of philosophy, and none of the apostles considered themselves philosophers. Justin's lack of emphasis on the traditional practices of Christian initiation suggests that whatever he believed about Christianity was much less informed by early church practices than by the schools of the philosophers. While it is possible Justin was baptized, it is this author's opinion that he was not. The fact that water baptism is not included in his written account of his conversion is compelling.

Nevertheless, Justin did write about water baptism in his *First Apology*, and for this reason, it is reasonable to assume that he was, perhaps, baptized. The reason I remain unconvinced of Justin's baptism is that his *First Apology* was a presentation of Christian doctrine as he understood it more broadly, and it is written regarding general beliefs, not necessarily Justin's personal experiences. Furthermore, Justin is unclear in his presentation of the methods surrounding baptism in his *First Apology*, and he is not consistent with the New Testament.

But once again, whether one believes Justin was baptized or not, in reading the *First Apology*, it is evident that whatever Justin believed about water baptism, it was not necessarily harmonious with the early Christian beliefs. Recall from the book of Acts that, in every scenario where both Jews and gentiles were converted, they were baptized in the name of Jesus Christ. Chapter five of this book references Matthew 28:19, when Jesus commanded His disciples to go into all the world, baptizing them in the name of the Father, and of the Son, and of the Holy Ghost. The disciples of

Jesus responded in every situation by performing water baptism in the name of Jesus Christ, thus illustrating to that the early Christians believed that the name of Jesus Christ was the name of the Father, and of the Son, and of the Holy Ghost. But in Justin's *First Apology*, he states specifically that water baptism must *necessarily* be performed in another manner.

> I will also relate the manner in which we dedicate ourselves to God when we had been made new through Christ; lest, if we omit this, we seem to be unfair in the explanation we are making. As many as are persuaded and believe that what we teach and say is true, and undertake to be able to live accordingly, are instructed to pray and to entreat God with fasting, for the remission of their sins that are past, we praying and fasting with them. Then they are brought by us where there is water, and are regenerated in the same manner in which we were ourselves regenerated. For in the name of God, the Father and Lord of the universe, and of our Saviour Jesus Christ, and of the Holy Spirit, they then receive the washing with water...in order that we may not remain the children of necessity and of ignorance, but may become the children of choice and knowledge, and may obtain in the water the remission of sins formerly committed, there is pronounced over him who chooses to be born again, and has repented of his sins, the name of God the Father and Lord of the universe; he who leads to the laver the person that is to be washed calling him by this name alone. For no one can utter the name of the ineffable God; and if any one dare to say that there is a name, he raves with a hopeless madness...[19]

There are two references to the mode of baptism by Justin in this chapter, so it can be confusing to determine just how Justin believed baptism ought to be performed. Early in the passage, Justin states that water baptism is performed in the "name of God, the Father and Lord of the universe, and of our Savior Jesus Christ, and of the Holy Spirit." But later in the passage, Justin says

---

[19] Justin Martyr, *First Apology*, (Ch. LXI).

that what is pronounced over the individual being baptized is simply the "name of God, the Father and Lord of the universe," and that the person who leads the would-be convert to baptism must call God by this name *alone*. In the first example, it seems that Justin approved of a three-fold formula. In the second, Justin seems to suggest that God can only be known as the Father and Lord of the universe, not by a name.

Justin goes on to say that there is no name by which a man can know God, and on this point, he is out of sync with the New Testament writers. The early Christians emphasized baptism in Jesus' name. They did so because they recognized that Jesus was the name by which human beings can know the Father[20] and that Jesus was the express image of the Creator that Justin referred to in his *First Apology*.[21] For Justin, God the Father and Lord of the universe was distinct from the Savior in a way that required separate names to be used in the baptismal formula. He did not believe that the name of Jesus was synonymous with the Creator God. He says this explicitly to Trypho later in their exchange. Justin's understanding of the nature of God will be discussed in greater detail from Justin's *Dialogue with Trypho*, but the high point of emphasis early in the examination of Justin's work is that it marked a significant step away from the practices and beliefs of the early Christians.

It is helpful to look at chapters 56-57 of his *Dialogue with Trypho* to understand why Justin's presentation of water baptism differed from the earlier Christians of the New Testament. These chapters offer some of the clearest insight into what Justin believed about the nature of God and explain why he did not believe that Jesus Christ could be equated with God the Father.

Moses, then, the blessed and faithful servant of God, declares that He who appeared to Abraham under the oak in Mamre is

---

[20] John 14:7-11.
[21] Colossians 1:15.

God, sent with the two angels in His company to judge Sodom by Another who remains ever in the supercelestial places, invisible to all men, holding personal intercourse with none, whom we believe to be Maker and Father of all things;...when I had made an end of quoting these words, I asked them if they had understood them...Then I replied, "I shall attempt to persuade you, since you have understood the Scriptures, [of the truth] of what I say, that there is, and that there is said to be, another God and Lord subject to the Maker of all things; who is also called an Angel."[22]

At this point in Justin's discussion with Trypho, he cites Genesis chapter eighteen, the story of Abraham's visitation from God, followed by three visitors, whom he feeds and then serves in his tent. Justin chose this passage as a proof text for his chief claim: "that there is, and that there is said to be, another God and Lord subject to the Maker of all things." The narrative in the book of Genesis begins with Abraham experiencing a divine visitation from God. Three visitors appear before him, and Abraham restrains them until he can serve them food, water, and shade for their journey. Jewish scholars have traditionally understood the story to mean that God granted Abraham favor because Abraham showed great hospitality to strangers. This interpretation is probably not without merit, as it was only after Abraham served his three visitors that he received a prophetic word that his wife Sarah would conceive a child in old age. God is present in the story, but He is referred to distinctly from the three visitors at Abraham's tent. Christian interpretation lends itself to the notion that God sent the three visitors to Abraham, likely angels, which are often used as the messengers of God throughout the Bible.[23]

Justin's interpretation fits neither the traditional Jewish nor Christian viewpoint. From Justin's perspective, what transpires in

---

[22] Justin Martyr, *Dialogue with Trypho* (Ch. LVI).
[23] The book of Acts chapter twelve illustrates that many early Christians believed that angels walked the earth in human form, sometimes even taking the form of familiar individuals (Acts 12:15). The book of Hebrews also admonishes the reader to remember that there are moments in life where one may entertain angels unaware, and so it is important to be kind to strangers, such as the example given in Genesis 18:1-8.

Genesis eighteen is the revelation that there are two gods of the Old Testament and that the second one is submitted to the first.

> Reverting to the Scriptures, I shall endeavour to persuade you, that He who is said to have appeared to Abraham, and to Jacob, and to Moses, and who is called God is distinct from Him who made all things,—numerically I mean, not [distinct] in will. For I affirm that He has never at any time done anything which He who made the world—above whom there is no other God—has not wished Him both to do and to engage Himself with...[24]

Thus, when the text says that God appeared to Abraham under the oak at Mamre, it is actually a reference to Jesus, the second God, and not the Creator. Justin goes on a lengthy discourse about the story of the destruction of Sodom and Gomorrah, claiming that the various references to the Lord signal that there is a God who is himself also an angel and that the angel-God is Jesus Christ.[25] After returning to the central discussion of who, precisely, appeared before Abraham at Mamre, Trypho objects to Justin's interpretation; if the one of the servants who appeared to Abraham was both a God and an angel, why then is he said to have eaten and been nourished? Justin responds:

> I would say that the Scripture which affirms they ate bears the same meaning as when we would say about fire that it has devoured all things; yet it is not certainly understood that they ate, masticating with teeth and jaws. So that not even here should we be at a loss about anything, if we are acquainted even slightly with figurative modes of expression, and able to rise above them.[26]

---

[24] Justin Martyr, *Dialogue with Trypho* (Ch. LVI).
[25] The generic use of the word "Lord" is consonant with other references to angels in the Old Testament, as the angel of the Lord is often given the honorific to disclose in whose authority he speaks. Judges chapter six illustrates this (the angel of the Lord appeared to Gideon), as well as Exodus chapter twelve (God sends the death angel into Egypt). Because the angels execute the will of God, it is not wrong to say that God was responsible for the act itself. But nowhere are the angels said to be equal with God.
[26] Justin Martyr, *Dialogue with Trypho* (Ch. LVII).

Justin's reliance on metaphor to interpret the story of Genesis is consistent with traditional Greek practices. "It is not certainly understood that they ate, masticating with teeth and jaws. So that not even here we should be at a loss about anything, if we are acquainted even slightly with figurative modes of expression, and able to rise above them." The practice of "rising above" what is explicitly stated in the text was implored by Philo of Alexandria as the highest mode of interpreting the Scriptures. The literal meaning was only valuable to the uninitiated. It was elementary for those who practiced philosophy to assume that the text could be understood in its most fundamental form. Thus, Justin avoids Trypho's objection altogether by claiming that although the text says one thing, it means another.

Justin's perspective on the nature of God and the personhood of Christ comes out again in chapter 127 of his *Dialogue with Trypho*, and it is here where he makes his clearest break with traditional Christian beliefs about Jesus of Nazareth.

> You must not imagine that the unbegotten God Himself came down or went up from any place. For the ineffable Father and Lord of all neither has come to any place, nor walks, nor sleeps, nor rises up, but remains in his own place, wherever that is...how then, could he talk with anyone, or be seen by anyone, or appear on the smallest portion of the earth...it must follow that the Father and Lord of all had not been in heaven when what Moses wrote took place.[27]

Justin's emphasis on the impassability of God the Creator and His distance from His creation is not in harmony with the presentations of God in the Old Testament. Although foolish to the Greek mind, reason alone cannot lead one to a sound

---

[27] Ibid. (8) (Ch. CXXVII).

understanding of the God of Israel from the Christian perspective. Although Justin objects to the idea of God moving, talking, and appearing before men, these are generally understood to be anthropomorphic expressions used by human writers to describe an otherwise not-human God. Furthermore, the principle that God is omnipresent does not seem to be significant to Justin. Omnipresence implies that, although God remains in His own place (as Justin says), He can also be in another. This presentation of God is explicitly described in the story of the tabernacle of the wilderness.[28] This concept was likely difficult for Justin to grasp due to his belief in Stoicism, a point which will be explained later in the reading.

In chapter 128 of his *Dialogue*, Justin distinguishes his understanding of God and Christ from another group of unnamed believers.

> And that Christ being Lord, and God the Son of God, and appearing formerly in power as Man, and Angel, and in the glory of fire as at the bush, so also was manifested at the judgement executed on Sodom has been demonstrated...And do not suppose, sirs, that I am speaking superfluously when I repeat these words frequently: but it is because I know that some wish to anticipate these remarks, and to say that the power sent from the Father of all which appeared to Moses, or to Abraham, or to Jacob, is called an Angel because He came to men...is called Glory, because He appears in a vision sometimes that cannot be borne; is called a Man and a human being, because He appears strayed in such forms as the Father pleases; and they call Him the Word, because He carries tidings from the Father to men; but maintain that this power is indivisible and inseparable from the Father...[but it] has been also amply demonstrated [this power] is not numbered [as different] in name only like the light of the sun but is indeed something numerically distinct.[29]

---

28 Exodus (Ch. 29).
29 Justin Martyr, *Dialogue with Trypho* (Ch. CXXVIII).

This passage is critical to our discussion. Justin describes a particular group of believers who claimed that, although there are many names and attributes by which God is called throughout the Scriptures, the descriptions do not suggest other persons of God at all. From the perspective of the unnamed believers, the names and attributes are inseparable from the identity of God the Father.

Whether or not the group described by Justin consisted of Jews, gentile Christians, or both is not necessarily clear. What can be known is that these believers were evidently familiar with the Scriptures, and common enough in the region that Justin lived to merit remarks in his written work. Using Justin's description, it appears that the unnamed believers were doctrinally very similar to the New Testament Christians. In the book of John, Jesus presented the Father and Son as inseparable. The unity of the Word of God and the creator is referred to in John chapter one as well. And as discussed in previous chapters, the early Christians possessed a high Christology that presented Jesus as the Creator of all things in heaven and earth in the book of Colossians.

Contrary to the Christians described in the New Testament, Justin did not believe that the Father and Son were one. According to his *Dialogue with Trypho*, Justin believed that the Son was subordinate in nature and power to the Father, something which he also details in his *First Apology*. Because of this belief, it is not surprising that he encouraged a three-fold formula in water baptism that invoked the Father and Lord of the universe before the Son. While it is sometimes assumed that the three-fold formula was intended to imply that all three titles summarized the fullness of the Godhead, that was not necessarily the case. The early Christians baptized exclusively in the name of Jesus Christ because they believed that the name of Jesus was the saving name of God. Justin thought that baptism ought to be performed using the three-fold formula because without the invocation of the Father and Lord of the universe, the power of the washing would be insufficient. To Justin, Father and Son were numerically distinct.

It is worth mentioning at this point that contemporaneous Christians of Justin's time did not seem to embrace his three-fold formula as a common practice in their faith. Although Justin's work has been revered in more recent generations for its apologetical value, Justin was not widely received by Christianity in his time. It is never recorded that Justin was ordained a minister. As stated in the earlier portions of this chapter, Justin Martyr died a philosopher. Although somewhat well versed in the Hebrew Bible, his novel interpretations of various passages suggest that, although familiar with the Scriptures of the Old Testament, his training was predominantly Greek and not informed by the religious population of Judaea. The Christians of Justin's era did not embrace his three-fold baptismal formula, evidenced by the fact that generations of Christians proceeding Justin continued to baptize primarily in the name of Jesus Christ.[30] As Leo Miller writes, "It is impossible to offer an apodictic historical proof the existence of the present formula [three-fold] of baptism in the first three centuries of the Church."[31] Nevertheless, the writings of early Apologists such as Justin Martyr were used in later generations to justify the precedent for changing the baptismal formula from a Jesus-centric model to a three-fold version.

Justin also introduced a new term in his *Dialogue with Trypho* that was a novel departure from other descriptions of the Christ. "God the Son of God" does not appear in the New Testament. Still, it was necessary to use in the mind of Justin because it denoted the existence of a subordinate God that was numerically different from the creator God. Remember that for Justin, the compatibility of Father and Son as one God was unacceptable. For this, he may be credited with providing some of the earliest examples of trinitarian thought, as the finalized form of the Nicene Creed used by Catholics to describe the disposition of God says that Jesus is "God from God" and "Light from Light."[32] "God the Son" is not a biblical phrase, but it is necessary to use if one assumes two pre-existent and distinct beings. Still, the Justinian presentation of God and Christ is not entirely

---

[30] Miller, Leo F. "The Formula of Baptism in the Early Church." *The Catholic Historical Review* 10, no. 4: (220).
[31] Ibid. (30).
[32] "Nicene Creed." Britannica. Accessed November 10, 2021. https://www.britannica.com/topic/Nicene-Creed.

compatible with later trinitarian developments, as he believed in an absolute subordination of God the Son to God the Father.

Justin Martyr differed from earlier Christians in his beliefs about the Jews as well, a topic on which he and Trypho argued extensively. At one point, Justin calls the Jews "utterly incompetent, foolish, and ridiculous," a characterization which angered Trypho greatly.[33] By the end of the exchange, Justin boasts that Christians are the new sons of God, and that the Jews have been cast away for their unbelief. The early Christians did not share this perspective on Christian identity. In the book of Romans, Paul warned against anti-Semitism and replacement theologies.[34] From the Pauline perspective, the Christians were grafted into the vine to provoke the Jews to jealousy so that they might turn back to God, but he explicitly states God had not cast off natural Israel, and that Christians who boasted against the Jews were in danger of damnation themselves.[35]

Justin's harsh criticism of the Jews is unsurprising given the timing and location of his writing. Justin was born in a Judaean province hated by the Roman authorities, and he was old enough to witness the Bar-Kokhba revolt at its height. Justin shows a familiarity with the Hebrew Bible in his *Dialogue with Trypho*, but almost never cites work from the New Testament writers. There may have been numerous reasons for this, but it is safe to assume that concerning his perspective on the identity of Christ, water baptism, or the treatment of the Jews, he had not become greatly familiarized with the book of Acts or the epistles to the Romans and Colossians.

Isolated as it may have been, examination of the works of Justin Martyr reveals a shift from prioritizing Semitic interpretations of the Scriptures to prioritizing Greek interpretations of the Scriptures among Christians in the second

---

[33] Ibid. (8) (Ch. CXXIII-CXXIV).
[34] Romans (Ch. 10-11).
[35] Romans 11:1-7; 16-21.

century C.E. In his *Dialogue with Trypho*, both Justin and Trypho admit that as recently as their written exchange, some Christians continued to worship in synagogues with the Jews, suggesting a more positive relationship between the two groups than is sometimes believed. The text also seems to imply that many Christians may have found common ground with the Jews on the nature of God, as far as the Old Testament was concerned. Although there were certain Jews who rejected the message that Jesus was the Messiah, it did not necessarily cause the final break between the two groups. There is some evidence to suggest that greater controversy stemmed from the fact that certain Jews wanted the Christians to remain observant of the Law of Moses. When they refused, they were asked to leave the synagogues.[36]

The lack of Christian observance of the Law of Moses combined with Roman animosity toward the Jews were likely the most significant contributing factors to the dissolution of relations between Jews and Christians. But on the nature of God, it appears that Justin Martyr was an outlier and not a representation of dominant Christian beliefs. By nearly all historical accounts, most Christians remained committed to the gospel and the message of salvation as it was described in the New Testament.[37]

Philosophy was not the only aspect of Hellenism that influenced the theology of Christianity in the first two centuries following the New Testament. Believers who saw outsized influence of Greco-Roman culture making its way into the church continued to fight battles with paganism. Recall from chapter three that as Judaism struggled to maintain its biblical identity during the rise of Hellenism in the region, even the rabbis were susceptible to

---

[36] Ibid. (8) (Ch. XLVII).
- Tension between Jews and gentiles over the essentiality of observance of the Law of Moses dated back to the New Testament, where in the fifteenth chapter of Acts it is said that many believers came together in a council at Jerusalem to discuss the issue.

[37] Whitaker, E C. "History of the Baptismal Formula." *The Journal of Ecclesiastical History* 16, no. 1 (April 1965): 5-6.

ideological capitulation on certain issues. Ornamentations of the Greek and Roman gods could be found adorning certain public facilities, bath houses, and even synagogues.[38]

*Figure 7.1*

Figure 7.1 depicts the image of a Roman God (possibly Venus), located on the Dionysus mosaic floor of the synagogue in Diocaesarea (Sepphoris), Israel, likely dating to the second century C.E.

Christianity was not immune to paganism either. Apologists and other Christian writers wrote extensively on the battles with the cult of Bacchus (Dionysus), highlighting the ideological struggles with those who opposed Christianity on the grounds that they, too, knew of a resurrected god. In some cases, the worlds of philosophy and paganism merged, creating a hybrid-theology that embraced Christian principles, but was informed by Greco-Roman traditions as well. This practice likely found its most meaningful expression in the writings of men such as Clement of Alexandria.

---

[38] Meyers, Eric M. "Jewish Culture in Greco-Roman Palestine." In *Cultures of the Jews*, edited by David Biale, 172-73. New York: Schocken Books, 2002.

Clement, of whom we know more, had been a learned pagan philosopher. In his search for knowledge he came to Alexandria and placed himself under the influence of Pantaenus, later succeeding him as a teacher. As compared to Origen, Seeberg notes, Clement was a "talented dilettante with the virtues and vices which belong to such character." A study of Clement's writings substantiates this...The situation in which Clement found himself explains the Hellenic form of much of his theology...Clement regarded philosophy as having the same pedagogical significance for the Greek world as law had for the Hebrew world. Philosophy is the light of reason which the Logos has imparted to mankind...Through Greek philosophy the soul is prepared for the reception of faith on which truth erects the edifice of knowledge. Philosophy is the means by which the real nature of Christianity is disclosed to the thinking man...Such were the thoughts of Clement, and they lay also at the foundation of the system of Origen.[39]

Philosopher Christians such as Clement of Alexandria can be difficult to unpack. On the one hand, they were supportive of the Christian plight and saw themselves as ambassadors for the Christian cause. On the other hand, much of their writing reflected poor knowledge of the Scriptures and was much more informed by Greek traditions than is sometimes admitted by modern Christian Apologists. Clement's belief about philosophy being the structure that informs Christian theology instead of the Law is evidence of the point. In the New Testament, the Law of Moses informed Jewish and Christian thought alike, not being divisible from Christianity as was supposed by Clement and the Apologists. Jesus is said to have taught the gospel from the books of Moses and the Prophets.[40] The apostles of the book of Acts are said to have done the same.[41]

[39] Heick, Otto. *A History of Christian Thought*. Vol. 1. Philadelphia, PA: Fortress Press, 1965. (p. 111-113).
[40] Luke 2:27.
[41] Acts 28:23.

> Wherefore the law was our schoolmaster to bring us unto Christ, that we might be justified by faith. But after that faith is come, we are no longer under a schoolmaster. For ye are all children of God by faith in Christ Jesus.[42]

Paul's letter to the Galatians emphasized the importance of the Law, not philosophy, as the pre-cursor to the Christian faith. Early Christians understood the context of Jesus' life and ministry through the framework of the Old Testament. Probably the most striking example of this can be found in the eighth chapter of the book of Acts, which narrates the conversion of one Ethiopian Jew to the gospel using the book of Isaiah as a reference point.

> And the angel of the Lord spake unto Philip, saying, Arise, and go toward the south unto the way that goeth down from Jerusalem unto Gaza, which is desert. And he arose and went: and behold, a man of Ethiopia, an eunuch of great authority under Candace queen of the Ethiopians, who had the charge of all her treasure, and had come to Jerusalem for to worship, Was returning, and sitting in his chariot reading Esaias the prophet. Then the Spirit said unto Philip, Go near, and join thyself to this chariot. And Philip ran thither to him, and heard him read the prophet Esaias, and said, Understandest thou what thou readest? And he said, How can I, except some man should guide me? And he desired Philip that he would come up and sit with him. The place of the Scripture which he read was this, He was led as a sheep to the slaughter; and like a lamb dumb before his shearer, so opened he not his mouth: In his humiliation his judgement was taken away: and who shall declare his generation? For his life is taken from the earth. And the eunuch answered Philip, and said, I pray thee, of whom speaketh the prophet this? of himself, or of some other man? Then Philip opened his mouth, and began at the same Scripture, and preached unto him Jesus. And as they went on their way, they came unto a certain water: and the eunuch said, See, here is water; what doth hinder me to be

---

[42] Galatians 3:24-26 (KJV).

baptized? And Philip said, if thou believest with all thine heart, thou mayest. And he answered and said, I believe that Jesus Christ is the Son of God. And he commanded the chariot to stand still: and they went down both into the water, both Philip and the eunuch; and he baptized him.[43]

This passage in the book of Acts is probably the most damning case against Clement of Alexandria's claim that it was philosophy, not the Law of Moses, which informed Christian thought. Early Christians were much less familiar with philosophy than with the Hebrew Bible. In cases where philosophy abounded in a particular area, the apostles warned believers to be cautious and not swept away by it.

Much like Justin, Clement of Alexandria believed Christianity to be the highest philosophy, and in this way, he may be understood to be an admirer of the early church. But his initiation into the church was not congruent with the practices of the first Christians. Clement is also said to have been a believer in *gnostikoi* Christians, which embraced knowledge as the epicenter of Christianity instead of faith and obedience to Jesus Christ. *Gnostikoi* (Gnostic) doctrine discusses the relation of Christian truth to philosophy and of faith to knowledge; the latter is emphasized in both cases (i.e., philosophy & knowledge > Christian truth & faith).[44] Although the early Christians did not accept this doctrine, it does offer insight into how Christian thought evolved under Greek influence. The New Testament Christians were greatly influenced by Semitic thought. Their emphasis on the Hebrew Bible as the primary source of Christian doctrine also kept them tethered to Jewish communities, even when gentiles became more prominent in the church. The more disconnected the church became from their Judaean roots, the more novelty appeared in Christian writings.

As stated earlier, synagogues were not the only houses of worship that the Greco-Roman world influenced. The image shown in figure 7.2 is a statue of Aphrodite, excavated from the

---

[43] Acts 8:26-38 (KJV).
[44] Ibid. (39) (p. 112).

Church of John the Baptist in Ein Kerem, dating roughly to the third century (200 C.E.).

*Figure 7.2*

I took this photo in 2016 at the Rockefeller Archeological Museum in Jerusalem. Though the head and arms are missing, the posture indicates that it was made in the style of Venus the Modest—in which the goddess is shown with her right hand covering her breasts and her left hand over her genitals.

Whether or not the statue served as ornamentation or was worshiped as an idol, it is difficult to know with certainty. But images of idols, ornamentation or otherwise, would have been unacceptable additions to houses of prayer and worship among the first Christians.

Second-century icons included in later Christian structures suggests a bifurcation in Christian thought. Although many Christians continued to worship in traditional ways, fellowship with both Jewish and gentile believers, baptize in the name of Jesus Christ, and rely on the books of the Hebrew Bible and the writings of the New Testament to inform their Christian beliefs, some did not. As evidenced by the work of Justin and Clement of Alexandria, there was another branch of Christianity emerging in the second and third centuries that brought traditional Greek elements into the framework of Christian thought. In some cases, the impact on Christian life was minor, amounting to little more than cultural differences. In others, it marked a significant change in how entire schools of theology approached the Scriptures. Writings of men such as Clement and Origen greatly impacted the school at Alexandria.45

In the years following the deaths of Justin and Clement, generations of Christian teachers and preachers believed it was their responsibility to rid Christianity of its Judaean roots so that it would no longer be perceived as a religion necessarily informed by the Hebrew Bible. Necessarily was the operative word for these thinkers. Because Christianity was universal in its approach to evangelism, Hellenized Christian thinkers began to interpret the character of Christianity as universal as well.46 Thus, the more exclusive elements of Christian doctrine, such as the essentiality of water baptism in the Jewish name of Jesus, being filled with the Holy Ghost made evident by speaking with new tongues, and even holy living, were re-cast in molds more acceptable to Greco-Roman lifestyles. The emphasis on creating a "universal" Christian character that was much more eclectic contributed to the rising popularity of the term "Catholic" in the post-Apostolic generation, and was likely used to describe Christians that identified with the movement.47 The terminology became prominent in the third century, although it can be found as early as the writings of Ignatius in the second century.48 The movement was also characterized by greater hostility to the Jewish roots of Christianity. Some post-Apostolic writers wanted Christians to break with the Jews entirely, claiming that Jews who continued to observe the Law and even spoke of Jesus Christ were monsters.49

---

45 Origen was a pupil of Clement at the school in Alexandria.
46 Ibid. (39) (p. 114).
47 Catholic simply means, "universal."
48 Ignatius, *Epistle to the Smyrnans*.
49 Ignatius, *Epistle to the Magnesians*.

This perspective was not cohesive with the New Testament, which states that Paul encouraged his disciple named Timothy to be circumcised, because he was ethnically a Jew.[50] The theological break with the early Christians coincided with a rise in anti-Semitism in later generations, to say nothing of the political climate that still raged against the Jews for their part in ending the Augustan Dynasty. Kurtz summarizes:

> When once the substantial truth of divine salvation had cast off the Judaistic husk in which the kernel had ripened, those elements of culture, which had come to maturity in the Roman-Greek world, were appropriated as the means for giving Christian ideas a fuller and clearer expression. The task now to be undertaken was the development of Christianity on the lines of Graeco-Roman Culture."[51]

Later Christian philosophers' movement against Judaean Christianity was not well received by all, or even the majority, of Christians in the second century. Evidence of the inter-Christian struggle can be seen in the writings of men such as Justin, as examined earlier in this chapter. But there is a great deal of evidence to suggest that the ideological battle between the two groups of Christians continued for centuries, culminating with accusations of "Sabellianism" against certain believers in the fourth century. This term will be discussed at length later in this book. Hellenism was the dominant secular culture of its time, so it is not surprising to find that Christians of the second century capitulated to it. The fight between religion and culture continues even today. Nevertheless, the Hellenistic culture's impact on the theology of Christianity in the first two centuries created a lasting

---

- The writings of Ignatius, as well as other post-Apostolic writers, was also characterized by a strong emphasis on paying honor to the bishops of the church and submitting to authority. While this is present in the New Testament as well, it plays a much more prominent role in the post-Apostolic writings. For more on this, see J.B. Lightfoot, *The Apostolic Fathers*.

[50] Acts 16:1-2.

[51] Ibid. (39) (p. 114).

- Kurtz, *op. cit.,* Par. 19; cf. Par. 7, 25-26.

dogma that would be codified in the next two. That dogma, known as the holy trinity, was expressed in its earliest form by the subject of our next chapter, Tertullian of Carthage.

# CHAPTER VIII

## The Riddle

## of

## Tertullian

> What indeed has Athens to do with Jerusalem? What concord
> is there between the Academy and the Church? What between
> heretics and Christians?[1]

Thus begins the riddle of Tertullian. Modern theologians and historians know him as the first post-Apologetic writer to bring the word "trinity" into the forefront of Christian thought. Others know him as the promising theologian of the second century who fell into an old heresy later in life. For the purposes of our discussion, Tertullian represents two competing conceptions of Christian thought in one person during the second century C.E. For on the one hand, Tertullian objected to the influence of Greco-Roman themes in Christianity, such as those described in our previous chapter. On the other, Tertullian presented challenges to the Judaean legacy of the church and did not shy away from using his own training in philosophy to become one of the most schismatic writers of the second century.

Tertullian was born sometime around 150 C.E. near the region of Carthage.[2] Unlike Justin before him, Tertullian was a recognized

---

[1] Tertullian, *Prescription Against Heretics*, (Ch. VII).
[2] Heick, Otto. *A History of Christian Thought*. Vol. 1. Philadelphia, PA: Fortress Press, 1965. (p. 123-124).

minister in the universal movement and served as a presbyter for some time.[3] He was likely influenced by the writings of Justin Martyr, as much of Justin's work comes out in the writings of Tertullian which will be examined shortly.[4] Tertullian and Justin differed in their appreciation for the influence of philosophy on Christian thought. Still, his hesitancy toward Greek themes did not hinder Tertullian from using his training from the school of North Africa to articulate his own beliefs about the nature of God.[5] It is important to understand that by the second century C.E., philosophy and religious thought were not easily separated, especially in the gentile communities. More than three hundred years before Tertullian was born, scores of disputations between religious and philosophical schools throughout Asia Minor and the Near East created webs of arguments between writers that cannot be quickly untangled. The introduction of Christianity to the conversation only augmented the tension between the different schools of thought, culminating in the examples given in the book of Acts concerning the Stoics and the Epicureans. Pagan philosophers used the cult of Dionysus to discredit the Christians. At the same time, Christians brought metaphysical interpretations of the Old and New Testament to support their claims about the identity of Jesus Christ. This is seen most evidently in the writings of the Apologists.

These written and oral disputations were passed down to future schools in Alexandria, Rome, and Athens, many of which the gentile Christians studied in. The best arguments were retained, while the less durable ones were thrown out and new ones were developed. If you can conceive of a generation of Christian thinkers who were taught to be generally critical of philosophy, but also inherited philosophical tools (even unwittingly) to combat greater Greco-Roman conceptions, this practice becomes more comprehensible. Philosophy came under criticism in Christianity as early as the New Testament writers, but gentile Christians who lacked the traditional Semitic

---

[3] Ibid. (2).
[4] Chalfant, William B. *Ancient Champions of Oneness*. Hazelwood, MO: Word Aflame Press, 1986. (p. 64).
[5] Ibid. (2) (p. 124).

understanding of the Hebrew Bible required an interpretative framework to view the Scriptures through. Without proper training in the Hebrew Bible, that interpretative framework was generally philosophy. The ambivalence of gentiles toward the Jews in the first two centuries following the death of Jesus also contributed to a diminishing appreciation for traditional approaches to the Hebrew Bible. The Jews were frequently treated as an outgroup in Christianity rather than as its original proponents.

Such abandonment of traditional Biblical training is why writers such as Justin Martyr or Clement could say that what the Law of Moses was to the Jews, philosophy was to the Christians. Their theory was not consistent with the behavior of the early church according to the book of Acts, but it provided the necessary tools to thoughtfully examine the Scriptures without essential attachment to the Judaean movement. Many Christians who were influenced by philosophy, wittingly or not, were also critical of the pagan cults. Thus, the same man who wrote, "What indeed has Athens to do with Jerusalem?" was also trained in the work of the Stoics while living in North Africa.

> Like Cyprian, who revered him as his teacher, he [Tertullian] belonged to the School of North Africa. His writings indicate the various influences to which he had been subjected. There was his own training in Stoicism, his reading in the early apologetic literature of the Church, and the strong influence of the tradition of Asia Minor transmitted through Irenaeus.[6]

In the mind of Tertullian, the cults, the philosophical schools, and the philosophers were not representative of his own beliefs. Like Justin, Tertullian framed Christianity as its own philosophy, not dependent on Athens for its identity. Yet, it was also Stoicism that informed Tertullian's belief about the nature and existence of God. Whether or not the inconsistency was intentional on the part of Tertullian is uncertain, but there is little doubt that it was the product of generational disputations and the hybridizing of

---

[6] Ibid. (2) (p. 124).

philosophical and religious ideas. Such cognitive dissonance abounded in the days of Tertullian because one's approach to reason was not necessarily believed to be dependent on one's religious beliefs. Tertullian may have borrowed Stoic ideas, but he was not a self-identified "Stoic." In generations past, the very use of Stoic ideas may have identified Tertullian as one of their kind. But by the second century, philosophy was essential to the psyche of Rome in a way that could not be reduced to a "school of thought." It was woven into the fabric of society. Thus, even those who were critical of philosophy generally may have owed their ideas to older philosophical beliefs long cemented within the culture itself.

The Stoicism in Tertullian's writing was one of the most important contributions to the development of the doctrine of the trinity. From the Stoic framework came his harshest criticisms against the highly Jesus-centric Judaean movement and his polemics against men like Praxeas and a group known as the Monarchians. *Against Praxeas* is one of the most well-known polemics of Tertullian. A brief examination of its primary themes is helpful in understanding how, precisely, Tertullian came to his articulation of the God of Israel in three distinct persons.

Not much is known about Praxeas, or even if that was actually his name.[7] Most of what can be known about Praxeas comes from what Tertullian wrote about him in his *Against Praxeas.* Undoubtedly, some of the accusations levied against Praxeas were probably exaggerated or, at least, slanted by Tertullian. The very title of the work suggests that Tertullian was attempting to paint Praxeas in a negative light. Nevertheless, Tertullian's work does situate Praxeas alongside other known Christian believers of the time. By comparison, we can come to some conclusions about why Tertullian took such an issue with Praxeas.

---

[7] Praxeas simply means "busybody," so it is entirely possible that the name was intended to be a disparaging descriptor of the individual that Tertullian was writing to.

Much of the debate in *Against Praxeas* is centered around one fundamental disagreement between the two men—the nature of God in relationship to the person of Jesus Christ. Their competing conceptions of God unfold in the arguments of Tertullian. From them, the modern reader can learn something about how the universal movement (to which Tertullian belonged) found itself at odds with other groups of Christians.

> For before all things God was alone—being in Himself and for Himself universe, and space, and all things. Moreover, He was alone, because there was nothing external to Him but Himself. Yet even not then was He alone; for He had with Him that which He possessed in Himself, that is to say, His own Reason. For God is rational, and Reason was first in Him...although it would be more suitable to regard Reason as the more ancient; because God had not Word from the beginning, be He had Reason even before the beginning...For although God had not yet sent out His Word, He still had Him within Himself, both in company with and included within His very Reason, as He silently planned and arranged within Himself everything which He was afterwards about to utter through His Word. Now, while He was thus planning and arranging with His own Reason, He was actually causing that to become Word which He was dealing with in the way of Word or *Discourse*.[8]

When attempting to dissect his beliefs about the nature of God and Christ, Tertullian's perspective on the creation account and the existence of God the Father is a good starting point. A reoccurring theme of Tertullian in the aforementioned passage is the relationship between "Reason" and "God" before creation. It may stand out to the reader that Tertullian wrote of reason as though it were another person altogether, possessing its own form apart from God. "Now, while He was thus planning and arranging with His own Reason..." Here lies one of the earliest examples of Stoic thought coming out in the writings of Tertullian.

---

[8] Tertullian, *Against Praxeas*, (Ch. V).

The Stoics were materialists, but not in the sense that is commonly understood in modernity. Materialism in the ancient world was not necessarily meant to be interpreted as hedonism or a belief in nothing beyond what could be seen; rather, it was understood in a corporeal sense. In other words, Stoicism embraced the notion that all things possess form, have their own body, and they consist of a discernable material makeup.[9] In this way, it was not rational for Stoics to conceive of things such as "spirit" or "reason" without observable material features to define them. To Tertullian, the "Reason" that he wrote about was distinct from God the Father in the corporeal sense, but its *corpus* was filled with something similar to whatever it was that composed God the Father. From this Stoic principle comes the bifurcation of "person" and "substance" in traditional trinitarian thought (three persons of the same substance), at least in the nominal sense. As will be examined shortly, Tertullian did not necessarily believe that the Father and Son shared substance, although he admits uncertainty on the point.

Tertullian also distinguished between "Reason" and "Word" in this chapter of his work, which is vital to his overarching disagreement with Praxeas. Recall that Tertullian believed that Reason should be regarded as more ancient than the Word because the former resided in God first. Although many today do not think of a person's words or reason as being independent of the person who speaks or thinks, for Tertullian they were numerically separable from the person in a tangible sense. Whatever was said to have emanated from God must be understood in the materialist sense—it had its own body, discernably and distinctly different. Because the Word proceeded from God, it was like God. But because it had no corporeal existence before God spoke, it was second in power and authority to God the Father. Thus, according to Tertullian, the Word was not in the beginning.

---

[9] "Stoicism." Standford Encyclopedia of Philosophy. Last modified April 15, 1996. https://plato.stanford.edu/entries/stoicism/.

Do you then, (you ask,) grant that the Word is a certain substance, constructed by the Spirit and the communication of Wisdom? Certainly I do. But you will not allow Him to be a really substantive being, by having a substance of His own; in such a way that He may be regarded as an objective thing and a person, and so be able (as being constituted second to God the Father,) to make two, the Father and the Son, God and the Word...How could He who is empty have made things which are solid, and He who is void have made things which are full, and He who is incorporeal have made things which have body?...For who will deny that God is a body...and while I recognize the Son, I assert His distinction as second to the Father.[10]

Here Tertullian distinguishes emphatically between Father and Son, God and Word. He takes issue with Praxeas' apparent claim that the Father and Son are not distinguishable concerning their substantive identity. "You will not allow Him to be really substantive being, by having a substance of His own." The accusation against Praxeas also illustrates the Stoic influence on Tertullian's thought. To a Stoic, everything *must* be made of its own substance, have its own form, possess its own body. "How could He who is empty have made things which are solid...He who is incorporeal have made things which have body?" In this way, Tertullian's Stoicism remained intact insofar as his theology was concerned, his comments about the danger of merging Athens and Jerusalem notwithstanding.

Tertullian's later assertion, "For who will deny that God is a body?" was especially foreign to the doctrine of the early Christians. The principle that "God is a Spirit"[11] informed the early church's understanding of the nature of God. While Tertullian believed that all spirits must possess a body in some form, it was not part of early church doctrine. For the Jews and the early Christians, God was omnipresent and not at all constrained by human reason.[12] Thus, even Tertullian's statement, "God is

---

[10] Tertullian, *Against Praxeas*, (Ch. VII).
[11] John 4:24.
[12] Jeremiah 23:24.

rational" in chapter five of *Against Praxeas*, was not necessarily consistent with early church doctrine. Rationality as a presupposed characteristic of God complicates the definition of rationality itself. For if God is said to be omnipresent, then omnipresence is the rational thing, not the Stoic view. Thus, while the principle of omnipresence may have seemed irrational to Tertullian, it was not inconsistent with early Christian interpretations of the Scriptures. However, Tertullian's assertion that the Son was subordinate to the Father in authority is more critical to our discussion. Although most trinitarian Christians no longer share this position, it was popular among universalists in Tertullian's time because the only other option was something like that of the Monarchians, a group that Tertullian despised.

> So it is either the Father or the Son, and the day is not the same as the night; nor is the Father the same as the Son, in such a way that Both of them should be One, and One or the Other should be Both—an opinion which the most conceited "Monarchians" maintain.[13]

While it is impossible to know with certainty what, precisely, the Monarchians believed in totality, it can be assumed from the writings of Tertullian that they were probably something akin to the those that Justin wrote about in his *Dialogue with Trypho*.[14] By Tertullian's own admission, the Monarchians claimed that the Father and Son were one (or both) and not as divisible in identity as Tertullian claimed. Such a belief is not necessarily incompatible with the writings of the New Testament, which include similar statements about Christ and His relationship to the Father.

> Philip saith unto him, Lord, shew us the Father, and it sufficeth us. Jesus saith unto him, Have I been so long time with you, and yet thou hast not known me, Philip? he that hath seen me hath seen the Father; and how sayest thou then, Shew us the Father? Believest thou not that I am in the Father, and the Father in me? the words that I speak unto you I speak not

---

[13] Tertullian, Against *Praxeas*, (Ch. X).
[14] Justin Martyr, *Dialogue with Trypho* (Ch. XXVIII).

of myself: but the Father that dwelleth in me, he doeth the works. Believe me that I am in the Father, and the Father in me...[15]

While the New Testament speaks of Jesus Christ as having a Father in heaven, it also refers to Him frequently as being one with the Father,[16] the express image of God,[17] and even the creator.[18] For the early Christians, Father and Son language was generally understood in the context of a human Messiah's submission to God, not as two eternal persons of the Godhead. Early Christian soteriology depended heavily on the principle that when the Messiah came, He would be properly submissive, obedient, and faithful to God in a way that mankind had not been throughout history.[19] Even Christ's crucifixion signaled His submission to earthly and heavenly judgement, and His followers understood it to be a principle of spiritual salvation, not a distinction of persons in the Godhead. By being an obedient servant to God, Jesus restored mankind's relationship to God.[20] by becoming obedient to death, He overcame death.[21] The revelation that God was manifested in the flesh to do this for mankind was, in many ways, at the epicenter of early Christian theology.[22]

Yet, Jesus-as-man was no less a part of early Christian theology than Jesus-as-God. John the revelator recorded the words of Jesus,

I am Alpha and Omega, the beginning and the ending, saith the Lord, which is, and which was, and which is to come, the Almighty...I am he that liveth, and was dead; and, behold, I am alive forevermore, Amen; and have the keys of hell and of death.[23]

---

[15] John 14:8-10 (KJV).
[16] Ibid. (15).
[17] Hebrews 1:3.
[18] Colossians 1:15-16.
[19] Romans 5:12-21.
[20] Philippians 2:5-7.
[21] Philippians 2:8.
[22] 1st Timothy 3:16.
[23] Revelation 1:11;18 (KJV).

Thus, the principle is reasserted—the first Christians possessed a high Christology that did not conceive of a lower office for Jesus than the creator. Tertullian's objection to the high Christology of Praxeas and the Monarchians was primarily motivated by his training in Stoicism. For Tertullian, Stoicism was incompatible with the notion that God could be simultaneously in heaven and manifested in the form of a man in the earth at the same time. Corporeal theology required them to remain distinct in substantive ways. Because of the different perspective of Tertullian regarding the nature of God, he asserted that it was not God that was manifested in the flesh, but the Son of God—the second person—that was manifested in the flesh. In the mind of Tertullian, the Son of God was the first or second emanation of God in creation, and that emanation could not be equated with the Father. Furthermore, according to Tertullian, God the Father did not participate in creation by Himself as the prophets claimed.

> ...and God also said, "Let there be lights (in the firmament); and so God made a greater and a lesser light." But all the rest of the created things did He in like manner make, who made the former ones—I mean the Word of God, "through whom all things were made, and without whom nothing was made." John 1:3 Now if He too is God...then you have two Beings—One that commands the thing to be made, and the Other that executes the order and creates.[24]

Although translation may have played a part in the error, it is worth noting at this juncture in Tertullian's polemic against Praxeas that he misquoted John 1:3, which does not say, "Through whom all things were made," but says, "All things were made by him." The words "through" and "by" are the operative terms here. Although they are quaint differences, they do present an important problem for Tertullian's argument. Colossians situates Jesus squarely in the context of the creator, and the Hebrew Bible does not appear to allow for the possibility that God had help in the creation narrative.

---

[24] Tertullian, *Against Praxeas*, (Ch. XII).

Thus saith the LORD, thy redeemer, and he that formed thee from the womb, I am the LORD that maketh all things; that stretched forth the heavens alone; that spread abroad the earth by myself;[25]

Tertullian presented Jesus as the second-in-command during the creation narrative because it was the only way to reconcile Stoicism with the book of Colossians. The early Christian's presentation of high Christology confounded Greek philosophy because it backed the materialists into an ideological corner. They either had to admit that the framework through which they were interpreting the Bible was wrong or try to rework portions of the Bible into something more compatible with corporeal theology. How could God be "here" and "there" simultaneously? If Jesus is referred to as the creator, then in what meaningful way was He separable from the Father?

...Is there any God beside me? yea there is no God; I know not any.[26]

The most repeated argument made against Praxeas in Tertullian's polemic is the disputation over the use of Father and Son language in the New Testament. According to Tertullian, Praxeas had committed himself to heresy by embracing only Jesus, and not the Father also.[27] There is some irony to the dispute, as it was the New Testament writers who assured the churches that those who embraced Jesus as the Son of God had the Father also.[28] Nevertheless, the arguments between Tertullian and Praxeas laid the groundwork for what would eventually turn into a completely codified doctrine of God by the universal movement, but not for another two centuries. By the second century, there was a

---

[25] Isaiah 44:24 (KJV).
[26] Isaiah 44:8 (KV).
[27] Tertullian, *Against Praxeas*, (Ch. XI).
[28] 1st John 2:23.

pronounced difference between those who described themselves as universalists and those who identified more with the traditional Judaean movement. Recall from our last chapter that Justin Martyr detailed a neo-model of water baptism that included three distinct titles by which the universalists could describe God. Justin's method differed from the model followed by the Monarchians and Praxeas, who continued to water baptize according to the more traditional manner—in the name of Jesus Christ. The rise of trinitarian theology made its earliest encroachment on traditional Christian doctrine through the alterations made to the formula of water baptism. There is no record of a three-fold formula being used by the early Christians insofar as the New Testament is concerned. When Jesus gave the command to His disciples that they ought to baptize people in the name of the Father, and of the Son, and of the Holy Ghost, they responded by baptizing converts in the name of Jesus Christ, lending credibility to the notion that early Christians did not interpret the words of Jesus in a way that observed three individual identities in the Godhead. The Judaean movement believed the Father, Son, and Spirit, were all disclosed in the person of Jesus Christ. In this way, they could write with the high Christology of Colossians while still acknowledging the humanity of the Messiah.

For in him dwelleth all the fulness of the Godhead bodily.[29]

Tertullian's closing chapter in *Against Praxeas* seems to suggest that the connection of the Monarchians and Praxeas to the Judaean movement was a greater issue for the universalists than has been historically assumed. The desire to create an eclectic Christian character that could assume the form of Greek culture necessarily required that the universalists push Christianity away from Judaea. To what extent Tertullian believed Praxeas was too connected to the Jewish root comes out in chapter thirty-one of his polemic.

---

[29] Colossians 2:9 (KJV).

But, (this doctrine of yours bears a likeness) to the Jewish faith, of which this is the substance—so to believe in One God as to refuse to reckon the Son besides Him, and after the Son the Spirit. Now, what difference would there be between us and them, if there were not this distinction which you are for breaking down? What need would there be of the gospel...if thenceforward the Father, the Son, and the Spirit are not both believed in as Three and as making One Only God?[30]

For Tertullian, the doctrine of the trinity ought to have been the signal difference between Jewish and Christian conceptions of God. But it was not the greatest point of distinction between Jews and Christians in the first century. Early Christians continued to worship alongside the Jews long after the resurrection of Jesus Christ. Though unlike the Jews, the Christians believed that Jesus was the Messiah, they did not deny that God was one. The first Christians presented Jesus Christ in a manner that was consonant with the oneness of God. By contrast, the universalist model was not compatible with Jewish beliefs about God. Tertullian accused Praxeas of adopting a likeness to the Jewish faith in his beliefs by his rejection of a distinction between the three persons of God. Tertullian's accusation reveals a major shift in gentile Christian thought in the second century.

Christians in the first century identified Jesus Christ as the God of Israel revealed in the flesh. Although their faith in Jesus as the Messiah put them at odds with the unbelieving Jews, they did not present their beliefs in a way that disassociated them from their Jewish roots completely. In fact, quite the opposite was the case. Even gentile Christians were encouraged by the apostles to interpret their faith in Christ through the lens of the Hebrew Bible, which was the source of monotheism in the Near East.

Moreover, brethren, I would not that ye should be ignorant, how that all our fathers were under the cloud, and all passed through the sea; And were all baptized unto Moses in the cloud and in the sea; And did all eat the same spiritual meat;

---

[30] Tertullian, *Against Praxeas*, (Ch. XXXI).

And did all drink the same spiritual drink: for they drank of that spiritual Rock that followed them: and that Rock was Christ. But with many of them God was not well pleased: for they were overthrown in the wilderness. Now these things were our examples, to the intent we should not lust after evil things, as they also lusted.[31]

The early Christians actively sought association with—not divorce from—the Jews. In his first letter to the Corinthian Church, the Apostle Paul used the Exodus story to illustrate New Testament principles with which his audience was familiar. He equated the crossing of the Red Sea[32] with water baptism. He called the rock from which they drank in the wilderness "Christ."[33] Thus, Paul built an indivisible relationship between the covenant of the Jews and that of the Christians. Another passage in the book of Galatians articulates a more explicit example of the interconnected nature of the covenant between the two groups.

For ye are all the children of God by faith in Christ Jesus. For as many of you as have been baptized into Christ have put on Christ. There is neither Jew nor Greek, there is neither bond nor free, there is neither male nor female: for ye are all one in Christ Jesus. And if ye be Christ's, then are ye Abraham's seed, and heirs according to the promise.[34]

In a single passage Paul unified all in Christ (neither Jew nor Greek), yet associated those who were in Christ with "Abraham's

---

[31] 1st Corinthians 10:1-6 (KJV).

[32] Although translated as "Red Sea" in the King James Version of the Bible, giving the sea its more popular historical name, Paleo-Hebrew called it the "Sea of Reeds." The change likely happened because there is no clear translation of the "ee" from the original. For more on this, see Joseph Telushkin's *Jewish Literacy*, p. 50-51.

[33] This is probably a reference to the twentieth chapter of the book of Numbers, which tells the story of Moses' disobedience against God for smiting the rock that he was told to speak to instead. God told Moses that if he lifted his rod and spoke to the rock, it would give water to the people so that they could drink while in the wilderness. But when Moses took the rod in his hand, he rebuked the people, and smote the rock twice with his rod instead. The water still came forth so the people could drink, but Moses was barred from leading the Israelites into Canaan for his behavior.

[34] Galatians 3:26-29 (KJV).

seed" as well, calling them heirs according to that promise. According to the Hebrew Bible, Abraham was the first Jew and the patriarch of the Jewish faith.[35] He was the first man to obey the commandment to be circumcised,[36] and his children in Isaac became the Israelites—the chosen people of God. Paul's decision to link the chosen-ness of Abraham with all who were in Christ— Jew and Greek alike—was associative, not dissociative. In other words, Paul's writing did not diminish the Christian relationship to the Jews or the Hebrew Bible—it bolstered it. If Christianity were intended to be a novel departure from the doctrine of the Hebrew Bible, it would not have been prudent for Paul to use the Jewish Scriptures to inform his teaching. The importance of the Hebrew background of the Christian faith was not a novelty in the New Testament. It was one of the most frequent themes used by New Testament writers. The high emphasis of the oneness of God in the Hebrew Bible does not appear to have been a point of confusion or debate for the early Christians. There are no disputes over the trinity anywhere in the writings of the New Testament. Had the early Christians intended to articulate a new conception of the nature of God that distanced them from the Jews *specifically* in a meaningful way, there is little doubt that it would have appeared somewhere in the writings of the first century. Furthermore, the fact that the early Christians baptized exclusively in the name of Jesus Christ only serves to emphasize the point that the oneness of God was not a significant area of dispute in the early church. God is referred to as the Holy One more than fifty times throughout the Old and New Testaments. The phrases "Holy three," "God is three," or, "three persons of God," are not used even once.

The highest point of distinction between early Christian theology and Jewish theology was not over whether God was one or three persons. The great controversy of the first century was whether Jesus was the Christ of God or not. The two debates were not the same, and Tertullian's claim that the trinity was the primary point of controversy between Christians and Jews is, at best, misguided. Tertullian was the first of the ancient writers to

---

35 Genesis 12:1-3.
36 Genesis 17:1-14.

use the term "trinity" to describe God.[37] This fact complicates his claim that the early Christians necessarily associated themselves with trinitarian theology. How could they have embraced a doctrine that had not even been articulated yet?

> It was Tertullian who first used the word "Trinity" and introduced the terms *substantia* and *persona* to describe the interrelation of the three persons of the Trinity. With Origen, and later Athanasius, he was a pioneer in paving the way for the Church's conceptions of the Trinity, even though he did not succeed in avoiding subordinationism.[38]

Without Stoicism to inform greater Christian theology, it is unnecessary to conceive of God in three bodies (persons) in the corporeal sense. Because the early Christians were averse to the influence of philosophy on Christian doctrine, it makes sense that the trinitarian conception of God did not appear in the early writings, even among the heretics. It took generations of ideological distance from Judaea and time spent away from the Jewish root to begin redefining the nature of God in a way that was more compatible with Hellenic thought. A conception of Christianity that specifically avoided dependence on the Jewish tradition was required to achieve a coherent trinitarian doctrine. On this point, Tertullian was correct: The Jewish claim that God is one is not compatible with trinitarian thought.

Another point of interest in Tertullian's closing remarks to Praxeas is the question, "What need would there be of the gospel...if thenceforward the Father, the Son, and the Spirit are not both believed in as Three and as making One Only God?" Tertullian seemed to suggest that the high point of the gospel was the revelation of the three-fold nature of God. If this was his intent, Tertullian once again put himself at odds with the early

---

[37] Tertullian, *Against Praxeas*, (Ch. IV).
[38] Ibid. (2) (p. 127).

Christians. Faith in Christ, repentance from old deeds, water baptism, and being filled with the Holy Ghost were all acts performed by Christians, not for a greater revelation of the nature of God, but for the salvation of the soul and freedom from the curse of sin. Tertullian's belief that the gospel is useless without the doctrine of the trinity is, perhaps, the most philosophical approach to the Bible in all his work.

Ironically, Tertullian's doctrine was determined to be heretical by later trinitarian thinkers because his subordination of Son to Father associated him with the doctrine of Arius. Arius was condemned by the First Council of Nicaea for claiming that Jesus was less than God, but more than man.[39] Tertullian also struggled to define the personhood of the Holy Spirit, something that was probably complicated by the fact that the New Testament writers did not distinguish between the Spirit of God and the Spirit of Christ in their writings. For example, in the book of Romans, Paul used the terms interchangeably to describe the Holy Spirit that resides within the Christian believer.

> So then they that are in the flesh cannot please God. But ye are not in the flesh, but in the Spirit, if so be that the Spirit of God dwell in you. Now if any man have not the Spirit of Christ, he is none of his. And if Christ be in you, the body is dead because of sin; but the Spirit is life because of righteousness. But if the Spirit of him that raised up Jesus from the dead dwell in you, he that raised up Christ from the dead shall also quicken your mortal bodies by his Spirit that dwelleth in you.[40]

Herein is one of the best examples of the early church's beliefs about the nature of the Spirit of God. At the outset of the passage, Paul referred to the Spirit as "the Spirit of God," saying that it is the Spirit that dwells within the Christian believer. Yet not more than a line passes before Paul called it "the Spirit of Christ" residing in the Christian as well, thus equating the two as one and the same. Going still further, Paul said that it was actually Christ Himself that dwelled in the Christian ("if Christ be in you"), and

---

[39] Ibid. (4) (p. 62).
[40] Romans 8:8-11 (KJV).

so it may rightly be said that Christ was both Spirit and flesh from the Judaean movement's perspective. Moving forward in the passage, Paul used yet another term—"the Spirit of him that raised up Jesus"—to describe He who lives in the Christian.

Taken at face value, early Christians either believed that three or four spirits resided in believers, or they understood that the Holy Spirit was not distinguishable from Christ or the Father in any meaningful way. Nominally perhaps, but no more. Given Paul's method of using the terms interchangeably, it is not surprising that Tertullian struggled to determine whether or not the Spirit as "the third person" of the trinity proceeded from the Father or the Son. Corporeal theology required that each possess their own body, distinguishable in substance from the others. The Stoic belief is, of course, not compatible with the eighth chapter of Romans, so it was likely inevitable that Tertullian came to the conclusions that he did.

> Tertullian admitted that Praxeas and his followers...considered themselves to possess the "pure truth." They thought that one could not believe "in only one God in any other way than by saying that the Father, the Son, and the Holy Ghost are the very selfsame Person." Tertullian, a disciple of Justin, could not accept that. He maintained a doctrine of derivation and subordination concerning the Son and the Holy Ghost: "The Son I derive from no other source but from the substance of the Father. The Spirit is third from God and the Son."[41]

Athens and Jerusalem found their fullest expression in the writings of the man who asked the question at the opening of our chapter, "What indeed has Athens to do with Jerusalem?" Modern historians consider Tertullian to be the founder of occidental theology,[42] largely due to the fact that although his articulation of

---

[41] Ibid. (4) (p. 61-62).
[42] Ibid. (2) (p. 127).

the trinity was rejected in the centuries following his death, he was the first to articulate a trinitarian doctrine that opposed the Judaean tradition. His writings mark one of the most significant breaks between the universal movement with the early Christians. Although he was never more than a presbyter during his lifetime, his writings became a line of demarcation between the old and new world theology. The universalist movement owed a great deal to the polemics of Tertullian. Sadly, one of those polemics also galvanized negative Christian sentiment toward the Jews, contributing to gentile anti-Semitism in future generations of the universalist movement. Tertullian taught that the *nova lex* (new law) served to set the gentiles as the replacement for the Jews as God's chosen people.[43] This was one of the earliest written expressions of replacement theology by a Christian. Replacement theologies vary, but they all teach that God cast off the Jews in the first century and replaced them with the gentiles. The earliest form of the doctrine was likely motivated by many socio-political factors of the first century surrounding the Judaean province that have been discussed in earlier portions of this book. In the second and third centuries, negative Christian attitudes toward the Jews became much more pronounced.

Replacement theology was not entirely novel for the first-century Christians, particularly in Rome. The Apostle Paul wrote to the church in Rome extensively about the issue, condemning the practice as antithetical to Christianity itself.

> I say then, Hath God cast away his people? God forbid. For I also am an Israelite, of the seed of Abraham, of the tribe of Benjamin. God hath not cast away his people which he foreknew...I say then, Have they stumbled that they should fall? God forbid: but rather through their fall salvation is come unto the Gentiles, for to provoke them to jealousy. Now if the fall of them be the riches of the world, and the diminishing of them the riches of the Gentiles; how much more their fulness? For I speak to you Gentiles, inasmuch as I am the apostle of the Gentiles, I magnify mine office: If by any means I may

---

43 Tertullian, *Against the Jews*, (Ch. III).

provoke to emulation them which are my flesh, and might save some of them. For if the casting away of them be the reconciling of the world, what shall the receiving of them be, but life from the dead? For if the firstfruit be holy, the lump is also holy: and if the root be holy, so are the branches. And if some of the branches be broken off, and thou, being a wild olive tree, wert grafted in among them, and with them partakest of the root and fatness of the olive tree; Boast not against the branches. But if thou boast, thou bearest not the root, but the root thee. Thou wilt say then, The branches were broken off, that I might be grafted in. Well; because of unbelief they were broken off, and thou standest by faith. Be not highminded but fear: For if God spared not the natural branches, take heed lest he also spare not thee.[44]

Whatever happened to the church in Rome that caused Paul to bring up the issue in his epistle to them cannot be known with certainty. But it is apparent from Paul's letter that he took the issue of replacement theology seriously. In total, the topic spans more than three chapters of his epistle.[45] Our excerpt specifically condemns remarks like those made by Tertullian in his *Against the Jews*. Namely, it dismisses the claim that God cast off the Israelites and that the gentile Christians were the new Israel. "Hath God cast away his people? God forbid. For I also am an Israelite, of the seed of Abraham, of the tribe of Benjamin." For Paul, his place as an apostle to the church was proof enough that God had not cast off the Jews as a people at all. Afterall, it was a Jew who was writing to the church in Rome. As concerns the church, all the first Christians were Jews. Tertullian's claim that the Christians were a replacement for the Jews is not consistent with history—the Jews were the first Christians. Christianity did not begin as a gentile movement. In fact, there is no evidence to

---

[44] Romans 11:11-21 (KJV).
[45] The ninth, tenth, and eleventh chapters of the book of Romans all deal specifically with Paul's affection for his brethren in the flesh (the Israelites) and his desire that Christians show kindness and benevolence toward them. His hope is that in emulating Christ, they might lead the unbelieving Jews to Christ.

suggest that there were any gentile Christians during the first decade of the movement.[46]

Concerning the unbelieving Jews, Paul did not appear to allow for the possibility that God had cast them away in the sense that Tertullian claimed either. From Paul's perspective, the gentile Christians were like wild olive branches, grafted into a vine that they did not originally belong to. The purpose of their grafting in was to provoke the natural branches (the Jews) to jealousy so that the natural branches might be restored to the vine. Although Paul emphasized that the unbelieving Jews needed Christ, it was not for Christians to boast themselves above the Jews.

> Thou wilt say then, The branches were broken off, that I might be grafted in. Well; because of unbelief they were broken off, and thou standest by faith. Be not highminded but fear: For if God spared not the natural branches, take heed lest he also spare not thee.[47]

The Pauline perspective on replacement theology situated it as a sinful mindset that was not coherent with Christian doctrine. "Be not highminded but fear: For if God spared not the natural branches, take heed lest he also spare not thee." According to Paul, it was the responsibility of the Christians to lead the Jews to Christ through compassion and love and not to become arrogant in their own election to grace. In fact, Paul seemed to suggest that the restoration of natural Israel would signal an even greater moment in the history of the world.

> Now if the fall of them be the riches of the world, and the diminishing of them the riches of the Gentiles; how much more their fulness?[48]

---

[46] The tenth chapter of the book of Acts is the first recorded instance of a gentile convert to Christianity.

[47] Romans 11:19-21 (KJV).

[48] Romans 11:12 (KJV).

In perhaps his most astounding assertion, Paul went even further to suggest that God would preserve Israel in such a way that placed them in the grace of God above any measure seen in other nations.

> For I would not, brethren, that ye should be ignorant of this mystery, lest ye should be wise in your own conceits; that blindness in part is happened to Israel, until the fulness of the Gentiles be come in. And so all Israel shall be saved: as it is written, There shall come out of Sion the Deliverer, and shall turn away ungodliness from Jacob: For this is my covenant unto them, when I shall take away their sins.[49]

Soteriological or eschatological debates notwithstanding, it is evident that Paul placed a high emphasis on the proper treatment of the Jews in the gentile communities. Paul referred to those who taught replacement theology as "wise in their own conceits." Tertullian's *Against the Jews* illustrates the culture-drift of the gentile church by the second century, at least where the universal movement was concerned. The relationship between unbelieving Jews and Christians had always been tense, but the early Christians believed it was their responsibility to be benevolent to the Jews, even in cases where the Christians were mistreated. Evidence of this is shown in Paul, one who had even been beaten and stoned by certain Jews,[50] yet continued to speak affectionately of his brethren in natural Israel.

> Brethren, my heart's desire and prayer to God for Israel is, that they might be saved.[51]

Anti-Semitism became much more pronounced in the universal movement in the centuries following the death of Tertullian. While there is no reason to believe that Tertullian would have

---

[49] Romans 11:25-27 (KJV).
[50] Acts 14:9.
[51] Romans 10:1 (KJV).

approved of abuses against the Jews, his work, wittingly or not, contributed to the dissolution of relations between the two groups. Tertullian's conception of the nature of God in *Against Praxeas* is related to his work in *Against the Jews* in many ways. Tertullian represented a generation of Christian thinkers that had no connection to their Judaean roots. By the time Tertullian was born, the Bar-Kokhba Revolt had been dismantled, and the land of Judaea was renamed Palestine. The greater culture of the Roman Empire was not favorable to the Jews, particularly where their relationship to Christianity was concerned. The fact that philosophy became the primary method of interpreting the Scriptures was likely an inevitable outgrowth of the greater culture in the empire. By the third century, persecution against Christianity would become reinvigorated to an intensity not seen since the time of Nero. Because Christianity was still understood by many to be a Judaean religion, a large part of the empire resented the Jews for bringing Christianity into existence. Recall that it was Tacitus writing in the second century who warned his readers of the Judaean origins of the most sinister of religions called Christianity.[52] The message that spiritual salvation could be (must be) obtained in the name of a Jewish rabbi from Nazareth named Jesus was, to say the least, revolting to the Roman authorities. The Christians were also hated for their radical approach to evangelism. They were known for converting Romans from the pagan cults and turning the religion of the empire on its head. The cults were powerful political entities in the Roman Empire, and the weakening of their influence in the eyes of the public was not met without resistance.

Tertullian's writings became useful to the universal movement over the next two centuries. A great deal of work would be done to redefine Christianity in terms more compatible with the Greco-Roman world. The doctrine of the trinity would eventually become the centerpiece around which the movement could unify. But in the second century, the universal movement still did not have the hearts of the greater Christian population. Many continued to baptize in the name of Jesus Christ,

---

[52] Tacitus, *Annals*, Book XV.

acknowledge the oneness of God, and abstain from the influence of Greek philosophy. Although the influence of the Apologists and writers such as Tertullian became more pronounced during this period, they were not the authoritative body of Christian thought as is sometimes assumed. That power remained in the hands of the bishops and overseers of the local assemblies. The localized distribution of power where church authority was concerned served to isolate heresies and factionalism in the church where it could not be eradicated completely. Although the Catholics (universalists), Monarchians, Montanists, and Patripassians continued to write polemics against one another, dispute in public, and organize their own movements, the church at large remained relatively stable. Even in the first century, there arose heretics and factionalists that the apostles warned the church to isolate from and not have fellowship with.[53] But their existence did not stop the majority of Christians from growing in number and influence.

The decentralized approach to Christian leadership would change in the generation following the persecution of Diocletian. The drastic shift in church authority created the catalyst for what became one of the most influential religious movements in the history of the world.

---

[53] 2nd Timothy 4:14 refers to one named Alexander the coppersmith of whom Paul warned Timothy to have no fellowship with, because he greatly resisted the words of the preachers. Revelation 2:6 references a group known as the Nicolaitans, whose doctrine Jesus hated.

# CHAPTER IX

## Persecution

&

## The Tetrarchy

Recall from chapter six that during the first eighty years of the third century, the crown of the Roman Empire changed hands more than twenty-six times. Barry Strauss, Professor of History and Classics at Cornell University, has posited that the number was probably much higher.[1] This period of instability was characterized by special interest groups vying for power through the vehicle of the Roman military. Many of the emperors who came to power during the run of twenty-six were generals, warriors, or prefects of the Praetorian Guard. In this way, the crown became more abstract than in generations past. Divine right did not exist in this era. Much like the situation following the death of Alexander the Great, the crown belonged to the strongest. Because "the strongest" was a fluid concept in the empire at the turn of the third century, this meant that when leaders were deemed "emperor" by the men that followed them, it amounted to little more than a vote of confidence to be the next captain of their team. But the status-quo of instability changed with the rise of one of Rome's most influential emperors, Diocletian.

Diocletian was born on December 22 around 240 C.E in Dalmatia.[2] His birth name was Diocles, Greek for "Glory of Zeus."[3]

---

[1] Strauss, Barry S. *Ten Caesars*. New York: Simon & Schuster, 2019. (p. 268).
[2] Grant, Michael. *The Roman Emperors*. New York: Simon & Schuster, 1985. (p. 203).
[3] Ibid. (1) (p. 264).

Diocletian came from a poor family and worked his way up through the military ranks to become one of the most respected commanders of his time. When he succeeded Numerian in 284 C.E., he had witnessed dozens of men attempt to seize control of the throne. Knowing that his reign, too, would likely be short-lived if he did not work to change the situation, Diocletian did something that no ruler before him had ever done. He named three co-rulers and set each one up as a localized authority between the East and West sides of the Roman Empire.

Diocletian restructured the empire with two primary rulers known as the Augusti and two lower-level leaders to assist them, known as the Caesars. This four-man structure became known as the tetrarchy ("rule by four"). It consisted of Diocletian and Maximian ruling as the two Augusti, with Galerius and Constantius as their Caesars. As each Augusti was assigned a Caesar for their region, Galerius served Diocletian in the East, while Constantius served Maximian in the West.[4] While the entire tetrarchy ultimately answered to Diocletian, each ruler played a significant role in reshaping the empire. All four members of the tetrarchy began life as poor peasants from the Balkans who proved their metal through service in the Roman military. The reign of these four men marked one of the most transitional periods in the history of the Roman Empire. They were also the conduits of the harshest persecution brought against the Christians since its inception in the Judaean province.

Restoring stability to the empire was not a simple task. Diocletian first had to restore faith in the institutions of the Roman Empire. This included obeisance to the gods whom many in Rome believed had been angered against them, causing much of their troubles. Diocletian called himself Iovius—Jupiter, the highest in the Roman pantheon. He gave his second Augustus, Maximian, the title of Hercules—the Roman iteration of the Greek Heracles. Just as Heracles was the son of Zeus to the Greeks, Hercules was the son of Jupiter to the Romans. The relationship illustrated a political tactic employed by Diocletian when he set up the tetrarchy. Maximian may have been an Augustus, but he was

---

[4] Ibid. (1) (p.270).

not equal to Diocletian. In the end, Jupiter was in charge. The titles were not arbitrarily picked either. Diocletian's decision to name himself Jupiter situated his role squarely in the context of supreme control. Hercules was the offspring of Jupiter, but so were many of the gods of Rome. Thus, why Hercules was picked for Maximian is more complex than just his tangential relationship to Jupiter. Hercules was the god who acts—the hero whose twelve labors promised immortality if he could accomplish his task.[5] So was the life of Maximian. Success alongside Diocletian offered the promise that Maximian's name would be cemented in the sands of time as one of Rome's greatest rulers, perhaps even synonymized with the salvation of the empire itself.

> Following standard Roman procedure going back to Augustus, Diocletian used marriage to cement political relations. He had Maximian marry his daughter to the Caesar Constantius, who was required to divorce his wife and then also had Maximian adopt Constantius as his son. A soldier-statesman, Constantius spent a large part of his career on military campaigns, with little noticeable desire to leave the field as he got older. Meanwhile, Diocletian married his only child, Valeria, to the Caesar Galerius, whom he also adopted as his son...She and Galerius had a baby girl, who was promised in marriage to Maximian's son.[6]

It is evident from the strategic marriages that Diocletian set in order that he attempted to re-institute the right of the throne through primogeniture, something that had been lost during the battle royal for the crown in recent years. The marriages between Maximian's daughter and Constantius, as well as Diocletian's daughter and Galerius were established to ensure that, should anything happen to the Augusti, the alliances between the Caesars would remain strong through family ties. The move was probably intended to lower the possibility of another coup in the military

---

[5] "The Twelve Labors of Heracles." Mythology Unbound. Accessed November 15, 2021. https://press.rebus.community/mythologyunbound/chapter/the-twelve-labors-of-heracles/.
[6] Ibid. (1) (p. 271-272).

and bring more legitimacy to the leadership of Rome as well. Diocletian's co-rulers are worth brief examination, as the role they played in stabilizing the empire set up their successor, Constantine the Great, for one of the most significant political moves in world history.

It is not known where Maximian was born precisely, but historians suggest somewhere around Sirmium, roughly the same time as Diocletian.[7] The ancient historian Eutropius described Maximian as a thoroughly coarse, savage, brutal, impatient, and impossible man to deal with. Although it is entirely possible that Eutropius' description was embellished, other historical accounts do seem to suggest that Maximian was not a man of great compassion. When the persecution against Christians began, those under the authority of Maximian were considered some of the worst.

Maximian was a military man at his core. His humble upbringing in the Balkans meant that he had very little in the way of nostalgic ties to the traditions of Rome. It also meant that his elevation to god-like status was probably not unwelcome. The journey from peasant to demi-god was enough to create sycophants out of the greatest skeptics. One writer of the time-period described witnessing Maximian and Diocletian side by side this way:

> What a vision your piety granted when those who had been admitted into the palace at Milan to adore your sacred faces caught sight of you both, and your twinned godhead suddenly threw into confusion the customary practice of single veneration.[8]

Maximian's protégé and son-in-law was no less honored in his time. Constantius I Chlorus hailed from the Danubian region, and like Maximian, he was a military man all his life. In the early 280s,

---

[7] Ibid. (2) (p. 209).
[8] *Panegyrici Latini* (Manuscript XI).

he fathered his son Constantine through an inn-keeper named Helena, though whether the two were ever married or not is unclear.[9] He joined the tetrarchy in 293 C.E. and was considered the senior of the two Caesars. After the arranged marriage with Maximian's daughter, Constantius was adopted by Maximian and assumed all the rights and responsibilities that accompanied the adoption, including taking on the association with Hercules. He assumed leadership over the regions of Gaul and Britain, proving important to his legacy. For generations, rebellion in Britain had been a thorn in the Roman's side, and consolidation of that region would have marked a huge victory for the Roman Empire. That task was given to Constantius.

The province of Britain attempted secession from the Roman Empire under Carausius. The movement passed to his successor Allectus who waged war with Constantius in 296 C.E.[10] Constantius crossed the British Sea (known today as the English Channel) and destroyed what remained of the British rebellion, cementing his legacy as one of Rome's greatest generals. Gold medallions still exist today that were minted by Constantius to commemorate his signature military victory in Britain. Inscriptions on the medallions become important to our discussion in this book.

> On one such piece, inscribed 'the Dutifulness of the Emperors'...Constantius, wearing the lionskin of Hercules, depicts himself offering his hand to a kneeling Britannia, while Victory places a crown on his head. An even larger medallion, bearing the inscription 'Restorer of Eternal Light' (REDDITOR LVCIS AETERNAE), shows the Caesar riding up to a city wall, in front of which a suppliant kneels; while a warship appears in waters nearby. The city is identified as LON (*dinium*).[11]

---

[9] Ibid (2) (p. 216).
[10] "Allectus: Roman Administrator." Britannica. Accessed November 15, 2021. https://www.britannica.com/biography/Allectus.
[11] Ibid. (2) (p. 217).

*Figure 9.1*

*Known as the Arras Medallion, this coin illustrates some of the earliest associations of the family of Constantine I the Great with the cult of light in the Roman Empire.[12]*

The depiction of Constantius in the lionskin of Hercules while exalting him as the "Restorer of Eternal Light" is telling. First, it must be noted that Hercules possessed an ancillary relationship to the cult of light, as Hercules was the offspring of one of the gods often associated with light according to Greco-Roman tradition. But the phrase *"restorer* of eternal light" is important as well. In the late third century, conflict in Britain was interpreted as the woeful triumph of barbarians over the otherwise civilized Roman Empire. Constantius brought Britain back into alignment with Rome and, in this way, reintroduced the order into a region that had become chaotic by rebellion. Restoration of the light of Rome to the barbaric region of Britannia was the signature victory of Constantius during his lifetime. "Rome as the light" would be a reoccurring theme in the tetrarchy, as Constantius' co-Caesar also possessed an important connection to the cults.

Galerius was born around 250 C.E. in a village near Florentiana in Dacia Ripensis. Although he was only a Caesar during the reign of

---

12 "Roman Coins About Britain-Constantius Chlorus." Collecting Ancient Coins. Accessed November 15, 2021. https://collectingancientcoins.co.uk/roman-coins-about-britain-constantius-chlorus/.

Diocletian, Galerius would become one of the most critical players in the tetrarchy before his death.

Galerius served under Diocletian in the Eastern portion of the empire. Although he was technically the junior Caesar between himself and Constantius, geography favored Galerius' legacy. Between the Eastern and Western halves of the empire, the East was much wealthier, and it was situated in a better strategic position to ward off one of Rome's greatest threats in the third century—the Sasanian Empire.[13] The legacy of Galerius primarily hung on two major events of the third century: the defeat of the Sasanians, and the last great persecution against the Christians. Of the first event, it may be said that Galerius first failed, only to succeed in the end. Of the second, precisely the opposite was the case. Where he had success in the beginning, he was ultimately forced to withdraw.

After Galerius became Caesar following the formation of the tetrarchy in 293 C.E., he did not feel that his talents were being used to their full potential. After spending a couple of years on the Danube frontier, he finally got a chance to prove himself when the Sasanians invaded the Roman province of Syria in 296 C.E.[14] The invasion of the Persian forces was an opportunity for Galerius to stand out above Constantius as a military leader, but his quest to stop the Sasanian forces ultimately failed. There is a fairly humorous story associated with Galerius' defeat—historians claim that after he failed to drive out the Sasanians from Syria, he also managed to lose the entire province of Mesopotamia in the process. Because of the humiliation this brought to Diocletian, he forced Galerius to run beside his chariot for over a mile, clad in scarlet robes while the two entered the city of Antioch together.[15]

Galerius had the last laugh though. In 298 C.E., he reorganized his army from the Balkans and went after the Sasanians again, this time with much more success. He captured the Sasanian royal harem and marched as far south as Iraq. He was able to use the harem he had captured as leverage against the

---

[13] The Sasanian Empire was centered in what is now Iran. The Sasanians are sometimes referred to as the "neo-Persians" by modern historians.
[14] Ibid. (2) (p. 219-220).
[15] Ammianus Marcellinus, *History*, Book XIV (Ch. XI).

Sasanian forces. The Sasanians withdrew from the region, and Diocletian resumed control over the once lost territory.[16] Galerius managed to restore Diocletian's confidence in his co-ruler, and his victory over the Sasanian's contributed to his elevation to the status of Augustus later in life. Still, Galerius' legacy is remembered in a negative light by historians, primarily due to his instigation of the final persecution against the Christians in the Roman Empire.

What motivated Galerius' hatred of the Christians is debated, but the most likely answer is that there was more than one contributing factor. First, it must be remembered that the era of the tetrarchy was a tumultuous time for the empire. Inflation was high because of the devaluation of the currency. Many wars spanning across the empire's borders meant that it was the responsibility of the people to make sacrifices to the gods on behalf of the empire and the emperor for their safety and success.[17] Christians did not participate in ritual sacrifices of any kind, let alone those made to the pagan gods on behalf of the emperor. Their hesitancy displeased Diocletian, who saw Christianity's influence growing throughout the empire, particularly in the army. Historians estimate that at least ten percent of the empire was Christian by the time that Diocletian ruled—a very large number.[18] Still, had Diocletian been acting alone, it is unlikely that he would have pursued a policy of persecution against the Christians. Although he was a pagan, there is no record of any specific religious devotion on the part of Diocletian. His Caesar in the East, however, was different.

Galerius' mother was named Romula. According to ancient historians, she was a fervent participant in the pagan cults and worshipped the god called Mars.[19] In a tale similar to that of Caesar Augustus, Seleucus I Nicator, or Alexander the Great

---

[16] Ibid. (1) (p. 274).
[17] M. Tullius Cicero, *For Marcus Fonteius*, Book XIII (Ch. XXX).
[18] Ibid. (1) (p. 279-280).
[19] Lactantius, *On the Deaths of the Persecutors*, (Ch. XI).

before them, it is said that Romula was the consort of a serpent possessed by Mars, and Galerius was conceived in this relationship with the serpent. The tradition of powerful pagan kings having been conceived through divine possession of serpents and sexual relationships with women was a reoccurring myth in the ancient world. Its reappearance in the life of Galerius is essential to understanding the era of persecution.

Romula was an ardent pagan and likely held a great deal of influence in the various cults of Rome. Being the mother of a Caesar had its benefits. It was probably not coincidental that she situated Mars into her son's legacy. Mars was the Roman expression of Ares, the god of war.[20] Mars was not popular in Greek myth, but according to the Romans, he was second only to Jupiter himself, casting Galerius in a glorious position—second only to Diocletian. It is recorded that in addition to Romula's persuasiveness, the cult of Apollo also pressured Diocletian to begin a policy of persecution against the Christians. Interestingly, it is also said that the Platonists asked Galerius and Diocletian to persecute the Christians as well, something which will be addressed later.[21] Of Diocletian's decision to pressure the Christians to sacrifice to the pagan gods, Lactantius offers this account:

> The mother of Galerius, a woman exceedingly superstitious, was a votary of the gods of the mountains.[22] Being of such a character, she made sacrifices almost every day, and she feasted her servants on the meat offered to idols: but the Christians of her family would not partake of those entertainments; and while she feasted with the Gentiles, they continued in fasting and prayer. On this account she conceived ill-will against the Christians, and by woman-like complaints instigated her son, no less superstitious than

---

[20] "Gods and goddesses of the Greek and Roman pantheon." The British Museum. Last modified , 1942. Accessed November 16, 2021. https://blog.britishmuseum.org/gods-and-goddesses-of-the-greek-and-roman-pantheon/.

[21] Ibid. (2) (p. 220).

[22] The phrase "gods of the mountains" may have been a reference generally to Mount Olympus, the dwelling place of the Greek and Roman pantheon.

herself, to destroy them...He [Diocletian] resolved, therefore, to take the opinion of his friends...Yet not even then could the emperor be prevailed upon to yield his assent. He determined above all to consult the gods; and to that end he [dispatched] a soothsayer to inquire of Apollo at Miletus, whose answer [was] such as might be expected from an enemy of the divine religion. So Diocletian was drawn over from his purpose. But although he could struggle no longer against his friends, and against Caesar and Apollo, yet still he attempted to observe such moderation as to command the business to be carried through without bloodshed; Whereas Galerius would have had all persons burnt alive who refused to sacrifice.[23]

Not by coincidence did the cult of Apollo specifically want to see the Christians removed from the empire. Recall from earlier reading that Apollo was the god of light and divine truth. He was also known as the healer, and he who slays the serpent,[24] two attributes associated with Christ in the New Testament.[25]

Apollo at Delphi was a purely beneficent power, a direct link between gods and men, guiding men to know the divine will, showing them how to make peace with the gods; the purifier too, able to cleanse even those stained with the blood of their kindred.[26]

Much like the cult of Dionysus, the cult of Apollo took issue with the Christians because believers were apt to draw converts out of the cults into the gospel of Jesus Christ. According to Christian doctrine, Christ was the mediator between God and men, leading them to the knowledge of truth.

---

[23] Ibid. (19).

[24] Hamilton, Edith. *Mythology*. New York: Grand Central Publishing, 1942. (p. 25-26).

[25] Mark, the oldest of the gospel accounts, introduces Jesus as one who heals the sick and delivers the possessed (Mark 1:30-34). In the book of Revelation, Christ is associated with the power that casts the serpent known as Satan—the accuser of the brethren—out of the heavens, ushering in the kingdom of God (Revelation 12:7-10).

[26] Ibid (24) (p. 26-27).

> For there is one God, and one mediator between God and
> men, the man Christ Jesus.[27]

Christianity is also characterized by the belief that only the blood of Jesus can cleanse someone who has sinned;[28] thus, Apollo's role as "the purifier... able to cleanse even those stained with the blood of their kindred" was also challenged. Christianity offered eternal redemption of the soul as well, something that was not necessarily consistent with the beliefs of the cults. The oracles had immense political power in the Roman Empire, as was shown by Diocletian's decision to consult one before making his final decision concerning the persecution of the Christians. The cults stood to lose a great deal of influence, to say nothing of financial gain, if Christianity continued to grow. The fact that the oracle of Apollo sought out Christian persecution informs the great tension between the cult of light and the Christians of the third century. The exclusivity of the Christian religion was also a likely point of offense to the cults. Recall that Romula set meats offered to idols before her Christian family members, who then refused to eat.[29] Other pagans may not have taken issue with the meal, even if the meats were offered to gods that they did not worship. The religion of the pagans was much more eclectic and inclusive, open to broad interpretations, and not in conflict with other cults. By contrast, the Christians claimed that only the God of Israel ought to be worshipped, and they refused to acknowledge the existence, let alone the power, of other gods. This could only have served to anger the pagans, who saw the Christian way as divisive to their lifestyle.

The Christian message of eternal salvation and reconciliation with God resonated with pagan converts who heretofore had only known the gods through appeasement and sacrifice. In the Greek and Roman traditions, human beings were made for the toil of the gods, always subject to their ever-changing wills. Christianity

---

[27] 1st Timothy 2:5 (KJV).
[28] 1st John 1:9.
[29] In Acts 15:28-29, a council of believers met at Jerusalem to discuss how much of the Law of Moses ought to be placed upon the gentile Christians. Their determination was that they ought to abstain from meats offered to idols, from blood, from strangled things, and from fornication.

presented a new conception of God that did not demand appeasement but offered reconciliation with God through the death of Jesus Christ. His will was not ever-changing, and He did not wish any harm to His creation. That was new as well—His *creation*. Remember that in the Olympian pantheon, the gods were not all-powerful, and, in some cases, could be challenged and even defeated. Nor were the gods ever said to be creators—they were not the originators of the universe, only the forces that governed it. According to the Christians, it was the creator God that loved His creation so much that He was manifested in the flesh to save them from their sins. The idea that God was more concerned with ethical behavior than with sacrifice annoyed the Romans as well. For pagans, appeasement happened through oblations, not through obedience to a spiritual law. In light of all of this, it is not difficult to see why the cults worked through Romula, Galerius, and Diocletian to bring down the Christians. At nearly every level, Christianity threatened the pagan way of life.

It was not just the cults that wanted the Christians gone either. The philosophers apparently had enough of Christianity as well, culminating with pressure from the Platonists to silence the movement. Tensions between philosophical thought and traditional Judaean Christianity have been illustrated in earlier portions of this book, but the animosity of the Platonists, especially toward believers, is interesting. Recall that Justin Martyr considered himself a Platonist, so drawing ideological divisions between the two groups in the third century becomes complicated.

Some Christians were sympathetic to philosophy, and those believers found their fullest expression in the universalist movement mentioned by writers such as Justin, Ignatius, and Tertullian. But those Christians were also at odds with other believers who did not embrace philosophy, typified by men such as Praxeas or the Monarchians. Because most Christians at the time still rejected the universal movement that advocated for changing the baptismal formula and distancing Christianity from Judaea, schools of philosophy such as the Platonists rejected Christianity, and believers experienced great persecution. When the dust settled, one of these Christian groups would rise to prominence in the Roman Empire, ending the persecution and reframing Christianity's relationship to the empire forever.

Christianity was also an affront to the emperors as individuals, and this is important to our discussion too. Diocletian synonymized himself with Jupiter, Maximian with Hercules, Constantius with Sol Invictus,[30] and Galerius with Mars. They demanded that the Christians sacrifice to the gods and, by extension, the emperors, on pain of death. When the Christians refused, their houses of worship were torn down, holy books confiscated, and in some cases they were sent to the flames to be burned.

> A series of orders proclaimed in 303 and 304 formed what Christians called the Great Persecution. The first orders targeted clergy as well as Christians in high office. Then the regime turned on ordinary Christians as well and demanded that they sacrifice to the pagan gods. Churches were torn down and holy books confiscated. Diocletian was particularly interested in driving Christians from the army. According to a Christian source, the persecution began in winter 303 with the destruction of a Christian church in Nicomedia near Diocletian's palace. The writer accuses Galerius of then setting fire to Diocletian's palace and blaming Christians, in order to inflame the emperor's enthusiasm for persecution...A veteran named Julius with twenty-seven years of military service and seven campaigns behind him preferred to be executed rather than offer incense to the gods. Crispina, a wealthy mother with children who lived in what is today Algeria, also accepted execution rather than sacrifice. Bishop Felix, in what is now Tunisia, refused to turn over his holy books and so was executed at the age of fifty-six.[31]

---

[30] Sol Invictus was another iteration of the cult of light, which will be discussed at length later in this book.
[31] Ibid. (1) (p.280).

Sources differ on just how harsh each of the tetrarchs were in their campaigns against the Christians. Galerius is often regarded as the most brutal, but Maximian and Diocletian were also adamant about restoring the order of the pagan cults to the empire. Their acts against the Christians were no less severe. One ancient historian named Eusebius, who will be examined in detail throughout the following two chapters, records that Constantius was the least harsh of the persecutors, refusing even to tear down a Christian house of worship.[32] This claim is not necessarily consistent with modern research on the subject, as defiance to his superior (Maximian) would have likely resulted in Constantius' own execution.[33] The reason for Eusebius' generous portrayal of this tetrarch is likely related to Eusebius' relationship with Constantius' son, Constantine the Great. Other portions of Eusebius' writing suggest a severe bias against Galerius in particular and a desire to cast the family of Constantine in the most favorable light possible.

When Romula died, she was declared a goddess, and buried in a mausoleum that her son had especially constructed for her.[34] She would be forever remembered as a vehement opponent of Christianity and the spark that lit the fuse leading to The Great Persecution.

Diocletian for his part enjoyed an early retirement, something no other emperor had ever done before him. The political savvy shown by Diocletian—particularly for his time—is impressive. Before Diocletian came to power, the empire was unstable, the throne changing hands dozens of times in just a few short years. While all his reasons for early abdication cannot be known with

---

[32] Eusebius Pamphilus, *The Life of the Blessed Emperor Constantine*, Book I (Ch. XVI-XVII).
[33] Ibid. (1) (p. 281).
[34] Srejovic, Dragoslav, and Cedomir Vasic. *Imperial Mausolea and Consecration Memorials in Felix Romuliana*. Belgrade, CS: The University of Belgrad, 1994. (p. 149-151).

certainty, it seems evident from the way that Diocletian ruled that he always had stability and continuity in mind. His decision to break the empire up into smaller portions, at least as far as governance was concerned, ensured that no one of his co-rulers could consolidate too much authority over a vast swath of territory. He kept the tetrarchy busy fighting wars, knowing that idleness among the rulers would not work to his benefit. Eventually, someone would try to seize power just as the generations of rulers before him had done. Keeping the tetrarchy on the war path kept them busy, but it also gave each of them a sense of purpose and pride in ownership. Results still mattered to Diocletian, as shown by his humiliation of Galerius following his defeat by the Persians. But he was also careful not to impose too harsh a penalty for failure. Balance characterized Diocletian's approach to politics, and, in this way, he managed to keep power for over two decades, something no Caesar had done for at least a century.

Just as he had insisted on shared power among the rulers of the empire, Diocletian restructured the provinces in a similar fashion. He redrew the map of the empire into twelve districts of provinces known as dioceses, a term still used by the Catholic Church to describe their territorial structure.[35] When it came time for his retirement, Diocletian exercised forethought again by refusing to allow Maximian's son Maxentius to be elevated to the status of Caesar or Augustus. He also insisted that Maximian retire alongside him. Diocletian's decision reflected his own desire to restore legitimacy to the throne of the Roman Empire. Although Maxentius was Maximian's son, Galerius and Constantius had proven themselves worthy of becoming the next Augusti. Diocletian (and the rest of the tetrarchy, for that matter) understood the principle of earned rank. They were military men, not professional politicians. Divine right by birth was a valuable tool to have in the arsenal in case of another coup against the emperor, but it was not the primary method of succession. At least, not to Diocletian. His carefully crafted tetrarchy had ensured that when the Caesars were ready to take their place as

---

[35] Ibid. (1) (p. 275).

Augusti, their intermarriage with the children of the leaders who were stepping down would keep the peace in the case of a sibling rivalry. Furthermore, Diocletian likely favored Galerius in any case, as Galerius had served at his side since the beginning of the tetrarchy. Although Maximian protested, in the end Diocletian had his way. Galerius and Constantius would be the new Augusti. At the same time, the Caesars would be Flavius Severus and Maximinus Daia, two soldiers from the Balkans who had been elevated in status through military strength, much like the tetrarchy itself.

Although he managed to secure the succession he wanted to see in the empire while remaining unscathed, Diocletian's orderly transfer of power was short-lived. Unexpectedly, Constantius died on July 35, 306 C.E. The West needed a new Augustus, and old habits die hard. Rebellion broke out in the armies of Constantius, who wanted his son Constantine to be the new Augustus. To further complicate the problem, the Praetorian Guard rejected Diocletian's decision to keep Maxentius, son of Maximian, out of the line of succession. They named Maxentius their leader, threatening Galerius' leadership. Diocletian's pick for Caesar named Severus was killed trying to put down Maxentius' power play. All of the infighting also motivated Maximian to come out of retirement, eventually challenging his own son for power.

Constantine was, perhaps, the most patient of the group. Although his troops wanted to raise him to the level of Augustus, Constantine conferred with Galerius and submitted to his authority, claiming only for himself the title of Caesar of the West, with Galerius remaining as the legitimate Augustus in the East. The move proved to be exceptionally beneficial to Constantine, as it was the East that represented the future of the empire. Challenging Galerius could have been a disastrous move. Both men likely realized the significance of ruling from the East by this point, as the city of Rome was losing influence in the empire. Most of the power in Rome was concentrated in the Balkans and other major Eastern territories. Diocletian chose to rule from the East for precisely the same reason, and his foresight was not lost on Galerius or Constantine. As for Maximian, his beginning was greater than his end. Realizing he no longer had the support of his former co-rulers, Maximian abdicated for a second time. Likely believing that Maximian would take another shot at the throne if he got the chance, Constantine chose to act. In 310 C.E., he resolved the unrest with Maximian once and for all by forcing him to commit suicide.[36] By this point, the most senior of the legitimate leaders was Galerius. One of his final acts as Augustus was to appoint a man named Licinius as Augustus, replacing Maximian's role. After a chaotic and confusing transition, the new power structure consisted of Licinius, Maxentius, Daia, and Constantine. What resulted was a free-for-all power struggle culminating in Constantine and Licinius joining forces against Maxentius and Daia for supremacy.

Galerius is remembered as one of the harshest persecutors of Christians in Roman history. Yet, in a stunning turnabout of character, Galerius' last act before his death was to cease the persecution against the Christians and order that they be allowed to worship freely.

In 311 C.E., Galerius was in the final stages of what some historians believe to have been cancer.[37] During April of that year, Galerius laid on his deathbed in Nicomedia, ready to turn the empire over to his successors. But before doing so, he issued a decree known as the Edict of Serdica, which canceled all persecution against the Christians that Galerius had been largely responsible for inciting. The edict was conditional, stating that the Christians were free to worship if they entreated their own God for the well-being of the emperors and the state in addition to the church.

---

[36] Ibid. (1) (p. 283-284).
[37] Ibid. (2) (p. 221).

Galerius and his colleagues instructed their provincial governors to grant members of the Church freedom of worship and legal tolerance and recognition—including the right to assemble together for common worship. Various reasons have been sought for this momentous *volte-face* by Galerius...But the most plausible explanation is that Galerius himself knew that the persecutions had failed. Far from creating a unified state by destroying the autonomy of the Christians, they had hardened and strengthened their will to pursue their own beliefs and ways of life—to the detriment of national unity and harmony.[38]

For Galerius, persecution of the Christians was only valuable insomuch as it galvanized support for the cults and unified the empire around one religion. This would become the express goal of future emperors—that all of Rome be as one in their religious beliefs. But the persecution of the Christians achieved precisely the opposite of what Galerius intended. The public was sympathetic to the plight of the Christians, and Christian abuse had not done a great deal to appease the gods of Rome.[39]

Galerius' edict offering freedom of worship to the Christians was an acknowledgement of defeat, but it was also intended to set Constantine and his contemporaries up for success. A religiously fractured empire was not a long tenable situation, particularly when legally enforced persecution was part of the equation. The Edict of Serdica was as much about quieting the unrest at the bottom as at the top—the empire would not survive another coup. Although political persecution against Christians ceased after 311 C.E., Christianity was far from a unified force. The church lacked institutional legitimacy in the Roman Empire, and factionalism still raged inside the Christian movement itself. The tension between Christians and pagans remained high in the empire, as well as between Catholic and Monarchian, Montanist and Arian.

---

[38] Ibid (2) (p. 221-222).
[39] Galerius' illness was attributed by contemporary writers to the anger of the God of the Christians against him, or perhaps a triumph of the Christian God over the Roman gods. Furthermore, instability at the top of the Roman hierarchy only spelled doom for the system that Galerius and Diocletian had worked so hard to build.

From an institutional perspective, no one did more to further the unification of Christianity under a single banner than Galerius' famous successor, Constantine the Great. Although it would be another seventy years before an official codified version of the trinitarian statement would be put on paper, the rise of Constantine may be considered the first domino to fall in the line of the institutionalizing Christianity in Rome.

*Figure 9.2*

Two-piece porphyry statue of the tetrarchs located on
the corner of the façade of St. Mark's Basilica, Venice, Italy.

As the reader may recall from the introduction of this book, the tetrarchy discussed in this chapter can be seen today on the corner façade of St. Mark's Basilica in Venice. The statue depicts the Augusti, bearded, embracing the Caesars next to them, each adorned in armor. Yet the location of the statue could not seem more out of place.

All of the tetrarchs were persecutors of a religion that later enshrined them on the corner of one of their most prolific basilicas. The question may rightly be asked, how did Diocletian, Maximian, Constantius, and, above all, Galerius, end up being venerated on such an iconic Christian structure? The answer to that question begins in our next two chapters. Thus far in this book, we have examined the introduction of Hellenism to the Near East and how that influence impacted monotheism on an ideological basis. We have seen how wars, economics, and politics shaped Roman and Christian sentiment against the Jews and how Judaean Christianity was separated from the gentile Christianity. A large portion of gentile Christianity in the Roman Empire eventually came to be known as the universal, or "Catholic," movement. The division between Judaean Christianity and Catholic Christianity had two primary causes—the introduction of Hellenistic philosophy to Christian thought, and the political influence of the Roman Empire. Still, traditional Christianity flourished in this time-period. It was not erased completely. Christian leaders continued to baptize in Jesus' name and practice traditional Christian liturgy.

But the turn of the fourth century marked a monumental shift in Christianity. And that shift began with the subject of our next chapter, Constantine the Great.

# CHAPTER X

## Unconquered
## Constantine

Constantine the Great was traveling through Gaul[1] in 310 C.E. when he is said to have seen a vision in the sky that changed the western world forever. The accuracy of the events surrounding said vision has been debated by historians for centuries—even the claim that the vision happened at all. Nevertheless, fact or fiction, the vision became the basis for turning an empire on its head and recasting the religion of Rome into a new mold entirely. Recall from our previous chapter that the father of Constantine the Great was Constantius I Chlorus and that through his elevation to Caesar and later Augustus, he was associated with Hercules, son of Jupiter. Upon his conquest of Britain, Constantius was hailed as the "Restorer of Everlasting Light," likely an homage to his own worship of the sun god and a recognition that Constantius had returned the light of Rome back to the barbaric provinces.[2]

At Gaul in 310 C.E., Constantine the Great likely sought the favor of the gods during his campaign with the army. Constantine's father worshipped an iteration of the sun god known as Sol Invictus (the Unconquered Sun). In Gaul, this god was worshipped alongside Apollo, the god of light. It was common for emperors to seek the blessing of their favorite gods before a conquest, and Constantine's family was well connected to the cult of light. Given his father's previous success in Britannia, it made

---

[1] Ancient Gaul was primarily comprised of what is now France, as well as portions of Italy, Germany, and Belgium.
[2] Strauss, Barry S. *Ten Caesars*. New York: Simon & Schuster, 2019. (p. 294).

sense for Constantine to seek the blessing of the Unconquered Sun in his battles on the Rhine against the Germanic tribes.[3]

When he arrived at Gaul, it is said that Constantine saw a dramatic light around the sun, perhaps a solar halo.[4] Interpretations of what the light meant would become the subject of much debate in the centuries following his death. But in 310 C.E., Constantine took the vision as a sign from the gods that he would have victory over the barbarian tribes, and indeed, his triumph in Gaul and the frontier regions of the empire only served to confirm his suspicions that he was destined for greatness. Had the vision at Gaul remained entirely pagan, it is unlikely that it would have become the issue of debate that it did among historians. But after the death of Galerius, Constantine claimed that what he had seen in Gaul the year before was actually a Divine visitation from the Christian God. The result? Constantine had converted to Christianity at that moment and re-oriented the empire into a pro-Christian position. The incident near the temple of Apollo and the Unconquered Sun became the catalyst for the most radical shift in Roman culture and politics since the death of Julius Caesar—the Christianization of the Roman Empire.

Constantine the Great was born in Naissus,[5] likely on February 27, 273 C.E. He was educated in Latin literature and Greek philosophy at a young age, as nearly all of Rome's elite classes were at that time. As a young man, he served in Diocletian's court at the behest of his father, becoming one of the Augustus' most effective military commanders. Because his father ruled in the West while he lived in the East, Constantine served in Galerius' army and

---

[3] The Unconquered Sun was recognized as a god that promised victory in military action as early as the days of emperor Aurelian.
[4] Accounts of what, exactly, Constantine saw differ widely among historians. Eusebius claims that it was a trophy of a cross that appeared above the sun with the inscription, "conquer by this." Others associated the vision with a ring around the sun. The reason for this discrepancy is that the first known written account of Constantine's vision was not recorded until after his death, nearly thirty years after the supposed incident. For more on this, see Strauss (Ch. 10).
[5] Modern Serbia.

witnessed some of the most brutal persecutions against Christians that occurred during the era of the tetrarchy. Constantine, married once before, took the daughter of Maximian named Fausta as his second wife, likely an attempt shore up alliances with Maximian and his family in the West.

It is important to remember that the tetrarchy was fairly stable at this point in history. It was not until Diocletian decided to abdicate that internal conflict within the tetrarchy caused the rule-by-four system to fracture. When it became clear that Maxentius would be cut out of any future opportunity to rule, Maximian rebelled against Diocletian's plan, and the two worked together to consolidate power. Constantius was worried that Constantine would not be safe if he remained in the East with Galerius. The young man was recalled to the West where he would eventually take over as Caesar after his father's untimely death. The factionalism inside the royal families culminated with special interest wars between Constantine and Licinius against Maxentius and Daia. Each pair had support on both sides of the empire. Constantine remained in the West while Licinius was his ally in the East, but the situation was not long tenable. Daia was put down quickly, but Maxentius proved a more challenging opponent for Constantine and Licinius.

The death of Galerius further complicated the situation. Because of Diocletian's abdication, the disgrace of Maximian, and the death of Constantius, it was Galerius that inherited the office of most senior Augustus among the tetrarchs. He was the last surviving connection to Rome's great political reformation. In 311 C.E., his mantle was the ultimate prize among the four junior rulers. When Galerius died, he did something unexpected that shifted the rulers' priorities, particularly for Constantine and Maxentius. Galerius issued the Edict of Serdica before his passing, giving the Christians reprieve from persecution in the empire. This was the last official act of the Augustus, so it may be understood as a "last will and testament" of sorts. Thus, whoever wanted to be considered the legitimate successor of Galerius would have to imitate his policy toward the Christians in order to be well received by the public.

Galerius' edict resulted in Constantine, Maxentius, and Licinius all issuing proclamations favoring Christians in the empire, attempting to position themselves as the true connection to Galerius—the next in line for the throne. The most famous of these proclamations was the so-called Edict of Milan in 313 C.E., issued by Constantine. Interestingly, the Edict of Milan was neither an edict, nor was it issued by Constantine. Although it is commonly credited to Constantine that he issued the great proclamation giving Christianity the freedom to worship in Rome for the very first time, historical accounts say otherwise. The Edict of Serdica had already given Christians recognition in the empire and the freedom to worship, suggesting that the overall tone toward Christianity was shifting in the Roman public. Even Galerius—the most hateful toward Christians—understood that this was the case. Thus, by the time the Edict of Milan was issued, it was little more than lip service paid to the Christians. The so-called Edict of Milan was actually a letter issued by Licinius favoring Christians in the East, likely motivated by a desire to unify the East and West.[6]

The competition between Constantine and Maxentius for Galerius' mantle culminated at the Battle of the Milvian Bridge in 312 C.E. This was the final battle between the brothers in law to consolidate power in the West and become the sole ruler of Western Rome.

The battle actually took place not on the bridge but north of it, on land. By coincidence, Constantine's army marshaled just under the hill on which Livia's suburban villa had stood. By that point, Constantine had enjoyed a string of victories, and Maxentius was so worried that he buried his regalia of office on the Palatine Hill, where archaeologists discovered them in 2006. The prize find was Maxentius's scepter, the only

---

[6] Ibid. (2) (p. 299).

imperial scepter ever uncovered. Imperial scepters often were two-to-three-foot ivory rods holding a globe or eagle. Maxentius's scepter features a blue orb representing the earth and held in place by a gold-colored brass alloy grip. In order to keep Constantine away from the city, Maxentius tore down enough of the Milvian Bridge to make it impassible. Then he changed his mind and decided to march out and fight Constantine, so he had a pontoon bridge put up as a replacement. Maxentius led his troops into battle and suffered a crushing defeat. Afterward, he tried to find safety back within the city's walls, but he fell off the bridge in the crush of refugees and was drowned in his armor. Maxentius's body later washed up to shore.[7]

It is worth noting that the Battle at the Milvian Bridge took place after Constantine's supposed conversion to Christianity mentioned in the opening of our chapter. This fact becomes relevant when discussing Constantine's behavior after the battle, of which it is said he paraded the head of Maxentius through Rome on a pike. It can be assumed that this likely grieved his wife, who was the sister of Maxentius. After his battle with Maxentius, Constantine continued to work alongside Licinius who still ruled the East. Although Constantine had conquered Rome, there was no doubt where the real power was in the empire—the East. It is difficult for the modern reader to imagine a Roman Empire in which Rome was a mostly irrelevant city, but that was precisely the case in the fourth century. Most of the political and economic activity was concentrated in the East. Its prominence was such that by the time of the tetrarchy, some of the Caesars and Augusti were declared rulers of the Roman Empire, yet had never been to Rome themselves. It is also important to our discussion to note that the East, not the West, was the most hostile toward Christians in the fourth century. Recall that Diocletian and Galerius, the harshest persecutors of Christians, ruled from the East. The majority of the empire remained pagan in the fourth century, while roughly ten percent considered themselves Christians.

---

[7] Ibid. (2) (p. 293).

Constantine may have scored a decisive victory over Maxentius at the Milvian Bridge. Still, it was by no means certain that his rise to total sovereignty over the empire would happen. Politics, economics, and religion happened in the East, and Licinius still had control of that region. To gain support over the more influential half of the Roman Empire, Constantine would need to utilize all his political and military instincts.

Understanding the religious climate of the Roman Empire in the fourth century is not a simple task. On the one hand, Christianity was considered a polarizing religion that the leaders of the pagan cults hated. This may be illustrated by the fact that it was the oracle of Apollo who pressured Diocletian to begin his great persecution against the Christians. The oracles held an immense amount of power in ancient Rome, much like the oracles of ancient Egypt and Greece. Acting in a displeasing manner to the oracles was tantamount to angering the gods.

On the other hand, the public attitude toward Christians was shifting. While many Romans remained pagan, they did not necessarily have the stomach for persecution either. The divide between Christianity and the pagan cults was real, but the conflict needed to be settled politically or ideologically, not with bloodshed. The Edict of Serdica issued by Galerius was proof enough of this fact—persecution was not going to end the conflict with Christians. The religion may have been a minority in the empire, but it was also growing. The existence of Christianity in the Roman military has been documented by many ancient historians, to say nothing of the fact that Lactantius seems to suggest that even some of Caesar's own house were Christians in the fourth century.[8] Thus, the problem remained even after the death of Galerius—how does one unify a religiously fractured empire?

---

[8] Lactantius, *On the Deaths of the Persecutors*, (Ch. XI).

Constantine was not oblivious to the religious situation in the empire. In 314 C.E., Constantine wrote a letter to a man named Ablavius (or Aelafius), emphasizing his desire to unite the empire under one religion.[9] The desire for all the empire to be one was not novel to Constantine. Antiochus IV Epiphanes had expressed the same desire for the Seleucid Empire in the second century B.C.E. But in a world where people have different religious views and are also willing to die for them, how does one achieve religious homogeny? The Edict of Serdica presented the next ruler of Rome with a real challenge—bridging the social gap between the pagan cults and the Christians. This brings us back to the subject of Constantine's vision near the temple of Gaul in 310 C.E. Whether or not Constantine had a vision in 310 C.E. or not is of little importance to history—it is the *story* of the vision that changed Rome forever. Or, perhaps more precisely, *when* the story was told. Although the incident in Gaul was said to have happened in 310 C.E., it was not associated with Constantine's conversion to Christianity until many years later. The question may rightly be posed: If Constantine experienced a dramatic spiritual conversion in Gaul, why was it not known by others at the time?

In 310 C.E., Christians were still under an immense amount of pressure by the Roman authorities to either forcibly convert or be killed. When Constantine traveled to Gaul, it is unlikely that he considered any Christian association with his vision in the sun at all. Constantine had a strong relationship with the cult of the sun god, and in 310 C.E. it would have been illegal for Constantine to convert to Christianity. It was not until 311 C.E., when Galerius issued his shocking edict, that Roman leaders began reframing the empire's religious conversation around tolerance toward Christians. Thus, associating the trip to Gaul with Christianity in 310 C.E. was political suicide, but by 312 C.E., it would have become advantageous to do so. By claiming to be an advocate for Christianity, Constantine built a tacit relationship between his own legacy and the last of the tetrarchs (Galerius). All the junior rulers in 311 C.E. attempted this association, but Constantine took it one step further than the rest. Because Christianity was viewed

---

[9] Optatus of Milevis, *Letter of Constantine to Ablavius (or Aelafius)*. For more on this, see *Against the Donatists*.

more favorably in the West, it made sense for Constantine to begin personal association with the Christians after his victory over Maxentius in 312 C.E. Thus, the first time the vision of 310 C.E. was associated with Constantine's conversion to Christianity was only after the Battle of the Milvian Bridge.

Fair enough, the modern reader might think; but why would Constantine choose the event in Gaul as the moment of conversion? The truth is, the story of the vision at Gaul was only detailed in later years by Constantine's personal friend and biographer named Eusebius. It is impossible to know with certainty whether or not contemporaries of Constantine associated the vision with the emperor's later sympathy toward Christians, let alone whether or not Constantine did so himself. Suppose one assumes that the vision happened when and how Constantine's biographers claim. In that case, the simplest answer is that Constantine identified the Christian deity with the sun because he was already a worshiper of the sun god himself. It is the opinion of this writer that, in all likelihood, the sun god received credit for Constantine's many military victories and not the God of the Christians. Coins minted in the years following the vision at Gaul depict Constantine's continued veneration of the Unconquered Sun, lending credibility to this theory.

*Figure 10.1*

Figure 10.1 shows the legend inscription on Constantine's coins, minted more than a decade after his supposed conversion. "TO

THE INVINCIBLE SUN, COMPANION OF THE EMPEROR UNCONQUERED CONSTANTINE."[10] The evidence of Constantine's continued worship of the sun god aligns with what we know about Constantine and his family—that they were advocates for the cult of light in Rome. Given the timing of Constantine's vision in Gaul and the archeological evidence uncovered in later centuries, it is safe to assume that whatever Constantine saw in the sky that day, he identified it with the Unconquered Sun, not Christ. The Christian association was probably only *ad hoc*. Further evidence that Constantine remained faithful to the sun god is revealed on perhaps the most famous of all tourist attractions bearing his name—Constantine's Arch in Rome.

*Figure 10.2*     *The Arch of Constantine in Rome, Italy.*

Beside the Colosseum in Rome sits the triumphal arch that bears the name of Constantine. Arches were a common feature of Roman royal architecture, similar to presidential libraries of the modern era. In the fourth century, the Roman Senate built the arch in honor of Constantine's victory over Maxentius at the Milvian Bridge. The artwork that adorns the arch is an amalgamation of other imperial monuments, commemorating

---

[10] For more coin images from this era, see Online Coins of the Roman Empire (OCRE).
- http://numismatics.org/ocre/id/ric.7.tri.135

Constantine's military victories. It also includes depictions of Trajan, Hadrian, and Marcus Aurelius. There are scenes of war displayed on the arch, as well as pagan sacrifices. If one were to look up into the central arch of the giant monument, one would find a colossal statue of the sun god—Constantine's great patron—standing overhead.[11] The depiction of pagan sacrifices on the arch also lends credibility to the notion that Constantine never abandoned his affection for the Unconquered Sun and considered the god to be his benefactor all his life.

The addition of scenery honoring Trajan, Hadrian, and Marcus Aurelius on the arch is also telling. Constantine's father ascended to the throne from a humble background. He was not a man of the nobility, and, by extension, neither was Constantine. It was common for rulers to fabricate ancestry for themselves to legitimize their reign, but the selection by Constantine paints an intriguing portrait of what legacy Constantine wanted. Trajan was a warrior and was awarded the title by the Senate the "Best Prince."[12] Hadrian was the most Greek of all the emperors. Constantine's desire to relocate the epicenter of the empire to the Greek city of Byzantium while abandoning the Western capital of Rome speaks to the longing for Greek revivalism inside of Constantine.[13] Marcus Aurelius was the philosopher-king, the most literary and thoughtful of Rome's rulers. Constantine wanted to frame his leadership in the context of the greatest emperors, and he found the most admirable qualities in Trajan, Hadrian, and Aurelius.

Constantine's conversion may also be questioned on other grounds. For example, it is well documented that Constantine refused to be baptized until his death, as he found it inconvenient

---

[11] Ibid. (2) (298).
[12] Bennett, Julian. *Trajan, Optimus Princeps*. Bloomington, IN: Indiana University Press, 1997. (p. 107).
[13] The official language of the Byzantine Empire became Greek in later generations, abandoning the Roman tradition of Latin.

to do so until he could sin no more.[14] Much like Justin, the story of Constantine's conversion to Christianity is not consonant with the early Christian experience. Water baptism in the name of Jesus Christ was an essential part of Christian initiation in the first century. The fact that Constantine refused to be baptized until his death illustrates a lack of familiarity with specific matters of Christian doctrine and theology in the life of Constantine. Furthermore, there is no record of Constantine ever having received the baptism of the Holy Ghost, made evident by the sign of speaking in other tongues, which characterized all early Christian conversions. I make the comparison between the conversion of Constantine and Justin because in both cases each man was said to have been moved to conversion by the forces that he already admired the most in his life. In the case of Justin, he had a conversation with a man who convinced him that Christianity was the greatest philosophy—the very thing that Justin already practiced. In Constantine's case, he is said to have seen a light around the sun—a sign that could be associated with the god he already worshipped, the Unconquered Sun. Neither Constantine nor Justin experienced Christian conversion as described in the book of Acts, yet both profoundly impacted Christian thought in their generations.

The question may be rightly asked, if Constantine continued to honor the sun god throughout the course of his life, what purpose did his overtures toward Christianity serve? For example, it is recorded that Constantine invested private funds into Christian building projects, including the construction of Saint John in the Lateran. Yet, public projects remained entirely pagan. There was a strong bifurcation between public and private works during this time, demonstrating that Constantine understood the greater population of the empire was still predominantly pagan. But Christian sentiment was growing in the empire, and Constantine knew that the first step to bringing the religiously divided empire together was to balance his appeal to both sides, honoring his old gods while attempting to embrace the new. Articulating his relationship with the Christian God and the pagan

---

[14] Grant, Michael. *The Roman Emperors*. New York: Simon & Schuster, 1985. (p. 231).

gods meant finding creative ways to express love for both in a way that appealed to the leadership of all sides. As one writer put it,

> Constantine continued to behave as a pagan in various ways for years after converting. For example, he still had to work out the relationship between his new god, Christ, and his old god, the Unconquered Sun. He saw no reason at first why he couldn't worship both...Yet when it came to reaching a wider pagan audience, it could be useful to blur the difference between the old gods and the new one.[15]

Between 311-313 C.E., Constantine's agenda of bringing together the pagan past and the Christian future was primarily expressed in terms of iconography, construction projects, and proclamations. But in 313 C.E., the relationship between the pagan emperor and the Christian movement passed the tangential to become intertwined.

Recall from earlier reading that Constantine once articulated in a letter his will that Roman religion ought to be unified under the banner of Christianity. That letter became the basis for what came to later be known as the Council of Rome in 313 C.E. This meeting in Rome between bishops of the Catholic Church and the emperor is the first historical example of one of Rome's sovereigns becoming actively involved in internal church affairs. Such action by a political ruler may seem strange, particularly for its time, but Constantine did not view himself as an outsider concerning church affairs. After his alleged conversion, he hailed himself as the thirteenth of the original twelve apostles. Before his death, he had the Church of the Holy Apostles built to immortalize his legacy as one of the first followers of Christ. The church operated as a mausoleum for Constantine, and his remains were interred there for a time.[16] In many cases, such a claim by a fourth-century

---

[15] Ibid. (2) (p. 296).
[16] Ibid. (14) (p. 231).

Christian would have been dismissed as foolish (if not heretical) by the majority of believers. But opposition to the emperor was not so simple. Constantine was the heir of the tetrarchy, His ignorance of Christian doctrines notwithstanding. Offending him would not have been prudent for church leaders who sought his favor.

> And so Constantine initiated, over a number of years, a whole series of measures favouring the Christians. Church and State were to work together in the closest association. Meanwhile, as the emperor became more and more convinced of his divine mission as God's champion, victorious by the divine grace, the successive Councils of Arelate of 314 and Nicaea of 325 made it very apparent that it was he who held the reins.[17]

There has been speculation in recent years as to whether or not Constantine actually considered himself the head of the Catholic Church. But examination of primary source materials from the time allows for little doubt that Constantine truly believed he was the successor of the early apostles.

> Many communications have been sent to me by Anulinus, the most illustrious proconsul of Africa, in which it is said that Caecilian, bishop of the city of Carthage, has been accused by some of his colleagues in Africa in many matters. It seems to me a very serious thing that in those provinces which Divine Providence has freely entrusted to my devotion...the multitude are found following ignoble course, and dividing, as it were, into two parties, and the bishops are at variance...At Rome, in the presence of yourselves and of Retecius and Maternus and Marinus, your colleagues, whom I have commanded to hasten to Rome for this purpose...[18]

This excerpt from Constantine's letter to the leaders of the Catholic Church in Rome illustrates what the primary concerns of

---

[17] Ibid. (14) (p. 231).
[18] Eusebius Pamphilus, *Church History*, Book X (Ch. V).
  • Constantine's Letter Summoning the Council of Rome, 313 C.E.

the Catholics (and the emperor) were at the turn of the fourth century. For Constantine, the primary issue was not necessarily the doctrinal error of Caecilian.[19] At least, not directly. The primary concern for Constantine was that there were bishops who disagreed on the legitimacy of the Catholic Church's appointment of certain bishops, creating a split, "dividing, as it were, into two parties." In his letter, Constantine does not seem to have been familiar with the specific accusations against Caecilian. It is also important to note that Constantine did not limit the purpose of his ordering a council together to the doctrinal disputes concerning Caecilian. Constantine justified the calling together of a council because there were multiple disputes in many provinces under Roman jurisdiction. Constantine, ever careful to balance his public pagan appearance with his private Christian overtures, claimed that "Divine Providence" had set the provinces in his charge. He found it wrong that the provinces were divided in matters of Christian doctrine. His reluctance to invoke the name of Jesus Christ directly bespeaks Constantine's Christian hesitancy at this point in his life and his desire to remain universal in his approach to religious affiliation. Although he may have been friendly to Christians, his version of Christianity was by no means congruent with traditional Christianity.

It is difficult to know with certainty what, precisely, Constantine meant by his claim that the church was being divided into "two parties." This claim was probably not a reference to the accusations against Caecilian, as Caecilian was later cleared of the allegations against him. More than likely, the reference was to a split between those Christians who favored the government's intervention in church affairs, and those who opposed to it. Those opposed to state interference in church matters were likely made up of factions such as the Montanists, Novatianists, Monarchians, and Donatists.[20] By contrast, those Christians who were in favor

---

[19] Both the Council of Rome in 313 C.E. as well as the Council of Arles (Arelate) in 314 C.E. were convened to discuss, among other things, the issue of appointing bishops. It is likely that Caecilian was accused of affiliation with heretics, although he was later confirmed innocent by the later council.
[20] "Council of Arles/Donatist." Britannica. Accessed November 21, 2021. https://www.britannica.com/topic/Donatists.

of Constantine's intervention in church matters were found primarily in the Catholic movement, which Constantine praised in his letter.

> For it does not escape your diligence that my reverence for the legitimate catholic church will not permit me to allow schism or division in any place. May the divinity of the great God preserve you, most honored sirs, for many years.[21]

Given that Christianity was already experiencing a real conflict between the universal movement and the Judaean-influenced movements before 313 C.E., it seems plausible that these were the primary competing factions at the Council of Rome in 313 C.E. Although later church officials justified the council as a simple dispute over Caecilian, it seems apparent from Constantine's letter that there was more at stake for the emperor.

Bringing Christianity together under the umbrella of the universal, or "Catholic," church was the was primary motivation of Constantine's intervention in Christian affairs. Remember that heretofore, no emperor had recognized Christianity as a legitimate religion in the state, let alone called an audience of its leaders together. The letter written by Constantine petitioning leaders from the Catholic church to meet in Rome was an olive branch that the universal movement could not dismiss. First, it may be rightly assumed that, had the leaders refused Constantine's request (or, in the words of Constantine, "command") to allow the emperor to become involved in church affairs, those who refused would have had every reason to fear for their own safety. Up until 311 C.E, Christians enjoyed no reprieve from persecution in the empire. Precedent suggested that, if the emperor was not allowed to have his way with the church, persecution against resistance could ensue. In 313-314 C.E., there was no reason to assume that Constantine would remain a lifelong friend of the Christians. Although he had offered public statements favoring the church, such as his endorsement of Licinius' edict, those statements could be easily reversed. Constantine's continued veneration of the

---

[21] Ibid. (18).

Unconquered Sun at this point in his life suggests that, although he was willing to extend a hand of friendship to the Christians, he was not ready to relinquish his favor in the rest of the empire to do so. Thus, Christianity could rise in rank throughout the empire, but only on his terms.

The Council of Rome in 313 C.E. offered church officials who were willing to allow the emperor to arbitrate the issue of division in Christianity something they had never had before—institutional legitimacy. For several reasons, Constantine likely found the Catholic Church more appealing than other competing Christian factions. First, the Catholic Church was much more eclectic than other movements, such as the Monarchians. The exclusivity of the doctrines of men such as Praxeas would not have been compatible with the emperor's vision for a universal religion. Constantine needed a Christianity that the rest of the empire could unify around. In order to stop pagan animosity toward Christians, it needed to be distanced from the traditions of Judaea as much as possible. (The attempt to distance Catholicism from Judaean Christianity will be discussed in later sections.) Catholic Christianity also possessed the appropriate structure and governmental organization throughout the empire that was needed to establish a universal religion, which was important to Constantine.[22] When the first two councils were convened in 313 C.E. and 314 C.E., they established a precedent that would be honored in the Catholic Church for generations—the state's legitimate authority in church matters. The decision to allow the emperor to make decisions concerning matters of Christian doctrine was, perhaps, the most significant leap of Christianity away from the Judaean movement described in the book of Acts.

After the councils of Rome and Arles, Constantine became the highest authority in the Christian Church. The Catholic Church's continued use of popes allowed it to maintain the image of an

---

[22] Ibid. (14) (p. 231).

internally led church, but there was no doubt as to who was really in charge.

> Constantine became the ruler of the Christian Church, or, to be more accurate, of the Christian *Churches*. Christianity as Constantine knew it was a diverse religion, an umbrella sheltering a great deal of regional variation and doctrinal choice. After nearly twenty years of hard-fought war and politics, Constantine had finally unified all Romans under the rule of one man. He equally insisted on unifying all Christians...Constantine wanted to impose an official or orthodox Christianity and to oppose other beliefs, which were labeled as heresy. But *heresy* comes from *hairesis*, a Greek word for "choice," and Christianity had a long tradition of freedom and decentralization. It proved resistant to central control.[23]

Since the first century, Christianity had honored the tradition of instituting apostles, pastors, and bishops to serve in positions of church governance and authority. These church officials were the arbiters of internal disputes over Christian doctrine, and they depended heavily on the Scriptures to guide their decisions. In instances where a church or an individual may have been out of alignment with the teachings of the Scriptures (and, by extension, the church) they were often corrected through written epistles or individual letters.[24] There are no examples in the New Testament of a king or local governor intervening in church affairs. The New Testament writers did not endorse secular governance as an approved ministry in the church. Heresy and apostasy were legitimate issues of concern to early Christians that needed to be addressed, but ex-communication was not a practice of the early church. In examples such as the one offered in the second chapter of the book of Revelation, those who had fallen into false doctrine

---

23 Ibid. (2) (p. 303-304).
24 In both of Paul's letters to Timothy, he was critical of a man named Alexander the coppersmith who apparently associated with the church at Ephesus. Paul operated as the chief apostle to the churches that he helped establish throughout Asia Minor, but Timothy was the local pastor/overseer, at least for a time.

were commanded to repent.[25] Although there are limited references to ostracization in cases where a believer may have been causing division in the church, the punishment does not appear to have been intended to be permanent.

> And if any man obey not our word by this epistle, note that man, and have no company with him, that he may be ashamed. Yet count him not as an enemy, but admonish him as a brother.[26]

Ex-communication became dogma in the Byzantine Empire through Constantine's opposition to sects of Christianity that did not align with the universal movement. To achieve a universal religion in the empire, all other interpretations of Christian doctrine had to be deemed illegitimate, and Constantine needed a version of Christianity that the empire could unify around. In the Catholic Church, he found favor with certain bishops who were willing to remain silent about the emperor's continued worship of the Unconquered Sun. This fact becomes most relevant when discussing Constantine's authoritative biographer, Eusebius Pamphilus, bishop of Caesarea.

Not much is known about the early life of Eusebius. He was born and raised in Caesarea, where he would later become a bishop in the Catholic Church. Eusebius' work is valuable to modern historians because it is some of the earliest primary source material available concerning the life and legacy of Constantine the Great. Eusebius is widely considered to be the first church historian, and his accounts of the events surrounding the fourth century are invaluable for modern research on the issue. But not always for the reasons that one might think.

Eusebius was a close friend of Constantine. Why the emperor chose to befriend a lowly bishop from the relatively unimportant

---

[25] Revelation 2:1-7.
[26] 2nd Thessalonians 3:14-15 (KJV).

town of Caesarea is a question that will be discussed in the next chapter. For now, it is important to note the friendship of the two men because upon the death of Constantine, Eusebius wrote *The Life of The Blessed Emperor Constantine*, which served as the foundation for generations of historical research on Constantine. The trouble with depending heavily on Eusebius for close examination of the early life of Constantine is that much of his biography of Constantine (particularly in the earliest portions of the book) is a reimagination of the emperor's life and family that does not necessarily line up with modern research.

For example, no mention is made by Eusebius of Constantine's early worship of the sun god or of the fact that he continued to honor the sun god until his death. In fact, Eusebius does not even acknowledge the pagan beliefs of Constantine's father, Constantius.

> The father of Constantine, then, is said to have possessed such a character as we have briefly described. And what kind of death was vouchsafed to him in consequence of such devotion to God, and how far He whom he honoured made his lot to differ from that of his colleagues in the empire, may be known to any one who will give his attention to the circumstances of the case. For after he had for a long time given many proofs of royal nobility of soul, in acknowledging the Supreme God alone, and condemning the polytheism of the impious, and had fortified his household by the prayers of holy men, he is said to have passed the remainder of his life in repose and tranquility...[27]

According to Eusebius, it was Constantius who first ruled his portion of the empire as a Christian.[28] There is, of course, no evidence that the father of Constantine was ever a Christian. There

---

[27] Eusebius Pamphilus, *The Life Of The Blessed Emperor Constantine*, Book I (Ch. XVII).

[28] Curiously, Eusebius associates the death of Constantius with evidence that he was blessed among the Augusti, unlike his fellow rulers. This was a strange comment by Eusebius, as it is known that Constantius was the first of the original tetrarchy to pass away. Galerius, the most pagan of the tetrarchs, outlasted his fellow rulers.

is a significant amount of archeological evidence to suggest that Constantius, like his fellow rulers, was a pagan and remained one all his life. Recall that upon his conquest of Britain, Constantius had himself depicted on the newly minted coins of the region in the skins of Hercules and that his own worship of the Unconquered Sun (unique in its time) led his son Constantine to honor the same god. Constantius regarded himself as the "Restorer of Everlasting Light," an homage to Apollo and the Unconquered Sun, and he emphasized Rome's role as the light among the barbaric nations. It was customary for pagans to honor the cults of their fathers, so Constantine's continued reverence for the sun god after the death of Constantius is consistent with what is known about the period.

The most likely reason for Eusebius' fictional depiction of Constantius relationship to Christianity was that it legitimized Constantine's own role as the head of the Catholic Church. Much like Constantine's Arch in Rome, creating an ancestry that favored the political priorities of the empire could be useful. Constantine was not related to any of the Antonine Emperors.[29] Still, by associating himself with one of the more stable dynasties in Rome's history on his arch, he could cultivate support from those who were otherwise skeptical of his rise to power. It was no different in the case of Christianity. Constantine did not have any legitimate claims to church authority, and the fact that he had no known association with Christianity probably did not help his case. From his perspective, solidifying his role as the thirteenth apostle required that he have some Christian background on which he could fall back. Furthermore, it was not acceptable to pagans for sons to abandon the religion of their fathers.[30] In Roman culture, the father operated as the priest of the home, and each family was devoted to a specific cult of the Roman pantheon. By regarding his father as a Christian, Constantine attempted to avoid criticism from those who would have interpreted his

---

[29] Trajan, Hadrian, and Marcus Aurelius all belonged to the Antonine dynasty. All three are depicted on Constantine's Arch in Rome.
[30] "Roman Religion." UNRV Roman History. Accessed November 22, 2021. https://www.unrv.com/religion.php.

behavior as disrespectful to his father's legacy. If it angered the gods to abandon the religion of the family, then the solution for Constantine was to suggest that he had not converted at all. Instead, his parents were also said to have been believers. Ironically, the problem of conversion away from the religion of one's family was a problem for pagans, but it was not an issue for the Christians. The New Testament is filled with stories of men and women who forsook the religion and the traditions of their fathers to follow Jesus Christ. Such behavior was not interpreted as disrespectful but as an act of faith. Thus, in an example of irony, the decision to re-cast his father in the mold of Christianity was not consistent with Christian behavior, but it was consonant with the behavior of the pagans.

The subject of the religion and behavior of his father was probably a more difficult gauntlet for Constantine to navigate than is sometimes assumed. Constantius had been party to one of the most brutal persecutions against Christians in the history of the empire. Furthermore, his father's veneration of the sun god complicated the situation for Constantine. If the sun god was to be given credit for his father's many victories in Britain and over the barbaric tribes, how could Constantine abandon the sun god in good conscience? It may have appeared irreverent to his family, to say nothing of his constituents in the empire, to claim that the god who had been responsible for elevating his father to the office of Augustus did not exist. Not for nothing was the vision near the temple of Apollo chosen as the associative moment of conversion for Constantine—honoring the Unconquered Sun was just as important to the emperor's legacy as unifying Christianity.

Some portions of Eusebius' biography of Constantine are suspect for other reasons as well. At the opening of his work, Eusebius briefly describes the formation of the tetrarchy, of which he says it was filled with the highest levels of barbarity. This description may seem accurate, but the ancient writer's summary is missing one critical individual—Caesar Galerius. Chapter eight of Eusebius'

*Life of Constantine* opens by informing the reader that at a time when four princes shared the administration of the Roman Empire, Constantius alone was the friend of the Supreme God. But the four princes mentioned by Eusebius are Diocletian, Maximian, Maxentius, and Constantius.[31] This, of course, was not the tetrarchy at the time of Constantius' reign. Maxentius was the son of Maximian, and his feuds with the son of Constantius would become famous in the generation following the tetrarchy, but he was not a ruler that could have been associated with the original four. Galerius is the only one of the original four tetrarchs not mentioned by Eusebius. In fact, Eusebius never mentions Galerius by name in the entirety of the book. Either one is left to assume that Eusebius was ignorant to the name of Constantine the Great's predecessor, or that Galerius was left out of the biography by design.

Eusebius probably had many reasons for refusing to mention the name of Galerius in his book, not the least of which was the fact that Galerius was the worst of the four tetrarchs when it came to his treatment of the Christians. His mother was a fervent pagan, and his devotion to the cults inspired an entire generation of persecution. In light of this, it would not be surprising to discover that Eusebius harbored animosity toward Galerius and did not want to legitimize his reign by documenting it in his histories.[32] Still, other tetrarchs were also abusive toward the religion of Eusebius, and they are accounted for in his histories. So, the question still begs, why not Galerius?

There is another theory that may explain Galerius' absence from the biography of Constantine. It relates to the issuing of the Edict of Serdica in 311 C.E. Throughout his work, Eusebius never mentions the idolatry of Constantius or Constantine the Great. If the ancient historian is to be believed, both men were pious

---

[31] Eusebius Pamphilus, *The Life Of The Blessed Emperor Constantine*, Book I (Ch. VIII).

[32] Eusebius seems to suggest that this is precisely his motivation in (Ch. XXIII) of Book I. "I have not thought it fit to give any distinct account of their downfall, nor to stain the memory of the good by mentioning them in connexion with those of an opposite character." Still, while Eusebius writes with equal animosity toward the other tetrarchs and even Maxentius, Galerius is the only one that he refused to mention by name.

Christians throughout the entire course of their lives, and it was Constantine alone who was responsible for bringing reprieve and recognition to the church when he came to power at the beginning of the fourth century. For Eusebius, Constantine is the political savior of the Christians after his defeat of Maxentius in 312 C.E.

The problem with Eusebius' presentation of Constantine-as-savior is that by the time Constantine joined Licinius' edict endorsing Christianity in 313 C.E., the Christians had already been granted the freedom to worship by Galerius two years earlier. This contradicts Eusebius' presentation of Constantine-as-savior. If one were to read only Eusebius on the matter, they would come away with the impression that Constantius and Constantine were responsible for the improved condition of the Christians in the fourth century. It could be that Eusebius saw fit to exclude any mention of Galerius or the Edict of Serdica in 311 C.E. to add legitimacy to the later Edict of Milan in 313 C.E. Furthermore, the two theories regarding the omission of Galerius from Eusebius' work are not mutually exclusive. It is entirely possible that Eusebius hated Galerius, and that hatred only served to fuel his desire to leave his proclamation in favor of the Christians out of the history books. One may easily have informed the other.

Constantine's intention to unify all of Christianity under one banner was repeated explicitly between 313-325 C.E. In a letter to Alexander the Bishop and Arius the Presbyter. Constantine wrote,

> I call that God to witness...that I had a two-fold reason for undertaking that duty which I have now effectually performed. My design then was, first, to bring the diverse judgements formed by all nations respecting the Deity to a condition, as it were, of settled uniformity; and secondly, to restore a healthy tone to the system of the world, then

suffering under the malignant power of a grievous distempter.[33]

Concerning our subject matter, Constantine's comment about the "diverse judgements formed by all nations respecting the Deity" is, perhaps, telling. Evidence that Christianity was not as uniform in its belief in the doctrine of the trinity as men like Tertullian would have us believe frequently reappears in this era. Discussions concerning the nature of God and the person of Jesus Christ abounded in the fourth century. But the influence of Constantine the Great changed the dynamics of the situation for Christians forever. Heretofore, no individual had the power to declare a universal doctrine in the church that, if not followed, would anathematize the dissenter. Although decidedly not a theologian, unconverted, and illiterate concerning the Bible, Constantine invested himself with the power to arbitrate the most crucial doctrines of the church, and to see to the excommunication of those who disagreed with his judgements. This incredible power was wielded most notably at the First Council of Nicaea in 325 C.E., of which Constantine the Great was the chairing official.

Constantine was not well educated in matters of Christian doctrine. In his same letter to the Christians in Egypt, Constantine wrote,

For since the power of Divine light, and the rule of our holy religion, which have illuminated the world by their sacred radiance, proceed in the first instance...as it were, of the East, I naturally believed that you would be the first to promote the salvation of other nations, and resolved with all energy of purpose and diligence of inquiry to seek your aid...And yet, having made a careful inquiry into the origin and foundation of these differences, I find the cause to be of a truly

---

[33] Eusebius Pamphilus, *The Life Of The Blessed Emperor Constantine*, Book II (Ch. LXV).
  • Constantine's letter to Alexander the bishop, and Arius the presbyter.

insignificant character, and quite unworthy of such fierce contention.[34]

Once again, Constantine spoke of God in generalities that could easily be associated with his older traditions. His reference to God as "the power of the Divine light" is consistent with his repeated emphasis on blurring the lines between the worship of Apollo and the Unconquered Sun with Jesus Christ. But the more interesting comment by Constantine in his letter to the Egyptian Christians concerns his dismissal of the problem that was dividing so many groups of Christians around the provinces—the debate over the nature of God and the person of Christ. "Having made a careful inquiry into the origin and foundation of these differences, I find the cause to be of truly insignificant character." This comment, more than any, illustrates Constantine's illiteracy and disconnection from the primary beliefs in Christian doctrine. The identity of God in Christ is one of the most dominant (perhaps the dominant) points of emphasis regarding the doctrine of Jesus in the New Testament. The exclusivity of the name of Jesus in water baptism throughout the New Testament, as well as the repeated claims to His divinity, depict an early Christianity that was deeply concerned with the identity of the Christ as God Himself manifested in the flesh.[35]

Debates between groups such as the Monarchians and Catholics have been detailed in earlier portions of this book, but they were not the only competing factions at this point in church history. A group known as the Arians sprung up in the early fourth century, claiming that Jesus was less than God but more than a man.[36] Although it came to be known as the Arian controversy, the name of the movement itself was a misnomer. The source of the doctrine was a man named Lucian, who was the founder of an

---

[34] Eusebius Pamphilus, *The Life Of The Blessed Emperor Constantine*, Book II (Ch. LXVII-LXVIII).
• Constantine's letter to Alexander the bishop, and Arius the presbyter.
[35] 1st Timothy 3:16.
[36] Pamphilus, Eusebius. "Ecclesiastical History." In *The Fathers of the Church*, Edited by Roy J. Deferrari and Rudolph Arbesmann, 6-7. Translated by Roy J. Deferrari. New York: Fathers of the Church, Inc., 1953.

exegetico-theological school in Antioch.[37] The movement became known as Arian because of its most popular proponent, Arius, whose doctrine was condemned at the First Council of Nicaea in 325 C.E.

Although Constantine considered such debates trivial, the implications of the arguments greatly impacted Christian theology. Take, for example, the claims made by those in the Arian movement at the time. If it were true that Jesus was less than God but more than a man, how could He rightly be credited with creating all things, as is explicitly stated in the book of Colossians?[38] If the Arians were correct that Christ was a participant in creation, yet was not the sole creator, then that would nullify the entirety of the Old Testament Scriptures, which repeatedly emphasize the oneness of God,[39] and stress the fact that God had no help in creation.[40] Just as the doctrine of the Arians would have been objectionable to the Catholics, the doctrine of the Catholics concerning the same principles would have been objectionable to the Monarchians and others. For the Monarchians, the Catholic idea that Jesus was another person of God, distinct from yet sharing authority or glory with God the Father created the same problem that the Arian controversy had created. Some Christian sects more highly prioritized the overarching emphasis on the oneness of God throughout the Scriptures than others in the fourth century. These disagreements forged "the diverse judgements formed by all nations respecting the Deity" that Constantine wrote about and was so ambivalent toward.

It is not surprising that Constantine trivialized the disagreements concerning the nature of God and the person of Jesus Christ. Constantine grew up in a world with many gods, and some gods

---

[37] Ibid. (36).
[38] Colossians 1:16.
[39] Deuteronomy 6:4.
[40] Isaiah 44:24.

had more than one iteration themselves. Thus, the cult of light could be represented in the person of Apollo and the Unconquered Sun alike, or even Jupiter and Hercules. They didn't need to remain completely distinct, as each possessed its own unique characteristics yet remained unified in their supremacy over man. The practice of amalgamating the identities of the gods was also not unique to the fourth century. In the opening chapter of this book, we briefly examined the conglomeration of the Greek Zeus with the Egyptian Ammon in the fourth century B.C.E. This was possible because although the Greeks and the Egyptians may have described their gods differently, they recognized that they represented the same powers in the earth.

Constantine did not see why those same principles could not be applied to the God of the Christians. In this way, it was probably not offensive to the mind of Constantine to equate the Christian God with the Unconquered Sun, or any of the other gods of Rome for that matter. Although he may have acknowledged that the Christian iteration represented the supreme form, that did not necessarily dismiss the pagan interpretations of His existence. Constantine's highest priority was not the dissolution of paganism from the empire. Constantine welcomed the veneration of the gods of Rome so long as the pagans acknowledged that the Christian God was superior. Although Constantine is often regarded as the emperor who was responsible for eradicating paganism from the empire. But pagan worship was not made illegal until the reign of Emperor Theodosius I after the death of Constantine.[41]

Whether the Catholic bishops accepted it or not, Constantine had established himself as the head of the church. The consequences would prove dramatic over the next decade. But the church was far from unified at this point in history, and no council or creed defining the Roman orthodox approach to Christianity had been issued yet. For a time, Constantine was content to be influential where he could and leave the rest to bishops that he

---

[41] "Christianity: The Alliance Between Church and Empire." Britannica. Accessed November 22, 2021. https://www.britannica.com/topic/Christianity/The-alliance-between-church-and-empire.

approved of. Constantine still had not solidified his control over the most important half of the empire, and appearing too openly Christian could create a boon of pagan support for Licinius in the East. Although Licinius offered tolerance to Christians, he remained a pagan until his death. The East was much more favorable to the religion of the pagans, and Licinius was not likely to relinquish power without a fight. Between 316 C.E. and 324 C.E., Constantine engaged in a series of wars with his co-ruler that culminated with Constantine's final victory over Licinius at Chrysopolis, modern Istanbul. It is probably not a coincidence that only after he had defeated Licinius did Constantine refuse to offer sacrifices to Jupiter. Half of Constantine's ambitions were realized with the empire now wholly under his control; the Roman Empire was one. Now it was time to return to the question of religion. Could Constantine unify the religion of Rome under a single banner just as he had done with the state?

The mission of creating one religion that the empire could unify around was challenging for two reasons. First, it must be remembered that many Romans remained pagan even after the commitments of Constantine to a Christian future. Getting Christians to honor the gods of the pagans was likely much more difficult than getting the pagans to honor the God of the Christians. On the whole, pagans were open to the idea that their gods were not the only gods, and the idea that the Christian God had triumphed over their own may have been disheartening, but it was not impossible to reconcile. Thus, Christianity was an easier banner to rally around than paganism when dealing with Romans who were otherwise not Christians themselves.

Because of the elasticity of certain pagan beliefs, some of the decisions made to universalize the religion of the empire were met with little or no resistance from the pagans. For example, Constantine decreed that Sunday, "the venerable day of the sun," become the official holy day of the week and that all worshipers celebrate it as the day of rest in the Roman Empire.[42] Before Constantine's decree, many Christians acknowledged the Jewish Sabbath (roughly from sundown Friday to sundown Saturday) as the day of regular weekly worship. As discussed earlier in this book, many Christians continued to worship in synagogues long after the first century, and this would have necessitated Saturday worship as a regular practice for these Christians. However, there is some evidence to suggest that Sunday had become popular among some Christians, particularly gentiles, as early as the second century.[43] The reason for Sunday's popularity as a day of worship among gentile Christians was likely for the same reason that Saturday was popular to the Jewish Christians—it was already the regular day of worship before their conversion. Pagans recognized Sunday as a holy day to the sun, so the principle of Sunday worship was not offensive to their culture. For pagan gentiles who converted to Christianity and had no connections to the traditions of Judaea, it made sense for them to practice weekly observance of their new religion on the same day as the rest of their peers.[44] Since most gentiles in Rome never practiced Sabbath observance to begin with, what day one worshiped was not necessarily considered a critical aspect of doctrine. While the earliest Christians of the New Testament Era almost certainly practiced weekly worship on Saturday, the gradual influx of gentiles to the Christian movement introduced Sunday as an alternative, particularly in the universal movement described by writers such as Justin and Tertullian. While the transition to Sunday worship was well received by the pagans in the empire, it took more than two generations for it to become a common practice throughout Christianity broadly. Some Christians protested the change so much that they left their churches in favor

---

[42] *Theodosian Code*, Book II (Sect. VIII).
[43] Justin Martyr, *First Apology*, (Ch. LXVII).
[44] Some have suggested that the reason for Sunday worship by early Christians was due to the fact that Jesus resurrected on a Sunday, however this claim is widely debated, as it is not entirely certain what day of the week Jesus resurrected. It is more likely that Sunday association with the resurrection of Christ became popular only after the decree by Constantine.

of the synagogues, an issue which will be discussed at length in the next chapter.[45]

While it is likely that Constantine chose Sunday as the day of worship for the Christians because he favored the practices of the universal movement over that of its detractors, it is entirely possible that the decree was also made to assuage the grievances of the pagans. Constantine himself already honored Sunday as the day of worship, so the fact that the Catholics and many gentile believers embraced it too only served to confirm his bias toward it. It was a way to bring together two religious groups who otherwise wanted nothing to do with each other. But overcoming the first challenge—the pagans—only augmented the tension between a second group of dissenters—non-Catholic Christians. This was the second great challenge for Constantine in his quest to unify the religion of the empire. Christianity was deeply divided in the fourth century. So the greater problem for Constantine was not getting the pagans to submit to a Christian future, but getting Christians to submit to one universal interpretation of a Christian empire. When it became apparent to the emperor that the doctrinal issues plaguing the churches would not be resolved through reason, he determined to resolve them through force. To his credit, Constantine issued a number of reforms that would have been favorable to even the most skeptical of Christians. Crucifixion was abolished as a form of execution in the empire. Divorce was discouraged, and Constantine made it much more difficult for those who sought a divorce to be able to do so. Money initially pledged to pagan temples was reappropriated for new Christian houses of worship.[46] But all the social reforms in the empire could not solve the greater problem looming over Constantine's one-empire-religion agenda: What was to be done with the various sects of Christians who disagreed over the fundamental doctrines of Christianity?

---

[45] Irshai, Oded. "Confronting A Christian Empire." In *Cultures of the Jews*, edited by David Biale, 202. New York: Schocken Books, 2002.
[46] Zosimus, *New History*, Book II (Ch. XXXII).

Despite his notion that it was a trivial issue plaguing the church, Constantine determined to have the argument over the identity of God and Christ settled at the First Council of Nicaea in 325 C.E. One year removed from his final victory over Licinius, the emperor had the latitude to institute grand sweeping reforms that would be met with little resistance.

In the events leading up to the First Council of Nicaea, Constantine wrote his letter to Alexander and Arius, two men who would become key figures at the Nicene Council shortly thereafter. Arius' claim that Jesus was less than God but more than man was a point of great controversy among other Christians, but it did not appear to be so for Constantine. In his letter to the two leaders, Constantine wrote,

> Let therefore both the unguarded question and the inconsiderate answer receive your mutual forgiveness. For your difference has not arisen on any leading doctrines or precepts of the Divine law, nor have you introduced any new dogma respecting the worship of God. You are in truth of one and the same judgement...For as long as you continue to contend about these truly insignificant questions, it is not fitting that so large a portion of God's people should be under the direction of your judgement, since you are divided between yourselves...You know that philosophers, while they all adhere to the general tenets of their respective sects, are frequently at issue on some particular assertion or statement: and yet, though they may differ as to the perfection of a principle, they are recalled to harmony of sentiment by the uniting power of their common doctrines. If this be true, is it not far more reasonable that you, who are the ministers of the Supreme God, should be of one mind respecting the profession of the same religion? But let us still more thoughtfully and with closer attention examine what I have said, and see whether it be right that, on the ground of some trifling and foolish verbal difference between ourselves, brethren should assume towards each other the attitude of enemies, and the august meeting of the synod be rent by

profane disunion, because we will wrangle together on points so trivial and altogether unessential?[47]

Here again, Constantine's primary point of emphasis is on the frivolous nature of the debates over the Godhead. Constantine goes as far as to say the disagreement concerned doctrines that were trivial and unessential to the core tenants of the church. "Your difference has not arisen on any leading doctrines or precepts of the Divine law..." This statement by Constantine not only reveals an unfamiliarity with the Scriptures, but with church history up to that point. Debates over the person of Jesus Christ were as old as the New Testament itself, to say nothing of the many letters and polemics written in the years following the first-century church. Beliefs about the nature of Christ greatly informed Christian soteriology, most notably in prayer and water baptism. Constantine likened the debate between Alexander and Arius to something amounting to a philosophical dispute, one that did not impact greater Christian doctrine. There is some irony to the flippancy with which Constantine handled the situation, as he was responsible for convening the most historic ecumenical council on the issue.

When they arrived in Nicaea in 325 C.E., any questions surrounding who was in charge of the council were dispelled quickly. Of the emperor's role in the meeting, Eusebius wrote,

> Now when the appointed day arrived on which the council met for the final solution of the questions in dispute, each member attended to deliver his judgement in the central building of the palace, which appeared to exceed the rest in magnitude...As soon, then, as the whole assembly had seated themselves with becoming gravity, a general silence prevailed, in expectation of the emperor's arrival. And first of all three of his immediate family entered in succession, and others also preceded his approach, not of the soldiers or guards who usually accompanied him, but only friends who avowed the faith of

---

[47] Eusebius Pamphilus, *The Life Of The Blessed Emperor Constantine*, Book II (Ch. LXX-LXXI).

- Constantine's letter to Alexander the bishop, and Arius the presbyter.

Christ. And now, all rising at the signal which indicated the emperor's entrance, at last he himself proceeded through the midst of the assembly, like some heavenly messenger of God, clothed in raiment which glittered as it were with rays of light, reflecting the glowing radiance of a purple robe, and adorned with the brilliant splendour of gold and precious stones...For the rest of his personal excellencies, he surpassed all present in height of stature and beauty of form, as well as in majestic dignity of men, and invincible strength and vigour...As soon as he had advanced to the upper end of the seats, at first he remained standing, and when a low chair of wrought gold had been set for him, he waited until the bishops had beckoned him, and then sat down, and after him the whole assembly did the same.[48]

Embellished though his descriptions may have been, Eusebius paints a vivid portrait of who was in charge at the First Council of Nicaea. In the opening portion of the previous excerpt, it may be noted that the meeting which Eusebius described did not take place in a church but in a palace. It is believed that the days-long council was probably initially held in a church, but when it came time for the final deliberations on the issue at hand, it convened at the palace. This once again signaled the emperor's authority in church matters—Constantine would have the final say.

Constantine opened the final day of the council with personal remarks, once again stressing the need for uniformity in doctrine, and his will that all sides come to an agreement on the most hotly contested issues.[49] By examining the events surrounding this council, the personal relationship between Constantine and Eusebius comes to life. Both men were present at the council, and Eusebius had the distinct honor of sitting at the emperor's right hand. Speculation abounds as to the reason for the special

---

[48] Eusebius Pamphilus, *The Life Of The Blessed Emperor Constantine*, Book III (Ch. X).

[49] Although the nature of God and the person of Christ are often considered the primary focus topics of the First Council of Nicaea, Eusebius makes mention of a more prominent issue in his writings on the council—the date for the celebration of Easter. The debates around this controversy will be discussed in greater detail in the next chapter.

treatment given to Eusebius, as he was only the bishop of a relatively unimportant region—Caesarea. The First Council of Nicaea thoroughly debated the issue of Easter celebration, and for this reason, Eusebius may have played a prominent role in the council. As Constantine's biographer, their professional relationship may have precipitated the special treatment of Eusebius as well. Whatever the reasons, Eusebius had the privilege of offering an opening address to the emperor, whereafter the topics of controversy were allowed one final day of debate.

From Eusebius' account of that day, one gathers that the emperor maintained a very mild demeanor throughout, offering his thoughts where he felt appropriate, but largely remaining out of the debates. Although they did not play a dominant role in the discussion, it is interesting to note the evidence of Monarchian-like beliefs at the council. There was present at Nicaea a bishop from Antioch named Eustathius. His bishopric of the Syrian region was significant in the fourth century, as Antioch, Rome, and Alexandria were considered three of the most important epicenters of Christianity at that time. Eustathius was a strong dissenter against the doctrine of Arius, and he did not appear to get along with Eusebius either. Some have speculated that Eusebius was a supporter of Arian beliefs, which precipitated the debates between Eustathius and Eusebius. Eustathius attacked the teachings of Origen,[50] and this infuriated Eusebius, who was himself a disciple of these teachings. In return, Eusebius accused Eustathius of Sabellianism.[51] Whether or not Eustathius actually adhered to the teachings of Sabellius or not is unknown. It is more likely that the accusation of Sabellianism was intended to be a slight against Eustathius. Nevertheless, the accusation itself seems to suggest that the theology of Arius was not the only one questioned at the First Council of Nicaea. Criticisms against Origen, one of the most significant proponents of the universal

---

[50] Origen was a disciple of Clement of Alexandria, one of the earliest writers to depart from the traditional Christian teachings about the person of Christ.

[51] Ibid. (36) (p. 11-12).

- Not a great deal is known about Sabellius, but it can be assumed from what historical data that has been gathered on him that his teachings were probably consistent with that of the Monarchians or early Jewish Christians.

movement, suggest there was representation at Nicaea from all sides of the theological spectrum.

A significant number of bishops present at Nicaea favored the teachings of men such as Clement of Alexandria, Origen, and Tertullian. Constantine favored the Catholics, and it was unlikely that anyone who gathered at Nicaea that day was willing to oppose the final decision of the emperor in any serious way. Why Constantine favored the Catholic position on certain matters of Christian doctrine is discussed at greater length in our next chapter. Before the close of the First Council of Nicaea, the terminology adopted for the creed that the council put forth was decidedly anti-Arian and greatly favored Catholic terminology surrounding the nature of the Godhead.

Those responsible for articulating the language of the creed at Nicaea determined that the Father and Son were distinct, consistent with the teachings of the universal movement. When a final version of the creed put forth by the council was presented to the emperor, he insisted on the insertion of a single word: *homoousion* (of the same substance). He then gave explanations of its meaning in order to assuage the concerns of those who thought the original form too unclear or perhaps too radical.[52] Of course, distinguishing between "person" and "substance" likely made Constantine's insertion all the more ambiguous. But then, ambiguity favored Constantine's ultimate goal. Thus, the first iteration of the Nicene Creed did not offend many. But it did not please many either.

> We believe in one God, the Father almighty, maker of heaven and earth, of all things visible and invisible; And in one Lord, Jesus Christ, the only begotten Son of God, begotten from the Father before all ages, light from light, true God from true God, begotten not made, of one substance with the Father...[53]

"Light from light" is an inclusion in the Nicene Creed, which bespeaks the murky relationship Christ had to the Unconquered Sun in the mind of Constantine. Constantine's father was regarded

[52] Ibid. (36) (p. 11).
[53] Nicene Creed, 325 C.E. (amended 381 C.E.).

as the "Restorer of Everlasting Light." It is probably not out of the question to wonder if Constantine believed that he had continued his father's legacy by uniting the empire under one religion in the person of Christ. If the light restored in the lifetime of Constantius I was Rome, perhaps the new religion of the empire, Christianity, could be thought of as the new light. Thus, Christ is the light of Rome, and Rome the light of the world.

Such an interpretation of the events surrounding the First Council of Nicaea may seem lofty but they are not necessarily overstated. In the next chapter, we will examine the specific attempts to recast Christ in a Roman role and the impact that this reimaging of Christianity's origins had on the church.

It is important to note that the First Council of Nicaea may have played a critical role in forwarding what would eventually become an official church doctrine concerning the trinity, but it was not the council that created it. An official statement articulating the belief that God existed in three distinct persons and that the third person, the Spirit, proceeded from the Father, was not written for another fifty-six years. The primary goals of the First Council of Nicaea were to quell the Arian controversy and to establish an official church position regarding the recognition of Easter.

Nevertheless, the First Council of Nicaea is exceptionally important to our subject matter, because it solidified the precedent of 313 C.E.—that the emperor had the power to oversee church affairs. Furthermore, it established the authority of Catholic interpretation in matters of Christian doctrine, something which was contested for years following the first of the ecumenical councils. The Catholic movement was more sympathetic to the influence of the early Apologists and philosophers on Christian thought than other factions, and they eventually adopted trinitarian theology as a result. While trinitarianism was still not the official or enforced theology by 325 C.E., it was elevated to a much higher status in the church through the advent of the universal movement.

Early Judaean Christianity suffered as a result of the councils convened by Constantine. In most cases, those who refused to acknowledge the authority of the emperor's councils were anathematized and ex-communicated. Catholic Christianity flourished after the fourth century because its movement had something that no Christian group had enjoyed heretofore— institutional legitimacy. With the support of the state, the universal movement could claim that they alone were the possessors of true Christian doctrine. Everything else was heretical. Thus, the most significant impact of the First Council of Nicaea was the ostracization of heterodoxy against the Catholic Church. Their pre-eminence in matters of doctrine was articulated clearly in the final published version of the Nicene Creed.

> [We believe] in the Holy Spirit, the Lord and life-giver, who proceeds from the Father, Who with the Father and the Son is together worshipped and together glorified, Who spoke through the prophets; in one holy Catholic and apostolic Church.[54]

But trinitarianism was not just elevated due to the theological conclusions of the 325 C.E. council. Recall that the council was not just convened to address Arianism, but also the observance of Easter. It was the conclusions reached concerning this second issue that largely contributed to a final break between the Judaean Christianity of the first century, and the Roman Christianity which followed it.

---

[54] Nicene Creed, 381 C.E.

# CHAPTER XI

## The Roman Christ

But before this time another most virulent disorder had existed, and long afflicted the Church; I mean the difference respecting the salutary feast of Easter. For while one party asserted that the Jewish custom should be adhered to, the other affirmed that the exact recurrence of the period should be observed, without following the authority of those who were in error, and strangers to the grace of the gospel as well in this as in other respects...No one appeared who was capable of devising a remedy for the evil, because the controversy continued equally balanced between both parties.[1]

The disputes at the First Council of Nicaea concerning the celebration of Easter have not been issues of significant discussion in recent decades, but they greatly inform our understanding of the prevailing Christian attitudes toward the Jews in the fourth century. In the first and second centuries, the Roman Empire harbored a great deal of hostility against the Jews for their revolts against the Roman government.[2] Recall that after the failure of the Bar-Kokhba Revolt, Emperor Hadrian had the Judaean province renamed Palestine in an effort to humiliate the Jews for their rebellion.

Whether or not such political sentiments were the driving force behind early Christian anti-Semitism or not, it is at least plausible to assume that it played a role in motivating some of the anti-Jewish rhetoric by certain Catholics of the fourth century. Judaea was considered a gem in the Roman crown at one time,

---

[1] Eusebius Pamphilus, *The Life Of The Blessed Emperor Constantine*, Book III (Ch. V).
[2] For more on the Jewish Revolt, see (Ch. 6).

Herod's Temple being the crown jewel. But by the fourth century, much of its former beauty had become desolate. Although Judaea was the ancestral homeland of the Jews and Jerusalem was their most holy city, many gentile Christians developed a sort of neo-nostalgia for the birthplace of Christianity, one that excluded the Jews from their reimagined history.

Nevertheless, despite opposition from certain groups that were hostile to the Jews, many Christians continued to worship alongside the Jews long after the first century. Furthermore, many continued to celebrate the traditional holy days of the Old Testament. Such continuity with the Jews displeased men like Eusebius and Constantine. When Eusebius was writing about the Easter dispute, he said, "For while one party asserted that the Jewish custom should be adhered to, the other affirmed that the exact recurrence of the period should be observed." The incongruity described by Eusebius between the two competing factions concerned the celebration date for Easter. The Jews used a lunar calendar consisting of 354 days rather than a solar calendar made up of 365. The Jewish lunar calendar has a nineteen-year cycle. During seven years out of those nineteen, there is an extra month added to ensure that the holidays occur in their appropriate seasons.[3] Furthermore, there are restrictions concerning when the various holidays within a given month may begin. For example, the spring holiday of Passover is held in the Hebrew month of Nisan, and it begins on a full moon.[4] Because moon's cycle dictates when the holiday begins, the holiday does not always occur on the same calendar date every year. The eight days of Passover fluctuate between the months of March and

---

[3] Telushkin, Joseph. *Jewish Literacy*. New York: William Morrow and Company, Inc., 1991. (p. 561).
  • The fluidity of celebration dates for the Jewish holidays has contributed to the statement, "the holidays came early this year" or, "the holidays are late this year" in Judaism. By contrast, the Roman Empire operated on what was known as the Julian Calendar in the fourth century. By the sixteenth century, the Gregorian Calendar was adopted which is still used today.
[4] Moss, Aron. "Why is Passover on a Full Moon?." Chabad.org. Accessed November 27, 2021.
https://www.chabad.org/holidays/passover/pesach_cdo/aid/4250850/jewish/Why-Is-Passover-on-a-Full-Moon.htm.

April, not necessarily landing on a specific day of the month each year.

Although popularly known among Christians as Easter, the holiday celebrating the resurrection of Jesus Christ is known in the Jewish calendar as Passover. The word "Easter" appears in the New Testament one time,[5] and it is the Greek word *pascha* (in Hebrew *pesach*), meaning "Passover." Thus, quite literally, Easter is Passover and Passover is Easter. They were not distinguishable holidays in the first century.

Christians celebrated the resurrection of Jesus Christ during Passover because according to the gospel writers, Jesus was said to have been crucified, buried, and resurrected during the week of Passover.[6] Because all of the first Christians were Jews, it is not surprising to discover that the traditional celebration was maintained long after the first century. Holy days of the Old Testament were not abandoned after Christian conversion.[7] When gentiles were converted to Christianity, many adopted the practice of celebrating the traditional week of Easter with their Jewish brothers and sisters. But as Judaism and Christianity became more fractured, there arose certain Christians who did not want to celebrate Easter according to the lunar calendar of the Jews. Eusebius writes,

> The other [those who wanted to break Passover celebration away from the Jews] affirmed that the exact recurrence of the period should be observed, without following the authority of those who were in error, and strangers to the grace of the gospel as well in this as in other respects.[8]

---

[5] Acts 12:4.

[6] Matthew 26:2; Mark 14;12.
- Passover is celebrated over the course of eight days. The gospel writers inform us that the episode known as "The Last Supper" between Jesus and His disciples happened on the first day of the Passover (Matthew 26:17).

[7] In Acts 20:16 Paul is said to have been eager to travel to Jerusalem to celebrate the day of Pentecost, which was held fifty days after Passover. This account happened long after his conversion to Christianity.

[8] Eusebius Pamphilus, *The Life Of The Blessed Emperor Constantine*, Book III (Ch. V).

Eusebius justified the behavior of the Christians who wanted to change the Easter celebration date by stating that they did not want to "follow the authority of those who were in error," likely a reference to the Jews who had rejected Jesus. However, the Scriptures, not Jewish traditions, set the date for the Passover celebration.[9] Interestingly, Antiochus IV Epiphanes used a similar strategy in the second century B.C.E. He attempted to force the Jews to honor a solar calendar and discontinue their observance of holy days.[10] The dispute between the two competing groups of Christians was apparently so significant that it warranted lengthy discussion and resolution at the First Council of Nicaea. Just as Tertullian had once accused Praxeas of relating too much to the Jews in his presentation of the Godhead, Constantine warned Christians against association with those he claimed were responsible for killing the Messiah. Constantine's letter to the churches respecting the First Council of Nicaea regarding the celebration of Passover marks some of the earliest known use of blood-libel against the Jews—the accusation that they were Christ-killers. Eusebius recorded the words of Constantine,

> At this meeting the question concerning the most holy day of Easter was discussed, and it was resolved by the united judgement of all present, that this feast ought to be kept by all and in every place on one and the same day...And first of all, it appeared an unworthy thing that in the celebration of this most holy feast we should follow the practice of the Jews, who have impiously defiled their hands with enormous sin, and are therefore deservedly afflicted with blindness of soul. For we have it in our power, if we abandon their custom, to prolong the due observance of this ordinance to future ages, by a truer order, which we have preserved from the very day of the passion until present time. Let us then have nothing in common with the detestable Jewish crowd; for we have received from our Saviour a different way...Beloved brethren, let us with one consent adopt this course, and withdraw ourselves from all participation in their baseness...For how

---

[9] Exodus 12:13-20.
[10] 2nd Maccabees (Ch. 6-7).

should they be capable of forming sound judgement, who, since their parricidal guilt in slaying their Lord, have been subject to the direction, not of reason, but of ungoverned passion, and are swayed by every impulse of the mad spirit that is in them...But supposing these reasons were not of sufficient weight, still it would be incumbent on your Sagacities to strive and pray continually that the purity of your souls may not seem in anything to be sullied by fellowship with the customs of these most wicked men.[11]

It is important to recognize that Constantine did not frame the discussion of Easter celebration in the context of finding a proper reoccurring date to celebrate the holiday in a historical sense. There is no specific dispute about two competing points on the calendar. According to the emperor, the primary motive behind shifting the date for the Easter celebration was to create distance between Christians and the Jews. This attitude was not consistent with the teachings of the early Christians, who stressed forbearance toward the unbelieving Jews.[12] The specific accusation that the Jews were responsible for killing the Christ is also curious. In the gospel accounts, Jesus emphasized that no one religious or racial group was responsible for His crucifixion. New Testament soteriology relied on the belief that the Messiah would offer Himself as a willing sacrifice, and that through His willing self-denial, He would set a precedent for Christians to do the same.

> Therefore doth my Father love me, because I lay down my life, that I might take it again. No man taketh it from me, but I lay it down of myself. I have power to lay it down, and I have power to take it again. This commandment have I received of my Father.[13]

---

[11] Eusebius Pamphilus, *The Life Of The Blessed Emperor Constantine*, Book III, (Ch. XVIII).
  - According to Eusebius, this inclusion is an excerpt from a letter written by Constantine.
[12] Romans (Ch. 11).
[13] John 10:17-18 (KJV).

Objection to the accusation that the Jews killed Christ may also be made on historical grounds. Crucifixion was not legal under Jewish law; it was a wholly Roman practice. While the Jews may have falsely accused Jesus of many acts that He did not commit,[14] it was technically the Romans who crucified Jesus on the cross. Thus, both Jew and gentile played their part in rejecting the Christ. Nevertheless, neither was responsible for the death of the Messiah in the truest sense. According to the New Testament, Jesus offered Himself as a willing sacrifice for both Jew and gentile, despite the fact that both the Jews and the gentiles rejected Him. Thus, salvation through the blood of Jesus was not for one racial or religious group; the death of Christ was for all mankind. The most obvious case to be made against the polemical statements made by Constantine is that Christianity itself exists only because of the death, burial, and resurrection of Jesus Christ. Thus, had He not been crucified, there could not have been a resurrection; had there not been a resurrection, there would be no church. From a Christian perspective, it is irrational to lament the death of Jesus Christ on the cross as a tragedy that should not have happened. The Scriptures suggest precisely the opposite—that His death was not a tragedy but a triumph. His death was cruel, but His resurrection granted access to the immortality that Constantine wrote so fondly of.

Constantine's apparent biblical illiteracy was probably not the only cause of his virulent attitude toward the Jews though. Considering the Jews in the political context of the fourth century is just as important as the religious context. Palestine was a black mark on the history of the Roman Empire. The ostracization of the Jews was an inevitable outgrowth of attempting to unify the empire under a single religious banner. The pagans could be swayed to acknowledge Christianity's supremacy over their own gods, because the two were not necessarily mutually exclusive in the pagan psyche. That was not the case for the Jews. Judaism's high emphasis on maintaining strict monotheism kept it diametrically opposed to making concords with the religions of surrounding nations. Antiochus IV Epiphanes of the second

---

[14] Mark 14:56.

century B.C.E. had the same problem as Constantine in the fourth century C.E. In a world where Judaism was allowed to thrive, how could a one-empire religion be achieved? Constantine wrote,

> For we have it in our power, if we abandon their custom, to prolong the due observance of this ordinance to future ages, by a truer order, which we have preserved from the very day of the passion until present time. Let us then have nothing in common with the detestable Jewish crowd...[15]

Perhaps more than any other, this statement by Constantine signaled an unfortunate motive behind formation of the Catholic Church—to recast Christianity into a mold that the Jews could no longer fit. When the new date for Easter was decided upon, it was done as a calculated re-ordering of the future of Christianity.

Constantine's letter to the bishops regarding the Easter controversy spans across three entire chapters of Eusebius' work, suggesting that the controversy was a much bigger problem for the Catholic Church than has perhaps been realized. Eusebius remarks that at least half of the bishops at Nicaea were opposed to abandoning the traditional celebration of Easter. Constantine mentions certain Roman cities and dioceses that had already adopted the new date for the Easter celebration, leaving out any mention of Antioch or Diocesis Orientis,[16] suggesting that those areas may have resisted the change.

> Since, therefore, it was needful that this matter should be rectified, so that we might have nothing in common with that nation of parricides who slew their Lord; and since that arrangement is consistent with propriety which is observed by all the churches of the western, southern, and northern parts of the world[17]...it is most fitting that all should unite in

---

[15] Eusebius Pamphilus, *The Life Of The Blessed Emperor Constantine*, Book III, (Ch. XVIII).
[16] Diocesis Orientis would have been the region covering Palestine after the provinces were re-drawn by Diocletian in the third century.
[17] Constantine is hesitant to mention all the eastern territories in this portion of his writing, as he later admits not all of the east—the older home of Christianity— was on board with his changes.

desiring that which sound reason appears to demand, and in avoiding all participation in the perjured conduct of the Jews.[18]

According to Constantine, the matter of Easter celebration needed to be rectified, not to establish a proper date for Easter, but to ensure that the future of Christianity no longer had any association with the Jews. Like the articulation of the doctrine of the trinity before it, the alterations made to the celebration of Easter were in part motivated by animosity toward the Jewish people. Nevertheless, it is significant to note that some Christians resisted the changes made by Constantine and his council. Although the twentieth chapter of Eusebius' work stressed the authority of the councils in settling such matters, it is evident that many Christians chose to ignore the decisions that were made at Nicaea.

At this juncture, it was Christians, not Jews, who were creating a headache for the Catholic leaders. There were no rabbis present at the First Council of Nicaea—only Christians. Thus, the struggle to separate Christianity from the traditions of the Jews happened within the framework of the believers, not outside them. That is important to our discussion. As late as the fourth century, there were believers who did not see eye to eye with the leadership of the universal movement, and they were often characterized as being too favorable to the Jews.[19] In some cases, the divide between the two groups of believers was expressed in dramatic fashion.

---

[18] Eusebius Pamphilus, The Life Of The Blessed Emperor Constantine, Book III (Ch. XIX).
- Although a controversial discussion in Christianity today, the fact that the dates for Passover were changed in the Christian tradition to avoid association with the Jews cannot be avoided. It is the opinion of this writer that it would be profitable for Jewish-Christian relations globally if Christians returned the celebration of Easter to its traditional dates.

[19] Recall the accusations of Tertullian, the writings of Justin Martyr, etc.

In the late fourth century, shortly after the First Council of Nicaea, an archbishop of Constantinople named John Chrysostom wrote at length about the issue of Christians fellowshipping with the Jews.[20] Interestingly, his homilies appear to be written to his own congregation. The writings were gathered into a polemic known as *Against Judaizing Christians*, in which his congregants were not accused of observing the Law of Moses, but of fraternization with the Jews.

> Another very serious illness calls for any cure my words can bring, an illness which has become implanted in the body of the Church. We must first root this ailment out and then take thought for matters outside...What is this disease? The festivals of the pitiful and miserable Jews are soon to march upon us as one after the other in quick succession: the feast of Trumpets, the feast of Tabernacles, the fasts. There are many in our ranks who say they think as we do. Yet some of these are going to watch the festivals and others will join the Jews in keeping their feasts and observing their fasts. I wish to drive this perverse custom from the Church right now...I am afraid that, because of their ill-suited association and deep ignorance, some Christians may partake in the Jews' transgressions; once they have done so, I fear my homilies on these transgressions will be in vain. For if they hear no word from me today, they will then join the Jews in their fasts; once they have committed this sin it will be useless for me to apply the remedy.[21]

There is some irony to the fact that Chrysostom called the holidays of the Jews "transgressions" and "sins." Jesus Christ participated in all such festivals, complicating the claim that the traditions of the Jews were somehow sinful. The apostles did not teach that the gentiles should observe the Law of Moses in order to merit

---

20 Irshai, Oded. "Confronting A Christian Empire." In *Cultures of the Jews*, edited by David Biale, 202. New York: Schocken Books, 2002.
21 John Chrysostom, *Against Judaizing Christians*, Book I, (Ch. I; Sect. IV-VI).
   - The last sentence of Chrysostom's excerpt seems to imply that such association with the Jews amounted to unforgivable blasphemy from the perspective of the Catholic Church.

salvation. But from a biblical perspective, the claim that the holy days were acts of transgression against God is without merit. The Apostle Paul continued to celebrate the holy days even after his conversion, further complicating Chrysostom's claims. As both a believer and Jew, Paul felt it was acceptable to reverence the Biblical holidays. From a New Testament perspective, many of Chrysostom's claims appear to have been misguided at best.

Chrysostom's assertion that many Christian joined the Jews in celebrating the Biblical holy days as late as the fourth century is astounding. The timing of the homily suggests that the First Council of Nicaea failed in establishing the grand sweeping reforms that it was aiming for.[22] As one reads through the homily, it appears that Chrysostom's greater concern was the attendance of synagogue services, as he describes at length the problem of his congregants attending such services.

> Since there are some who think of the synagogue as a holy place, I must say a few words to them. Why do you reverence that place? Must you not despise it, hold it in abomination, run away from it?...So it is that I exhort you to flee and shun their gatherings...For when they see that you, who worship the Christ whom they crucified, are reverently following their rituals, how can they fail to think that the rites they have performed are the best and our ceremonies are worthless?...Therefore, flee the gatherings and holy places of the Jews. Let no man venerate the synagogue because of the holy books; let him hate and avoid it because the Jews outrage and maltreat the holy ones, because they refuse to believe their words, because they accuse them of the ultimate impiety.[23]

According to the book of Acts, early Christians preached and fellowshipped in synagogues, both Jews and gentiles.[24] This practice likely continued for generations. The fact that some Christians living during the time of John Chrysostom apparently

---

[22] Chrysostom was born in 347 C.E. and died in 407 C.E.
[23] John Chrysostom, *Against Judaizing Christians*, Book I, (Ch. V; Sect. I-VIII).
[24] Acts 14:1.

revered the synagogue and actively attended it seems to suggest that the earliest forms of Christian liturgy continued well into the fourth century. This behavior was likely not intended to bolster support for Christian observance of the Law of Moses but to maintain unity with the Judaean heritage of Christianity. Christianity worships a Jewish savior, reads Jewish holy books, and began on a Jewish holy day.[25] Chrysostom makes no mention of Christian observance of the Law of Moses.[26] His primary complaint concerns Christian association with the Jewish people. This lends credibility to the notion that Catholic Christianity wanted to disassociate from the earliest presentations of Christian doctrine, including strict monotheism, the celebration of Passover, and water baptism in Jesus' name.

Chrysostom repeated the trope that the Jews were Christ-killers, evidence that perhaps Constantine's accusation at the First Council of Nicaea had some staying power in the Catholic Church.[27] The archbishop went further than earlier writers in his criticism of the Jews, crossing into the sort of anti-Semitic rhetoric that would eventually lead to persecution against the Jews.

> When brute animals feed from a full manger, they grow plump and become more obstinate and hard to hold in check; they endure neither the yoke, the reigns, nor the hand of the charioteer. Just so the Jewish people were driven by their drunkenness and plumpness to the ultimate evil; they kicked about, they failed to accept the yoke of Christ, nor did they pull the plow of his teaching. Another prophet hinted at this when he said: "Israel is as obstinate as a stubborn heifer". And still another called the Jews "an untamed calf". Although such beasts are unfit for work, they are fit for killing.[28]

---

[25] Most Christian scholars agree that Christianity began on the day of Pentecost as described in the book of Acts.

[26] Synagogues are not mentioned in the Law of Moses because at the time of the giving of the Law at Mt. Sinai, synagogues did not yet exist.

[27] Recall that Chrysostom was the archbishop of Constantinople at the time he wrote his polemic. Thus, as an archbishop Chrysostom appeared to possess a very elementary understanding of the greater principles of the New Testament.

[28] John Chrysostom, *Against Judaizing Christians*, Book I, (Ch. II; Sect. V-VI).

"Although such beasts are unfit for work, they are fit for killing." While many Catholics are supportive of the land of Israel and the Jewish people today, it is apparent that some of the earliest Catholic writers harbored a great deal of hostility against the Jews and wanted to disassociate Christianity from them completely.

There is a great deal of evidence to suggest that the project of recasting Christianity in a Roman mold was broadly applied in fourth-century Catholicism. To create a universal church, Constantine needed a version of Christianity that the empire could unify around. The First Council of Nicaea greatly aided the effort by articulating a presentation of the Godhead that pleased the Catholics but was not necessarily offensive to the pagans. In order to shape the new religion in the image of Rome, Christianity needed to be divorced from its Judaean roots completely.

*Figure 11.1*

Mosaic located in Basilica of St. Pudentiana, Rome. This fourth century depiction of Christ includes Jesus seated upon a golden throne and wearing a Roman toga. The halo surrounding the head of Jesus was a feature of Apollo and the Unconquered Sun. It was re-appropriated for depictions of Christ sometime around 390 C.E., making it one of the earliest amalgamations of pagan iconography with the Christian world.

A grand sweeping campaign led by Constantine's mother was put together to reshape the history of Christianity in a way that was more palatable to gentiles everywhere. Nothing was off-limits—not even Jesus of Nazareth.

Figure 11.1 illustrates a fourth-century mosaic found in St. Pudentiana's Basilica in Rome. The mosaic depicts Christ in a Roman toga, seated on a gaudy throne in the midst of what are believed to be some of His disciples. The background of the painting includes large colonnade structures that typified the Greco-Roman world. There is also a halo around the head of Jesus, an icon that was completely foreign to Jewish and Christian imagery.

The halo was commonly included in icon representations of Apollo and other iterations of the sun god such as Jupiter or the Unconquered Sun. Such presentations of Christ may have assuaged pagan predations against Christianity, but they also distanced Christianity from more Jewish expressions of Jesus. In a world where the Jews were said to have been the religious enemy of Jesus Christ and the Christians, a Jewish representation of Jesus was unacceptable to many Catholics. Recasting Jesus as a citizen of Rome was useful to the cause of creating a unified religion of the Roman Empire. The representation of Jesus in the Basilica of St. Pudentiana also betrays the claim that Constantine's Byzantine Empire abandoned all affection for older presentations of the gods. Just as the Jews of the first century B.C.E. struggled to maintain autonomy from the Greco-Roman world, the Christians were in Hellenism, and Hellenism in Christianity. The tacit relationship between Christianity and idols created in the fourth century would have unforeseen consequences throughout the history of the Byzantine Empire.

Perhaps the most impactful feature of the Romanization of Christianity was the mission of Constantine's mother, Helena, in Palestine. Constantine sent his mother into Palestine in 327 C.E. to set up Christian holy sites that could be venerated instead of the traditional Jewish sites. With nearly an unlimited number of resources, Helena traveled into the Holy Land with the mission of building new churches in Bethlehem, the Mount of Olives, and Jerusalem.[29] The most significant architectural project of this

[29] Strauss, Barry S. *Ten Caesars*. New York: Simon & Schuster, 2019. (p. 305-306).

period was the construction of the Church of the Holy Sepulcher where Constantine imagined that the resurrection of Jesus Christ took place. Although renovated many times throughout the centuries, part of the original structure still stands today.

*Figure 11.2*

Church of the Holy Sepulcher, located in Jerusalem. Although Catholic tradition maintains that this was the site of the resurrection of Jesus Christ, the geography is highly questionable. The Romans were not apt to perform crucifixions in the middle of larger cities, and the Church of the Holy Sepulcher is not located near Golgotha where Jesus was crucified. The geography of the crucifixion site is significant because it is known from the New Testament writers that Jesus was buried in a garden tomb not far from the site of His crucifixion, diminishing the likelihood of the Catholic tradition. Tourists who travel to Israel today may visit another site known as The Garden Tomb, which is largely considered a more likely site for the resurrection of Jesus, as it is situated only walking distance from Golgotha.

During the rise of the Byzantine Empire, imperial laws were later set in order to ban the construction of synagogues as well.[30]

> After the Romans destroyed Jerusalem as punishment for the Jewish revolt, they rebuilt it under Hadrian but as a pagan city rather than a Jewish city; Aelia Capitolina instead of

---

[30] Ibid. (20) (p. 194).

Jerusalem. Now they rebuilt it as Jerusalem but, again, not a Jewish city; Jerusalem was now a Christian city.[31]

The fourth century reshaped the identity of Christianity from a Jewish or Judaean-influenced religion into a Roman one. Drastic steps were taken to reimagine Christianity as a religion of the empire and retell its history in a way that shed favorable light on Catholic beliefs.

The role that Constantine played in reshaping the identity of Christianity in the Roman Empire cannot be overstated. Although he may have been ignorant concerning matters of doctrine, Constantine was a shrewd politician. He understood the importance of image and perception. While his legacy as the second savior of Christianity may have been fictitious, Constantine's ability to retell the story of Christianity through the narrative of Roman culture set the stage for the rise of one of the most powerful religious sects in the world—the Roman Catholic Church.

Nevertheless, Constantine was also prone to rash behavior that would put a black mark on his memory too. Because of the honor he has received from Christians in church history, it is important for readers to understand the character of Constantine. Constantine's goal was to be remembered as the founder of the Christian empire, and he accomplished that—but he was not a Christian in the traditional sense. At no point in his life did Constantine experience a moment of conversion consistent with the New Testament experiences. His continued worship of the Roman gods through iconography on coins and arches long after the supposed vision in 310 C.E. is proof enough of this fact. Idolatry, even if practiced passively, was completely forbidden by the early Christians. Furthermore, his refusal to be baptized until his death suggests that Constantine remained quite shallow in his

---

[31] Ibid. (29) (p. 306).

understanding of basic Christian beliefs until the end of his life. But all his theological misgivings aside, there are much more important reasons to question the sincerity of Constantine's Christianity. After the First Council of Nicaea, Constantine's legacy was thrown into chaos when he ordered the execution of his second wife Fausta, along with his son from his first marriage named Crispus. This led many to believe that the emperor's overtures toward Christianity were motivated more by politics than by personal convictions.

Events surrounding the executions are not entirely clear, and opinions vary widely among modern historians as to the reason for the killings. What can be known is that in 326 C.E., one year after the First Nicene Council, Constantine ordered his son Crispus to be executed.[32] The accusation against Crispus was likely treason, as it was common for emperors to suspect their families (particularly fathers and sons) of trying to usurp power.[33] That same year, Fausta suffered similar accusations, and in a bout of paranoia, Constantine arranged to have her killed as well. Ancient historians are not precise in detailing the circumstances of her death, but many claim that Constantine either had her drowned in a scalding bath or had her suffocated in a bathhouse.[34]

Crispus and Fausta were not the only two relatives that Constantine had executed. By the end of his reign, Constantine had arranged for the deaths of his son, father-in-law, two brothers-in-law, nephew, and wife. Ancient historians also state that Constantine had numerous friends executed during this time,

---

[32] The ancient writer Sidonius Apollinaris (C.A. 440-485 C.E.) records that Crispus was executed by poisoning. Modern historians have surmised that he was drowned in a bath house, however this theory is probably a conflation of the death of Fausta and Crispus together, either confusing the two or combining them. It is the opinion of this writer that Sidonius' account is the more accurate. For more on this, see:
- Sidonius Apollinaris, *Letters*. Translated by O.M. Dalton, 1915.

[33] Grant, Michael. *The Roman Emperors*. New York: Simon & Schuster, 1985. (p. 233-234).

[34] Varying accounts surrounding the death of Fausta can be found in:
- Burkhardt, Jacob. *The Age of Constantine the Great*. New York: Pantheon Books, Inc., 1949.
- Balsdon, John P. *Roman Women*. New York: John Day Company, 1962.
- The ancient historian Eutropius also records that Constantine had his wife and son slain in his *Breviarium*, composed sometime around 369 C.E. (Book X).

evidentially motivated by his paranoia that there was a conspiracy to remove him from the throne.[35] Constantine's brutality should not go unnoticed when examining his influence on the Christian movement throughout the empire. By all available evidence, a man who was not converted to Christianity had the final say in the direction of the Christian church during his lifetime. A man who claimed to be the thirteenth apostle and demanded quasi-worship at his death was also a man given to impressively immoral behavior and ideologies that were not consistent with traditional Christianity.

Second to his reshaping of Rome toward Christianization, Constantine's greatest achievement throughout his lifetime was his decision to relocate the center of power in the Roman Empire to the East. Like many emperors before him, Constantine had little interest in Rome itself, and after the fall of Licinius, the East was ripe for the taking.

The ancient Greek city of Byzantium had his interest. Byzantium was founded around the seventh century B.C.E. and served as a military outpost for rulers even as late as the wars between Constantine and Licinius. Situated on the coast of the Sea of Marmara toward the southern end of the Bosporus, Byzantium sat directly between the borders of Europe and Asia, making it one of the most strategically valuable locations in the ancient world.[36]

> The new city was dedicated on May 11, 330. The emperor built on a grand scale. Constantinople had a new palace, a circus (that is, horse-racing venue), a forum surrounded by porticoes, a Senate, and a series of churches. In the center of the forum stood a tall porphyry column, part of which still

---

[35] Ibid. (31) (Eutropius, Breviarium).
[36] Norwich, John J. *A Short History of Byzantium*. New York: Alfred A. Knopf, Inc., 1997. (p. xxxvii, preface-p. 3).

stands. On the tope was a large, nude statue of Constantine himself wearing a crown with rays coming out of it.[37]

Figure 11.3

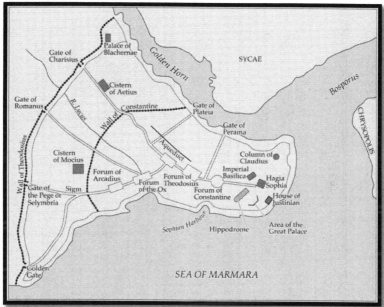

Map of Byzantine Constantinople. The Byzantine Empire survived for approximately 1,000 years, making it one of the most enduring empires in the history of the world.

When Constantine relocated the capital of the empire to the East, he renamed Byzantium as Constantinople (Constantine's City).

> The new city was dedicated on May 11, 330. The emperor built on a grand scale. Constantinople had a new palace, a circus (that is, horse-racing venue), a forum surrounded by porticoes, a Senate, and a series of churches. In the center of the forum stood a tall porphyry column, part of which still stands. On the tope was a large, nude statue of Constantine himself wearing a crown with rays coming out of it.[38]

---

[37] Ibid. (29) (p. 308).
[38] Ibid. (29) (p. 308).

Constantinople was founded two decades after Constantine's alleged conversion, once again raising questions about his Christian legacy.

*Figure 11.4*          *Figure 11.5*

While much of the original structure (left) has deteriorated, Constantine's Column can still be seen today in the ancient city. Figure 11.5 (right) shows an artistic rendering of what the original structure probably looked like.

According to historical descriptions, figure 11.5 shows an artistic rendering of what the original porphyry pillar that Constantine had constructed would have looked like. In the center of his new forum, the emperor constructed a sizable nude statue of himself cast in the form of the ancient gods, holding an orb in one hand and a scepter in the other. Nude statues glorifying the human physique typified Greek art and were later adopted by the Romans. One of the most common features of Greco-Roman sculptures that depicted the gods was the orb and scepter, most commonly associated with Zeus and Jupiter (see figure 11.6). The fact that Constantine chose these features for his own statue perhaps illustrated his belief even late in life that he had taken on the mantle of his predecessor Diocletian, assuming the role of supreme ruler. Recall that Diocletian chose Jupiter as his sponsor and used iterations of Jupiter and Hercules to promote the legacy of the tetrarchy. Furthermore, close examination of figure 11.5 reveals the crown of rays upon the head of Constantine, regarded by historians as an associative display of veneration of the Unconquered Sun or Apollo.

*Figure 11.6*

Hermitage Replica of the Statue of seated Zeus, located in Olympia, Greece. The orb in the right hand and scepter in left was a posture used for many sculpted works of similar style. When Caesar Augustus had a statue of himself constructed in the likeness of Zeus, he used a similar pose, again incorporating the use of orb and scepter.

Even toward the end of his life, Constantine did not completely cast off his relationship to the cult of light. When Constantinople was constructed, it retained much of its Greek identity. Not long after its founding, Greek was adopted as the official language of the empire, signaling the desire for Greek revivalism in

Byzantium.[39] Constantine's ability to obscure the relationship between the gods of the Roman Empire and the Christian God allowed him to bridge the gap between two worlds that had been in conflict for centuries. His decision to institutionalize the Catholic Church set a precedent for the increasingly murky relationship between church and state in generations following his death, the consequences of which would not be fully realized for centuries.

The re-imagining of Christianity in a Roman light was not just a natural consequence of the religion becoming predominantly practiced by gentiles as is often assumed. Although gentile participation in Christianity could be traced back to the first two decades of the church,[40] their entry into Christianity was perceived by the earliest Christians to be an adoption of a way that had already been established, not the formation of a new one. Geographically speaking, early gentile Christians were closely associated with Jewish believers who founded the movement, so it made sense for those same gentiles to adopt the practices and customs of the Jews. Hence, observance of Easter, synagogue attendance, and Saturday worship all characterized early Christian practices in and around Judaea by Jew and gentile alike. As Christianity expanded into the larger gentile communities, the customs of the gentiles were less influenced by Jewish believers, so it once again made sense for certain practices to become more normative in these Christian communities than in others (Sunday worship instead of Saturday, living by a 365-day solar calendar instead of a 354-day lunar calendar, etc.). But in both instances, the Judaean origins of Christianity were respected. Those who wanted to worship on Saturday were free to do so, and those who wanted to worship on Sunday could do that too. Some celebrated Easter following the lunar calendar; others followed the solar. Regardless of their differences, the communities maintained correspondence and fellowship and did not appear to disassociate from one another. In this way, the early Christians practiced the

---

39 Ibid. (33) (p. 230).
40 While it is not known precisely when Cornelius converted, the timeline of seven to thirteen years after the birth of the church in Acts chapter two is generally accepted.

kind of forbearance with one another on cultural issues that the Apostle Paul seemed to allude to in his epistles.

> For though I be free from all men, yet have I made myself servant unto all, that I might gain the more. And unto the Jews I became as a Jew, that I might gain the Jews; to them that are under the law, as under the law, that I might gain them that are under the law; To them that are without law, as without law, (being not without law to God, but under the law to Christ,) that I might gain them that are without law. To the weak became I as weak, that I might gain the weak: I am made all things to all men, that I might by any means save some. And this I do for the gospel's sake, that I might be partaker thereof with you.[41]

The rise of the Catholic Church and the influence of the Roman Empire changed the relationship between believers. Under the influence of Constantine, there was an articulated motive to distance the Christian religion from its birthplace—Judaea. Even the province itself needed to be remodeled. Thus, while even gentile Christians acknowledged the value of the Jewish roots of Christianity before the fourth century, after the fourth century, it became anathema to do so. Recall that in John Chrysostom's writings to his church, he acknowledged that there were those in his congregation who only wanted to watch the festivals of the Jews, not necessarily participate. According to Chrysostom, they wanted to do so because they respected the Jews for preserving the holy books of the church and because they were the founders of the Christian movement.[42] But Chrysostom responded to the wishes of the congregants by commanding them to hate the Jews, and reject their feasts as an abomination unto the Lord. His specific instructions are essential to our discussion, because this was not a case of Christians reverting to the Law of Moses as a means of salvation, such as those cases discussed by the Apostle

---

[41] 1st Corinthians 9:19-23 (KJV).
[42] John Chrysostom, *Against Judaizing Christians*, Book I (Ch. I; Sect. IV-VI).

Paul in the book of Galatians.[43] It was a simple ban on association—a command to stay away from the Jews.

This sort of behavior by Catholic leaders could not help but impact later Christian interpretations of Scripture concerning the Godhead. Early Christianity was characterized by a high-monotheism, something stressed in both the Old and New Testaments. It was an extension of the covenant of Abraham into Christian doctrine. The exclusivity of the name of Jesus in water baptism signaled the early church's belief that in Him dwelled "all the fulness of the Godhead bodily." As went the connection to the Judaean roots of the church, so went the emphasis on upholding the practices of the early Judaean Christians. Maintaining the older traditions was not useful to the Romans who wanted to refashion Christianity. Thus, new customs were created that were entirely novel to the early Christians.

Nevertheless, many of the reforms made by the Catholic Church to Christian doctrine were rejected by a great number of Christians. It would take generations of councils, creeds, and coercion to establish fundamental doctrines of the Catholic Church such as papal supremacy, Marian veneration, and trinitarian water baptism. There is strong evidence to suggest that there were Christian groups all over the empire that did not acquiesce to the demands of the Catholic Church throughout the Middle Ages. Nevertheless, the Catholicism that was institutionalized in the fourth century held the political reigns of religion in the empire for the next eleven centuries (roughly speaking). In the next chapter, we will examine how the doctrine of the trinity came to reach an articulated form and was codified as official Catholic Church doctrine, as well as the unforeseen impact that Constantine's paganism had on the generations following his death in 337 C.E.

---

43 In his epistle to the Galatians, Paul addressed certain believers who, after having already come to Christ through the new birth, wanted to revert to the Law of Moses as a means of sanctification, something which the apostle forbade.

# CHAPTER XII

## The Triumph

## of

## Byzantium

The thirty years immediately following the death of Constantine the Great were characterized by vicious sibling rivalry. His three sons, Constantius II, Constantine II, and Constans I, all vied for power and failed to establish lasting dominance over the others.[1] None managed to create a sustainable legacy as their father had done, and in 361 C.E., Constantine the Great's nephew took the throne. Although his reign was exceptionally short, Julian the Apostate—as he would later come to be known—fomented a great deal of religious controversy in the empire that would eventually culminate with a codified and tyrannical Christian doctrine being instituted as Roman law over the next three decades. But Christianization was not Julian's aim.

Not for nothing was he known as Julian "the Apostate." Like all of the house of Constantine in the fourth century, Julian professed Christianity out of obeisance to Constantine the Great. But his heart was far from the religion of his family. Julian was a devout pagan, and he resented the Christianization of the empire. Unlike much of his family, which remained in and around the epicenter of the empire during the reign of Constantine, Julian spent his most formative years studying abroad in cities such as Athens and Cappadocia.[2] Although Julian was not well respected by the other members of his family, his services became necessary in 355 C.E. when Constantius II realized that if he did not appoint

---

[1] Grant, Michael. *The Roman Emperors*. New York: Simon & Schuster, 1985. (p. 240-247).
[2] Norwich, John J. *A Short History of Byzantium*. New York: Alfred A. Knopf, Inc., 1997. (p. 21-22).

another Caesar to replace his dead brothers, the empire was certain to destabilize.

Julian was called to Milan, whereafter he assumed command of his own army and was named Caesar, serving under Constantius II. Julian proved to be a more able ruler than Constantius, securing military victories in Cologne and the region of Strasbourg that Constantius had not. Although Julian was little more than a philosopher, he won favor with the armies that he controlled, and they soon wanted to name him as the new Augustus of the empire. Military factionalism characterized the unstable leadership of the empire before the advent of the tetrarchy, and it seemed to return after the death of Constantine. It is entirely possible that the army admired the pro-pagan tendencies of Julian and their motivation for elevating him was partially religious. By the time Julian came to power, much of the Roman military was not actually Roman in the truest sense. Many soldiers had been pressganged into service from the barbaric regions of Gaul, Britain, and the Danube frontier, not a few of which were pagans. After the army petitioned for his elevation in rank (in essence calling for the end of Constantius' supreme rule) Julian claimed that he prayed to Zeus for a sign, asking whether or not he should challenge his cousin. The gods (remarkably favorable to the will of the emperors) responded in affirmation, telling Julian to accept the will of the army.[3] Julian traveled to the East in hopes of securing peace with Constantius, although he knew such a peace was unlikely given the quasi-mutiny in the military. However, his concerns quickly became irrelevant. While Julian resided in Naissus, he received word that Constantius had died of illness while in Tarsus.[4] Thus, Julian secured supremacy over the empire without engaging in a civil war.

With Constantius out of the way, Julian could begin the religious reforms he desired in the empire. His pagan-revivalism was made easier because Christianity continued to be divided throughout Rome on many key issues, not the least of which was

---

[3] Ibid. (2) (p. 23).
[4] "Constantius II: Roman emperor." Britannica. Accessed December 1, 2021. https://www.britannica.com/biography/Constantius-II.

the Arian controversy mentioned in chapter ten of this book. In the fourth and fifth centuries, the Arians made up a much larger percentage of Christendom than is sometimes assumed. To make matters more complicated for the Christians, Constantius II was himself a believer in Arianism.[5] With the emperor on their side, the Arians had no reason to capitulate to the Catholic dogma. Constantine the Great had vested the Catholics with institutional legitimacy, so they had no reason to give in to Arianism. Bitter disputes ensued between the two groups for many years. When Julian came to power, Christianity could not easily present a united front against his pagan agenda.

Yet, Julian was no fool. Christianity had succeeded in supplanting paganism in the empire for a reason. It was not just a simple exercise in might over right—Christianity had also managed to win the war of hearts and minds. Pagans became docile toward Christianity because the elasticity of early credal statements by the church were murky enough to be ignored, and because pagans no longer had the stomach for persecution. The Christians may have encroached on the pagan way of life in matters of liturgy and doctrine, but they were also benevolent caretakers of their communities. Throughout the fourth century, the empire had become accustomed to pro-Christian policies. The Christians, for their part, had done a great deal to institute social reforms by giving money to the poor, building hostels for the homeless, and offering food to the hungry. Julian understood that if the empire were to be reverted to paganism, it would have to be done through the framework of Christian behaviors that were

---

[5] Ibid. (1) (p. 244-245).

- There is some evidence to suggest that Constantine the Great was also sympathetic to Arianism, perhaps made evident by his trivialization of the doctrinal disputes as discussed by Eusebius. Some have speculated that he embraced Arianism but was encouraged to remain silent about the belief for the sake of political unity. It does not seem unreasonable to assume that Constantine may have believed in Arianism. Given his complicated relationship to the Unconquered Sun and his continued participation in certain pagan practices, it would not be unrealistic to believe that he embraced a version of Christianity that lowered the status of Jesus from God Almighty to a sort of demi-god. "More than man but less than God" was a common belief about great rulers in the ancient world. It is the opinion of this writer that the idea that such a belief could be applied to Jesus Christ in the mind of Constantine is not so far-fetched.

enjoyed by the public. Thus, just as Constantine needed to maintain an obscure relationship with the pagans in order to consolidate the empire under a single religion, Julian needed paganism to imitate Christianity in order to justify his policy of reversion. Around 362 C.E., Julian wrote a letter to a pagan priest in which he said,

> The religion of the Greeks[6] does not yet prosper as I would wish, on account of those who profess it. But the gifts of the gods are great and splendid, better than any prayer or any hope...Why then do we think that this is sufficient and do not observe how the kindness of Christians to strangers, their care for the burial of their dead, and the sobriety of their lifestyle has done the most to advance their cause? Each of these things, I think, ought really to be practiced by us. It is not sufficient for you alone to practice them, but so must all the priests in Galatia without exception. Either make these men good by shaming them, persuade them to become so or fire them...Secondly, exhort the priests neither to approach a theater nor to drink in a tavern, nor to profess any base or infamous trade. Honor those who obey and expel those who disobey. Erect many hostels, one in each city, in order that strangers may enjoy my kindness, not only those of our own faith but also of others whosoever is want of money...For it is disgraceful when no Jew is a beggar and the impious Galileans[7] support our poor in addition to their own...Teach also those who profess the Greek religion to contribute to such services, and the villages of the Greek religion to offer the first-fruits to the gods. Accustom those of the Greek religion to such benevolence, teaching them that this has been our work from ancient times.[8]

---

[6] It is perhaps worthy of mention that Justin referred to the pagan cults of the empire as "the religion of the Greeks." In the Roman Empire, the deities of Rome were not distinct from their Grecian origin. Thus, Hellenism was not just tacitly adopted by the Romans, but explicitly.

[7] This was an early term for Christians.

[8] Julian the Apostate, *Letter to Arsacius*, C.A. 362 C.E.

- This excerpt is based on the translation of Edward J. Chinnock, *A Few Notes on Julian and a Translation of his Public Letters*, London: David Nut, 1901.

Julian continually stressed the need for social reforms through the religion of the Greeks as a means of winning back support from the public for the older religion of Rome. It is evident from his letter to Arsacius that Julian understood the Christian foothold in the empire could not be moved through simple persecution or by using force. The sectarian divisions of the church helped his cause, but they alone could not be counted on to dissolve the influence of Christianity in the empire. Julian needed more.

> Where Julian stands alone is in his convinced and dedicated paganism...It was as a professed pagan that he settled down to frame the laws which, he was convinced, would ultimately eliminate Christianity and re-establish the worship of the ancient gods throughout the Roman Empire...The first thing to do was to repeal the decrees closing the pagan temples.[9] An amnesty would then be proclaimed for all those orthodox churchmen whom the pro-Arian government of Constantius had sent into exile. Orthodox and Arian would soon be at each other's throats again, for, as Ammianus notes, 'he had found by experience that no wild beasts are so hostile to men as are Christian sects in general to one another'. After that it would be only a question of time before the Christians saw the error of their ways.[10]

Julian understood that politics are often downstream of culture, and culture is often downstream of religion. His decision to grant amnesty to the Catholics who had been dismissed by the Arian government of Constantius II was shrewd. By bringing back into the fold those who honored the Nicene faith, Julian ensured that the Arian controversy would spring up once again inside the church as it had during the time of Constantine. A divided church worked to his advantage as he pressed for pagan restoration throughout the Roman Empire. One of the more interesting actions taken by the emperor against Christianity was an edict

---

[9] Pagan temples were not closed by Constantine the Great, so it is to be assumed that the closing of pagan temples began during the reign of his sons between 337-361 C.E.
[10] Ibid. (2) (p. 25).

issued in 362 C.E. forbidding Christians to teach in schools of philosophy and rhetoric. The mandate also demanded that any Christian minister attempting to seek ordination for their calling must be first approved of by the state so as to ensure that they did not intend to continue teaching Greek literature.[11] A great deal of outrage was expressed by the Christian communities at this order, suggesting that the relationship between Christianity and the schools of philosophy throughout the Roman Empire was strong at the time. Julian's order seems to confirm that the early introduction of Greek philosophy into Christian thought had some staying power in the Catholic Church throughout the fourth century.

Ambitious though he was, Julian's time on the throne was short-lived. Throughout the summer of 363 C.E., the Roman army was pressing into Persian-occupied territory, attempting to fend off the incursions of the Persian king named Shapur. On June 26, 363 C.E., the emperor and his army were near Samarra when suddenly their army came under heavy attack. Julian bravely jumped into the fray himself to inspire his men, fighting alongside them. But he never strapped on his breastplate before doing so, and a flying spear caught him in the chaos of the Persian retreat. He died in the late hours of the evening, bringing an end to the pagan revivalism of the Byzantine Empire and making way for a new era of Catholic dominance.[12] That great movement of Catholicism was precipitated by yet more internal struggles for power over the empire. After the unexpected death of Julian's successor named Jovian, men such as Valentinian I, Valens, and Gratian all struggled to maintain control over the rising Byzantine Era of the empire. No single ruler would consolidate power as Constantine had done until the rise of Theodosius I the Great in 379 C.E. When he came to power, Theodosius joined hands with the Catholic

---

[11] Julian the Apostate, *Rescript on Christian Teachers*, C.A. 362 C.E.
[12] Ibid. (2) (p. 27).

Church to make the most extensive concerted effort to unify the empire under the Nicene faith since 325 C.E.

Theodosius did not profess to be a Christian before he began to reign. Yet, he furthered the spread of Catholicism in the empire more than any other emperor of Rome, second only to Constantine. During this time, the idea of a universal church that could serve as the vehicle for all religion in the Roman Empire remained as controversial as it had ever been. Although Constantine did a great deal to promote a universal religion in Rome, it did not last everywhere that it was tried. During the reign of Julian, the conflict between Catholicism and Arianism nearly destroyed the institutionalization of Christianity throughout the empire. If the kingdom was going to unify under a single religious banner, more drastic actions had to be taken to define Catholicism's boundaries and to ex-communicate dissenters from the movement. Theodosius was up to that task. Although he is often regarded as a benevolent ruler, he had a tyrannical side as well.[13] In order to reassert the authority of the Catholic Church in the empire, Theodosius issued a series of radical laws designed to root out heretics and establish the supremacy of the universal movement. There was even an edict issued that prohibited the discussion of any religious question whatsoever, likely intended to inhibit the possibility of conversion through debate. Other heretics were driven into underground movements or ostracized from society altogether. The Catholicism of the First Council of Nicaea was confirmed as the only legitimate faith in the empire, and all other iterations of Christianity were deemed illegal for the first time.[14] The emperor was determined to send a message to all those who professed to be Christians: if they did not adhere to the authority of the Catholic bishops, they would be ex-communicated.

---

[13] One incident which stained his memory was his response to a mob outside a garrison headquarters in Thessalonica. When a captain of the imperial garrison was killed in the incident, Theodosius ordered troops in the city to reassert their authority in whatever way they saw fit. In response, the soldiers waited until the people of the city were gathered in the Hippodrome for the games. Once they were trapped, the army attacked, killing more than seven thousand citizens. The massacre is regarded as the low point of Theodosius reign.
[14] *Edict of Thessalonica*, C.A. 380 C.E.

In 380 he pronounced that the faith professed by Pope Damasus and the bishop of Alexandria, based on the Catholic Nicene Creed, was the only true religion. In the following year he ordered that every church should be placed in the hands of Catholic bishops—whose claim to be regarded as Catholics he himself would define.[15]

Strangely, when Theodosius began his reforms, he did not immediately call for the end of pagan sacrifices or liturgy. It is entirely possible that this was a purely political decision designed to keep would-be pagan dissenters at bay until Christianity could once again achieve a firmer foothold in the empire, but this is entirely speculation. Eleven years after he issued his decree favoring the Catholic Church, he reversed course on the pagans. He began closing their shrines, perhaps lending credibility to the theory that his forbearance toward them in the first decade of his reign was primarily political.

Concerning Christian doctrine, the most significant contribution of Theodosius I to the Christianization of the empire was his formation of the First Council of Constantinople in 381 C.E. There is probably some irony to the fact that the council which codified the doctrine of the trinity as the only acceptable theology of the Catholic Church, convened in an ancient Greek city that honored the gods that Christianity had struggled against for so long.

Although the first creed issued by the Council of Nicaea in 325 C.E. confirmed the Catholic Church's position that the Father and Son were distinct persons yet unified in the Godhead, it did so primarily as a condemnation of Arianism. Furthermore, the First Council of Nicaea assembled to discuss other issues that were not necessarily about Christian presentations of the Godhead, although it may be argued that the debates over the celebration of

---

[15] Ibid. (1) (p.272).

Easter were related to the issue. Regardless, it was evident to Theodosius that a new council needed to convene and settle the Arian controversy in the empire once and for all. He was also determined to expel other heretics that had been a thorn in the side of the Catholic Church for a long time.

When the council was convened in 381 C.E., it set out to discuss the term implemented by Constantine in Nicaea, "*homoousion,*" and how it could be used to settle the Arian controversy.[16] Remember that the Catholic Church endorsed the theology of writers such as Justin and Tertullian, who spoke of God in three persons. Many also endorsed a trinitarian model of water baptism. But the First Council of Nicaea did not settle the issue of whether or not God was a trinity because there was never any real discussion over the third person of the trinitarian Godhead, The Holy Spirit. In order to identify the advocates of heretical positions who needed to be ex-communicated, the universal position first needed to be clearly defined. Heretofore, it was not. So, the council came together to do just that. Between May and July, Catholic bishops sat together to discuss settling the debate over the godhead to prevent further sectarian divine in the church. Because one of the motives of the First Council of Constantinople was to abolish heretical views, it is possible to learn a little bit about what the Catholic Church believed was heretical to Christianity at that time based on the groups that they dismissed in 381 C.E. One such group that was condemned in Constantinople was the Sabellians.

You may recall from chapter ten that the term "Sabellian" was used at the First Council of Nicaea in 325 C.E. in a derogatory sense by the Catholic bishop Eusebius. The term was used as an insult against those who resisted the influence of the Catholic

16 "Council of Constantinople (AD 381)." Wisconsin Lutheran College: Fourth Century Christianity. Last modified , 2021. Accessed December 1, 2021. https://www.fourthcentury.com/council-of-constantinople-ad-381/.

Church. The Sabellians received their namesake from a man who was a dissenter against the doctrine of the trinity.

Not much is known about Sabellius, but it is believed that he was born somewhere near the Libyan city of Ptolemais around 180 C.E.[17] Late in the second century, Africa was becoming an epicenter of power in the Roman Empire and many Christian bishops arose in the area during that time who wrote and spoke extensively on church matters. Given the period and geography, Sabellius likely spoke Greek and Latin. As a young man, Sabellius traveled to Rome where he engaged many prominent Christian thinkers of his time, including Victor and Praxeas.[18] During his stay in Rome, Sabellius stirred up great controversy among the Catholic leadership because, unlike the Catholics, Sabellius opposed the doctrine of the trinity as described by Justin and Tertullian. Some writers have suggested that Sabellius was a student of Praxeas, the theologian that Tertullian so greatly despised.[19] Given what can be known about Sabellius' beliefs, it seems reasonable to assume that he may have found harmony with men such as Praxeas. Whether or not he was ever a student of Praxeas, it is apparent from his writings that the men were cut from the same cloth.

Remember that throughout the second century, Christianity was still not a welcome institution in the Roman Empire. Many divergent groups of Christians did not see eye to eye with one another, and no ecumenical councils had yet been called to settle doctrinal disputes. The universal movement, which later became the Catholic Church, was still in its infancy. The doctrine of the trinity, although present, was not yet a dogma. Disagreements abounded between Christian scholars, as believers struggled to define Christianity in a strictly gentile sense. Those who were dismissive of trinitarian thought were sometimes accused of being too sympathetic to the beliefs of the Jews, as was the case in the polemics of Tertullian in his *Against Praxeas*. Sabellius found

---

[17] "Sabellius." New World Encyclopedia. Accessed December 6, 2021. https://www.newworldencyclopedia.org/entry/Sabellius.
[18] Recall from chapter eight that Praxeas was the subject of much controversy, as he apparently opposed the beliefs of men such as Justin and Tertullian.
[19] For more on this subject, see R.B.B. Tollinton's *Clement of Alexandria: A Study in Christian Liberalism*.

himself in the camp of the accused. Nevertheless, the second century was characterized by many such disputes, so accusations against men like Sabellius had little effect. As one writer points out,

> Sabellius returned to Libya c. AD 235. He is said to have pastored a church at Ptolemais. He became a district leader of some sort and preached throughout the area...Schleiermacher stated that "many bishops in the neighboring countries of [Cyrenaica] and Egypt received his opinions." Fairweather acknowledged that "Sabellianism...found favor with the bishops of Egypt." The writings of Sabellius were extant up through at least the fifth century.[20]

The suggestion that Sabellius was an influential thinker for his time may be corroborated by the fact that even as late as 381 C.E.— more than a century after his death—the teachings of Sabellius had a broad enough influence to merit condemnation by the Catholic Church at the First Council of Constantinople. Although most of his writings and homilies are nearly impossible to come by in the modern era, there is compelling evidence that Sabellius was not an inconsequential thinker of his time.

It is also probably not a coincidence that the influence of Sabellius was most prominent in the East, especially in the region of Syria and North Africa. Constantine's letter calling for the convocation of a council of Christian leaders to settle the Arian controversy said that bishops from the north, south, and west were essentially in agreement over the doctrine of the trinity—but not the east. Not only did Constantine leave out the eastern bishops in his comments, but a bishop from the Syrian city of Antioch was accused of Sabellianism by Eusebius at the First Council of Nicaea. Although speculative, such evidence does seem to suggest that eastern Christians were much more reluctant to embrace the doctrine of the trinity as the church's new dogma, and

---

[20] Chalfant, William B. *Ancient Champions of Oneness*. Hazelwood, MO: Word Aflame Press, 1986. (p. 96-97).

it had been that way long before the First Council of Constantinople in 381 C.E.

In the fourth century, a French Catholic Bishop named Hilary of Poitiers wrote about the beliefs of the Sabellians, characterizing them as those who believed that the Father and Son were one. Some have suggested Sabellius himself wrote the following quotation by Hilary:

> Nothing except the nature of God produces the miracles which have been performed. From God alone comes the forgiveness of sins, the cure of diseases, the walking of paralytics, the sight of the blind, the dead coming to life. No other Nature, except that which is conscious of what it is, would say, "I and the Father are one" (John 10:30). Why do you force me into another substance? Why do you endeavor to make me another God? The one God has performed the deeds which are characteristic of God.[21]

The operative phrase in the excerpt is the question, "Why do you force me into another substance?" The suggestion being that the bifurcation of the identity of God the Father and the Christ was something with which Sabellius took issue. Other writers in the fourth century made similar statements about Sabellius, corroborating the idea that even as late as 381 C.E., Sabellianism still posed significant opposition to the Catholic Church. Writing around 375 C.E., Epiphanius of Salamis wrote that the Sabellians claimed that,

> [they] hold that the Father is the same, the Son is the same, and the Holy Spirit is the same, so that there are three names in one entity...They use all the Scriptures of the Old and New Testaments, but [especially] certain texts which they select themselves in keeping with the idiocy and stupidity of their own which they have introduced. First, God's words to Moses,

---

[21] Hilary of Poitiers, "The Trinity." In *The Fathers of the Church*, Edited by Bernard Peebles, Translated by Stephen McKenna. Washington, DC: Catholic University Press, 1970 (25:134).

"Hear, O Israel, the Lord thy God, the Lord is one." "Thou shalt not make to thyself other gods." "There shall not be unto thee new gods," for "I am God, the first and the last, and beside me there is no other."...Again, [they use] the saying from the Gospel, "I am in the Father and the Father in me, and we two are one."[22]

Epiphanius' remark that the Sabellians used "all the Scriptures of the Old and New Testaments" is curious. This may have been a passing remark, but it also could suggest that Epiphanius interpreted their behavior as a novelty in the fourth century. By 375 C.E., it may not have been common practice for Christians to quote the Old Testament in particular. As has been discussed in earlier portions of this book, Christian thinkers in this era dismissed the Old Testament as antiquated, amounting to little more than a historical record of the failures of the Jews. Nevertheless, it is apparent from Epiphanius' comments that the Sabellians were very similar to the Monarchians mentioned by Justin and the man named Praxeas who was condemned by Tertullian.[23]

There were contemporaries of Sabellius who also wrote about his beliefs. Sometime around 250 C.E., Gregory Thaumaturgus recorded that,

Some treat the Holy Trinity in an awful manner, when they confidently assert that there are not three Persons...Wherefore we clear ourselves of Sabellius, who says the Father and the Son are the same. For he holds that the Father is He who speaks and the Son is the Word that abides

---

[22] "The Panarion of Epiphanius of Salamis Books II and III." In *Nag Hammadi and Manichaean Studies*, Edited by Johannes van Oort and Einar Thomassen, 123-24. Translated by Frank Williams. Boston: Brill, 2013.

[23] Further reading of his comments about the Sabellians reveals that Epiphanius did not approve of their beliefs about water baptism either. He specifically cites Matthew 28:19 as evidence for the legitimacy of trinitarian water baptism. This is interesting, as it documented throughout both the New Testament and historical records that the use of the single name of Jesus was the dominant method of water baptism for the early Christians.

in the Father, and becomes manifest at the time of creation, and thereafter reverts to God on the fulfilling of all things.[24]

Whether or not Gregory characterized the beliefs of the Sabellians accurately or not, in principle the broad strokes are clear—they did not embrace the doctrine of the trinity as presented by the universalists.

Despite opposition by Catholic leaders, Sabellius apparently maintained a steady following his entire life. This fact only serves to confirm what historical examination already suggests—that Catholicism, while popular, was by no means in charge of the direction of greater Christianity until it was institutionalized in the fourth century. Chalfant writes,

> Sabellius died c. AD 257-61, but his followers continued his work in North Africa and elsewhere. Ammonius, pastor of the church at Berenice (modern Benghazi, a port on the Mediterranean), was a follower of Sabellius. So was Euphranor, a pastor in the Libyan Pentapolis area of Cyrene, as well as Telephorus and Euporus.[25]

Sabellius was never ex-communicated or removed from the ministry during his lifetime. The practice of anathematizing believers who did not obey Catholic doctrine was not instituted until the development of the ecumenical councils, once again confirming the notion that the Catholic Church was only one of many competing factions in Christianity before the fourth century.

---

[24] Gregory Thaumaturgus, *A Sectional Confession on Faith*, (Sect. VII).
  • It is worth noting that what can be gathered about the Sabellians, Monarchians, and even Praxeas comes to us in the form of writings by men who largely despised them. What Sabellius and Praxeas believed in their own words is extremely difficult to come by, and so the polemical statements by those who disagreed with them should probably be taken with a grain of salt. History is written by the victors.
[25] Chalfant's record of the various followers of Sabellius comes from Charles Bigg's, *The Christian Platonists of Alexandria*, Oxford: Clarendon Press, 1913.

Given what can be known about Sabellius and the teachings of his followers, it is altogether unsurprising to find him counted among the condemned at the First Council of Constantinople in 381 C.E.[26] The council convened by Theodosius abolished any recognition of Christians who dissented from the authority of the ecumenical councils. Interestingly, the Sabellians were explicitly commanded to be rebaptized if they wanted to be received into the Catholic Church.[27] No such requirement was placed upon the Arians, which seems astounding in its own right. It is possible that the command was motivated by the belief that the Sabellians rejected the legitimacy of the trinitarian model of water baptism while the Arians did not, although this suggestion is only speculative. Whatever the reasons, it is apparent that the Catholic bishops that convened at Constantinople were committed to ending opposition to their authority.

When the council came together in 381 C.E., it was understood that the attempt by the First Council of Nicaea to end the Arian controversy had failed. In large part, this was because the First Council of Nicaea claimed to uphold the doctrine of the trinity, yet neglected to define what that doctrine was. In fact, the failure of the First Council of Nicaea likely contributed to the revival of Arianism after the death of Constantine the Great. Because the Nicene Council never offered any definitive statement about the existence and role of the Holy Spirit in the trinity, there arose widely diverging interpretations of the Nicene Creed. Arians, including Constantine's son, continued to claim that there was a time when Christ was not. They believed that although He proceeded from the Father, He was not God. The ambiguity of the Nicene Creed only augmented the problem for the Catholic leaders. It was apparent to the First Council of Constantinople that until the doctrine of the trinity was articulated clearly, there would be no universal church in the empire.

When the First Council of Constantinople convened, almost no leaders from the Arian, Sabellian, or Apollinarism movements

---

[26] "First Council of Constantinople." New World Encyclopedia. Accessed December 6, 2021. https://www.newworldencyclopedia.org/entry/First_Council_of_Constantinopl e.

[27] Ibid. (26). (Seventh canon of the council).

were invited. The decision to include primarily Catholic bishops in the meeting suggests that the council's purpose was not to have a debate, but to end the controversy. Without representation of the dissenting movements, it was much easier to reach a consensus. The Nicene Creed of 325 C.E. was amended at Constantinople in 381 C.E. in an effort to end any ambiguity in Catholic beliefs about the Godhead. Ironically, this only created more problems for the Catholics, as will be discussed shortly.

The first Nicene Creed from 325 C.E. reads:

> We believe in one God, the Father Almighty, Maker of all things visible and invisible. And in one Lord Jesus Christ, the Son of God, begotten of the Father [the only-begotten; that is, of the essence of the Father, God of God], Light of Light, very God of very God, begotten, not made, being of one substance with the Father; by whom all things were made [both in heaven and on earth]; who for us men, and for our salvation, came down and was incarnate and was made man; he suffered, and the third day he rose again, ascended into heaven; from thence he shall come to judge the quick and the dead. And in the Holy Ghost. [But those who say: 'There was a time when he was not;' and 'He was not before he was made; and 'He was made out of nothing,' or 'He is of another substance' or 'essence,' or 'The Son of God is created,' or 'changeable,' or 'alterable'—they are condemned by the holy catholic and apostolic Church.][28]

Although determined to define the Father and Son in specific terms, the First Council of Nicaea was not concerned with defining the third person of the trinity, the Holy Spirit. This was in part because verbally separating the Spirit of God from God the Father was difficult if not meaningless ("God *is* a Spirit" according to John 4:24). There was also no reason to believe that leaving the third person of the trinity ambiguous in 325 C.E. would cause the Catholic Church problems. Eventually, of course, it did, and so the creed was amended in 381 C.E. to further define the Catholic

---

[28] Ibid. (26).

beliefs about the Holy Spirit. The creed adopted at Constantinople reads:

> We believe in one God, the Father Almighty, Maker of heaven and earth, and of all things visible and invisible. And in one Lord Jesus Christ, the only-begotten Son of God, begotten of the Father before all worlds (aeons), Light of Light, very God of very God, begotten, not made, being of one substance with the Father; by whom all things were made; who for us men, and for our salvation, came down from heaven, and was incarnate by the Holy Ghost of the Virgin Mary,[29] and was made man; he was crucified for us under Pontius Pilate, and suffered, and was buried, and the third day he rose again, according to the Scriptures, and ascended into heaven, and sitteth on the right hand of the Father; from thence he shall come again, with glory, to judge the quick and the dead; whose kingdom shall have no end. And in the Holy Ghost, the Lord and Giver of life, who proceedeth from the Father, who with the Father and the Son together is worshiped and glorified, who spake by the prophets. In one holy catholic and apostolic Church; we acknowledge one baptism for the remission of sins; we look for the resurrection of the dead, and the life of the world to come. Amen.[30]

The claim that the Holy Spirit "proceeded from the Father" became a controversial statement for the ecumenical councils that convened in later centuries. By making the Holy Spirit exclusive to the Father, the First Council of Constantinople unwittingly put themselves at odds with the New Testament writers who refer to the Holy Spirit as proceeding from the Christ as well.[31] It is not difficult to understand why the placement of the Holy Spirit in the trinity stumped the early Catholic thinkers. On the one hand, in order for the trinity to be defined as three individual persons, the Holy Spirit needed a unique identity that could be easily

---

[29] It is interesting that Mary is not mentioned in the first iteration of the Nicene Creed but was added to the later one. This became an issue of import in the next century.
[30] Ibid. (26).
[31] Romans 8:9-11.

334

distinguished from the Father and the Son. On the other hand, by making such a distinction, the Catholic bishops appeared to contradict the writings of the earliest Christians. Not wanting to err in either direction, the trinity was largely characterized as a mystery that remains unsolvable.

Of further interest regarding the Nicene Creed of Constantinople was the affirmation by the bishops that they only acknowledged one baptism. Given the Catholic Church's opposition to the Sabellians (and, by extension, the teachings of Praxeas, the Monarchians, etc.), it seems likely that that this was the first time the trinitarian model of water baptism was explicitly identified as dogma of the Catholic Church. Of course, it is not clear from the creed what, precisely, was meant by the statement. Ancillary historical examination suggests that this was probably an attempt to condemn the mode of water baptism that was practiced by dissenting groups. This is made evident by the fact that the seventh canon of the First Council of Constantinople explicitly stated that the Sabellians, among others, needed to be rebaptized if they desired entry into the Catholic Church.

As with the First Council of Nicaea, the First Council of Constantinople created more problems for the Catholic Church than it solved. The theological game of whack-a-mole against dissenting beliefs opposed to Catholicism continued for centuries. When one was squashed, another would spring up in a different place. Each time one sprang up, a new council was convened to deal with the issue. In some cases, such councils found themselves debating the same issues that the earliest councils had already discussed. In others, new issues arose that created new doctrinal statements, creating new heresies, which only produced the need for more councils. Thus, the cycle continued for the next four hundred years.

When Epiphanius wrote concerning the beliefs of the Sabellians, he took issue with the argument by Sabellius that, left to its own devices, the doctrine of the trinity would eventually lead to polytheism in Christianity.[32] The earliest trinitarians held their theology together through allegory and—knowingly or not—a significant amount of dependence of the philosophy of Justin. But philosophy and theology were not the only principles holding the Catholic Church's beliefs together in the fourth century. Politics and culture were deeply intertwined with the formation of the Catholic Church as an institution as well, and they played a vital role in forming Catholic thought in the centuries following the first ecumenical councils.

The next council to convene after the First Council of Constantinople was the Council of Ephesus in 431 C.E. Like Constantinople, the Ephesian Council came together with the intent of ending controversy and creating uniformity in Christian thought. But, like Constantinople, Ephesus created more problems for the Catholic Church than it solved. Although it is most remembered for its discussions surrounding the nature of Christ, the Council of Ephesus in 431 C.E. had little to do with that subject.[33] However, the Council of Ephesus in 431 C.E. did introduce one entirely new concept to Christianity that still distinguishes Catholicism from other denominations of Christianity today—Marian veneration.

As it later came to be known, The Third Ecumenical Council was held at the Church of Mary in Ephesus, Asia Minor. Unlike the First Council of Nicaea or the First Council of Constantinople, this council did not convene to discuss the nature of God or the proper mode of water baptism. The Council of Ephesus in 431 C.E. assembled in order to condemn one patriarch named Nestorius of Constantinople for his refusal to use the term *theotokos* (Mother of God) to describe the virgin Mary.[34] Nestorius preferred to use the term *Christotokos* (Christ-bearer) for Mary rather than the phrase implored by the Catholic Church. Nestorius' reservations

---

[32] Ibid. (22) (p. 124).
[33] The confusion stems from the fact that there were multiple meetings of the Ephesian council. The first ecumenical council convened in Ephesus happened in 431 C.E., but the second occurred in 449 C.E. The second of these two councils is the more well known, and it was the council which primarily debated the nature of Christ.
[34] "Council of Ephesus." New World Encyclopedia. Accessed December 7, 2021. https://www.newworldencyclopedia.org/entry/Council_of_Ephesus.

about the designation "mother of God" for Mary stemmed from his belief that, although Mary may have given birth to the man Christ Jesus, she did not give birth to the Spirit of God. From the perspective of Nestorius, just as it would not be proper to say that God died on the cross and ceased to exist for three days, so too would it be improper to say that Mary gave birth to God instead of saying she gave birth to Christ.

This position infuriated many contemporaries, such as Cyril of Alexandria, who actively pursued his excommunication over the issue. Christian thinkers such as Cyril thought that Nestorius' refusal to honor Mary as the mother of God brought his acceptance of the trinity into question. From the trinitarian perspective, it was not difficult to call Mary the mother of God. If the Son existed distinct from the Father in personhood, then the Son could die, Spirit and body, and the Father continue to live. The premise of Stoic-corporeal theology is that each thing possesses its own form, body, and material. Thus, one person of the trinity could cease to exist, and the other two remain alive. But Nestorius seemed to disagree with the premise. From his perspective, to say God died in Christ was nonsensical. God is a Spirit, and of course, the Spirit could not be crucified. In this way, Nestorius' theology shared some similarities with that of early dissenters against the Catholic Church, such as Sabellius and Praxeas, although it is doubtful that Nestorius would have found agreement with such men.[35] Regardless, it is evident that Nestorius believed that the Father and Son were identifiable with the same Spirit. To crucify the Spirit in the Son was no different than saying God the Father died as well. The two were completely intertwined in the mind of Nestorius. Because of this, he also refused to call Mary the mother of God. The principle was the same in both cases—Jesus of Nazareth was fully man and fully God. The man was born and crucified, but God was not. Therefore, Mary may be said to be the mother of Christ, but she was not the mother of God.

---

[35] Being a patriarch of the Catholic Church in Constantinople would have meant that Nestorius could not have been confirmed as a minister in such a city without adhering to the Nicene Creed. Nevertheless, he did object to the Catholic Church on other issues.

It is unclear when Marian veneration first entered the Catholic psyche, but it seems from reading the New Testament and historical writers that it was a later development. It is possible that it began around the time the Council of Ephesus was convened in 431 C.E. Mary was not reverenced in her lifetime to the degree that she was later honored by the Catholic Church. Biographical materials concerning her life before the birth of Jesus are essentially non-existent. Early in the gospels, Mary is visited by an angel who foretells of the miraculous birth of Christ, and she is periodically present in the gospels during the ministry of Jesus. After the crucifixion, it is recorded that John the beloved took care of Mary after the departure of Jesus.[36] Mary was also present in the upper room with the rest of the disciples on the day of Pentecost, awaiting the outpouring of the Holy Ghost.[37] She fades from the New Testament early in the book of Acts and is never said to have played a significant role in the formation of the early church. Given her legacy as the mother of the Messiah, her absence from much of the New Testament is surprising. It is evident that the writers—while acknowledging her significance— were not fixated on Mary as a central figure in the gospel itself. She is never portrayed as an intermediary between men and Christ and is nearly characterized as a disciple in certain instances. Outside of the nativity narrative, the role of Mary in the New Testament is relatively muted.

Consistent with the gospel writer's brevity on the subject, Paul never acknowledged a need for specific veneration of Mary in his letters to the churches or the pastoral epistles either. Given that Cyril and his supporters sought total ex-communication against Nestorius over the matter, it seems reasonable to assume that precedent for the practice could be found somewhere in the New Testament. Surely if Marian veneration were a priority of the early Christians, it would have been mentioned at least once in the gospels or the epistles. The fact that the issue never arose in the

---

[36] John 19:25-27.
[37] Acts 1:14.

earliest writings of the Christians does lend credibility to the notion that the acknowledgement of Mary as the mother of God was not a doctrine of the early church but a later development in Catholic theology.

The origin of Marian veneration in Christian thought may possess some relationship to the debates between Christians and the cult of Dionysus shortly after the first century as well. Recall from chapter five that early Christians found themselves at odds with Greek thinkers who saw in Christ the story of their own Bacchus (Dionysus). In the story of Dionysus, it is said that as the last of the gods of Greece to enter the pantheon, he was the only one born to one divine parent and one human.[38] Of Dionysus, it is said that,

> Everywhere he taught men the culture of the vine and the mysteries of his worship and everywhere they accepted him as a god until he drew near to his own country.[39]

In the eyes of the pagans, particular descriptions of Dionysus likely augmented the relationship between Jesus and Dionysus. Jesus taught many parables using agrarian allegory, and—a prophet not welcome in His own country—His ministry was the least accepted among the most religious Jews of the first century.[40] But the cult of Dionysus may also have had something to do with later Christian interpretations concerning Mary, the mother of Jesus.

According to Greek mythology, after the mother of Dionysus died, he determined within himself to rescue her from the depths of hades.

---

[38] The father of Dionysus was Zeus, the greatest god of Olympus. His mother was Semele, the princess of Thebes.

[39] Hamilton, Edith. *Mythology*. New York: Grand Central Publishing, 1942. (p. 63).

[40] According to Matthew's account, the ministry of Jesus began in the region of Galilee among the settlements where many inter-married Jews lived that were not religious. As He drew closer to Jerusalem—the epicenter of Jewish life—He became less welcome, culminating with His crucifixion at the behest of the religious and political leadership of the city.

The mother whom he had never seen was not forgotten. He longed for her so greatly that at last he dared the terrible descent to the lower world to seek her. When he found her, he defied the power of Death to keep her from him; and Death yielded. Dionysus brought her away, but not to live on earth. He took her up to Olympus, where the gods consented to receive her as one of themselves, a mortal, indeed, but the mother of a god and therefore fit to dwell with immortals.[41]

The exaltation of Semele is an episode that bears a striking resemblance to Catholic Marian veneration in later centuries. There is no doubt that the cult of Dionysus engaged actively with the early Christians, attempting to build a relationship between the two religions that Christianity expressly forbode. Comparisons between Jesus and Dionysus were common, and it is not out of the question to assume that similar comparisons were made between Mary and Semele in an effort to dilute the efficacy of Christianity. The portrayal of Dionysus as one who descended into the depths of hell and defied death to save his mother was likely viewed by the pagans as synonymous with the death, burial, and resurrection of Christ. Nevertheless, while the cult of Dionysus exalted Semele as a mother of a god, the early Christians did not portray Mary in like fashion. In fact, the refusal to situate Mary as a deity herself was one significant difference between the early Christians and the cult of Dionysus.

He took her up to Olympus, where the gods consented to receive her as one of themselves, a mortal, indeed, but the mother of a god and therefore fit to dwell with immortals.[42]

Later Marian veneration was built on the premise that Mary was indeed the mother of God. Although the early Catholics regarded her as mortal, her lofty place in the Catholic psyche situated her as a tacit contemporary of the trinity itself. Given early Byzantium's constant struggle to unify and divide the relationship between Christianity and the pagan cults, it is not unreasonable to

---

[41] Ibid. (39) (p. 65).
[42] Ibid. (41).

assume that the Catholic Church developed Marian veneration to imitate the practices of pagan converts to Christianity in an effort to assuage their transition to the new state-enforced religion. This, however, is only speculative. What can be known with certainty is that Marian veneration was not a dogma of the earliest Christians.

Ironically, Marian veneration owes a great deal of its prominence in Catholic theology to the doctrine of the trinity. Nestorius' primary objection to the practice was that it denied the principle that there was only one Spirit of God. By separating the Father and Son into distinct persons of the Godhead possessing their own natures, the trinitarians were able to make the logical next step of claiming that Mary was the mother of God without giving her preeminence over God the Father. Instead, she was the mother of God the Son. Of course, this thin line was not long tenable for the Catholics.

Throughout the next three centuries, the practice of veneration that was applied to Mary was extended to the disciples, apostles, and other Christian leaders. Images of Christ, Mary, and the various saints of the Catholic Church were erected in homage to the individuals they represented. Although the practice likely began as an attempt to adorn Christian edifices in ways that reflected the Byzantine culture that adopted them, it quickly turned into what many characterized during the time as idolatry. Icons became the centerpieces of Christian houses of worship throughout the sixth and seventh centuries. In some cases, iconographic veneration was extended to other individuals of import in Catholic history who had no connection to the early church at all, such as Saint Theodore of Amasea. Saint Theodore the Dragon-Slayer, as he later came to be known, is said by Catholics to have been a Christian of the fourth century who refused to convert to paganism.[43] Upon his refusal, he was

[43] "Saint Theodore: Warrior Saint and Dragon-Slayer." Reliquarian . Accessed December 8, 2021. https://reliquarian.com/2013/03/23/saint-theodore-warrior-saint-and-dragon-slayer/.

martyred, and his memory was preserved in iconographic representations as early as the seventh century.[44] Sometimes iconography extended into physical representations of the traditions or fables that were told about the people they represented.

*Figure 12.1*                    *Figure 12.2*

(Figure 12.1) This fourteenth-century depiction of St. Theodore can be found outside St. Mark's Basilica in Venice. Here the saint is depicted with the halo seen in early Byzantine iconography of Christ, standing atop a crocodile (the serpent). (Figure 12.2) illustrates a more famous dragon slayer in English and Catholic tradition—Saint George. Saint George became so popular in Catholic tradition that he received his own feast day, celebrated each year in the spring.

Figures 12.1 and 12.2 offer some examples of how iconography morphed over time, culminating with fantastic images of the saints as warriors and adventurers. As the veneration of saints through artistic representation expanded, aspects of their

---

[44] Interestingly, St. Theodore the Dragon-Slayer is a bit of a misnomer. Nowhere in his story is he said to have slayed a dragon. The presentation of Theodore as the killer of serpents likely comes from a panegyric delivered by Saint Gregory of Nyssa in the fourth century, wherein he said that "devils were expelled and distempers cured" by the martyred saint. Because the serpent is commonly associated with devils in Christian thought it, it is likely that the presentation of St. Theodore as a dragon-slayer evolved into its present form over generations of Christian interpretation. Later adaptations of the dragon slayer motif were applied to other saints in Catholic thought, most famously of which is Saint George.

sainthood were eventually incorporated into the Catholic religion itself. For example, each year in the spring, Catholics celebrate the feast day of Saint George, honoring his martyrdom and sainthood.[45] Over the centuries, more than twenty-five such feast days were added to the Catholic calendar, commemorating the various saints, offering prayers for a fruitful harvest, and recognition of the virgin Mary.[46]

By 787 C.E., it was also believed that objects associated with Christian piety could also be honored. These objects were known as relics and were often incorporated into the altars of various basilicas and cathedrals. In some cases, these relics were objects that were identifiable with the early Christians or the crucifixion, such as the crown of thorns, pieces of the cross on which Jesus was crucified, or the spear that pierced His side. In other cases, relics were much more curious objects. Body parts were often incorporated as relics, such as human hair or bone fragments. George's Chapel of Windsor Castle is said to have possessed two fingers of Saint George, as well as portions of his heart and skull.[47] In much the same way that the earliest proponents of the doctrine of the trinity disassociated the three persons of the Godhead from the pagan practice of tri-theism, later developments in Catholicism applied the same logic to the saints and relics. Although much of their behavior imitated early pagan rituals such as the institution of feasts and prayers for harvest and iconography, they did not perceive their behavior as out of step with Christian doctrine.

In much the same way that each of the gods in the Roman pantheon possessed unique attributes that were honored by the public, the various saints of the Catholic Church were said to be the patron saints of unique domains. Thus, St. Christopher is the patron saint of travelers, and those who travel pray to him for safety and guidance. Saint Anthony is known as the patron saint of lost things, and adherents pray to him for the things that cannot be found. Offering prayers to saints that possessed the ability to

---

assist in individual disciplines of life is a practice entirely of the Catholic Church's own making, and it has no recognizable precedent in the New Testament. Although many Christians of the early Middle Ages did not perceive the practice as idolatry, there is little doubt that it was the inevitable outgrowth of forcibly Christianizing a pagan empire. Although it was illegal to be a pagan nominally by the fifth century, many of the traditions and practices of pagan culture were either incorporated or modified into the Catholic Church. Such adaptations were the only way to bring a primarily pagan empire under the umbrella of Christianity without causing more religious conflict.

It is important to note that separating culture from religion was not an easy task in Rome or Byzantium. To say that the Catholic Church sought out active participation in paganism throughout the Middle Ages is probably not correct. Although much of their behavior during this period would have been rejected by the apostles and certainly may be said to have become idolatry by biblical standards, the Catholics likely did not see it that way. From their perspective, Christianity was simply adapting to the needs of the greater culture. A culture that, until the middle of the fourth century, was wholly pagan. Transitioning an entire empire of people out of their holidays, liturgy, and religious rituals could not be done with a mandate or a council. Compromises had to be made with the greater psyche of the people to create a universal religion of the empire. Christian iconography and saint veneration were, in all likelihood, not offensive to pagans. Although pagan temples were eventually razed, their sacrifices ceased, and their gods defamed, the liturgical culture of the empire was still framed around its pagan past. In this way, pagans had an opportunity to recast their own faith in the mold of Christian traditions if they were willing to do so. Thus, if a pagan was once a devout member of the cult of Mercury—the god of merchants and travel—he was given the opportunity through Catholicism to pray to Christopher instead—the patron saint of travel. This practice could be applied broadly to almost every cult of the Greco-Roman world. And as long as the pagans acknowledged that Christ (and, by extension, the Catholic

Church) had supremacy over the empire, their way of life remained effectively undisturbed.

Not all Christians accepted the new practices of the Catholic Church in the Byzantine Empire. Many perceived iconography to be nothing more than pagan idolatry with a bit of a Christian face-lift. The practice of incorporating human body parts into the altars of churches was abhorrent to more conservative believers. Their opposition to the apostasy of the Catholic Church culminated in what became known as the Iconoclastic Controversy.

Throughout the eighth and ninth centuries, Christians protested the novel practices of Catholicism that diverged from the New Testament through a protest known as iconoclasm (literally, "the smashing of icons").[48] When Emperor Leo III came to power around 717 C.E., the empire was in a fierce war with Maslama, brother of the Caliph of the Muslim invaders. Himself hailing from eastern Anatolia, it is entirely possible that Leo was influenced by more traditional understandings of Christianity. Such influence may have contributed to his behavior in 726 C.E.

> For some time the cult of icons had been growing steadily more uncontrolled, to the point where holy images were openly worshipped in their own right and occasionally even served as godparents at baptisms. It was thus as a protest against what they considered flagrant idolatry that a number of bishops in Asia Minor adopted an iconoclast manifesto. Leo himself had given no early indication of similar tendencies. It seems that his change of heart was the result of a combination of Muslim and Jewish influences, together with others exerted by a number of his own Christian subjects. In 725 he preached a series of sermons in which he pointed out some of the more flagrant excesses of the iconodules—as the image worshippers were called—which he held to be in open disobedience of the

---

48 Ibid. (2) (p. 111).

Law of Moses as laid down in the Second Commandment. Then, in 726, he decided to set an example. Facing eastwards towards St Sophia was the principal gateway to the Imperial Palace, known as the Chalke; and above the great bronze doors that gave the building its name there rose a vast golden icon of Christ. It was this, the largest and most prominent icon in the whole city, that Leo selected as the first to be destroyed.[49]

Upon Leo's destruction of the most venerated image of Christ in Byzantium, riots broke out. Evidence that pagan converts to Christianity favored icon worship may be revealed in the fact that when factions formed in favor of or against the actions of Leo, the European subjects tended toward the side of defending the icons. As long-time adherents of the pagan cults, the Europeans were not as quick to relinquish their images as other portions of the empire. Pope Gregory II, along with other high officials in the Catholic Church, was furious with Leo. Monasteries were hit the hardest, where vast quantities of ancient relics of precious value were kept. Some icons were hidden from the authorities; others were sent away for safe keeping.

But all of the efforts of Leo III could not stop the momentum of the Catholic Church for long. Like it or not, the church of the state had been instituted as a favorable compromise featuring various aspects of many religious traditions, and it was going to remain that way. In 787 C.E., the Second Council of Nicaea was called together to resolve the Iconoclastic Controversy. Convened by Empress Irene, it solidified the Catholic Church's position that icons should once again be venerated and revered.[50] Although banned by Leo III, images and relics would be re-instituted into the Catholic Church and their honor as holy images restored. Going one step further, the council decreed that every altar in the Catholic Church should include a relic. So the various objects once

---

[49] Ibid. (2) (p. 112).
[50] "Second Council of Nicaea." Britannica. Accessed December 8, 2021. https://www.britannica.com/event/Second-Council-of-Nicaea-787.

removed from the basilicas and cathedrals would also be restored, including human remains.[51]

There is some irony to the fact that it was the Second Council of Nicaea that galvanized Catholic support for iconography in Christian liturgy. Nicaea was, therefore, home to two of the greatest controversies to ever arise in Christianity—the doctrine of the trinity, and the worship of idols. For the believers who dissented against each movement, the issues discussed at Nicaea I and Nicaea II may have been different in degree but not in kind. Early proponents of the formalized doctrine of the trinity were accused by those opposed to it of quasi-idolatry. In some cases, the accusation was explicitly made that the trinitarian proponents worshipped three gods. Less enthusiastic dissenters may not have accused the trinitarians of being polytheistic, but they still maintained that the doctrine was not original to the New Testament and could become dangerous. At the very least, it manipulated the traditional formula for water baptism as practiced by the early Christians. Trinitarian proponents defended their position by claiming that each person of the Godhead was honored in the others; therefore, dividing the Godhead as they had was a non-issue.

When the protests of the Iconoclastic Controversy began, they were motivated by the belief that the veneration of saints and the reverence of images amounted to idolatry, even if it was done in the name of Christ. In many ways, this was similar to the accusation levied against the trinitarians. While the iconodules would probably not have claimed that their behavior had any precedent in the New Testament, they would have justified it by saying that Christ was honored *through* their veneration of the images. Much like the doctrine of the trinity, the worship of one becomes the tacit acknowledgement of the other. The distinction is, of course, murky, but not unprecedented. Before the Catholic

---

[51] Ibid. (50).

version of such religious amalgamation, there was Constantine's reconciliation of the sun god and Christ. Before Constantine, the Apologists performed a similar balancing act with Greek philosophy and Christianity, attempting to bridge the gap between two worlds (Hellenic and Semitic) through the prioritization of knowledge over faith. Before the Apologists, the cults of the first century attempted the same thing with the teachings of the early Christians, finding Christ in Bacchus or Bacchus in Christ. Under the Seleucid Greeks and the Romans, the Jews redefined their own religion in Hellenic terms, rewriting the stories of their holy books to include Biblical figures but in Greek media. And, before the Jews, there was Alexander the Great, walking out of the oracle of Ammon in Egypt with a new iteration of his favored cult, Zeus-Ammon. Each group struggled to reconcile their beliefs with the world around them. And, to a large extent, all managed to succeed and fail. For on the one hand, many proved that it was possible to redefine one's religion in terms more palatable to the greater culture and in doing so create large-scale institutional support for one's beliefs. On the other hand, each was responsible for diluting the fundamental form of their beliefs to the degree that in just a few generations, the religion they first loved was unrecognizable.

There is probably something to be said for the fact that, had the doctrine of the trinity never been articulated the way that it was, Marian veneration would have likely never begun. Had it not started, perhaps the Iconoclastic Controversy would not have existed either. Slippery slopes notwithstanding, the connection between the three movements is at least recognizable. It is not difficult to see why both incidents—the institutionalization of trinitarianism and icon worship—were rejected by more conservative branches of Christianity, particularly those informed by a more eastern or Semitic understanding of the Scriptures. Acknowledging the authority of others to receive and answer prayers—even saints— in relationship to the power of God may have kept the peace in the Roman Empire, but it did not satisfy the fervent monotheism of Christianity. Eventually, that fervency began to fight back.

Like the Byzantine Empire that created it, image worship in Catholicism began to fade throughout the centuries. The stories of the Crusades against the Turks that grace our history books end in the thirteenth century with the victory of the Muslims, ushering in a new era of political dominance—the Ottoman Empire. But the influence of Byzantium on Christianity is forever sealed in the councils and creeds of emperors and popes who worked for more than five centuries to harmonize the relationship between two competing conceptions of religion in the world. If one were to travel to Venice today, situated on the corner façade of Saint Mark's Basilica, they would find one statue of the Byzantine Era that, perhaps better than any other, illustrates the continuing struggle to discover authentic Christian identity throughout a non-Christian history. The challenge continues to reconcile generations of religious and political upheaval with the most fundamental of all Christian beliefs.

To wit, that God was in Christ, reconciling the world unto himself...[52]

---

[52] 2nd Corinthians 5:19 (KJV).

# CODA

In the year 1511, perhaps around Tudela in Navarre, Spain,[1] a boy was born to a devout Catholic family known to many as the Reves. The father, whose name was Antonio, served as a royal notary to the Spanish government. A brother named Juan was a priest in the Catholic Church. The boy's mother was known as Catalina Conesa.[2] The family was well off, likely due to the father's relationship to the Spanish crown. When the boy was still in infancy, the family moved to Villanueva de Sijena, just north of Sargossa, where the family home can still be visited today.[3]

The young boy from Spain took a keen interest in theology at a time of tremendous religious upheaval throughout Europe. When he was just six years old, a religious reformer by the name of Martin Luther penned his Ninety-Five Theses and nailed it to the door of the church in Wittenberg, Germany. He was protesting certain injustices of the Catholic Church, and sparking a new movement across the land known as Lutheranism. Not many years later, another reformer named John Calvin from Noyon, Picardy, France, just two years older than himself, would become a critical figure in the boy's life. The sixteenth century proved to be one of the most exciting times in history for a man to become a Christian. And yet, it was also among the most dangerous. Just over fifty years before the birth of our subject, the Gutenberg Press delivered the first mass-produced Bible in the history of the world. The production of this Bible set the world ablaze with new religious fervor, calling into question the many extra-biblical traditions of the state-enforced church. Not willing to relinquish its power, the Catholic Church waged war on the Protestant movement. It was a war that would continue for centuries, creating unforeseen ripple effects into future generations,

---

[1] Sources differ on this point, some pointing to Villanueva de Sijena, others to Tudela.

    • *All dates included in this Coda are C.E. (Common/Christian Era).*

[2] "Michael Servetus." New World Encyclopedia. Accessed December 9, 2021. https://www.newworldencyclopedia.org/entry/Michael_Servetus.

[3] See figure C.1

including the formation of religious colonies in what became known as the New World.

Religious reform was the topic of the day in sixteenth-century Europe and Spain was at its epicenter. As the Catholic boy from Navarre grew, he resolved to become the pupil of a Franciscan friar named Juan Quintana.[4] Quintana would go on to become confessor to Emperor Charles V. But the boy was filled with wonder for many disciplines of learning throughout his life, and quickly became uninterested in the priesthood. He traveled to the University of Toulouse and began to study law instead. While at the university, the boy—now nearing eighteen years old—read the Bible himself for the first time.[5] For the young student who had once entertained the notion of life as a priest, discovering the Bible was like waking up from a bad dream. He found forms of what he had been taught his entire life in its pages, but forms only. The more he read, the more he came to believe that the Christianity of the Bible bore little resemblance to the Catholicism that he had been taught as a child. There were no references to the confessionals, the monasteries, or the popes. There was not one indulgence sold, not one saint so sacred as to merit the prayers of the believers, nor one hailing of Mother Mary. And, to his astonishment, not one reference to the holy trinity.

The lad was filled with a fervor that betrayed his age. A man now of his late-teens or early twenties, he began to write and speak with a passion that caused him to fall out of favor with those around him that did not share his indignance toward the traditions of the Catholic Church. In 1530, he traveled with his Franciscan mentor

4 Serveto, Michael. "The Two Treatises of Servetus on the Trinity." In *Harvard Theological Studies XVI The Two Treatises of Servetus on the Trinity*, edited by James H. Ropes and Kirsopp Lake, xx. translated by Earl M. Wilbur. Eugene, OR: Wipf and Stock Publishers, 2013.
  • Previously published by Harvard University Press, 1932.
5 "Michael Servetus." Britannica. Accessed December 9, 2021. https://www.britannica.com/biography/Michael-Servetus.

to the coronation of Charles V in Bologna. There it may be said that the final break with his father's religion occurred. At the coronation he saw the corruption of the Catholic Church through their near worship of the pope, and the immorality hidden behind the pomp and showmanship.

Over the next few years, he traveled far and wide searching for fellow reformers who would hear his case concerning the many errors of the Catholic Church. Of special interest was the young man's ardor regarding the error of the doctrine of the trinity. He wrote two dominant works on the subject still extant today. *On the Errors of the Trinity* and *Dialogues on the Trinity*, both served to dispel the notion that the doctrine of the trinity was an original belief of the early Christians. It was the hope of the young reformer that ridding the church of the dogma of the trinity would serve to improve relations between Jews and Christians, uniting them in the belief that there was only one God.[6] He acquainted himself with the writings of the Apologists, perceiving them to be the primary cause of the great stumbling block called the doctrine of the trinity. He read the work of Sabellius and the disputes with Arius of the fourth century. He concluded that there was no occasion in the New Testament wherein Jesus was ever called the eternal Son, God the Son, or the Second Person of God. He found many of the phrases of the Greek and Roman writers to be extra-biblical and without theological merit. In the opening portions of his work *On Errors of the Trinity*, he wrote:

> Seeing that the pronoun indicates a man, whom they call the human nature, I shall admit these three things: first, this man is JESUS CHRIST; second, he is the Son of God; third, he is God.[7]

The young theologian from Spain was adamant in his belief that the doctrine of the trinity failed to present God in a genuinely monotheistic fashion, and for this cause, the church had slipped into a form of pantheism. He contended that the humanity of

---

[6] Ibid. (2).
[7] Michael Servetus, *On Errors of the Trinity*, Book I.
  • Taken from the Wilbur translation.

Christ was truly human and not merely an abstract human form as some contemporary scholars of the sixteenth century suggested. He argued that the phrase "Son of God" referred not to the second person of the trinity but to the miraculously begotten Word of God; not a *hypostasis* or person who shared a substance with the Father, but the spoken Word of the Father Himself.[8] He was adamant that Jesus was fully God, that He was God manifested in the flesh, and that His was the only saving name. Concerning the third person of the trinity, he wrote that the Holy Spirit was not a separate being or person of God at all, as a belief in two Spirits would be nothing more than atheism or idolatry. Instead, he argued that Scripture proved there was not a unity of three persons in the Godhead, but a threefold (in some cases more than three-fold as he would later argue) description of the disposition, attributes, and character of God.

> There is not one word in the whole Bible about a Trinity, nor about such things as persons, essence, substance, or hypostases. The scholastics [Greek Apologists] have confused the matter by introducing such terms. They are imported from Greek philosophy, lead to countless difficulties, and hinder the spread of Christianity...if we held to one divine essence existing in three separate beings, we should have not a Trinity but a Quaternity.[9]

To his disappointment, the young scholar did not find a great deal of support for his writings against the trinity. In fact, more than one attempt was made to have him arrested and charged with heresy, a crime punishable by death.[10] He fled to Lyon, where for four years, he made great strides in other academic disciplines, publishing works in geography, astrology, and anatomy. It was during these four years that he devoted himself to medical studies and became the first man in history to publish his findings on the pulmonary circulation of blood through the lungs, from the right

---

[8] Ibid. (4) (p. xii).
[9] Ibid. (4) (p. xiii).
[10] Ibid. (5).

to the left side of the heart.[11] Although widely successful across a range of fields, it was theology that captured the young Spaniard's attention more than any other discipline. Over the next ten years, he returned to writing on the subject of biblical studies and published a great number of works, including more dialogues and treatises on the trinity.

Through his passionate writing, the still young theologian had made an enemy in one of history's most well-known reformers, John Calvin.[12] Calvin sought the arrest of the Spaniard for his writings against the trinity. The authorities came for the young man while he was living in Lyon, but he escaped and fled to Naples, where he believed he would be safe from persecution and could practice his newfound beliefs in peace.

It is not known why he chose to do so, but the Spanish theologian who had spent so much of his life writing critically of the beliefs of so many Catholics and Protestants chose to travel to Geneva and listen to John Calvin preach one day in 1553 C.E.[13] He was quickly recognized in the crowd and arrested on charges of obstinate and persistent heresy.[14] A small gesture was made to give the Spaniard an opportunity to defend his positions by petitioning local churches and councils through writing on his behalf. Both Calvin and the Spaniard would have an opportunity to present their cases to the church authorities and a

---

[11] Harvard University's publication on the work of Michael Servetus notes that while disputed by later pioneers in the field, it is clear today that Servetus was indeed the first to publish his findings on the anatomy of the heart. It is likely that his work was suppressed for many years due to his later conviction as a heretic.

[12] Before the death of Servetus, John Calvin was known as "The Prince of Geneva" as he had established a quasi-religious dictatorship over Geneva in the sixteenth century. After the death of Servetus, he fell out of favor with the public and was reprimanded for his treatment of the Spanish reformer.

[13] It is known that John Calvin maintained some level of written correspondence with Servetus throughout his life, so it is conceivable that the Calvin, determined to have the man arrested, feigned friendship (or, at least, cordiality) until the opportunity arose to have him captured.

[14] Ibid. (4) (p. xxv).

determination would be made based on consensus. But Calvin held a great deal of political influence in Geneva and warned the churches before the debates began not to listen to the Spaniard. At the end of all arguments, the young theologian of Villanueva de Sijena was convicted of denying the dogma of the trinity and rejecting the baptism of infants. He was sentenced to death by burning. For his part, John Calvin never apologized for the harshness with which he treated the Spaniard. He wrote,

> Whoever shall maintain that wrong is done to heretics and blasphemers in punishing them makes himself an accomplice in their crime and guilty as they are. There is no question here of man's authority; it is God who speaks, and clear it is what law he will have kept in the church, even to the end of the world. Wherefore does he demand of us a so extreme severity, if not to show us that due honor is not paid him, so long as we set not his service above every human consideration, so that we spare not kin, nor blood of any, and forget all humanity when the matter is to combat for His glory.[15]

On October 27, 1553, the Spanish doctor, geographer, astrologist, and theologian was executed. He was burned at the stake at Champel, just outside Geneva. It is recorded that he remained steadfast until the end, refusing to recant his belief that God was indivisibly one.

The Spanish theologian who is the subject of our story was a man named Michael Servetus *alias* Reves. Although history has been kind to men such as Martin Luther and John Calvin for their part in the Protestant Reformation, it is probably not an overstatement to say that Michael Servetus was truly history's greatest reformer

---

[15] Calvin, Jean. *Defensio orthodoxae fidei de sacra Trinitate contra prodigiosos errores Michaelis Serveti...* (Defense of Orthodox Faith against the Prodigious Errors of the Spaniard Michael Servetus...). Geneva, 1554.

of the sixteenth century. Vilified for his theology, Servetus presented the Godhead in a way that the Catholic Church had long since abandoned; but his ideas were not new to Christianity. While Martin Luther sought reforms primarily with regards to the sale of indulgences, Michael Servetus was fixated on a much more fundamental doctrine of Christianity—the mighty God in Christ. This is to say nothing of the fact that Servetus stood head and shoulders above his fellow reformers through his contributions to the fields of medicine and geography as well. Much like his presentation of the Godhead, the value of his work in the field of medicine would not be recognized until many years after his death. In short, Michael Servetus lived and thought well beyond the boundaries of his generation. For this, he may rightly be considered one of the most consequential thinkers of the Protestant Reformation.

*Childhood home of Michael Servetus, Villanueva de Sijena*

*Figure C.1*

The tragedy of Michael Servetus typified the greatest controversies surrounding the development of the doctrine of the trinity nearly twelve centuries before he was born. Erroneous doctrines; Catholic Church authority; suppression of dissent;

politics; all of these were subjects of discussion in the fourth-century councils. Michael Servetus represented the most critical problem that had faced the Catholic Church for over a thousand years. First, his discovery of the Scriptures for himself led him to conclude that the doctrine of the trinity was foreign to the earliest Christians, and this was a problem with which the Catholics had always struggled. This was also the primary objection to the articulation of the trinity as presented by men such as Praxeas and Sabellius in the second century. It continued to be a point of contention for centuries after their deaths. Dissent against the doctrine of the trinity was a primary feature of the first two ecumenical councils. When an agreement could not be reached, the empire attempted a new strategy. In 381, Emperor Theodosius made it difficult for anyone to defy Catholic Church doctrine through his proclamations, anathematizing all interpretations of the Scriptures that were not supported by the Catholic Church. When the church and state became essentially inseparable entities, Catholicism was the standard by which all Christians were compared; disloyalty to the church was tantamount to disloyalty to the state. Those who refused to renounce other beliefs were initially excommunicated, but by the eleventh century, execution became the preferred method of dealing with heresy.

In many ways, the early controversies sparked by the doctrine of the trinity were the catalyst that set the Catholic Church on the authoritarian path in the Middle Ages. The relationship of the trinity to one another and the nature of Christ were the most emphasized topics of discussion at nearly every Ecumenical Council of the Middle Ages. But when one point reached a resolution, two more would spring up in its place. The desire for uniformity of religion in the empire motivated much of the harsh behavior against non-Catholic Christians, as well as those of other religious beliefs. Ultimately, when agreements could not be reached, force was used to compel dissenters into submission.

When the Protestant Reformation began, it was done in the context of reforming the Catholic Church, not the complete dissolution of it. Because of this, much of Protestant liturgy and doctrine remained consistent with the basic traditions of the Catholic Church. This included rigidity in matters of doctrine and intolerance toward dissent. Hence, Michael Servetus was arrested at the behest of a Protestant leader and executed at the order of a Protestant council. But after the death of Servetus, many Protestants sought more radical reforms in the church. Many wanted to leave the severity of the Catholic Church behind, including the execution of heretics. As Protestantism grew, more radical changes were made in areas of doctrine. Salvation by grace and not by works became the mantra of those professing Protestantism. The sale of indulgences was abandoned entirely. Marian veneration ceased. Prayers were no longer made to the saints. Doctrines surrounding water baptism were revisited, many choosing to abandon the practice of infant baptism as Servetus had done, emphasizing the free-will of converts instead.

In short, nearly every essential doctrine of the Catholic Church was challenged in the generations immediately following the Protestant Reformation. Yet, the doctrine of the trinity stayed. Nearly all Protestant denominations continued to profess belief in the trinity for nearly four hundred years. And yet, paradoxically, the issue remained unsettled in Catholic and Protestant ranks. Michael Servetus was not the only one of his kind. From Monarchians and Sabellians in the early centuries to the Anabaptists and Racovians of the Reformation, the discussion of the nature of God and the proper mode of water baptism remained pervasive in Christian thought. The question may rightly be asked, why, if so willing to challenge the extra-biblical doctrines of the Catholic Church, did the most prominent reformers not dismiss the doctrine of the trinity as well? It is possible that the death of Michael Servetus set a precedent for gagging those who professed similar beliefs during the reformation. Many may have been unwilling or too afraid to openly affirm a doctrine that one of the most prominent reformers had been executed for. Whether or not the actions taken against Servetus stymied or delayed the growth of his teaching is plausible; however, it remains uncertain.[16] What can be known is that, at a time when many were becoming skeptical of the teachings of the Catholic Church and turning back to the Bible for answers to their religious questions, Michael Servetus was not afraid to challenge one of the oldest beliefs of the Catholic Church: That God exists in three co-eternal, consubstantial, and co-equal persons. In his work *On Errors of the Trinity*, Servetus wrote,

> For CHRIST after the inward man (to speak in the manner of Paul) means something divine, resulting from an inward anointing divinely done. According to the flesh, he is man; and in the spirit he is God, because *that which is born of the Spirit is spirit,* and, *God is a Spirit.* And, *Unto us a child is born...his name shall be called...Mighty God.* See clearly that both the name and the might of God are attributed to a child that is born, unto whom *hath been given all authority in heaven and on earth.* And Thomas calls him, *My God, my Lord.* And Christ is called, God in all things to be praised and blessed.[17]

His willingness to challenge the belief that Jesus was merely the second of three persons in the Godhead cost him his life. He was, without question, one of the bravest religious reformers in history. Servetus was so convinced of his faith, so possessed by his convictions, that even amid the flames, he refused to admit that debates over the trinity were something trivial or semantical. He was willing to die for his belief that God is one, and to do so at a time when it only served to mar his reputation in the eyes of so many Christians. Whatever the cost, the Spanish theologian believed it was a necessary reform to the doctrine of the church. To Servetus, the doctrine of the trinity was one of the most embarrassing aspects of the Christian faith.

---

[16] It is known that most of Michael Servetus' written works were destroyed after his execution to prevent them from being circulated throughout the public. Thus, again, history is written by the victors.
[17] Michael Servetus, *On Errors of the Trinity*, Book I (9a).

Furthermore, and worse than all this, how much this tradition of the Trinity has, alas! been a laughing-stock to the Mohammedans, only God knows. The Jews also shrink from giving adherence to this fancy of ours, and laugh at our foolishness about the Trinity; and on account of its blasphemies they do not believe that this is the Messiah who was promised in their law. And not only Mohammedans and Hebrews, but the very beasts of the field, would make fun of us did they grasp our fantastical notion, for all the works of the Lord bless the one God.[18]

Far from semantical, the doctrine of the trinity was an irreconcilable point between Christians, Jews, and Muslims. It prevented Christianity from being an effective witness in the world and, in all cases, kept Christianity diametrically opposed to the teachings of the early church.

Servetus did not start the debate against the doctrine of the trinity but he was probably its greatest champion during the height of the Protestant Reformation. The great controversy surrounding the doctrine of the trinity stirred up by Michael Servetus in the sixteenth century outlived him. Dreams of the New World also characterized this era, and as the Reformation grew, it expanded into the Western Hemisphere, landing on the shores of the Americas in Jamestown, Virginia, 1607. In the newly formed colonies, bold religious ideas that contradicted the Roman Catholic Church and the Church of England were more welcome. While in Europe, opposition to the dogma of the trinity was a heresy punishable by death, newfound liberty in the Americas ensured that those who desired to practice Christianity as it was done by the earliest Christians could do so without fear of persecution. The fervency of early religious revivals in the Americas has been well documented, but their contribution to the

---

[18] Michael Servetus, *On Errors of the Trinity*, Book I (42b-43a).

formation of a well-articulated non-trinitarian expansion in Christian thought cannot be overstated. At the turn of the twentieth century, an urgency sprung up in America to see a large-scale return to Christianity as it had been presented by the early church. This included a thoughtful re-examination of the veracity of the doctrine of the trinity. Largely finding its home in what became known as the Oneness Pentecostal movement, non-trinitarian Christianity began to spread quickly in the United States after 1913.[19] The early Oneness Pentecostal movement in America was comprised of advocates for Spirit baptism as described in the book of Acts that was associated with the various holiness movements throughout the country. Between 1906-1909, a ministry known as the Azusa Street Mission in Los Angeles, California, arose that bore witness to large-scale Spirit baptism as the New Testament writers had described it. One historian recorded,

> The Azusa revival sparked the worldwide spread of the movement, as scores of ministers and missionaries flocked to the meetings to experience glossolalia [tongues] and left to spread the message. Entire organizations were swept into the movement.[20]

The holiness movements that comprised the Azusa Street revival became strong advocates for a return to biblical Christian conversion as described in the New Testament. According to the book of Acts, the outpouring of the Holy Spirit made evident by speaking in new tongues was the signal of authentic conversion to Christianity. Spirit baptism was coupled with water baptism in Jesus' Name by the earliest Christians and this became the logical next step for the Azusa Street revivalists.

---

[19] Talmadge French records that as early as 1910, Pentecostal leaders such as Andrew D. Urshan began water baptizing in the name of Jesus Christ as opposed to the trinitarian formula. For more on this, see:
- French, Talmadge L. *Early Interracial Oneness Pentecostalism*. Eugene, OR: Pickwick Publications, 2014. (p. 59).

[20] French, Talmadge L. *Our God is One*. Indianapolis, IN: Voice & Vision Publications, 1999. (p. 47).

Those who identified with the movement and advocated for the sign of tongues as the primary and essential sign of Spirit baptism eventually became known as Pentecostals,[21] deriving their name from the experience of the earliest Christians on the Jewish holiday of *Shavuot* (Pentecost) in the second chapter of the book of Acts. But the movement soon split between those who wanted to retain the trinitarian form of water baptism that they inherited from their respective denominations, and those who wanted to abandon the practice in favor of water baptism in Jesus' name as practiced by the first Christians.

Those who advocated for water baptism in Jesus' name became known as the Oneness Pentecostals, having the modifier "oneness" added to their belief in Pentecostalism for their refusal to baptize in any other way than the way that it was done in the New Testament. The term "oneness" may be said to refer to their belief in one God, but it is important to note that by this point in history, there were not many trinitarian believers who claimed to believe in three gods either. Just as Marian veneration, prayers to the saints, indulgences, and sacraments had been reformed in the centuries following the death of Michael Servetus, so too had the articulation of the trinity undergone its own renovations. Many Christians who professed faith in the trinity did not perceive the doctrine to be extra-biblical or in violation of monotheism. Generations of dilution from its original form had reduced the doctrine of the trinity to little more than a description of the historical presentation of the Godhead. While trinitarians still defended their belief and strongly advocated for the trinitarian baptismal formula, it was not based on higher philosophy or hermeneutical accuracy but tradition. A desire to retain tradition, even neo-tradition, is a difficult habit to break. Thus, from the perspective of the Oneness Pentecostals in contrast to their trinitarian counterparts, the problem created by the doctrine of

---

[21] Some advocates for the sign of tongues did not believe the experience to be essential to conversion. This belief was known as "second-works doctrine." Thus, while they may be called Pentecostal in the most general sense because they identified with the experience of the day of Pentecost, many ceased from fellowshipping with those who believed the act to be essential, known as "finished-works doctrine." Finished-works believers were found most commonly among the Oneness Pentecostals.

the trinity in the twentieth century was not necessarily one of idolatry but of a lack of biblical originalism. When describing the earliest presentations of Oneness Pentecostalism at the turn of the century, Talmadge French writes,

> Oneness Pentecostalism is that theologically distinctive branch of the Pentecostal movement which emphasizes what it views as the Scriptural formula for water baptism—baptism 'in the name of Jesus'—and the absolute, indivisible 'Oneness' of God revealed in the full Deity of Jesus Christ. It emerged within the context of the fervor of restorationism and "back to the Bible" literalism at the turn of the century. Classical Pentecostalism's argumentation for a return to "the Bible" regarding speaking with tongues and spiritual gifts was simply applied to the issues of baptism and the Godhead.[22]

The Oneness Pentecostals saw their advocacy for water baptism in Jesus' name as an extension of their desire to point Christianity back to the beginning. Much like Michael Servetus, the Oneness Pentecostals believed that the doctrine of the trinity created an unnecessary and costly barrier between the church of today and the church of yesterday.

To date, there are more than 42,000 churches in the United Pentecostal Church International alone, with more than five million constituents worldwide.[23] One hundred ninety-seven of the world's 210 countries[24] have a Oneness Pentecostal movement within their borders.[25] This is to say nothing of the numerous other Oneness Pentecostal organizations across the globe that have seen a great deal of expansion in the twentieth and twenty-

---

[22] Ibid. (20) (p. 15).
[23] "About the UPCI." United Pentecostal Church International. Accessed December 13, 2021. https://www.upci.org/about/about-the-upci.
[24] This number recognizes the sovereignty of countries such as Taiwan, which is not represented in the United Nations list of recognized countries.
[25] Ibid. (23).

first centuries as well. Yet, the doctrine of the trinity remains the primary staple uniting so many denominations of Christianity all over the world that otherwise have very little in common. Wesleyans and Lutherans disagree on sanctification; Catholics and Baptists disagree on water baptism; Presbyterians and Evangelicals disagree on free will and the predestination of the soul. But all have found ways to reconcile their belief in the tradition of the trinity.

It is possible that, perhaps, trinitarians have been historically motivated to resist the pull of the doctrine of oneness believers for the same reason that the Oneness Pentecostals resisted the Trinitarian Pentecostals at the turn of the twentieth century. What is that motivation? Perhaps it is a desire to be connected to something older—something of more traditional sacredness. Tradition is a powerful thing. When many denominational Christians think of the doctrine of the trinity today, they do not think of something Catholic that their forefathers fought against but something they embraced. (Hence, the doctrine of the trinity may not be characterized as an original tradition of Christianity but a neo-tradition.) Although it is true that, like the Catholics, their Protestant forefathers failed in many ways to bring about the reforms in the church that they desired, they did so with the best of intentions. Despite their various theological, soteriological, or eschatological disagreements, those who wanted to separate themselves from the Catholic Church found agreement on the principle that Christianity needed to return to biblical originalism. To their credit, they advocated for the dissolution of many practices introduced to Christianity through the Catholic Church that were foreign to the Bible. But many failed where Michael Servetus succeeded—that is, in expelling the notion that the doctrine of the trinity is something original to the Christian Church.

The doctrine of the trinity found a home in schools of thought that predate the Council of Nicaea by more than a century, but its originalism stops there. To discover a genuinely biblical articulation of the nature of God and the person of Jesus Christ, it is essential that one examine the Bible itself and not later developments. The Bible represents the earliest primary source material concerning the beliefs of the first Christians. The early Protestants knew this, and many succeeded in cleaving Catholicism from Christianity in their respective movements. But the doctrine of the trinity, deeply engrained in the psyche of the church, was not moved so easily. But with time, it appears the doctrine of the trinity, like so many staple beliefs of the Catholic Church, is beginning to lose credibility in Christianity across the globe. Even the doctrine's most passionate advocates have come to terms with the fact that it is an articulation of God that is of the church's own making and not necessarily one that is original to the Scriptures.[26] Whether or not this realization will lead them into the camp of groups such as the Oneness Pentecostals remains to be seen. However, there is some evidence to suggest that many trinitarian denominations are beginning to accept the originalism of the oneness believers.[27] Nevertheless, many remain unconvinced. Thus, the struggle between the two competing conceptions of the Godhead—one God in three co-equal, consubstantial, co-eternal beings, and the fullness of the Godhead in Christ bodily—continues today. It is the estimation of this author that only a fervency for biblical originalism and a rekindled desire to see Christianity recast in the mold of the first-century church will spark a new movement to close the book on disputes surrounding the veracity of doctrine of the trinity for good and to bring manifold believers back into alignment with the earliest Christians, as it was at the beginning.

---

[26] Dunn, James D. *Christology in the Making*. Philadelphia, PA: The Westminster Press, 1980. (p. 63).

[27] In 2018, Trinity Bible Network (TBN) invited a Oneness Pentecostal pastor named Anthony Mangun onto their program to discuss his new book, in which he was allowed to openly advocate for his belief in the oneness of God. More than the discussion, it was the invitation which signaled one example of the dissolving hostility of trinitarians against oneness believers. The interview may be viewed at the following link:

- https://www.youtube.com/watch?v=XFtctvvGAqM

ONENESS PENTECOSTALISM

&

THE ROLE OF SEPARATION

## Contributor
# Esther Gill Hipes

### Editor for the 2021 Edition
#### Steven N. Gill

ASPECTS OF THE ONENESS PENTECOSTAL MOVEMENT

A HARVARD DIVINITY SCHOOL SYMPOSIUM

JEFFREY GILL, COORDINATOR

SUMMER, 1984

## Separation: A Historic Response to Conflict

The final break of the Oneness Pentecostals from the Trinitarians was officially pronounced at the General Council of the Assemblies of God in St. Louis, 1916. Fred J. Foster, quoting Brumback in *Suddenly From Heaven*, wrote "By the adoption of the statement of basic beliefs, this 1916 council forced the Oneness adherents to propagate their message from outside the Assemblies of God."[1] The focal point of the separation was reportedly the insistence of Oneness people on baptizing in Jesus' name. Although this terminology has been used from time to time in Church history, it had not been emphasized as a necessity.[2] To the Oneness, the New Testament emphasis on this mode of baptism was significant of a comprehensive and vital truth; Jesus had revealed Himself to be more than a second person in the Trinity. The ethics of separation as a means of coping with conflicts never arose; it was an unquestioned historical method of solving differences within the Church.

Beginning with the reluctant and painful separation of the Eastern Orthodox and Roman Catholics, protesting and separation had gained momentum until they reached epidemic proportions by 1900. To the Eastern Orthodox, the Roman Catholics were the first Protestants.[3] Lutherans, Anglicans, and Calvinists soon followed. These led to the secession of Anabaptists, Congregationalists, and Methodists in the seventeenth and eighteenth centuries; and the Holiness and Pentecostals in the nineteenth and twentieth centuries. Initially based on political and economic issues, later on issues of Church government, and finally on doctrine, the separations eventually led to the fragmentation of Christendom.[4]

---

[1] Foster, Fred J. *Think It Not Strange: A History of the Oneness Movement.* St. Louis, MO: Pentecostal Publishing House, 1965. p. 68.
[2] Golder, Morris T. *History of the Pentecostal Assemblies of the World.* Indianapolis, IN: 1973. p. 41.
[3] Ware, Timothy. *The Orthodox Church.* Suffolk, England: Richard Clay and Company Ltd., 1964. p. 10.
[4] Harper, Michael. *Let My People Grow.* Plainfield, NJ: Logos International, 1977. P. 111.

The Church has recently experienced a new kind of independence, the 'house-church movement', people who have set up worship centers, but who want to maintain their links with other Churches.5 George W. Forell has appropriately described Protestantism as a church at war with the powers of evil, both within and without the gates, resulting in numerous divisions.6 These divisions are often the result of deep convictions which reunitive solutions do not fulfill.7 They are also the result of deep spiritual need which mere separation does not provide.

In his classic *Pilgrim's Progress*, John Bunyan points to our mutual need of understanding by leading Christian behind the wall:

> Then I saw in my dream that the Interpreter took Christian by the hand, and led him into a place where was a Fire burning against a wall, and one standing by it always casting much water upon it to quench it; yet did the Fire burn higher and hotter. Then said Christian, What means this? So he had him about to the back side of the wall, where he saw a man with a vessel of Oil in his hand, of which he also did continually cast (but secretly) into the Fire.8 [See editor's note, 8.]

A trip behind the wall will reveal the sources of the Oneness Pentecostal convictions and the fuel which has kept the Trinitarian controversy alive for nearly twenty centuries.

---

5 Ibid. (4) (p. 12).

6 Forell, George W. The Protestant Faith. Philadelphia, PA: Fortress Press, 1960. p. 201.

7 Marty, Martin E. A Short History of Christianity. Philadelphia, PA: Fortress Press, 1959. p. 344.

8 Caird. G.B. *A Commentary on the Revelation of St. John the Divine*. New York, NY: Harper & Row Publishers, 1966. p. 8.

- Hipes cites Carid's commentary here. The quotation from John Bunyan may be found in: Bunyan, John. *Pilgrim's Progress*. Uhrichsville, OH: Barbour Publishing, Inc., 1988. (p. 36-37). *Pilgrim's Progress* was originally published in 1678.

## Sources of Oneness Pentecostal Separation

The Oneness Pentecostals hold to the early monotheistic position that Jesus Christ is: the image of the invisible God (Colossians 1:15); Creator of all things (Colossians 1:16); the fulness of the Godhead bodily (Colossians 2:9); Father (John 14:7-11); Son of God (John 1:34); Son of Man (John 5:27); Holy Ghost (John 14:18;26). He is the Almighty (Revelation 1:8) and the I Am of the Old Testament (John 8:58) tabernacled in the flesh (John 2:19, Revelation 21:3), the Alpha and Omega (Revelation 21:6).

Raymond E. Brown has drawn our attention to the unique way in which the Apostle John depicted the disciples' growing revelation of Jesus. A first disciple addressed him as "Rabbi," a second as "Messiah," another as "Son of God," and finally, after the resurrection, Thomas called Him "My Lord and My God" (John 1:38-51; 20:28).[9] Jesus has been called "Divine Fatherhood disclosed"[10] and "the genuine revelation of the mystery of existence."[11]

The Oneness Pentecostals do not claim their revelation (God's self-disclosure to men) came by ontological or historical research. God's Truth was hidden to the wise and prudent and revealed to babes (Matthew 11:25) just as Jesus' birth was revealed to shepherds rather than to Gamaliel (Luke 2:8). They further disclaim their exaltation of Jesus Christ to exceed the primacy and supremacy accorded to Him in the Scriptures.[12]

The pre-existence and glory of Christ are assigned to the foreknowledge of God who declared the end from the beginning (Isaiah 46:10) in the same manner as the Lamb was slain from the foundation of the world (Revelation 13:8).

The Oneness Pentecostals closely parallel the very early post-Apostolic writers in their doctrine of the Godhead. Early

---

[9] Brown, Raymond E., S.S. *The Anchor Bible, Vol. 29, The Gospel According to St. John.* Garden City, New York: Doubleday and Company, 1966. p. 73-88.
[10] Rusch, William G., Editor, *The Trinitarian Controversy.* Philadelphia, PA: Fortress Press, 1980 p. 2.
[11] Trueblood, Elton. *A Place to Stand.* New York, NY: Harper & Row Publishers, 1969. p. 39.
[12] Haywood, G.T. *Victim of the Flaming Sword.* Indianapolis, IN: Christ Temple Book Store, Undated. P. 62-63.

monotheism held to the unity of God with little reflection on the analysis of His Being. Christ is the image of the invisible God...the fullness of His glory...The Word of God incarnate. The International Bible Encyclopedia states:

> Jesus Christ affirmed a unity between Himself and the Father...but He reveals no category which would construe the unity of the Godhead in a manifoldness of manifestation. The experience of the first Christians as a rule found Christ so entirely sufficient to all their religious needs, so filled with all the fullness of God, that the tremendous problem which has arisen for [philosophical] though did not trouble them.[13]

J.N.D. Kelly states that, "the classical creeds of Christendom opened with a declaration of belief in one God, which was the demarcation line between the Church and paganism."[14] Kelly further states that the doctrine of one God, the Father and Creator, formed the background and premise of the Church's faith; that God had made Himself known in the person of Jesus and later in the pouring out of His Spirit upon the Church;[15] and that the Apologists, all ardent monotheists, struggled to preserve this truth.[16] [See editor's note, 16.]

The Oneness Pentecostals believe that later writers defined monotheism in a way that exceeded Biblical authority. The following concerns are illustrative:

1.  Biblical authority was supplemented by creeds, councils, and traditions which exceeded and sometimes contradicted the Scriptures.

---

[13] *International Bible Encyclopedia, Vol. 2.* Grand Rapids, MI: W.B. Erdman's Publishing Co., 1943. p. 1264.
[14] Kelly, J.N.D. *Early Christian Doctrines.* New York, NY: Harper & Row Publishers, 1978. P. 83.
[15] Ibid. (14) (p. 87).
[16] Ibid. (14) (p. 95).

- Kelly's analysis of the writings of the Apologists appears to be incomplete. Early Apologists such as Justin Martyr deviated significantly from the earliest presentations of Christ mapped out in the New Testament, even introducing novelty to the mode of water baptism.

2. A new vocabulary was needed for the formulation of the Trinity.[17] The International Bible Encyclopedia states, "The term Trinity is not a Biblical term and we are not using Biblical language when we define what is expressed by it."[18] When referring to what he called the "baffling doctrines of the Trinity," Dr. Hugo Thompson agreed that there is no doctrine of the Trinity in the New Testament.[19]

3. Concessions to Greek philosophy were believed to have been made which corrupted the Christian message. Although the Apologists were cautious lest the Church's faith be destroyed, they set the future course for Trinitarian theology by making Christianity appealing to Greco-Roman culture, and conversely enabled Christianity to take seriously the presuppositions of Greek philosophy.[20] From the beginning Christianity spoke to and in a world deeply influenced by Greek thought and culture. Trinitarian theology and institutions were molded by Greek thought and culture.[21]

4. Concessions to polytheistic religions was a charge made based upon the suppositions that the Trinitarian formula made Christianity more acceptable to many religions having triads of divinities.[22]

5. Thy Mystery of the Trinity appeared to conflict with the Scriptural insistence on revelation, light, and fulfillment in Jesus Christ. The Trinity has been referred to as "beyond human understanding"[23] and "admittedly complicated"[24] by its own proponents. The Oneness Pentecostals point to "the mystery revealed" (1st Corinthians 2:10); "the mystery

---

[17] Ibid. (10) (p. 7).
[18] *International Bible Encyclopedia, Vol. 5.* p. 3012.
[19] Thompson, Hugo. *Love-Justice.* North Quincy, Massachusetts: Christopher Publishing House, 1970. p. 175, 244.
[20] Ibid. (10) (p. 6).
[21] Ibid. (19) (p. 123).
[22] *International Bible Encyclopedia, Vol. 5.* p. 3012.
[23] Ibid. (3) (p. 28).
[24] Ibid. (6) (p. 193).

manifest in the flesh" (1st Timothy 3:16); "the mystery is Christ in you" (Colossians 1:26-27); and "the mystery is finished" (Revelation 10:7).

6.  The Baptismal formula used by the Trinitarians was not used in the New Testament according to the Acts and Epistles of the Apostles. Baptisms recorded in the New Testament after the Day of Pentecost were administered "in the name of the Lord Jesus" (Acts 2:38); "into the name of the Lord Jesus" (Acts 8:16); and "into Christ" (Romans 6:3, Galatians 3:27).[25] In Acts 19:5 believers were baptized in the name of the Lord Jesus.

In addition to limiting the doctrinal authority to the Bible, and rejecting the Trinitarian interpretation of the one God, a third factor facilitated the Oneness Pentecostal separation. They held to the historic precedent that the only alternative to conflict was either compromise or divide. Error must be condemned and judged, the final human judgement being withdrawal or expulsion. Most dissenting groups claimed their doctrine to be a "revelation"; persons not being enlightened were rejected as willful sinners. Church history is replete with examples of breakdown in human relations on the basis of diverse understandings of the Bible; these separations sometimes took the extreme form of executing the non-conformist.[26]

Impoverished understandings have been a constant in all divisions. Conflicting events and beliefs are set in such restricted contexts that no intelligent relationships can be developed. Theissen reminds us it is impossible to reform a group and put its identity in question.[27] The Oneness Pentecostals repeated the pattern of former separatists by denouncing the parent group and abrogating responsibility for them.

"The Christian community did not formulate its (Trinitarian) doctrine of God as a purely theological exercise, divorced from

---

[25] *International Bible Encyclopedia, Vol. 1.* p. 396.
[26] Qualben, Lars. P. *A History of the Christian Church*. New York, NY: Thomas Nelson & Sons, 1942. p. 272.
[27] Theissen, Gerd. *Sociology of Early Palestinian Christianity*. Philadelphia, PA: Fortress Press, 1977. p. 113.

other pressures."[28] Doctrines and ecclesiastical structures all arose within specific historic contexts, and were responses to historical demands.[29]

The first diversity entered the Christian faith when it was rejected in Palestine and more readily accepted in Hellenistic communities.[30] Here it met new languages, religions, and philosophical thought with which East and West struggled in their efforts to reconcile theological patterns. Western theology had emphasized the unity of God; Eastern theologians, who were influenced by Greek thought, emphasized the distinctions in the Godhead.[31] The Trinity was thought to be an acceptable answer.

A second difficulty arose with the rapid spread of Christianity which added to the multitude of interpretations, and consequent dilution of the message. Heresies abounded even before the completion of the New Testament and were warned against in its pages (2nd Peter 2:1).

The constantly repeated essential truth was Christ must be fully God and fully man.[32] This was the affirmation by which doctrinal heresies were measured, and rejected. Arianism concluded Christ was a created Son, and therefore, inferior to God the Father. Nestorianism held Christ's manhood to be so divided He actually became two persons. Monothelitism taught that Christ had no human will: therefore, He was not wholly man. Gnosticism argued Jesus was a Spirit, not truly flesh. These and other heresies seemed to require a concise statement of Christian faith.

A third and difficult problem for Christianity was the subservience of the early Church to the fortunes of emperors and empires. As mass "conversions" accompanied political alliances of kings and countries, political power and church authority became the conscience of the Christian. Michael Harper writes that the Church for many centuries had no divisions on doctrinal grounds.[33] This dubious unity was affected by monarchs and

---

[28] Ibid. (10) (p. 1).
[29] Weaver, Mary Jo. *Introduction to Christianity*. Belmont, CA: Wadsworth Publishing Company, 1984. p. 53.
[30] Ibid. (27) (p. 114).
[31] Ibid. (10) (p. 16).
[32] Ibid. (3) (p. 29).
[33] Ibid. (4) (p. 110).

clergy reigning over a near illiterate laity. Eventually political entanglements, clerical corruption, and an enlightened laity threatened this imposed unity. But creeds and councilor judgements had been deeply ingrained in the fiber of Christian thought, and remained to do battle with the dissenters.

It was in these early years of Church-state alliances, and within the context of differing cultures, that the quickly dispersed Christianity attempted to formulate its basic faith in terms understandable to its adherents.

The efforts of the Apologists to preserve the Truth was considered by many to be more sincere than what their opponents gave them credit for. One theme predominated: How is the Church to integrate the doctrine of One God with the disclosure of Himself in Jesus and the coming of the Holy Spirit?[34]

Judgements on the development and final formulation of the doctrine of the Trinity vary. For some it is the high point of theological achievement, allowing it to win the Greco-Roman world. Others, including Oneness Pentecostals, see it as a capitulation of Biblical revelation.[35]

It is noteworthy that many Oneness Pentecostals spoke avidly against "three Gods," which denoted a misinterpretation of the Trinitarian position of "One God in three persons." It is probable that the distinction between Tritheism (three gods) and Trinitarianism (One God, three persons) was not clearly demarcated by the early Oneness Pentecostals.[36] [See editor's note, 36.]

The magnitude of the responsibility of the Oneness Pentecostals lies before them. They stand apart from both Trinitarians and Tritheists. As previously stated, they stand very close in doctrine to the New Testament and early post-Apostolic writers. Their belief could be called, in the very true sense, a primitive Christianity. The Oneness Pentecostals have placed

---

[34] Ibid. (10) (p. 1-2).

[35] Ibid. (10) (p. 27).

[36] While it is true that some Oneness Pentecostals have accused trinitarians of tritheism, modern historical examinations suggest that early controversies between Oneness Pentecostals and trinitarians were primarily characterized by their disagreements over the proper mode of water baptism. For more on this, see *Early Interracial Oneness Pentecostalism* by Talmadge French.

their defense on the anvil of history. They may yet have the secret which will unlock the larger world, which has so far rejected Trinitarianism.

## The Role of Separation

Throughout the history of humankind, God has separated "chosen" people to be instructed and disciplined for service. Abraham and his descendants were chosen and set apart for the purpose of becoming God's instrument of self-revelation to the world. Later, the Church was chosen to continue God's work on the earth; and they too, were set apart. God's self-revelation in Christ and the use of a chosen people to witness this truth became a fundamental concept in Christianity.

However, a second and problematic kind of separation entered Christianity. Because humankind so easily falls from the lofty calling of sanctification, periods of renewal and restoration became necessary. Desire for a return to New Testament doctrine and for spiritual fulfillment culminated in protests and unlimited separation. Now many Christians are asking, "Are separations the solution?" The Danish philosopher Kierkegaard believed Lutheranism to have been meant for a corrective to Christianity, but that men made it normative.[37] Once the separations were made, responsibility and relationship to "other" groups became lost in the building and maintaining of walls. There is still serious need for the re-examination of the validity of this second kind of separation as a means to Church perfection.

## Maintaining Separation

When the ultimate goal of separation is not clarified, instruments for maintaining that separation become the center of activity. The history of the Jews offers one example of a people who having set the instruments of separation in place, became estranged from

---

[37] Ibid. (4) (p. 112).

their mission.[38] Some of the effective means by which the "chosen" people were kept chosen are:

1.  The crowing of a priest (authority without secular conflict).

2.  Setting of spiritual boundaries (making of codes and laws).

3.  Marriage restrictions.

4.  Written authority.

5.  Interpreters of that authority.[39]

A similar parallel can be seen in the maintenance of the various factions of Christianity. Gerd Theissen points out that the Church was not only identified with God's chosen, but that they also adopted Jewish ethno-centrism,[40] coming short of the righteousness that should have exceeded the righteousness of the Pharisees.[41] Mary Jo Weaver charges the Pentecostal people with psychological withdrawal from the world, and of creating their own world within the Church.[42] The withdrawal itself becomes a part of the separation reinforcement.

Since the advent of the Reformation each divided group bears its Scriptural emphasis as a badge of identification. Since most beliefs are not seriously examined, the emphasized "part-truth" is embraced as the whole truth and the variety of emphases become lines of demarcation between Christian groups. The Roman Catholics remember "Thou art Peter"; the Lutherans; "By grace, through faith'" the Baptists; "Eternal-security"; the Methodists,

---

[38] Throughout the first four chapters of *The History & Development of the Doctrine of the Trinity*, detailed examination is made concerning how the greater culture of the Jews was heavily impacted by the Greeks, and how Hellenism only served to augment the issue of maintaining separation among the Jews.
[39] Dimont, Max I. *Jews, God and History*. New York, NY: The New American Library, p. 70.
[40] Ibid. (27) (p. 118).
[41] This behavior by Christians is most clearly demonstrated throughout the fourth century, in which Jews were specifically targeted as people unfit for Christian fellowship.
[42] Ibid. (29) (p. 143-144).

"Wholly sanctified"; the Pentecostals; "Tongues"; the Oneness Pentecostals; "Baptism in Jesus' name"; the Charismatics; "Gifts of the Spirit." Such identifications are not without limitations, but they do point to emphases which serve to maintain the divisions.

Before the days of hopeful mergers, the diversity of Christianity was sometimes explained by comparing it to a tree of many branches. Just as a tree would suffer violence if the branches were severed or grafted into one, so the Church would be disfigured if coerced into one. Unity and strength, it was thought, should derive from mutual recognition and good will, and occasional pruning.[43] But the Church in its many divisions does not seem to bear the unity of a tree. Despite ecumenical councils, the Church is still at war with itself.

## Dangers and High Cost of Separation

The most lethal danger in separation is that God becomes a localized "god" which is the essence of polytheism.[44] A god adapted to the local needs becomes non-negotiable and nontransferable, resulting in the need for many gods. But our God is not localized; He is the God of all.

A deceptive danger is the exaltation of a part-truth to the whole truth. One definition of a fanatic is "one who exalts on part of the truth to the exclusion of another equally important part." In separation we deprive ourselves of valuable contributions made by the estranged group. Each library, each music store is an indication of the tremendous contribution of people we might claim do not "belong."

Separation deprives believers of the corrective tension which a diversity of ideas and personalities brings to a group. The rock-hound uses a method to polish his stones which should be instructive to the Church. It is in the rubbing and grinding against each other that the rocks become polished. "Forbear one another" becomes a meaningless commandment if our separation prevents

---

[43] Ibid. (26) (p. 621-622).
[44] Here Hipes refers to the secondary form of separation discussed in prior sections (isolationism) as opposed to the first form of separation which is characterized by holiness and chosen-ness.

us from associating with anyone who might disagree with us. Another danger and high cost of separation is the loss of communication with divergent groups whose membership no longer reflect the original conflict. There is a temptation to dispense unequal judgement to members of divergent groups. Thompson says that Reinhold Niebuhr, in his *Moral Man and Immoral Society*, contends that "men tend to exhaust their moral sensitivity in their loyalty within groups, so that the group itself becomes nonmoral in relations with other groups."[45] Distance removes the reality of our responsibility. We are our brother's keeper, even at a distance.

The psychological damage to a severely restricted group is evident. The narrower the circle of love, the broader the field of fear, hate, and anxiety beyond the group.[46] The danger of the church remaining isolated from the lost is that while hoping the world will come to it, the world remains aloof. Thus, the essence of exclusivity is rejection.[47] Few people today would condemn Wesley for separating from the Church of England. "The obtuseness of the English bishops demanded it!"[48] But dividing begat dividing; and the results have left the church still unfulfilled.

Without universal communication, contribution, and responsibility, we are all unfulfilled and lonely. Each [group] faces problems insoluble in terms of its own traditions yet feels insecure and directionless apart from them.[49]

## A New Priority

In his book *Love-Justice* Dr. Hugo Thompson has impressively re-emphasized the basic Christian concept of redeeming love. By defining the love that redeems as "affirmation of our interdependence, evidenced by forgiveness and sacrificial service to the unworthy, even the enemy"[50] he makes a case for an

---

45 Ibid. (19) (p. 15).
46 Ibid. (19) (p. 15).
47 Synan, Vinson, Editor. *Aspects of Pentecostal-Charismatic Origins*. Plainfield, NJ: Logos International, 1975. p. 31.
48 Ibid. (4) (p. 13).
49 Ibid. (19) (p. 17).
50 Ibid. (19) (p. 29; 87-89).

unshakable ethic which should go far to solve the problem of division without incurring the problem of compromise.[51]

Christianity began with a vision of love and reconciliation which faded with the involvement of the Roman Empire.[52] Under Greco-Roman influence, the language of the Church lost its original meaning and shifted toward legalistic interpretations.[53] A return to the Biblical concept of love-justice should restore broken bonds. Love as inter-dependence is a bond beyond differences, which encourages us to discover new ways of resolving conflicts and solving common problems.[54]

Dr. Thompson states that when dependence and independence mature into interdependence, an adult becomes an infantile slave of no person nor institution yet is debtor to all. He fears only God; but acknowledges interdependence with all men.[55]

> To restore broken bonds and heal hurt relations...something extraordinary is called for. The extraordinary thing that will startle weary eyes to a second look, stimulate tired hearts to an extra beat, will be to sacrifice for those who do not love us, who are scarcely aware of our existence.[56]

Sydney F. Alhstrom has indicated a growing awareness of a need for a deeper kind of Christian earnestness. He credits Barth for having drawn men back to the strange world of the Bible; and states that having recovered the words of Jesus, we do not judge them by some philosophical system.[57] The love ethic becomes a positive part of code morality leading to a re-evaluation of diversity in the Church and revised foundations of belief.[58]

---

[51] Here again, Hipes draws a distinction between separation which promotes holiness and separation which encourages isolation from the people that Christians are called to evangelize. In the mind of the writer, the two are distinct. One is an act of holiness, the other is not.
[52] Ibid. (27) (p. 119).
[53] Ibid. (19) (p. 123).
[54] Ibid. (19) (p. 32-33).
[55] Ibid. (19) (p. 58-59).
[56] Ibid. (19) (p. 97).
[57] Alhstrom, Sydney E. A Religious History of the American People. New Haven and London: Yale University Press, 1972. p. 933-935.
[58] Ibid. (57) (p. 944; 1087).

## Conclusion

Diversity is a product of human hunger for fulfillment. In our relentless pursuit of Jesus, the Truth, we have become divided over doctrine. In our search for Jesus the Life, the "free spirits" have become estranged from the institutions. But Jesus is first the Way, and his more excellent Way is redeeming love.

Redeeming love is God's indisputable essence and nature. Not yet mentioned in the creeds and rules of faith, it is the dynamic of which unity is the certain by-product. Redeeming love is the instrument by which each group can release both its revelation and responsibility to other groups without compromise. It is the province in which divergent groups can belong until unity of faith matures. Perhaps all the separations for perfection will not be in vain if they, like the Law of the Old Testament, not only point to the Perfect,[59] but lead us to the desperate realization that our ultimate need, our ultimate loyalty is the grace of God which was revealed at the coming of Jesus Christ.

---

- Alhstrom's anaylsis is not an endorsement of upending the foundations of Christian doctrine, but a reminder in how to return to those foundations when one has departed from them. Hence, the love-justice ethic is framed as a first century Christian principle, and not as a later development. In cultivating an ethic of forbearance, Christians can lead others to the truth. It is not the truth that changes nor the doctrines of the church, but the heart of the believer toward the unbeliever. Or, in Alhstrom's specific example, the heart of the believer toward other Christians with whom they might disagree.

[59] I spoke with Ms. Hipes shortly before the publication of this book about this particular passage of her writing. The "Perfect" to which she refers is Jesus Christ, as it is Galatians which teaches us that the Law is our schoolmaster that leads us to Christ (Galatians 3:24).

# ACKNOWLEDGEMENTS

I would like to extend my most sincere thanks to a few people who were tremendously supportive during this project. The subject matter of this book may be enjoyed by a wide variety of readers, from those interested in history and archeology, to those who study theology and hermeneutics. The surface level analysis covering numerous academic disciplines ideally makes the book more accessible to more people. Nevertheless, because of the need for accuracy and specificity regarding the more esoteric aspects of the research in the book, it was needful that I seek out oversight in certain matters.

First, I would like to thank David Brown of Indiana Bible College (IBC) in Indianapolis, Indiana, who offered such valuable guidance during the earliest stages of this work. Professor Brown has served IBC in numerous capacities over the last thirty years, including as Dean of Students, a position which he held for eleven years. He continues to teach church history and global Christianity at the college and his expertise as an educator in this field assisted me greatly. When *The History & Development of the Doctrine of the Trinity* was still just an idea formulating in my mind, I was invited to speak on the subject at the Oneness & Baptism Symposium during the General Ministry Conference of the Assemblies of the Lord Jesus Christ (ALJC) in Chattanooga, Tennessee in the summer of 2021. During my preparation for that symposium, I began organizing my thoughts for the appropriate boundaries concerning the subject matter of the book. Balancing scope and brevity is a difficult task for anyone writing in the field of historical studies. Realizing the challenge before me, I reached out to Professor Brown for his thoughts on my discussion, requesting his advice on where to focus the most attention. Furthermore, I wanted to know what areas he felt were the most critical to the subject matter generally. His willingness to offer such counsel assisted me greatly on the topic of the earliest Christian philosophers and the Apologists. Chapter seven of this book was greatly inspired by my discussions with Professor Brown, and for that I am especially grateful.

When it came time to take a thorough inventory of all that would be said in my own book regarding the land of Judaea and the influence of Judaism on Christian thought, it became apparent to me that scope would once again become challenging. Anyone who knows Jeremy Lang understands precisely why his advice on this project was valuable. After completing his undergraduate studies at the University of Southern Indiana (USI) as well as Parkersburg Bible College, Jeremy Lang received his Doctor of Divinity from Biblical Apostolic Theological Seminary. During that time, he devoted an incredible amount of time to Judaica studies, becoming an expert in the Hebrew language. Remarkably, he received his certificate in advanced Hebrew from Hebrew University of Jerusalem in 2012, a certification that has been achieved by an exceptionally small number of Americans.[1] He served as a missionary of the ALJC to India for nearly ten years, during which time he learned to speak Tamil and Mizo as well. After returning to the United States, Jeremy Lang became a regional field supervisor for the World Mission Department of the ALJC, serving the Asia and South Pacific regions. In 2019, he founded Biblical Hebrew Academy Online, a school that I have also been blessed to participate in upon the completion of this book. Jeremy Lang's willingness to oversee the broad strokes of this project, as well as guide my examination of the greater Jewish psyche just before, during, and after the time of Christ was especially helpful throughout chapters five and six of this book. Furthermore, I have had the pleasure of knowing Jeremy Lang personally for the better part of the last fifteen years, and his influence on my life has been invaluable. My earliest memories of discussion and debate over church history almost invariably include time spent with him.

I would also like to extend my sincerest gratitude to Pastor Luke St.Clair and his wife TJ St.Clair for their support throughout the formation of this book. 2021 was characterized by a great deal of personal uncertainty in my life, and the St.Clair family epitomized compassion and support during that time. Throughout

---

[1] Hebrew University of Jerusalem was founded by Albert Einstein and Chaim Weizmann in 1918, making it one of the oldest universities in Israel. It is currently ranked as the number one university in Israel.

the last five years I have had the privilege of serving in First Pentecostal Church of Anderson, a phenomenal church that has been pastored by the St.Clairs since 2012. During that time, I have been allotted the opportunity to teach in their weekly Bible class at the church, expanding and exploring many ideas to the congregation that contributed to the completion of this book. Their willingness to allow me that privilege has fueled a great deal of my personal development in academia and ministry, and for that I thank them. One-God preaching stands at the core of what we believe as Pentecostals. Pastor Luke St.Clair has been and remains one of the strongest advocates for the Jesus name message that I have ever met. I am thankful to be connected to a pastor who I can say with confidence is a One-God preacher.

Special thanks to Jordon Frye for all of his hard work surrounding the artwork and preparation for the publication of this book. His skills in design as well as his personal friendship to me have been critical to the finished product. Both Jordon and his wife Katlyn were made to listen to the at times lengthy untangling of my thoughts surrounding the content of the book over dinner tables and car rides. And, whether they knew it or not, it was helping me finish the work as much as any book I may have been reading at the time.

As well to my editor, Elizabeth Williams. I highly recommend her services to anyone seeking assistance in editing and presentation.

# GUIDE TO NOTES & SOURCES

## Source Guide for the Reader:

The traditional abbreviation "Ibid." has been used where appropriate to indicate when a previously referenced source has been used. However, I have added corresponding footnote numbers to help the reader find the source material referenced with more ease. Thus, a footnote labeled: "Ibid. (2) (p. 20)." would indicate that the source (Ibid.) can be found in footnote number two (2) of the same chapter, on the twentieth page of the referenced source (p. 20). If the referenced page or chapter is the same a previous reference, the Ibid. will only include a reference number. (Example: Ibid. (8) would refer to footnote number 8 within the chapter, all information being included on the same page number/chapter as the original citation.) Where ancient sources have been cited, I have chosen to limit my use of the Ibid. abbreviation to assist the reader in finding primary source material and quotations with more ease.

# INTRODUCTION

1 Paris, Natalie. "Venice mulls ticketing system for St. Mark's Square to combat overcrowding." The Telegraph. Last modified May 3, 2017. https://www.telegraph.co.uk/travel/news/venice-to-charge-tourists-ticket-enter-st-marks-square/#:~:text=The%20city%20attracts%20more%20than,how%20better%20to%20protect%20it.

2 "Basilica di San Marco." Last modified , 2021. http://www.basilicasanmarco.it/storia-e-societa/la-basilica-funzione-politica-e-religiosa/?lang=en.

3 Ibid. (2) (The Doges and the Basilica).

4 Ibid. (2) (The Fourth Crusade).

5 Smarthistory: YouTube. Last modified May 1, 2013. https://www.youtube.com/watch?v=Dui5V8TZYbE.

6 Strauss, Barry. Ten Caesars. New York: Simon & Schuster, Inc., 2019. (p.265).

7 Foxe, John. The New Foxe's Book of Martyrs. North Brunswick, NJ: Bridge-Logos Publishers, 1997. (p.28).

8 Ibid. (6) (p.272).

9 Grant, Michael. The Roman Emperors. New York City: Simon & Schuster, Inc., 1997. (p.221).

10 Ibid. (6) (p.278-280).

11 Ibid. (6) (p.176) (Hadrian the Greek).

12 Hamilton, Edith. Mythology. New York: Grand Central Publishing, 1942. (p.46).

# CHAPTER I: ALEXANDER THE GREAT & THE PERSIAN CAMPAIGN

1 Cummings, Lewis V. Alexander the Great. New York: Grove Press, 1940. (p.7).

2 Demosthenes, Olynthiacs II, (p.15).

3 Ibid. (1) (p.53-54).

4 Athenaeus, XIII, (p. DLVII).

5 Ibid. (1) (pp. 136-137).

6 The *Iliad*, Homer (scroll VIII, line I).

7 Daniel (Ch.5).
- It is not known with certainty that the King Darius mentioned in Daniel chapter six was Darius I of the Achaemenid Dynasty, however it seems plausible that he was indeed the same Darius. In Daniel chapter five it is said that Daniel traveled out of Israel during the Babylonian exile in 586 B.C.E. with many other Jews. Given the fact that Darius I reigned from 522-486 B.C.E., it is entirely possible that Daniel was a man of his mid to late seventies by the time the Babylonian Empire fell to the Persians, and that Darius knew Daniel personally as the Bible seems to suggest.

8 Ibid. (1) (p.128).

9 Arrian, *Anabasis,* Book I, (Ch. XV).

10 Strauss, Barry. "Issus." Antiquitas. Last modified November 7, 2019. https://podcasts.apple.com/us/podcast/antiquitas/id1442027700?i=100045619 3534.

11 Ibid. (1) (p.162-165).

12 Ibid. (1) (p.164).

13 It is difficult to know with certainty which prophecy Alexander was shown that softened his heart to the Jewish religion. However, it very likely that the prophetic reading came from Daniel chapter eight. In Daniel 8:5, the prophet is shown a he goat that conquers a ram in battle. Later, in Daniel 8:19-21, the prophet is told by the angel Gabriel that the goat represented the Grecian Empire, while the ram represented the Persians and the Medes. Another prophecy of interest during Alexander's encounter with the Jews is Zechariah chapter nine, which tells of a day in which the city of Tyre will be sacked and destroyed. Furthermore, the prophecy specifically mentions a Jewish conflict with the people of Greece.

14 Josephus, *Antiquities of the Jews*, Book XI, (Ch. XII).

15 Peterson, Jordan B. Kings, Ideals, and Marduk. Last modified August 18, 2020. https://youtu.be/BfqYGhncoeE.

16 Peterson, Jordan B. The Jordan B. Peterson Podcast-Introduction to the Idea of God. Last modified April 20, 2020. https://podcasts.apple.com/us/podcast/the-jordan-b-peterson-podcast/id1184022695?i=1000471222601.

[17] Ibid. (1) (p.191).

[18] Hamilton, Edith. *Mythology*. New York: Grand Central Publishing, 1942. (p.21).

[19] Strabo, *Geography,* Book XVII (Ch. I, Sect. XLIII).

[20] "Deities in Ancient Egypt - Amun." Rosicrucian Egyptian Museum. Last modified , 2021. https://egyptianmuseum.org/deities-amun.

[21] Sacks, Jonathan. *Covenant & Conversation - Exodus: The Book of Redemption.* Jerusalem: Maggid Books, 2010.
> The Egyptian Pharaohs known as Rameses were an expression of this belief. The suffix "meses" being interpreted "son of." Quite literally, the Rameses were the "sons of Ra."

[22] Ibid. (20).

[23] Ibid. (18).

[24] Liebieghaus Skulpturen Sammlung. Last modified , 2010. https://www.liebieghaus.de/en/antike/head-zeus-ammon.

[25] Strauss, Barry. *Ten Caesars*. New York: Simon & Schuster, Inc., 2019. (p.176).

[26] Wilcken, Ulrich. Alexander der Grosse. Germany: Quelle & Meyer, 1931.

[27] Kapadia, Shapurji A. *The Teachings of Zoroaster*. London: Aziloth Books, 2013. (p.16).

[28] Qualben, Lars P. *A History of the Christian Church*. New York: Nelson and Sons Pub., 1958. (p.105-106).

[29] Ibid. (27) (p.24).

[30] The book of Genesis leads the reader to understand that Noah, a gentile, was a righteous man who feared the God of heaven.

[31] In Genesis, Noah is depicted as a god-fearing man in an otherwise godless world. In Exodus, the reader is made to understand that two Egyptian women named Shiphrah and Puah who worked as midwives to the Hebrews refused to carry out an immoral order against the Jews. Again, in Exodus there is made mention of Jethro, the father-in-law of Moses, who was a priest in Midian that feared the God of Moses yet was not a Hebrew himself. In the book of Joshua, the reader finds Rahab the Canaanite harlot who acknowledges the power of the Israelite God. Furthermore, the patriarch of the dominant monotheistic peoples of today (Abraham) was a man from Ur of Chaldees who, according to Hebrew tradition, was the son of an idol merchant.

32 Khordah-Avesta is the prayer book of the Parsi people, who are modern observers of Zoroastrianism from the Indian subcontinent.

33 (Yaîçna I).

34 Ibid. (27) (p.22-23).

35 Ibid. (1) (p.424).

36 Ibid. (1) (p.440).

37 Arrian, *Anabasis,* Book VII, (Ch. XXVIII).

## CHAPTER II: THE SELEUCID GREEKS

1 Kosmin, Paul J. *The Land of the Elephant Kings: Space, Territory, and Ideology of the Seleucid Empire.* Cambridge, MA: Harvard University Press, 2018. (p.31).

2 The Hellenistic Age Podcast: The Seleucid Empire - Syrian Nights, Macedonian Dreams. Last modified November , 2020. https://podcasts.apple.com/us/podcast/the-hellenistic-age-podcast/id1377920930?i=1000500359954.

3 Ibid. (1). (p. 33).

4 Ibid. (2).

5 "The Hellenistic Age Podcast." Hellenistic Cities-Colonization, Urbanization, & Hellenization. Last modified December 9, 2019. https://podcasts.apple.com/us/podcast/the-hellenistic-age-podcast/id1377920930?i=1000459147232.

6 Ibid. (1) (p.183).

7 Ibid. (1) (p.62).

8 Pliny the Elder, *The Natural History*, Book VI (Ch. XVIII).

9 Ibid. (1) (p.62).

10 Ibid. (1) (p.63).

11 Hamilton, Edith. *Mythology*. New York: Grand Central Publishing, 1942. (p.25).

[12] Dr. Jordan Peterson's discussions on the relationship between light and darkness and the example used in the story of *The Lion King* greatly informed my understanding of this principle as an archetype in history. For more on the subject, I highly recommend his latest book *Beyond Order* as well as its companion volume, *12 Rules for Life.*

[13] Ibid. (11) (p.26-27).

[14] Marcus Junianus Justinus, *Epitome of the Philippic History of Pompeius Trogus.* Book XV, (Ch.IV).

[15] Ibid. (1) (p.118).

[16] Britannica. Accessed October 15, 2021.
https://www.britannica.com/biography/Antiochus-IV-Epiphanes

[17] Ibid. (16).

[18] Ibid. (1) (p.228).

[19] Polybius, *Histories*, Book XXX, (Ch. XV).

[20] Livy, *Periochae*, (XLI).

[21] Ibid. (16).

[22] Ezra 3:11-13 says that the foundation of the new temple was much smaller than that of Solomon's Temple. Furthermore, it can be drawn from the second book of Maccabees that the Ark of the Covenant was never restored to the Second Temple. In fact, it is still missing to this day. Historical accounts such as Josephus also record that the Second Temple was largely empty by the first century, and was missing the seven golden candlesticks as well.

[23] I took this photo in October, 2016. Although constructed long after the deaths of the men which they honor, these memorials constitute some of the clearest examples that archeology has to offer concerning the influence of Hellenism in Seleucid and Roman occupied Jerusalem. Large colonnade structures typified Greek style and was later adopted by the Romans.

[24] Diaspora refers to the dispersion of Jews outside of their ancestral homeland of Israel. Still today, Jews who choose not to live in Israel are referred to as diasporic communities.

[25] Gruen, Erich S. "Hellenistic Judaism." In *Cultures of the Jews*, edited by David Biale, 78-79. New York: Schocken Books, 2002.

[26] 1st Maccabees 1:7-12 (KJV).

[27] This act of "becoming uncircumcised" is likely a reference to the wearing of false foreskins by Jewish men so that they might participate in the gymnasiums of the Greeks. Activities such as athletic competition, theatrical productions, etc. were often performed in the nude. Because circumcision was not practiced by the greater culture, it was revolting to the Greeks to look upon. In an effort to conceal their Jewish identity and become more accepted members of the Hellenized culture, Jewish men would practice the buying and selling of artificial foreskins. For more on this, see Eric Meyers in *Cultures of the Jews* (p.170).

[28] 1st Maccabees 1:13-15 (KJV).

[29] 1st Maccabees 1:20-22;39-49 (KJV).

[30] 1st Maccabees 1:41-43 (KJV).

[31] Exodus 20:1-5.

[32] Leviticus 7:19.

[33] Exodus 20:8-9.

[34] Exodus 11:7. According to the Exodus account, the plague of the death of the firstborn was specifically to separate the Jews from the Egyptians. "That you may know how the LORD does put a difference between the Egyptians and Israel."

[35] 1st Maccabees 2:1-24.

[36] It is interesting to note that the miracle of the oil does not appear in the books of the Maccabees from which the story of Hanukkah is most popularly known. The traditional story of the oil that burned for eight days has been preserved in other texts such as the Talmud, but it was not included in the historical account of the Maccabean Revolt.

[37] Telushkin, Joseph. *Jewish Literacy*. New York: William Morrow and Co., 1991. (p.575-576).

[38] 1st Maccabees 1:60-61 says Antiochus had women and children put to death who participated in the act of circumcision. Mothers were executed, while the infants were hung from their necks.

[39] Ibid. (1) (p.248).

## CHAPTER III: HELLENISM & JEWISH THOUGHT

*Image 3.1*

Photo credit/creator: Eyal Bartov
Image credit: Getty Images

Image taken from: "Caesarea Roman Theater." Getty Images. Getty Images. Accessed November 15, 2021. https://www.gettyimages.com/detail/video/aerial-view-of-the-theatre-in-the-ruins-of-caesarea-stock-footage/1291608829?adppopup=true.

Dead Sea Scrolls translations taken from:
"The Dead Sea Scrolls." 49-55. Translated by Michael Wise, Martin Abegg, Jr., and Edward Cook. New York: HarperCollins Publishers, 1996.

[1] *Mishnah* is a compilation of rabbinic literature including legal opinions and debates that was assembled likely in 200 C.E. by Rabbi Judah the Prince.

[2] Deuteronomy 13:17.

[3] Meyers, Eric M. "Jewish Culture in Greco-Roman Palestine." In *Cultures of the Jews*, edited by David Biale, 135. New York: Schocken Books, 2002.

[4] Gruen, Erich S. "Hellenistic Judaism." In *Cultures of the Jews*, edited by David Biale, 80. New York: Schocken Books, 2002.

[5] "Hasmonaean" refers to the family clan of Hashman, from whom the Maccabees descended. For more on this, see Meyers in *Cultures of the Jews* p.143.

[6] *Hegemenos* was a Greek term used to refer to the supreme leader. Alexander the Great bore this title, as well as his father Philip of Macedon.

[7] 1st Maccabees 14:41-42 (KJV).

[8] While often thought of as a Jewish office because of its role in the New Testament, the sanhedrin was not a Jewish creation. It was a term for jurisprudential and private political council created by Alexander the Great in the fourth century B.C.E.

[9] Ibid. (3) (p.145-146).

[10] Aaron was from the tribe of Levi, hence all priests were Levites. However, not all Levites were priests.

[11] Wolbe, Yaakov. "Heresy, Hedonism and Hatred: The Rise of The Sadducees." The Jewish History Podcast. Last modified January 11, 2017.

https://podcasts.apple.com/us/podcast/the-jewish-history-podcast-with-rabbi-yaakov-wolbe/id1151634104?i=1000379837347.

- It is estimated that the office of the High Priest was sold more than three hundred times during this era.

12 Ibid. (11).

13 Downs, David J. "Hellenism." In *Dictionary of Jesus and the Gospels*, edited by Joel B. Green, Jeannine K. Brown, and Nicholas Perrin, 376. Nottingham, England: InterVarsity Press, 2013.

14 Although not included in the biblical account of Abraham's life, the *Midrash* says that Abraham's father named Terah was a seller of idols. To prove the powerlessness of such idols, Abraham destroys the statues and icons in his father's shop and blames it on one of the idols. When Terah objects to Abraham's story, saying that there is of course no way that an idol came to life and destroyed the other idols, Abraham responds with agreement, and questions his father's willingness to worship idols that are indeed so powerless.

15 James, M. R. (2000). Testament of Job. In *Wesley center online*. Retrieved from http://wesley.nnu.edu/sermons-essays-books/noncanonical-literature/noncanonical-literature-ot-pseudepigrapha/testament-of-job/

- The phrase, "thou must wrestle like an athlete" almost certainly places the *Testament of Job* in the category of books written to reshape the stories of Judaism into Greek forms. Athletic competitions were foreign to Judaea until the influence of the Seleucids.

16 The closing chapters of Job not only emphasize the unknowable nature of Job's trials, but also offer criticisms of Job for his insistence on trying to know such answers at all (see Job ch.37-ch.40).

17 Ibid. (4) (p.81-82).

18 Jethro, also known as Reuel, was the father-in-law of Moses according to Exodus 3:1.

19 Genesis 37:9.

20 1st Samuel 9:15.

21 2nd Samuel tells the story of David's moral failings concerning his affair with Bathsheba and his murder of Uriah. In 1st Kings 16, Ahab is regarded as a king that was more evil than any other in Israel. Even the most well-regarded kings in the history of Israel such as Hezekiah have their faults recorded in the books of the kings as well. Indeed, no other nation seems to have recorded their failures so thoroughly as the ancient Israelites.

22 Deuteronomy 17:14-20.

23 Edersheim, Alfred. *The Life and Times of Jesus the Messiah.* 3rd ed. Vol. 1. Grand Rapids, MI: Wm. B. Eerdmans Publishing Co.,, 1973. (p.43).

24 This is akin to Plato's "shadowy cave" analogy. For more on this, see:
- Schenck, Kenneth. *A Christian Philosophical Journey.* Marion, IN: Triangle Publishing, 2014. (p.8).

25 See (Ch. 1).

26 Ibid. (22) (p.50-51).

27 Hamilton, Edith. *Mythology.* New York: Grand Central Publishing, 1942. (p.17-18).
- According to the Greeks, some of the Titans were only known by the pre-existent forces that they embodied, such as Ocean.

28 Ibid. (22) (p.46).

29 Josephus, *Antiquities of the Jews*, Book XIII, (ch. XII.).

30 Ibid (29). (ch.XI).

31 Iturea was situated just north of Galilee, southwest of Damascus. At its peak, the Davidic kingdom of Israel stretched as far north as Sidon, and slightly further east than Ramoth Galaad.

32 Matthew 2:1-17.

33 Telushkin, Joseph. *Jewish Literacy.* New York: William Morrow and Co., 1991. (p.429).
- According to Jewish law, one is only a Jew by birth if their mother is a Jew. Thus, even if one is born to a Jewish father, intermarriage with a non-Jewish woman would prevent the child from being a Jew halakhically.

34 Ibid. (3) (p.147).

35 Josephus, *Antiquities of the Jews*, Book XV (Ch. VIII).

36 See (Ch. 2) (Note 26).

37 Ibid. (29).

38 Ibid. (29).

39 *Mishnah Parah* (3.5a).

40 Ezra 3:9-13.

41 According to 2nd Maccabees, the prophet Jeremiah buried the Ark of the Covenant and the Altar of Incense in a cave before the Babylonian invasion of 586 B.C.E. Josephus' *Antiquities of the Jews* also records that the Second Temple was largely empty compared to Solomon's Temple.

42 Gurtner, Daniel M. "Temple." In *Dictionary of Jesus and the Gospels*, edited by Joel B. Green, Jeannine K. Brown, and Nicholas Perrin, 940. Nottingham, England: InterVarsity Press, 2013.

43 Josephus, *Antiquities of the Jews*, Book XV (Ch. XI).

44 Ibid. (42).

45 Geniza A+B, 4Q268, *The Damascus Document.*
  - (4) refers to the cave number in Qumran the scroll was discovered in. (268) refer to the manuscript number taken from that cave.

46 Ibid. (45) 4Q266, *The Damascus Document.*

47 John 19:20. The writer states that the inscription written above the cross of Jesus was done in Hebrew, Greek, and Latin. However, the word "Hebrew" here likely refers to Aramaic, which was a Syrian dialect of the Hebrew language that contemporary speakers used. Paleo-Hebrew was not in common use during the first century, however religious communities probably continued to use it in liturgy and other isolated instances.

## CHAPTER IV: EARLY CHRISTIAN OPPOSITION TO HELLENISM

Dead Sea Scrolls translations taken from:
"The Dead Sea Scrolls." 49-55. Translated by Michael Wise, Martin Abegg, Jr., and Edward Cook. New York: HarperCollins Publishers, 1996.

1 Matthew 3:1-2 (KJV).

2 According to Luke's Gospel, John the Baptist was the cousin of Jesus (see Luke 1:36).

3 Isaiah 40:1-3. This prophecy is explicitly said to have referred to John the Baptist according to John's Gospel (John1:15-23).

4 Mark 6:24-38.
5 Luke 1:80; Matthew 3:1.

6 See notes (45-46) in chapter three.

7 1QM, 4Q491-496, *The War Scroll*, 4Q285, 11Q14, *The War of the Messiah*.

8 *Mikvah*, was the act of ritual cleansing by water immersion in Judaism. Given its consistent use by John the Baptist in the gospels, it is fair to assume that John belonged to one of the Essene communities which practiced ritual cleansing. As a matter of religious rite, *mikvah* was likely the forerunner for Christian water baptism as well. The Christian baptism practiced by the followers of Jesus Christ was associated with the actions of John the Baptist (see Acts 19), thus lending credibility to the theory that *mikvah* was the earlier form of spiritual cleansing through water immersion.
  - Figures 4.2 and 4.3 were taken in 2016 on an excursion to the ancient Dead Sea communities. Ritual baths were discovered just a short walk from the Qumran caves in which the Dead Sea Scrolls were discovered. Figure 4.2 includes an entry by Josephus in his work on the war of the Jews in which he details the ritual bathing practices of the separatists.

9 Matthew 3:6.

10 Acts 19:3-5.

11 Matthew 3:7-8.

12 In Matthew's account of the same story, the writer specifically states that there were Pharisees and Sadducees among the crowd that came to listen to John (Matthew 3:1-10).

13 Luke 3:1-3; 7-8; 10-14 (KJV).

14 According to the book of Genesis, Abraham had at least eight children (Genesis 25:1-12), although only one was in the covenant of God (Isaac). Thus, being a child of Abraham alone did not constitute a covenantal relationship with God.

15 In the book of Joshua, two tribes of Israel named Gad and Reuben and one half-tribe named Manasseh decided not to establish residence in the land of Canaan which had been promised to them by God as their ancestral homeland. Because of this, they were disconnected from the altar of sacrifice used by the Jews to fulfill their ritual obligations according to the book of Leviticus. Because they still wanted to be considered Jews but did not want to live in the Jewish homeland, they set up a faux altar called *Ed*, nearly causing a civil war among the Israelites. *Ed* served to remind their children that they were still Jews, even though they did not live in the borders of Canaan.

16 Leviticus 20:10-21 details the various commandments concerning an unholy marriage according to Jewish law. Herod violated Leviticus 20:21 which says, "and if a man shall take his brother's wife, it is an unclean thing..."

17 Scheidel, Walter. "Monogamy and Polygyny." Princeton Ed.. Last modified January , 2009. https://www.princeton.edu/~pswpc/pdfs/scheidel/010903.pdf.

18 Josephus records the death of Herod the Great in 4 B.C.E. (the thirty-seventh year of his reign) in *Antiquities of the Jews*, Book XVII (Ch.VIII).

19 A date this early for the birth of Christ would conflict with the traditional belief that Jesus was crucified in 33 C.E. Nevertheless, it can be known with a reasonable amount of certainty that Herod the Great died in 4 B.C.E. Given the fact that Herod issued an edict to have all children in the region of Bethlehem under two years old killed, and that Mary and Joseph fled to Egypt after this order was given and returned with their child after Herod's death, an early date for the birth of Christ fits the timeline of the New Testament.

20 Luke 2:1.

21 Matthew 23:1-4 (KJV).

22 The specific wording and pattern of the response of Jesus is interesting in Matthew 22:37-40. The first century B.C.E. Rabbi named Hillel was once approached by a would-be convert to Judaism and asked a similar question. Hillel gave the response, "Whatever is hateful unto you, do not do unto your neighbor. The rest is commentary, now go and study." The act of summing up the whole Torah in a single axiom was common to the schools of Hillel and Akiva in the generations following their deaths, of which Jesus may have been a part.

23 Jeremiah 7:22-23.

24 "Remember the sabbath day, to keep it holy" (Exodus 20:8 KJV) is the only commandment given in the original ten that concerns a form of ritual observance. It is interesting to note that many modern Christian denominations have adopted all the original Ten Commandments as essential to their own spiritual purity as well, except the one regarding the Sabbath day. Some regard the weekly attendance of their local church assembly as a symbolic fulfillment of this commandment.

25 Matthew 22:23-32 (KJV).

26 The statement by Jesus in Matthew 22:32 is probably a reference to Exodus 3:6, in which God said that He was still the God of Abraham, Isaac, and Jacob, long after the three patriarchs had passed away. The continued reference to the patriarchs in the Old Testament in the present tense suggests that their existence continues in a spiritual form, although physically they are gone.

27 In Matthew 22:34, the writer says that only after Jesus had left the Sadducees speechless did the Pharisees call him "master" and ask Him more sincere questions.

[28] Matthew 21:12-13 (KJV).

[29] See (Ch. 2).

[30] Doves were a traditional fowl offering according to Levitical Law (Leviticus 1:14).

[31] "Who Invented the Synagogue?." Chabad.org. https://www.chabad.org/library/article_cdo/aid/74339/jewish/Who-Invented-the-Synagogue.htm.

[32] Wolbe, Yaakov. "Rabbis, Renaissance and Reclamation: Jewish History of the Mishnaic and Talmudic Eras." The Jewish History Podcast. Last modified April 13, 2021. https://podcasts.apple.com/us/podcast/the-jewish-history-podcast-with-rabbi-yaakov-wolbe/id1151634104?i=1000375348977.
- It has been argued convincingly by some historians that the survival of rabbinic Judaism explains why the books of Maccabees were left out of the Hebrew Bible during the later canonization process. The books of the Maccabees tell the story of the reclaiming of the temple, culminating with the rise of the Hasmonean kings. Because the Sadducees were an outgrowth of Hasmonean influence, it makes sense that the rabbis chose not to include the stories of their heroic deeds in the Hebrew Bible. After the temple was destroyed by the Romans in the first century, the Sadducees no longer had political power and eventually dissolved as a sect completely. Rabbinic Judaism supplanted the temple order as the religious ruling class of the Jews. The rabbis were responsible for the final canonization process of the Hebrew Bible. Leaving out the tales of the Maccabees may be understood as a final slight against the Sadducee order, which the rabbis believed to be a grotesque movement of assimilation and compromise. Thus, history was written by the victors.

[33] Strong's number: g5330, *Pharisaios*: a separatist, i.e. exclusively religious.

[34] See note 19.

[35] Matthew 15:1-6 (KJV).

[36] In Mark's gospel this tribute is called "Corban." This was probably a temple offering and likely refers to a monetary pledge made to the priesthood in exchange for the responsibility of caring for one's parents in old age. According to Jewish law, children must care for their parents when they become too old to care for themselves. However, it seems that in this context, the Pharisees endorsed an effective legal "loophole" allowing children to offer their parents money rather than care through the form of temple offerings.
[37] Matthew 15:8 (KJV).

[38] Luke 12:48.

39 Xenophon, *Anabasis,* Book I (Ch. II Sect. XXIII).

40 Acts 22:25. Paul's invocation of this right lends credibility to the notion that Tarsus enjoyed greater privileges than Judaea in the Roman Empire, and that Paul was from the upper-crust of Tarsus. No such invocation is seen in the case of any of the other Christian apostles who were known to have lived in Judaea.

41 See A.N. Sherwin-White, *The Roman Citizenship* (Oxford,[2] 1973).

42 While it is often believed that only the tribe of Judah was spared after the Exilic Period of Israel's history, the Bible actually names three tribes of Israel that remained vibrant in the post-Exilic Period. According to 2nd Kings, the entire Northern Kingdom of Israel was wiped out in the eighth century by the Assyrian armies. There were eleven tribes of the Israelites represented in The Northern Kingdom of Israel (Reuben, Simeon, Levi, Issachar, Zebulun, Ephraim/Manasseh, Gad, Asher, Dan, Naphtali, and Benjamin). On the surface, this would mean that only the descendants of Judah could have survived into the first century. However, it is known from the books of Chronicles that a portion of the tribe of Benjamin seceded from the Northern Kingdom and chose instead to dwell in Judah after the civil war between the loyalists to Saul and the followers of David (1st Chronicles 12:29). Furthermore, the tribe of Levi was not allotted any land of its own in the book of Joshua. Instead, it was spread out across the lands occupied by the Northern Kingdom and Judah alike (Joshua 13:14), thus there would have been Levites living in Judah during the Assyrian exile as well. Although confusing at first glance, the Bible is very clear in the end: The tribes of Judah, Levi, and Benjamin all had representation in first century Judaea.

43 Philippians 3:4-5 (KJV).

44 1st Corinthians 10:1-11.

45 Acts 14:8-15 (KJV).

46 Hamilton, Edith. *Mythology.* New York: Grand Central Publishing, 1942. (p.30-31).

47 Acts 14:15-17 (KJV).

48 Ibid. (45).

49 Acts 17:16-20 (KJV).

50 Rutledge, David. "The Rise of Modern Stoicism." ABC's The Philosopher's Zone. Last
modified November 17, 2014.
https://www.abc.net.au/radionational/programs/philosopherszone/modern-day-stoicism/5896364.

51 Ibid. (50).

52 Hanselman, Stephen. "Stoicism vs. Epicureanism." Daily Stoic. https://dailystoic.com/stoicism-vs-epicureanism/.

53 Becker, Lawrence. *A New Stoicism*. Princeton, NJ: Princeton University Press, 1997.

54 Ibid. (52).

55 Acts 17:22-29 (KJV).

56 Epimenides, *Cretica*.

57 Acts 16:11.

58 Acts 19:9.

59 Although tradition says he ran to his own execution, it is not actually known precisely when or how the Apostle Paul died. The book of Acts closes with Paul on house arrest, awaiting his opportunity to give an appeal of his arrest to Nero. Historians have surmised that perhaps Paul made his appeal, whereupon he was released and continued to travel into the area of Britain or Spain, preaching the gospel until his death. Others have embraced the idea that Paul's request was never heard in Nero's final years as Caesar, and he was executed during the Jewish Revolt (see chapter 6). For more on these discussions, see F.F. Bruce's *Paul: Apostle of the Heart Set Free*.

60 Colossians 2:8.

61 Acts 23:2-10 (KJV).

62 Acts 16:17; 18:26; 22:4 all refer to the followers of Jesus as belonging to something known as "the way." In Acts 24:14 and Acts 24:22 Paul uses the phrase to refer to the sect to which he belonged. While general, this was probably a common method of referring to followers of Jesus before the word "Christian" came into common usage.

63 1st Corinthians 1:20-24 (KJV).

## CHAPTER V: FIRST CENTURY PERSPECTIVES ON JESUS OF NAZARETH

1 Matthew 16:13-16 (KJV).

² Strong's number: g5547

³ Isaiah 40:9.

⁴ Proverbs 30:1-3.

⁵ Isaiah 12:2-3.

⁶ Isaiah 9:6-7 (KJV).
- Interestingly, in recent years it has become more common among scholars to be skeptical of Isaiah 9:6 with regards to its messianic references. Some have suggested that the passage was only a reference to the son of the prophet himself. However, the more traditional interpretation of the passage does seem to be more in consonance with messianic beliefs. There are two direct references to an everlasting kingdom in Isaiah 9:6-7, something which does not seem to fit neatly if referring to an earthly ruler in the time of Isaiah. Furthermore, the description of the king to come as "the mighty God" and "the everlasting Father" are exceptionally lofty terms that do not appear often in the Hebrew Bible, and almost never reference a king. In any case, if Isaiah 9:6 was intended to refer to an earthly ruler of Israel, it is apparent that the words of the prophet were not fulfilled in his lifetime, as no king of Israel is ever said to have established an everlasting government of peace. The major historical events immediately following the death of Isaiah were largely characterized by the Babylonian Exile in 586 B.C.E.

⁷ Lang, Jeremy L. "From the Foundation of the World: The Establishment of the Oneness in Genesis." In *ALJC Oneness & Baptism Symposium 2021*, edited by Nathan S. Whitley, 30-31. Memphis, TN: Assemblies of the Lord Jesus Christ, 2021.

⁸ Isaiah 12:2-6 (KJV).

⁹ Isaiah 40:3.

¹⁰ Isaiah 43:11 (KJV).

¹¹ Isaiah 35:3-6 (KJV).

¹² John 21:25.

¹³ Luke 5:17-39.
¹⁴ John 9:6.

¹⁵ Mark 7:33-36.

¹⁶ John 11:38-44.

¹⁷ Hosea 11:1.

[18] Acts 3:19-23 (KJV).

[19] Deuteronomy 18:15.

[20] Acts 4:4.

[21] The first gentile convert to Christianity is described in the tenth chapter of Acts. It is estimated that the conversion of Cornelius occurred somewhere between seven and fourteen years after the birth of Christianity.

[22] 1st Timothy 3:16 (KJV).

[23] Concerning the doctrine of salvation.

[24] Acts 2:38; Acts 10:48; Acts 19:5.

[25] Colossians 2:8-10 (KJV).

[26] John 14:9 sums up the "Father and Son" discussion well in the New Testament. Certain disciples of Jesus were also uncertain of the relationship between the two. Jesus clarified the confusion by stating that He and His Father were one, and if you had seen Jesus, then you had seen the Father as well.

[27] Colossians 2:1-2 (KJV).

[28] Later Christian developments emphasized a distinct identity between Father, Son, and Spirit, but never between God and Father.

[29] James 1:26-27(KJV).

[30] Ephesians 4:4-5.

[31] Matthew 22:36-40.

[32] Colossians 1:9-19 (KJV).

[33] Acts 15:5 informs the reader that there were believers in Christ from the Pharisee sect. Of course, it is also known that Paul was himself a Pharisee. In fact, the book of Acts closes with Paul doing a home-Bible study with the chief of the Jews while on house arrest. By contrast, some of the greatest conflicts between Christianity and Judaism happened during the apostles encounters with the Sadducee sect (See Acts chapters three and four).

[34] Scott, James M. "Gods, Greek and Roman." In *Dictionary of Jesus and the Gospels*, edited by Joel B. Green, Jeannine K. Brown, and Nicholas Perrin, 329-334. Nottingham, England: InterVarsity Press, 2013.

[35] 2nd Maccabees 6:7.

[36] Ibid. (34) (p.330).

[37] See discussion on Philo, (p.72-73).

[38] Hamilton, Edith. *Mythology*. New York: Grand Central Publishing, 1942. (p.62).
  - Other heroes of Greek myth were said to have both human and divine parents, but none of them were identified with the elite gods of Olympus.

[39] Ibid. (38).

[40] John 2:1-11.

[41] Ibid. (38) (p.63).

[42] Mark 6:3-5 (KJV).

[43] Ibid. (38) (66).

[44] Ibid. (38) (p.68-69).

[45] Matthew 26:57-64 (KJV).

[46] Acts 8:32.

[47] Matthew 27:43.

[48] Ibid. (38) (p.69-70).

[49] Matthew 27:29-37 (KJV).

[50] Matthew 27:23.

[51] 1st Corinthians 1:20-24 (KJV).

[52] Psalm 22.

[53] Isaiah 9:6; Isaiah 43;11.
  - In the book of Acts, the disciple named Philip taught the Ethiopian eunuch that Jesus was the Christ using the book of Isaiah.

[54] Although Christian theology emphasizes that the salvation of God is spiritual, and that sin was the foe that Christ defeated on the cross, it is also commonly believed among Christians that Christ will return to the world He created and rule the earth as a king as well. In this way, the Jewish perspective on the coming of the Messiah is, perhaps, not completely incompatible with Christian theology.

55 Acts 1:4-7 (KJV).

## CHAPTER VI: THE JEWISH REVOLT

*Image 6.1*

Taken from: "Ancient Coins: Bar Kokhba." Coin Archives. Accessed November 15, 2021. https://www.coinarchives.com/a/results.php?search=bar+kochba.

1 Strauss, Barry. *Ten Caesars*. New York: Simon & Schuster, 2019. (p. 109).

2 Josephus, *Wars of the Jews*, Book III (Ch.VII)

3 Ibid. (1) (p. 117).

4 Ibid. (1) (p. 117).

5 Tacitus, *Annals*, Book XV.

6 Ibid. (1) (p.103).

7 Tacitus, *The History*, Book I (Ch. IV).

8 See (Ch. 3).

9 Josephus, *Wars of the Jews*, Book II (Ch.IV).

10 Ibid. (9) (Ch. IV).

11 Ibid. (9) (Ch. V).

12 Recall that it was Herod the Great who ordered the execution of all children under the age of two due to his paranoia of losing control of the kingdom.

13 Ibid. (9) (Ch. VI).

14 Ibid. (1) (p.96).

15 Ibid. (5).

16 Given his propensity for narcissistic behavior and his flair for the dramatic, the acting out of the destruction of Troy was viewed by many to be Nero's unique way of romanticizing what he had done to Rome. If Nero did not set fire to the city, the production of the destruction of Troy was, at the very least, poorly timed.

17 Ibid. (15).

18 Ibid. (15).

19 Although there is no record of the death of either Peter or Paul in the New Testament, the historical account of Peter's execution handed down by Hegesippus

does seem to correlate with the prophecy of Jesus regarding the manner in which Peter would be martyred (John 21:18-19).

[20] Foxe, John. *The New Foxe's Book of Martyrs*. North Brunswick, NJ: Bridge-Logos Publishers, 1997. (p.7-8).

[21] Bernard, David K. *A History of Christian Doctrine*. Vol. 1. Hazelwood, MO: Word Aflame Press, 1995. (p.44).

[22] Acts 14:1; Acts 17:10-12.

[23] Meyers, Eric M. "Jewish Culture in Greco-Roman Palestine." In *Cultures of the Jews*, edited by David Biale, 169. New York: Schocken Book, 2002.

[24] Ibid. (23) (p.168-169).
- For primary source evidence concerning these sorts of encounters between Jewish Christians and the early rabbinate, see *Tosefta Hullin* 2:24.

[25] Romans (Ch. 11).

[26] Ibid. (1) (p. 116).

[27] Ibid. (9) Book III (Ch. VII).

[28] Ibid. (9) Book IV (Ch. IX).

[29] Grant, Michael. *The Roman Emperors*. New York: Simon & Schuster, 1985. (p. 51).

[30] Galba, Otho, and Vitellius.

[31] Ibid. (9) Book VI (Ch. V).

[32] Telushkin, Joseph. *Jewish Literacy*. New York: William Morrow and Company, Inc., 1991. (p. 141-142).

[33] Ibid. (32) (p.145).

[34] Ibid. (23) (p. 163).

[35] Bar-Kokhba coin image taken from *coinarchives.com*, Bar-Kokhba second revolt, 133-134 C.E.

[36] Ibid. (32) (p.146).

[37] See (Ch. 5).

[38] *Palestina*, or, in Hebrew, *Pelesheth*, which means, "Land of the Philistines." As a last slight against the Jews for the trouble they had caused for the Romans, Hadrian renamed the province after the historical enemies of the Davidic Kingdom of Israel, the Philistines.

39 In Matthew 24:24, Jesus warned that there would come a time when false Christs would arise in the earth, and that they would deceive many people after His death. In 2nd Corinthians 11:4, Paul warned the church not to receive another Jesus, another spirit, or another gospel than the one which was preached in the New Testament—the gospel of Jesus Christ.

40 "List of Roman Emperors." Britannica. Accessed November 8, 2021. https://www.britannica.com/topic/list-of-Roman-emperors-2043294.


# CHAPTER VII: HELLENISM IN CHRISTIAN LIFE


*Image 7.1*

https://commons.wikimedia.org/wiki/File:The_%22Mona_Lisa_of_the_Galilee_%22_(possibly_Venus),_part_of_the_Dionysus_mosaic_floor_in_Sepphoris_(Diocaesarea),_Israel_(15004387483).jpg

*Image 7.2*

Photo taken at the Rockefeller Archeological Museum, Sultan Suleiman St. 27 Jerusalem, Israel. Archeological dating/information taken from display information associated with the statute.

1 Telushkin, Joseph. *Jewish Literacy*. New York: William Morrow and Company, Inc., 1991. (p. 509-510).

2 Galatians 1:8-9 (KJV).

3 Bernard, David K. *A History of Christian Doctrine*. Vol. 1. Hazelwood, MO: Word Aflame Press, 1995. (p. 43).

4 Kelly, John D. "Apologist." Britannica. Last modified October 20, 2021. https://www.britannica.com/topic/Apologist.

5 "Saint Justin Martyr Christian Apologist." Britannica. Accessed November 9, 2021. https://www.britannica.com/biography/Saint-Justin-Martyr.
6 See notes (Ch. 4).

7 Colossians 2:8.

8 Justin Martyr, *Dialogue with Trypho,* (Ch. XLVII).

9 Ibid. (8) (Ch. II).

10 The explanation has been abbreviated from the cited text in this work for brevity's sake, but it is interesting to note that Justin seemed to consider the Pythagorean school to be the worthiest of his attention. He only dismissed it

because he felt he did not have the proper skills necessary to utilize it, such as training in music, astronomy, and geometry.

[11] Ibid. (8) (Ch. III).

[12] Ibid. (8).

[13] Ibid. (8).

[14] Ibid (8) (Ch. VIII).

[15] Acts 10:44-48 (KJV).

[16] Acts 2:1-12; 38-41 (KJV).

[17] Acts 19:1-6 (KJV).

[18] The reason for this being that the unknown man instructed Justin in the wisdom of the prophets, juxtaposed with Greek philosophy in their conversation. For more on this, see *Dial.* (Ch. III-V).

[19] Justin Martyr, *First Apology*, (Ch. LXI).

[20] John 14:7-11.

[21] Colossians 1:15.

[22] Ibid. (8) (Ch. LVI).

[23] The book of Acts chapter twelve illustrates that many early Christians believed that angels walked the earth in human form, sometimes even taking the form of familiar individuals (Acts 12:15). The book of Hebrews also admonishes the reader to remember that there are moments in life where one may entertain angels unaware, and so it is important to be kind to strangers, such as the example given in Genesis 18.

[24] Ibid. (8) (Ch. LVI).

[25] The generic use of the word "Lord" is consonant with other references to angels in the Old Testament, as the angel of the Lord is often given the honorific to disclose in whose authority he speaks. Judges chapter six illustrates this (the angel of the Lord appeared to Gideon), as well as Exodus chapter twelve (God sends the death angel into Egypt). Because the angels execute the will of God, is not wrong to say that God was responsible for the act itself, but nowhere are the angels said to be equal with God.

[26] Ibid. (8) (Ch. LVII).

[27] Ibid. (8) (Ch. CXXVII).

[28] Exodus (Ch. 29).

[29] Ibid. (8) (Ch. CXXVIII).

30 Miller, Leo F. "The Formula of Baptism in the Early Church." *The Catholic Historical Review* 10, no. 4: (220).

31 Ibid. (30).

32 Nicene Creed." Britannica. Accessed November 10, 2021. https://www.britannica.com/topic/Nicene-Creed.

33 Ibid. (8) (Ch. CXXIII-CXXIV).

34 Romans (Ch. 10-11).

35 Romans 11:1-7; 16-21.

36 Ibid. (8) (Ch. XLVII).
  • Tension between Jews and gentiles over the essentiality of observance of the Law of Moses dated back to the New Testament, where in Acts 15 it is said that many believers came together in a council at Jerusalem to discuss the issue.

37 Whitaker, E C. "History of the Baptismal Formula." *The Journal of Ecclesiastical History* 16, no. 1 (April 1965): 5-6.

38 Meyers, Eric M. "Jewish Culture in Greco-Roman Palestine." In *Cultures of the Jews*, edited by David Biale, 172-73. New York: Schocken Books, 2002.

39 Heick, Otto. *A History of Christian Thought*. Vol. 1. Philadelphia, PA: Fortress Press, 1965. (p. 111-113).

40 Luke 2:27.

41 Acts 28:23.

42 Galatians 3:24-26 (KJV).

43 Acts 8:26-38 (KJV).

44 Ibid. (39) (p. 112).

45 Origen was a pupil of Clement at the school in Alexandria.

46 Ibid. (39) (p. 114).

47 Catholic simply means, "universal."

48 Ignatius, *Epistle to the Smyrnans*.

49 Ignatius, *Epistle to the Magnesians*.
  • The writings of Ignatius, as well as other post-Apostolic writers, are also characterized by a strong emphasis on paying honor to the bishops of the church and submitting to authority. While this is present in the New Testament as well, it plays a much more prominent role in the post-Apostolic writings. For more on this, see J.B. Lightfoot, *The Apostolic Fathers*.

50 Acts 16:1-2.

51 Ibid. (39) (p. 114).
- Kurtz, *op. cit.,* Par. 19; cf. Par. 7, 25-26.

# CHAPTER VIII: THE RIDDLE OF TERTULLIAN

1 Tertullian, *Prescription Against Heretics*, (Ch. VII).

2 Heick, Otto. *A History of Christian Thought.* Vol. 1. Philadelphia, PA: Fortress Press, 1965. (p. 123-124).

3 Ibid. (2).

4 Chalfant, William B. *Ancient Champions of Oneness.* Hazelwood, MO: Word Aflame Press, 1986. (p. 64).

5 Ibid. (2) (p. 124).

6 Ibid. (2) (p. 124).

7 Praxeas simply means "busybody," so it is entirely possible that the name was intended to be a disparaging descriptor of the individual that Tertullian was writing to.

8 Tertullian, *Against Praxeas*, (Ch. V).

9 "Stoicism." Standford Encyclopedia of Philosophy. Last modified April 15, 1996. https://plato.stanford.edu/entries/stoicism/.

10 Tertullian, *Against Praxeas*, (Ch. VII).

11 John 4:24.

12 Jeremiah 23:24.

13 Tertullian, Against *Praxeas*, (Ch. X).

14 Justin Martyr, *Dialogue with Trypho* (Ch. XXVIII).

15 John 14:8-10 (KJV).

16 Ibid. (15).

17 Hebrews 1:3.

18 Colossians 1:15-16.

19 Romans 5:12-21.

20 Philippians 2:5-7.

21 Philippians 2:8.

22 1st Timothy 3:16.

23 Revelation 1:11;18 (KJV).

24 Tertullian, *Against Praxeas*, (Ch. XII).

25 Isaiah 44:24 (KJV).

26 Isaiah 44:8 (KV).

27 Tertullian, *Against Praxeas*, (Ch. XI).

28 1st John 2:23.

29 Colossians 2:9 (KJV).

30 Tertullian, *Against Praxeas*, (Ch. XXXI).

31 1st Corinthians 10:1-6 (KJV).

32 Although translated as "Red Sea" in the King James Version of the Bible, giving the sea its more popular historical name, Paleo-Hebrew called it the "Sea of Reeds." The change likely happened due to no clear translation of the "ee" being possible from the original. For more on this, see Joseph Telushkin's *Jewish Literacy*, p. 50-51.

33 This is probably a reference to the twentieth chapter of the book of Numbers, which tells the story of Moses' disobedience against God for smiting the rock that he was told to speak to instead. God told Moses that if he lifted his rod and spoke to the rock, it would give water to the people so that they could drink while in the wilderness. But when Moses took the rod in his hand, he rebuked the people, and smote the rock twice with his rod instead. The water still came forth so the people could drink, but Moses was barred from leading the Israelites into Canaan for his behavior.

34 Galatians 3:26-29 (KJV).

35 Genesis 12:1-3.

36 Genesis 17:1-14.

37 Tertullian, *Against Praxeas*, (Ch. IV).

38 Ibid. (2) (p. 127).

39 Ibid. (4) (p. 62).

40 Romans 8:8-11 (KJV).

41 Ibid. (4) (p. 61-62).

42 Ibid. (2) (p. 127).

43 Tertullian, *Against the Jews*, (Ch. III).

44 Romans 11:11-21 (KJV).

45 The ninth, tenth, and eleventh chapters of the book of Romans all deal specifically with Paul's affection for his brethren in the flesh (the Israelites) and his desire that Christians show kindness and benevolence toward them, that in emulating Christ they might lead the unbelieving Jews to Him.
46 The tenth chapter of the book of Acts is the first recorded instance of a gentile convert to Christianity.

47 Romans 11:19-21 (KJV).

48 Romans 11:12 (KJV).

49 Romans 11:25-27 (KJV).

50 Acts 14:9.

51 Romans 10:1 (KJV).

52 Tacitus, *Annals*, Book XV.

53 2nd Timothy 4:14 refers to one named Alexander the coppersmith of whom Paul warned Timothy to have no fellowship with, because he greatly resisted the words of the preachers. Revelation 2:6 references a group known as the Nicolaitans, whose doctrine Jesus hated.

## CHAPTER IX: PERSECUTION & THE TETRARCHY

*Image 9.1*

Taken from: *https://collectingancientcoins.co.uk/roman-coins-about-britain-constantius-chlorus/*

*Image 9.2*

Taken from: https://21h007.wordpress.com/2018/12/11/the-portrait-of-the-four-tetrarchs/

1 Strauss, Barry S. *Ten Caesars*. New York: Simon & Schuster, 2019. (p. 268).

2 Grant, Michael. *The Roman Emperors*. New York: Simon & Schuster, 1985. (p. 203).

3 Ibid. (1) (p. 264).

4 Ibid. (1) (p.270).

5 "The Twelve Labors of Heracles." Mythology Unbound. Accessed November 15, 2021. https://press.rebus.community/mythologyunbound/chapter/the-twelve-labors-of-heracles/.

6 Ibid. (1) (p. 271-272).

7 Ibid. (2) (p. 209).

8 *Panegyrici Latini* (Manuscript XI).

9 Ibid (2) (p. 216).

10 "Allectus: Roman Administrator." Britannica. Accessed November 15, 2021. https://www.britannica.com/biography/Allectus.

11 Ibid. (2) (p. 217).

12 "Roman Coins About Britain-Constantius Chlorus." Collecting Ancient Coins. Accessed November 15, 2021. https://collectingancientcoins.co.uk/roman-coins-about-britain-constantius-chlorus/.

13 The Sasanian Empire was centered in what is now Iran. The Sasanians are sometimes referred to as the "neo-Persians" by modern historians.

14 Ibid. (2) (p. 219-220).

15 Ammianus Marcellinus, *History*, Book XIV (Ch. XI).

16 Ibid. (1) (p. 274).

17 M. Tullius Cicero, *For Marcus Fonteius*, Book XIII, (Ch. XXX).

18 Ibid. (1) (p. 279-280).

19 Lactantius, *On the Deaths of the Persecutors*, (Ch. XI).

20 "Gods and goddesses of the Greek and Roman pantheon." The British Museum. Last modified , 1942. Accessed November 16, 2021. https://blog.britishmuseum.org/gods-and-goddesses-of-the-greek-and-roman-pantheon/.

21 Ibid. (2) (p. 220).

22 The phrase "gods of the mountains" may have been a reference generally to Mount Olympus, the dwelling place of the Greek and Roman pantheon.

23 Ibid. (19).

24 Hamilton, Edith. *Mythology*. New York: Grand Central Publishing, 1942. (p. 25-26).

[25] Mark, the oldest of the gospel accounts, introduces Jesus as one who heals the sick and delivers the possessed (Mark 1:30-34). In the book of Revelation, Christ is associated with the power which casts the serpent, known as Satan who accuses the brethren, out of the heavens, ushering in the kingdom of God (Revelation 12:7-10).

[26] Ibid (24) (p. 26-27).

[27] 1st Timothy 2:5 (KJV).

[28] 1st John 1:9.

[29] In Acts 15:28-29, a council of believers met at Jerusalem to discuss how much of the Law of Moses ought to be placed upon the gentile Christians. Their determination was that they ought to abstain from meats offered to idols, from blood, from strangled things, and from fornication.

[30] Sol Invictus was another iteration of the cult of light, which will be discussed at length later in this book.

[31] Ibid. (1) (p.280).

[32] Eusebius, *The Life of the Blessed Emperor Constantine*, Book I (Ch. XVI-XVII).

[33] Ibid. (1) (p. 281).

[34] Srejovic, Dragoslav, and Cedomir Vasic. *Imperial Mausolea and Consecration Memorials in Felix Romuliana*. Belgrade, CS: The University of Belgrad, 1994. (p. 149-151).

[35] Ibid. (1) (p. 275).

[36] Ibid. (1) (p. 283-284).

[37] Ibid. (2) (p. 221).

[38] Ibid (2) (p. 221-222).

[39] Galerius' illness was attributed by contemporary writers to the anger of the God of the Christians against him, or, perhaps, a triumph of the Christian God over the Roman gods. Furthermore, instability at the top of the Roman hierarchy only spelled doom for the system that Galerius and Diocletian had worked so hard to build.

## CHAPTER X: UNCONQUERED CONSTANTINE

*Image 10.1*

Taken from http://numismatics.org/ocre/id/ric.7.tri.135

*Image 10.2*

Taken from www.britannica.com

[1] Ancient Gaul was primarily comprised of what is now France, as well as portions of Italy, Germany, and Belgium.

[2] Strauss, Barry S. *Ten Caesars*. New York: Simon & Schuster, 2019. (p. 294).

[3] The Unconquered Sun was recognized as a god that promised victory in military action as early as the days of emperor Aurelian.

[4] Accounts of what, exactly, Constantine saw differ widely among historians. Eusebius claims that it was a trophy of a cross that appeared above the sun with the inscription, "conquer by this." Others associated the vision with a ring around the sun. The reason for this discrepancy is that the first known written account of Constantine's vision was not recorded until after his death, nearly thirty years after the incident. For more on this, see Strauss (Ch. 10).

[5] Modern Serbia.

[6] Ibid. (2) (p. 299).

[7] Ibid. (2) (p. 293).

[8] Lactantius, *On the Deaths of the Persecutors*, (Ch. XI).

[9] Optatus of Milevis, *Letter of Constantine to Ablavius (or Aelafius)*. For more on this, see *Against the Donatists*.

[10] For more coin images from this era, see Online Coins of the Roman Empire (OCRE).
  - http://numismatics.org/ocre/id/ric.7.tri.135

[11] Ibid. (2) (p. 298).

[12] Bennett, Julian. *Trajan, Optimus Princeps*. Bloomington, IN: Indiana University Press, 1997. (p. 107).

[13] The official language of the Byzantine Empire became Greek in later generations, abandoning the Roman tradition of Latin.

[14] Grant, Michael. *The Roman Emperors*. New York: Simon & Schuster, 1985. (p. 231).

[15] Ibid. (2) (p. 296).

[16] Ibid. (14) (p. 231).

[17] Ibid. (14) (p. 231).

[18] Eusebius Pamphilus, *Church History*, Book X (Ch. V).
  - Constantine's Letter Summoning the Council of Rome, 313 C.E.

19 Both the Council of Rome in 313 C.E., as well as the Council of Arles (Arelate) in 314 C.E. were convened to discuss, among other things, the issue of appointing bishops. It is likely that Caecilian was accused of affiliation with heretics, although he was later confirmed innocent by the later council.

20 "Council of Arles/Donatist." Britannica. Accessed November 21, 2021. https://www.britannica.com/topic/Donatists.

21 Ibid. (18).

22 Ibid. (14) (p. 231).

23 Ibid. (2) (p. 303-304).

24 In both of Paul's letters to Timothy, he was critical of a man named Alexander the coppersmith who apparently associated with the church at Ephesus. Paul operated as the chief apostle to the churches that he helped establish throughout Asia Minor, but Timothy was the local pastor/overseer, at least for a time.

25 Revelation 2:1-7.

26 2nd Thessalonians 3:14-15 (KJV).

27 Eusebius Pamphilus, *The Life Of The Blessed Emperor Constantine*, Book I (Ch. XVII).

28 Curiously, Eusebius associates the death of Constantius with evidence that he was blessed among the Augusti, unlike his fellow rulers. This was a strange comment by Eusebius, as it is known that Constantius was the first of the original tetrarchy to pass away. Galerius, the most pagan of the tetrarchs, outlasted his fellow rulers.

29 Trajan, Hadrian, and Marcus Aurelius all belonged to the Antonine dynasty. All three are depicted on Constantine's Arch in Rome.

30 "Roman Religion." UNRV Roman History. Accessed November 22, 2021. https://www.unrv.com/religion.php.

31 Eusebius Pamphilus, *The Life Of The Blessed Emperor Constantine*, Book I (Ch. VIII).

32 Eusebius seems to suggest that this is precisely his motivation in Ch. XXIII of Book I. "I have not thought it fit to give any distinct account of their downfall, nor to stain the memory of the good by mentioning them in connexion with those of an opposite character." Still, while Eusebius writes with equal animosity toward the other tetrarchs and even Maxentius, Galerius is the only one that he refused to mention by name.

33 Eusebius Pamphilus, *The Life Of The Blessed Emperor Constantine*, Book II (Ch. LXV).
- Constantine's letter to Alexander the bishop, and Arius the presbyter.

[34] Eusebius Pamphilus, *The Life Of The Blessed Emperor Constantine*, Book II (Ch. LXVII-LXVIII).
  • Constantine's letter to Alexander the bishop, and Arius the presbyter.

[35] 1st Timothy 3:16.

[36] Pamphilus, Eusebius. "Ecclesiastical History." In *The Fathers of the Church*, Edited by Roy J. Deferrari and Rudolph Arbesmann, 6-7. Translated by Roy J. Deferrari. New York: Fathers of the Church, Inc., 1953.

[37] Ibid. (36).

[38] Colossians 1:16.

[39] Deuteronomy 6:4.

[40] Isaiah 44:24.

[41] "Christianity: The Alliance Between Church and Empire." Britannica. Accessed November 22, 2021. https://www.britannica.com/topic/Christianity/The-alliance-between-church-and-empire.

[42] Theodosian Code, Book II (Sect. VIII).

[43] Justin Martyr, *First Apology*, (Ch. LXVII).

[44] Some have suggested that the reason for Sunday worship by early Christians was due to the fact that Jesus resurrected on a Sunday, however this claim is widely debated, as it is not certain what day of the week Jesus resurrected. It is more likely that Sunday association with the resurrection of Christ became popular after decree by Constantine, and not earlier.

[45] Irshai, Oded. "Confronting A Christian Empire." In *Cultures of the Jews*, edited by David Biale, 202. New York: Schocken Books, 2002.

[46] Zosimus, *New History*, Book II (Ch. XXXII).

[47] Eusebius Pamphilus, *The Life Of The Blessed Emperor Constantine*, Book II (Ch. LXX-LXXI).
  • Constantine's letter to Alexander the bishop, and Arius the presbyter.

[48] Eusebius Pamphilus, *The Life Of The Blessed Emperor Constantine*, Book III (Ch. X).

[49] Although the nature of God and the person of Christ are often considered the primary focus topics of the First Council of Nicaea, Eusebius makes mention of a more prominent issue in his writings on the council—the date for the celebration of Easter. The debates around this controversy will be discussed in greater detail in the next chapter.

[50] Origen was a disciple of Clement of Alexandria, one of the earliest writers to depart from the traditional Christian teachings about the person of Christ.

51 Ibid. (36) (p. 11-12).
- Not a great deal is known about Sabellius, but it can be assumed from what historical data that has been gathered on him that his teachings were probably consistent with that of the Monarchians or early Jewish Christians.

52 Ibid. (36) (p. 11).

53 Nicene Creed, 325 C.E. (amended 381 C.E.).

54 Nicene Creed, 381 C.E.

## CHAPTER XI: THE ROMAN CHRIST

*Image 11.1*
Taken from: https://www.bbc.com/news/magazine-35120965
- Article written by Joan Taylor of King's College, London. December 24, 2015.

*Image 11.2*
Taken from: https://commons.wikimedia.org/wiki/File:Jerusalem-Grabeskirche-14-vom_Erloeserkirchturm-2010-gje.jpg

*Image 11.3*
Taken from: http://www.mmerlino.com/Byzantium/Constantinople.html

*Image 11.4*
Taken from: www.livius.org

*Image 11.5*
Taken from: Cambridge Elements: The Statues of Constantinople by Albrecht Berger. Published online by Cambridge University Press, June 18, 2021.

*Image 11.6*
Taken from: https://www.worldhistory.org/Statue_of_Zeus_at_Olympia/
- Andrew Bossi, (CC BY-NC-SA)

1 Eusebius Pamphilus, *The Life Of The Blessed Emperor Constantine*, Book III (Ch. V).

2 See (Ch. 6).

3 Telushkin, Joseph. *Jewish Literacy*. New York: William Morrow and Company, Inc., 1991. (p. 561).
- The fluidity of celebration dates for the Jewish holidays has contributed to the statement, "the holidays came early this year" or, "the holidays are late this year" in Judaism.

4 Moss, Aron. "Why is Passover on a Full Moon?." Chabad.org. Accessed November 27, 2021. https://www.chabad.org/holidays/passover/pesach_cdo/aid/4250850/jewish/Why-Is-Passover-on-a-Full-Moon.htm.

5 Acts 12:4.

6 Matthew 26:2; Mark 14;12.
- Passover is celebrated over the course of eight days. The gospel writers inform us that the episode known as "The Last Supper" between Jesus and His disciples happened on the first day of the Passover (Matthew 26:17).

7 In Acts 20:16 Paul is said to have been eager to travel to Jerusalem to celebrate the day of Pentecost, which was held fifty days after Passover. This account happened long after his conversion to Christianity.

8 Eusebius Pamphilus, *The Life Of The Blessed Emperor Constantine*, Book III (Ch. V).

9 Exodus 12:13-20.

10 2nd Maccabees (Ch. 6-7).

11 Eusebius Pamphilus, *The Life Of The Blessed Emperor Constantine*, Book III, (Ch. XVIII).
- According to Eusebius, this inclusion is an excerpt from a letter written by Constantine.

12 Romans (Ch. 11).

13 John 10:17-18 (KJV).

14 Mark 14:56.

15 Eusebius Pamphilus, *The Life Of The Blessed Emperor Constantine*, Book III, (Ch. XVIII).

16 Diocesis Orientis would have been the region covering Palestine after the provinces were re-drawn by Diocletian in the third century.

17 Constantine is hesitant to mention all the Eastern territories in this portion of his writing, as he later admits not all of the East—the older home of Christianity—is on board with his changes.

18 Eusebius Pamphilus, The Life Of The Blessed Emperor Constantine, Book III (Ch. XIX).

19 Recall the accusations of Tertullian, the writings of Justin Martyr, etc.

20 Irshai, Oded. "Confronting A Christian Empire." In *Cultures of the Jews*, edited by David Biale, 202. New York: Schocken Books, 2002.

21 John Chrysostom, *Against Judaizing Christians*, Book I, (Ch. I; Sect. IV-VI).
- The last sentence of Chrysostom's excerpt seems to imply that such association with the Jews amounted to unforgivable blasphemy from the perspective of the Catholic Church.

22 Chrysostom was born in 347 C.E. and died in 407 C.E.

23 John Chrysostom, *Against Judaizing Christians*, Book I, (Ch. V; Sect. I-VIII).

24 Acts 14:1.

25 Most Christian scholars agree that Christianity began on the day of Pentecost as described in the book of Acts.

26 Synagogues are not mentioned in the Law of Moses, because at the time of the giving of the Law at Mt. Sinai, synagogues did not yet exist.

27 Recall that Chrysostom was the archbishop of Constantinople at the time he wrote his polemic. Thus, as an archbishop Chrysostom appeared to possess a very elementary understanding of the greater principles of the New Testament.

28 John Chrysostom, *Against Judaizing Christians*, Book I, (Ch. II; Sect. V-VI).

29 Strauss, Barry S. *Ten Caesars*. New York: Simon & Schuster, 2019. (p. 305-306).

30 Ibid. (20) (p. 194).

31 Ibid. (29) (p. 306).

32 The ancient writer Sidonius Apollinaris (c.a. 440-485 C.E.) records that Crispus was executed by poisoning. Modern historians have surmised that he was instead drowned in a bath house, however this theory is probably a conflation of the death of Fausta and Crispus together, either confusing the two or combining them. It is the opinion of this writer that Sidonius' account is the more accurate. For more on this, see:
- Sidonius Apollinaris, *Letters*. Translated by O.M. Dalton, 1915.

33 Grant, Michael. *The Roman Emperors*. New York: Simon & Schuster, 1985. (p. 233-234).

34 Varying accounts surrounding the death of Fausta can be found in:
- Burkhardt, Jacob. *The Age of Constantine the Great*. New York: Pantheon Books, Inc., 1949.
- Balsdon, John P. *Roman Women*. New York: John Day Company, 1962.
- The ancient historian Eutropius also records that Constantine had his wife and son slain in his *Breviarium*, composed sometime around 369 C.E. (Book X).

35 Ibid. (31) (Eutropius, Breviarium).

36 Norwich, John J. *A Short History of Byzantium*. New York: Alfred A. Knopf, Inc., 1997. (p. xxxvii, preface-p. 3).

37 Ibid. (29) (p. 308).

38 Ibid. (33) (p. 230).

39 While it is not known precisely when Cornelius converted, the timeline of seven to thirteen years after the birth of the church in Acts chapter two is generally accepted.

40 1st Corinthians 9:19-23 (KJV).

[41] John Chrysostom, *Against Judaizing Christians*, Book I, (Ch. I; Sect. IV-VI).

[42] In his epistle to the Galatians, Paul addressed certain believers who, after having already come to Christ through the new birth, wanted to revert to the Law of Moses as a means of sanctification, something which the apostle forbade.

# CHAPTER XII: THE TRIUMPH OF BYZANTIUM

*Image 12.1*
Taken from: https://reliquarian.com/2013/03/23/saint-theodore-warrior-saint-and-dragon-slayer/

*Image 12.2*
Taken from: Saint George and the Dragon, tempera, gold leaf, and ink on parchment by the Master of Sir John Fastolf, c. 1430–40; in the J. Paul Getty Museum, Los Angeles.
J. Paul Getty Museum (object no. 84.ML.723.33v); digital image courtesy of the Getty's Open Content Program

- https://www.britannica.com/biography/Saint-George

[1] Grant, Michael. *The Roman Emperors*. New York: Simon & Schuster, 1985. (p. 240-247).

[2] Norwich, John J. *A Short History of Byzantium*. New York: Alfred A. Knopf, Inc., 1997. (p. 21-22).

[3] Ibid. (2) (p. 23).

[4] "Constantius II: Roman emperor." Britannica. Accessed December 1, 2021. https://www.britannica.com/biography/Constantius-II.

[5] Ibid. (1) (p. 244-245).
- There is some evidence to suggest that Constantine the Great was also sympathetic to Arianism, perhaps made evident by his trivialization of the doctrinal disputes as discussed by Eusebius. Some have speculated that he embraced Arianism but was encouraged to remain silent about the belief for the sake of political unity. It does not seem unreasonable to assume that Constantine may have believed in Arianism. Given his complicated relationship to the Unconquered Sun and his continued participation in certain pagan practices, it would not be unrealistic to believe that he embraced a version of Christianity that lowered the status of Jesus from God Almighty to a sort of demi-god. "More than man but less than God" was a common belief about great rulers in the ancient world. It is the opinion of this writer that the idea that such a belief could be applied to Jesus Christ in the mind of Constantine is not so far-fetched.

[6] It is, perhaps, worthy of mention that Justin referred to the pagan cults of the empire as "the religion of the Greeks." In the Roman Empire, the deities of Rome

were not distinct from their Grecian origin. Thus, Hellenism was not just tacitly adopted by the Romans, but explicitly.

7 This was an early term for Christians.

8 Julian the Apostate, *Letter to Arsacius*, C.A. 362 C.E.
   • This excerpt is based on the translation of Edward J. Chinnock, *A Few Notes on Julian and a Translation of his Public Letters*, London: David Nut, 1901.

9 Pagan temples were not closed by Constantine the Great, so it is to be assumed that the closing of pagan temples began during the reign of his sons between 337-361 C.E.

10 Ibid. (2) (p. 25).

11 Julian the Apostate, *Rescript on Christian Teachers*, C.A. 362 C.E.

12 Ibid. (2) (p. 27).

13 One incident which stained his memory was his response to a mob outside a garrison headquarters in Thessalonica. When a captain of the imperial garrison was killed in the incident, Theodosius ordered troops in the city to reassert their authority in whatever way they saw fit. In response, the soldiers waited until the people of the city were gathered in the Hippodrome for the games. Once they were trapped, the army attacked, killing more than seven thousand citizens. The massacre is regarded as the low point of Theodosius reign.

14 *Edict of Thessalonica*, C.A. 380 C.E.

15 Ibid. (1) (p.272).

16 "Council of Constantinople (AD 381)." Wisconsin Lutheran College: Fourth Century Christianity. Last modified , 2021. Accessed December 1, 2021. https://www.fourthcentury.com/council-of-constantinople-ad-381/.

17 "Sabellius." New World Encyclopedia. Accessed December 6, 2021. https://www.newworldencyclopedia.org/entry/Sabellius.

18 Recall from chapter eight that Praxeas was the subject of much controversy, as he apparently opposed the beliefs of men such as Justin and Tertullian.

19 For more on this subject, see R.B.B. Tollinton's *Clement of Alexandria: A Study in Christian Liberalism*.

20 Chalfant, William B. *Ancient Champions of Oneness*. Hazelwood, MO: Word Aflame Press, 1986. (p. 96-97).

21 Hilary of Poitiers, "The Trinity." In *The Fathers of the Church*, Edited by Bernard Peebles, Translated by Stephen McKenna. Washington, DC: Catholic University Press, 1970 (25:134).

22 "The Panarion of Epiphanius of Salamis Books II and III." In *Nag Hammadi and Manichaean Studies*, Edited by Johannes van Oort and Einar Thomassen, 123-24. Translated by Frank Williams. Boston: Brill, 2013.

23 Further reading of his comments about the Sabellians reveals that Epiphanius did not approve of their beliefs about water baptism either. He specifically cites Matthew 28:19 as evidence for the legitimacy of trinitarian water baptism. This is interesting, as it documented throughout both the New Testament and historical records that the use of the single name of Jesus was the dominant method of water baptism for the early Christians.

24 Gregory Thaumaturgus, *A Sectional Confession on Faith*, (Sect. VII).
- It is worth noting that what can be gathered about the Sabellians, Monarchians, and even Praxeas comes to us in the form of writings by men who largely despised them. What Sabellius and Praxeas believed in their own words is extremely difficult to come by, and so the polemical statements by those who disagreed with them should probably be taken with a grain of salt. History is written by the victors.

25 Chalfant's record of the various followers of Sabellius comes from Charles Bigg's, *The Christian Platonists of Alexandria*, Oxford: Clarendon Press, 1913.

26 "First Council of Constantinople." New World Encyclopedia. Accessed December 6, 2021. https://www.newworldencyclopedia.org/entry/First_Council_of_Constantinople.

27 Ibid. (26). (Seventh canon of the council).

28 Ibid. (26).

29 It is interesting that Mary is not mentioned in the first iteration of the Nicene Creed by was added to the later one. This became an issue of import in the next century.

30 Ibid. (26).

31 Romans 8:9-11.

32 Ibid. (22) (p. 124).

33 The confusion stems from the fact that there were multiple meetings of the Ephesian council. The first ecumenical council convened in Ephesus happened in 431 C.E., but the second occurred in 449 C.E. The second of these two councils is the more well known, and is the council which primarily debated the nature of Christ.

34 "Council of Ephesus." New World Encyclopedia. Accessed December 7, 2021. https://www.newworldencyclopedia.org/entry/Council_of_Ephesus.
1 Being a patriarch of the Catholic Church in Constantinople would have meant that Nestorius could not have been confirmed as a minister in such a city without adhering to the Nicene Creed. Nevertheless, he did object to the Catholic Church on other issues.

35 John 19:25-27.

36 Acts 1:14.

37 The father of Dionysus was Zeus, the greatest god of Olympus. His mother was Semele, the princess of Thebes.

38 Hamilton, Edith. *Mythology*. New York: Grand Central Publishing, 1942. (p. 63).

39 According to Matthew's account, the ministry of Jesus began in the region of Galilee among the settlements where many inter-married Jews lived that were not religious. As He drew closer to Jerusalem—the epicenter of Jewish life—He became less welcome, culminating with this crucifixion at the behest of the religious and political leadership of the city.

40 Ibid. (39) (p. 65).

41 Ibid. (41).

42 "Saint Theodore: Warrior Saint and Dragon-Slayer." Reliquarian . Accessed December 8, 2021. https://reliquarian.com/2013/03/23/saint-theodore-warrior-saint-and-dragon-slayer/.

43 Interestingly, St. Theodore the Dragon-Slayer is a bit of a misnomer. Nowhere in his story is he said to have slayed a dragon. The presentation of Theodore as the killer of serpents likely comes from a panegyric delivered by Saint Gregory of Nyssa in the fourth century, wherein he said that "devils were expelled and distempers cured" by the martyred saint. Because the serpent is commonly associated with devils in Christian thought it, it is likely that the presentation of St. Theodore as a dragon-slayer evolved into its present form over generations of Christian interpretation. Later adaptations of the dragon slayer motif were applied to other saints in Catholic thought, most famously of which is Saint George.

44 "St. George: Christian Martyr ." Britannica. Accessed December 8, 2021. https://www.britannica.com/biography/Saint-George.

45 "The Major Church Calendars." Britannica. Accessed December 8, 2021. https://www.britannica.com/topic/church-year/The-major-church-calendars.

46 Ibid. (45).

47 Ibid. (2) (p. 111).

48 Ibid. (2) (p. 112).

49 "Second Council of Nicaea." Britannica. Accessed December 8, 2021. https://www.britannica.com/event/Second-Council-of-Nicaea-787.

50 Ibid. (50).

51 2nd Corinthians 5:19 (KJV).

# CODA

*Image C.1*
Taken from:
https://museos.wiki/villanueva-de-sigena/c-chijlaqrdgmdwa0rfniubk714fi

¹ Sources differ on this point, some pointing to Villanueva de Sijena, others to Tudela.
  • *All dates included in this Coda are C.E. (Common/Christian Era).*

² "Michael Servetus." New World Encyclopedia. Accessed December 9, 2021. https://www.newworldencyclopedia.org/entry/Michael_Servetus.

³ See figure C.1.

⁴ Serveto, Michael. "The Two Treatises of Servetus on the Trinity." In *Harvard Theological Studies XVI The Two Treatises of Servetus on the Trinity*, edited by James H. Ropes and Kirsopp Lake, xx. translated by Earl M. Wilbur. Eugene, OR: Wipf and Stock Publishers, 2013.
  • Previously published by Harvard University Press, 1932.

⁵ "Michael Servetus." Britannica. Accessed December 9, 2021. https://www.britannica.com/biography/Michael-Servetus.

⁶ Ibid. (2).

⁷ Michael Servetus, *On Errors of the Trinity*, Book I.
  • Taken from the Wilbur translation.

⁸ Ibid. (4) (p. xii).

⁹ Ibid. (4) (p. xiii).

¹⁰ Ibid. (5).

¹¹ Harvard University's publication on the work of Michael Servetus notes that while disputed by later pioneers in the field, it is clear today that Servetus was indeed the first to publish his findings on the anatomy of the heart. It is likely that his work was suppressed for many years due to his later conviction as a heretic.

¹² Before the death of Servetus, John Calvin was known as "The Prince of Geneva" as he had established a quasi-religious dictatorship over Geneva in the sixteenth century. After the death of Servetus, he fell out of favor with the public and was reprimanded for his treatment of the Spanish reformer.

¹³ It is known that John Calvin maintained some level of written correspondence with Servetus throughout his life, so it is conceivable that the Calvin, determined to have the man arrested, feigned friendship (or, at least, cordiality) until the opportunity arose to have him captured.

¹⁴ Ibid. (4) (p. xxv).

15 Calvin, Jean. *Defensio orthodoxae fidei de sacra Trinitate contra prodigiosos errores Michaelis Serveti...* (Defense of Orthodox Faith against the Prodigious Errors of the Spaniard Michael Servetus...). Geneva, 1554.

16 It is known that most of Michael Servetus' written works were destroyed after his execution to prevent them from being circulated throughout the public. Thus, again, history is written by the victors.

17 Michael Servetus, *On Errors of the Trinity*, Book I (9a).

18 Michael Servetus, *On Errors of the Trinity*, Book I (42b-43a).

19 Talmadge French records that as early as 1910, Pentecostal leaders such as Andrew D. Urshan began water baptizing in the name of Jesus Christ as opposed to the trinitarian formula. For more on this, see:
  • French, Talmadge L. *Early Interracial Oneness Pentecostalism.* Eugene, OR: Pickwick Publications, 2014. (p. 59).

20 French, Talmadge L. *Our God is One.* Indianapolis, IN: Voice & Vision Publications, 1999. (p. 47).

21 Some advocates for the sign of tongues did not believe the experience to be essential to conversion. This belief was known as "second-works doctrine." Thus, while they may be called Pentecostal in the most general sense because they identified with the experience of the day of Pentecost, many ceased from fellowshipping with those who believed the act to be essential, known as "finished-works doctrine." Finished-works believers were found most commonly among the Oneness Pentecostals.

22 Ibid. (20) (p. 15).

23 "About the UPCI." United Pentecostal Church International. Accessed December 13, 2021. https://www.upci.org/about/about-the-upci.

24 This number recognizes the sovereignty of countries such as Taiwan, which is not represented in the United Nations list of recognized countries.

25 Ibid. (23).

26 Dunn, James D. *Christology in the Making.* Philadelphia, PA: The Westminster Press, 1980. (p. 63).

27 In 2018, Trinity Bible Network (TBN) invited a Oneness Pentecostal pastor named Anthony Mangun onto their program to discuss his new book, in which he was allowed to openly advocate for his belief in the oneness of God. More than the discussion, it was the invitation which signaled one example of the dissolving hostility of trinitarians against oneness believers. The interview may be viewed at the following link:
  • https://www.youtube.com/watch?v=XFtctvvGAqM

## ONENESS PENTECOSTALISM & THE ROLE OF SEPARATION: ESSAY BY ESTHER GILL HIPES, PRESENTED AT HARAVARD UNIVERSITY, 1984

[1] Foster, Fred J. *Think It Not Strange: A History of the Oneness Movement.* St. Louis, MO: Pentecostal Publishing House, 1965. p. 68.

[2] Golder, Morris T. *History of the Pentecostal Assemblies of the World.* Indianapolis, IN: 1973. p. 41.

[3] Ware, Timothy. *The Orthodox Church.* Suffolk, England: Richard Clay and Company Ltd., 1964. p. 10.

[4] Harper, Michael. *Let My People Grow.* Plainfield, NJ: Logos International, 1977. P. 111.

[5] Ibid. (4) (p. 12).

[6] Forell, George W. The Protestant Faith. Philadelphia, PA: Fortress Press, 1960. p. 201.

[7] Marty, Martin E. A Short History of Christianity. Philadelphia, PA: Fortress Press, 1959. p. 344.

[8] Caird. G.B. *A Commentary on the Revelation of St. John the Divine.* New York, NY: Harper & Row Publishers, 1966. p. 8.
  - Hipes cites Carid's commentary here. The quotation from John Bunyan may be found in: Bunyan, John. *Pilgrim's Progress.* Uhrichsville, OH: Barbour Publishing, Inc., 1988. (p. 36-37). *Pilgrim's Progress* was originally published in 1678.

[9] Brown, Raymond E., S.S. *The Anchor Bible, Vol. 29, The Gospel According to St. John.* Garden City, New York: Doubleday and Company, 1966. p. 73-88.

[10] Rusch, William G., Editor, *The Trinitarian Controversy.* Philadelphia, PA: Fortress Press, 1980 p. 2.

[11] Trueblood, Elton. *A Place to Stand.* New York, NY: Harper & Row Publishers, 1969. p. 39.

[12] Haywood, G.T. *Victim of the Flaming Sword.* Indianapolis, IN: Christ Temple Book Store, Undated. P. 62-63.

[13] *International Bible Encyclopedia, Vol. 2.* Grand Rapids, MI: W.B. Erdman's Publishing Co., 1943. p. 1264.

[14] Kelly, J.N.D. *Early Christian Doctrines.* New York, NY: Harper & Row Publishers, 1978. P. 83.

[15] Ibid. (14) (p. 87).

[16] Ibid. (14) (p. 95).

- Kelly's analysis of the writings of the Apologists appears to be incomplete. Early Apologists such as Justin Martyr deviated significantly from the earliest presentations of Christ mapped out in the New Testament, even introducing novelty to the mode of water baptism.

[17] Ibid. (10) (p. 7).

[18] *International Bible Encyclopedia, Vol. 5.* p. 3012.

[19] Thompson, Hugo. *Love-Justice*. North Quincy, Massachusetts: Christopher Publishing House, 1970. p. 175, 244.

[20] Ibid. (10) (p. 6).

[21] Ibid. (19) (p. 123).

[22] *International Bible Encyclopedia, Vol. 5.* p. 3012.

[23] Ibid. (3) (p. 28).

[24] Ibid. (6) (p. 193).

[25] *International Bible Encyclopedia, Vol. 1.* p. 396.

[26] Qualben, Lars. P. *A History of the Christian Church*. New York, NY: Thomas Nelson & Sons, 1942. p. 272.

[27] Theissen, Gerd. *Sociology of Early Palestinian Christianity*. Philadelphia, PA: Fortress Press, 1977. p. 113.

[28] Ibid. (10) (p. 1).

[29] Weaver, Mary Jo. *Introduction to Christianity*. Belmont, CA: Wadsworth Publishing Company, 1984. p. 53.

[30] Ibid. (27) (p. 114).

[31] Ibid. (10) (p. 16).

[32] Ibid. (3) (p. 29).

[33] Ibid. (4) (p. 110).

[34] Ibid. (10) (p. 1-2).
[35] Ibid. (10) (p. 27).

[36] While it is true that some Oneness Pentecostals have accused Trinitarians of Tritheism, modern historical examinations suggest that early controversies between Oneness Pentecostals and Trinitarians were primarily characterized by their disagreements over the proper mode of water baptism. For more on this, see *Early Interracial Oneness Pentecostalism* by Talmadge French.

[37] Ibid. (4) (p. 112).

38 Throughout the first four chapters of *The History & Development of the Doctrine of the Trinity*, detailed examination is made concerning how the greater culture of the Jews was heavily impacted by the Greeks, and how Hellenism only served to augment the issue of maintaining separation among the Jews.

39 Dimont, Max I. *Jews, God and History*. New York, NY: The New American Library, p. 70.

40 Ibid. (27) (p. 118).

41 This behavior by Christians is most clearly demonstrated throughout the fourth century, in which Jews were specifically targeted as people unfit for Christian fellowship.

42 Ibid. (29) (p. 143-144).

43 Ibid. (26) (p. 621-622).

44 Here Hipes refers to the secondary form of separation discussed in prior sections (isolationism) as opposed to the first form of separation which is characterized by holiness and chosen-ness.

45 Ibid. (19) (p. 15).

46 Ibid. (19) (p. 15).

47 Synan, Vinson, Editor. *Aspects of Pentecostal-Charismatic Origins*. Plainfield, NJ: Logos International, 1975. p. 31.

48 Ibid. (4) (p. 13).

49 Ibid. (19) (p. 17).

50 Ibid. (19) (p. 29; 87-89).

51 Here again, Hipes draws a distinction between separation which promotes holiness and separation which encourages isolation from the people that Christians are called to evangelize. In the mind of the writer, the two are distinct. One is an act of holiness, the other is not.

52 Ibid. (27) (p. 119).

53 Ibid. (19) (p. 123).

54 Ibid. (19) (p. 32-33).

55 Ibid. (19) (p. 58-59).

56 Ibid. (19) (p. 97).

57 Alhstrom, Sydney E. A Religious History of the American People. New Haven and London: Yale University Press, 1972. p. 933-935.

58 Ibid. (57) (p. 944; 1087).

- Alhstrom's analysis is not an endorsement of upending the foundations of Christian doctrine, but reminder in how to return to those foundations when one has departed from them. Hence, the love-justice ethic is framed as a first century Christian principle, and not as a later development. In cultivating an ethic of forbearance, Christians can lead others to the truth. It is not the truth that changes nor the doctrines of the church, but the heart of the believer toward the unbeliever. Or, in Alhstrom's specific example, the heart of the believer toward other Christians with whom they might disagree.

59 I spoke with Ms. Hipes shortly before the publication of this book about this particular passage of her writing. The "Perfect" to which she refers is Jesus Christ, as it is Galatians which teaches us that the Law is our schoolmaster that leads us to Christ (Galatians 3:24).

# Index

## B

## C

## D

## G

# H

## I

## J

## M

## N

# O

## P

# S

# T

## U

Index

Printed in Great Britain
by Amazon